CORRECTING THEMES

D1499809

M. 9:30 -11
J. 9:30 - 10, 3-4
W. 1-2
Th. 9:30 - 10, 3-4
F. 1-2

An American Rhetoric

An American
Rhetoric

By WILLIAM W. WATT

LAFAYETTE COLLEGE

RINEHART & COMPANY, INC.
NEW YORK · TORONTO

Ninth Printing, September 1955

Library of Congress Catalog Card Number: 52–5601

To James and Mary Tupper

Preface

This book is primarily addressed to college students in the elementary composition course. It is based on the assumption that such students need a guide to good writing, not merely a code for theme correction, need sympathetic understanding of educated usage in the middle of the twentieth century, not reluctant obedience to traditional rules and regulations. I have therefore supplemented the dos and don'ts with considerable discussion of the whys and wherefores. On the other hand, I have not plunged into the vast sea of problems that can be adequately treated only in separate courses in semantics, linguistics, remedial reading, creative writing, speech, or the introduction to literature.

I have frankly slanted the book toward the kind of good writing that is appropriate for most occasions today: informal but not careless, plain but not flat, light but not jazzy. But I have tried not to clip any genuine wings or mislead the student into assuming that any book can prescribe appropriate usage for all occasions. I have included the essential rules for writing "correct English," but wherever those rules no longer apply, except in the most formal writing, I have tried to make clear-cut distinctions among levels of usage. I have tried to tell the truth about educated writing today without giving the student the dangerous impression that anything goes.

Since the book was written to be read, not merely consulted or assigned, I have attempted to make it readable for students to whom composition is not a feature attraction in the curriculum, but only a selected short subject. Although I disagree with those who believe that techniques can be intelligently discussed without technical terms, I have tried to avoid the deadliest sin of the textbook style: the proliferation of trade jargon. I have also tried to steer a treacherous middle course between the extremes of text-book tone: solemn omniscience and playful condescension. And I have not cluttered up the page with so many typographical "study aids" that there is no room for reading.

The order of the chapters is not arbitrary. Chapter One is an informal orientation lecture designed to destroy secondary school illusions and strike the keynote of the book. Chapter Two is intended to counteract first-theme inertia: it contains a handful of hints to get the student going and a minimum of mechanical information about the manuscript. The problem of organization is placed next on the assumption that a student can and should understand the general blueprint for a well-built theme before he starts worrying about the struts, joists, and ornaments. Chapters Four (Grammar), Five (Sentences), and Six (Punctuation) come naturally in that order because sound sentence structure is applied grammar and intelligent punctuation presupposes some understanding of sentence structure. The short chapter on Spelling (Chapter Seven) deals with an elementary aspect of words, which are discussed in more detail in the next two chapters. Chapter Eight is an introduction to the use of the dictionary, and Nine is a detailed consideration of words in context. Chapters Ten (Style and Tone) and Eleven (Clear and Cloudy Thinking) consider on a broader scale a number of points made in earlier chapters; and hence serve partly for review. The final chapter (The Library Research Paper) contains detailed instructions for preparing the one assignment that nearly all elementary composition courses have in common. Of course, the chapters need not be taken up in this order. It's the instructor's privilege to shuffle them any way he likes.

To make the book convenient for reference as well as reading, I have supplied a list of grammatical terms, accompanying Chapter Four, an end-paper key for correcting and revising themes, a comprehensive index to Chapters One through Twelve, and a Glossary of Usage. The glossary is placed at the back of the book just before the index, where it should be more useful than if tucked away in a chapter on words. A number of grammatical teapot tempests traditionally included in the main discussions of grammar or diction (the split infinitive, *shall* and *will,* the preposition at the end of a sentence) have been demoted to the glossary, addressed only to whom they may concern.

I have furnished exercises after all but four chapters. They would be superfluous after Chapters One and Two; in Chapter Seven they are replaced by two spelling lists, on which most students should exercise regularly; and the best exercise on the principles of Chapter Twelve is to write a research paper. Elsewhere I have tried to make the exercises useful and generous in the hope that teachers will have no need for perforated workbooks. Although I must confess to some manufacturing, most of the exercises and other illustrations have been taken verbatim from student themes or contemporary books and periodicals. I believe that authentic illustrations of English as she is written are more convincing than synthetic sentences about John and Mary. In casting about for a wide variety of selections from contemporary prose, I have tried to choose, not mere pedagogical props, but passages that make lively reading in their own right.

All appreciable quotations are acknowledged in a special section. I am grateful to all the publishers and writers who have given me generous permission to reprint selections on which they hold the copyrights. I also want to express my special gratitude to Mr. Robert J. Geist for his careful reading of the manuscript; to Professor Emeritus James W. Tupper, who taught me Freshman English when I was fresh from the graduate school; and to Professor Gerhard H. Magnus, who gave me much neighborly help and encouragement en route.

WILLIAM W. WATT

Easton, Pennsylvania
January, 1952

Acknowledgments

I am grateful to the following persons and companies for permitting me to quote from their publications:

The Atlantic Monthly for permission to use passages from the following articles: Archibald MacLeish, "Humanism and the Belief in Man"; Howard Mumford Jones, "Patriotism—But How?"; James Truslow Adams, "Sweetness and Light—Sixty Years After"; and Gertrude Stein, "Your United States."

The Estate of the late ARNOLD BENNETT, the owners of the copyright, for permission to use the paragraph from "Seeing Life," from *The Author's Craft.*

MRS. CHESTON BENNETT for permission to use the passage from *The Journals of Arnold Bennett.*

BRANDT & BRANDT for permission to use Zachary Gold's "Spring over Brooklyn," copyright, 1939, by Curtis Publishing Company.

CAMBRIDGE UNIVERSITY PRESS for permission to use the passage from F. L. Lucas, *The Decline and Fall of the Romantic Ideal.*

CHATTO & WINDUS for permission to quote the paragraph from Lytton Strachey's essay on Florence Nightingale from *Eminent Victorians.*

DODD, MEAD & COMPANY for permission to quote the passage from *Imaginary Obligations* by Frank Moore Colby. Copyright, 1904, by Dodd, Mead & Company.

JOHN DOS PASSOS, for permission to quote the passage from *U.S.A.*, copyright, 1930, 1932, 1933, 1934, 1935, 1936, 1937, by John Dos Passos.

DOUBLEDAY & COMPANY, INC., for permission to use the passage from *The Author's Craft* by Arnold Bennett.

DUELL, SLOAN & PEARCE, INC., for permission to use the passage from Erskine Caldwell, *Jackpot,* copyright, 1931, 1933, 1935, 1938, 1940, by Erskine Caldwell; and the passage from *Kneel to the Rising Sun* by Erskine Caldwell, copyright, 1935, by Erskine Caldwell.

E. P. DUTTON & CO., INC., for permission to use the passages from

C. E. M. Joad, *Return to Philosophy,* copyright, 1936, by E. P. Dutton & Co.; and from Cleveland Amory, *The Proper Bostonians,* copyright, 1947, by Cleveland Amory.

ALBERT HALPER for permission to use the paragraph from *On the Shore.*

HARCOURT, BRACE AND COMPANY, INC., for permission to use the following excerpts: From *The Autobiography of Lincoln Steffens,* copyright, 1931, by Harcourt, Brace and Company, Inc.; from *The Common Reader* by Virginia Woolf, copyright, 1925, by Harcourt, Brace and Company, Inc.; from *Definitions* by Henry S. Canby, copyright, 1922, by Harcourt, Brace and Company, Inc.; from *Babbitt* by Sinclair Lewis, copyright, 1922, by Harcourt, Brace and Company, Inc.; from *Science and Man* edited by Ruth Nanda Anshen, copyright, 1942, by Harcourt, Brace and Company, Inc.; from *Little Children* by William Saroyan, copyright, 1937, by Harcourt, Brace and Company, Inc.; and from *Eminent Victorians* by Lytton Strachey, from Lewis Mumford, *Story of Utopias,* from E. M. Forster, *Abinger Harvest,* and from Katherine Anne Porter, *Pale Horse, Pale Rider,* all by permission of Harcourt, Brace and Company, Inc.

HARPER & BROTHERS for permission to use the passages from Henry Steele Commager, "Who Is Loyal to America?"; from E. B. White, *One Man's Meat;* from James Harvey Robinson, *The Mind in the Making;* from Frederick Prokosch, *The Asiatics;* from Thomas Hornsby Ferril, *I Hate Thursday;* from Frederick Lewis Allen, *Only Yesterday;* and from Frances Winwar, *The Romantic Rebels.*

HARVARD UNIVERSITY PRESS for permission to quote the passage from Zechariah Chafee, Jr., *Free Speech in the United States.*

HENRY HOLT AND COMPANY for permission to use the passage from *Brave Men* by Ernie Pyle.

HOUGHTON MIFFLIN COMPANY for permission to use the passages from *Mr. Roberts* by Thomas Heggen, from *Young Man with a Horn* by Dorothy Baker, and from *Essays in Appreciation* by John Livingston Lowes.

BURGES JOHNSON for permission to use a passage from his *Campus vs. Classroom.*

ALFRED A. KNOPF, INC., for permission to use passages from H. L. Mencken, *In Defense of Women;* from Katharine Mansfield, *The Doves' Nest;* and from E. M. Forster, *The Collected Tales of E. M. Forster.*

JOSEPH WOOD KRUTCH for permission to use the passage from his *The Modern Temper,* copyrighted by the author.

LITTLE, BROWN & COMPANY. The selections from *Teacher in America* by Jacques Barzun, by permission of Little, Brown & Company and The Atlantic Monthly Press.

LIVERIGHT PUBLISHING CORPORATION for permisison to use the passage from *Death in the Woods* by Sherwood Anderson, copyright, 1933, Sherwood Anderson.

McCLELLAND AND STEWART LIMITED for permission to use the passage from *Blood, Sweat and Tears* by Winston Churchill.

THE MACMILLAN COMPANY for permission to use the passages from Alfred North Whitehead, *Science and the Modern World,* copyright, 1925, by The Macmillan Company; and from James Michener, *Tales of the South Pacific,* copyright, 1947, by James Michener.

G. &. C. MERRIAM COMPANY for permission to use the entry from *Webster's New Collegiate Dictionary,* copyright, 1949, 1951, by G. & C. Merriam Company.

CLYDE R. MILLER for permission to use the passage from "How to Detect Propaganda."

New Republic for permission to reprint the passage from George Orwell, "Politics and the English Language," which appeared in *New Republic,* June 24, 1946.

New York Herald Tribune for permission to use material which appeared in its columns.

The New Yorker for permission to reprint material from Richard Lockridge, "The Grammarian"; John Hersey, "Hiroshima"; Peter DeVries, "Through a Glass Darkly"; H. L. Mencken, "Scented Words"; James Thurber, *My Life and Hard Times;* and the two paragraphs from "The Talk of the Town."

W. W. NORTON & COMPANY, INC., for permission to reprint material from H. A. Overstreet, *A Declaration of Interdependence,* and from Everett Dean Martin, *Psychology.*

HAROLD OBER ASSOCIATES for permission to reprint the passage from "The Bear" by William Faulkner. Copyright, 1942, by The Curtis Publishing Company.

ODHAMS PRESS LIMITED, proprietors of the British Copyright, for permission to reprint the paragraph from *My Early Life* by Winston Churchill.

OXFORD UNIVERSITY PRESS for permission to reprint passages from Arnold J. Toynbee, *Civilization on Trial,* and Chauncey B. Tinker, *On Going to College: A Symposium.*

G. P. PUTNAM'S SONS for permission to use the passage from *Blood,*

Sweat and Tears by Winston Churchill, and the passage from *Apes, Men, and Morons* by Ernest A. Hooton.

RANDOM HOUSE for permission to use the passages from *The Young Lions* by Irwin Shaw, from *Other Voices, Other Rooms* by Truman Capote, from *People on Our Side* by Edgar Snow, and from "How Writing Is Written" by Gertrude Stein.

RINEHART & COMPANY for permission to use the passage from Philip Wylie, *Generation of Vipers*. Copyright, 1942, by Philip Wylie.

The Saturday Review of Literature for permission to use the passages from Pearl Buck, "Literature and Life," and Mortimer J. Adler, "How to Read a Book."

CHARLES SCRIBNER'S SONS for permission to use the excerpts from Ernest Hemingway, *A Farewell to Arms;* from Thomas Wolfe, *Look Homeward Angel;* and from Winston Churchill, *My Early Life—A Roving Commission*.

SHEED & WARD, INC., for permission to use the passage from *The Well and the Shallows* by G. K. Chesterton. Copyright, Sheed & Ward, Inc., New York.

WILLIAM SLOANE ASSOCIATES, INC., for permission to use the passage from *Off Broadway* by Maxwell Anderson. Copyright, 1947, by Maxwell Anderson.

JAMES THURBER for permission to use the selections from *My Life and Hard Times*.

THE VIKING PRESS for permission to use the passages from *The Journal of Arnold Bennett;* from Thorstein Veblen, *The Higher Learning in America;* from John Steinbeck, *The Grapes of Wrath;* and from D. H. Lawrence, "The Rocking-Horse Winner."

Contents

An American Rhetoric

CHAPTER ONE

Good Writing and Correct English

Good writing is where you find it, whether in *Variety's*
headlines or in the reports of the Coast and Geodetic Survey.
—Bernard De Voto.

A cartoon in a recent magazine depicts a disheveled scrub-
woman knocking at a door labeled *Professor of the English Language* and saying timidly: "It is I." Although the professor is not
in the picture, he is obviously a bearded patriarch who has
devoted a lifetime to unsplitting infinitives and undangling
participles. He is a handy man to have around to settle occasional
moot points of usage ("My buddy and I have been having an
argument. What is it, *ice* tea or *iced* tea?"). But the rest of the
time he is about as useful to society as the harmless hobbyist who
gets his picture in a magazine by spending seven years building
a miniature Statue of Liberty with 7,496 pieces of burnt toast.

Of course, all grown-up students know that this species of
academic monster is almost extinct on the college campus. But
the tradition which he represents (or she, for the monster may
also be a "schoolmarm") still haunts the classroom. Many a
student still enters college under the illusion that the whole duty
of the English professor, at least in the freshman year, is to teach
him, not good writing, but "correct English." Correct English
consists solely of observing a solemn list of thou-shalt-nots; literary
skill is in indirect ratio to the expenditure of red pencil in the
margins; the unsullied page is perfection. "Only one measly
spelling error and he gives me a C minus!" The common campus
war cry betrays the illusion.

Another illusion follows from the first: that there is a yawning gap between writing "themes" for the English department and writing under any other set of circumstances. The English professor is a hawk-eyed detective eager to mistake a flyspeck for a misplaced comma, but easily soothed by an overwrought metaphor or a fifty-cent word. The biology professor—so goes the undergraduate myth—doesn't care how you say it as long as you get it all down somehow. One wants embroidery, the other wants facts; the student writes English for one class, his own private jargon for the other. The English teacher may explain patiently that English is a language, not merely a technique for passing a six-credit course in theme-writing scheduled Monday-Wednesday-Friday at eleven; that theme-writing is simply the most practical method of developing a student's powers of expression—which are related, not only to writing, but to speaking, reading, thinking, and listening as well. The biology teacher may turn out to be a highly literate purist who insists that if the student can't explain the amoeba clearly he hasn't proved that he knows an amoeba when he sees one. A philosopher may even contend that no idea can be said to exist until it has been clothed in well-ordered words. Still the illusion persists. Writing for an English course, especially writing themes, is in a lonely, unreal world of its own.

Closely related to the other two is a third illusion: that the student in an English composition course must always adapt his writing, not only to a rigid departmental code which differs vastly from all others, but also to the peculiar eccentricities of the instructor he has drawn in the registration lottery. This notion is invariably revealed in the very first class of the semester when a hand pops up and a well-meaning voice says, "Professor, can you give us some idea of what *you* want on these themes?" If he can keep his equanimity, the teacher might answer something like this: "I admit I have my idiosyncrasies. I happen to have a special aversion to students who encase all colloquialisms in apologetic 'quotes' or label irony with question marks in parentheses (?) or call all persons *individuals* I am highly allergic to the expression *due to the fact that* and to the words *factor, integration, activation,* and *implementation.* Although I don't know any logical reason why we shouldn't have such a verb, I grow warm under the collar whenever somebody gets *enthused* about something. And I writhe when I see *contact* used, in the loose commercial fashion, as a verb meaning anything from waving a dotted line under a business prospect's nose to sending him a transatlantic cablegram. These things I don't want. But in the last analysis I hope I want the same kind of writing that anybody wants if he knows good writing when he sees it."

The student is not entirely to blame for his illusions. Too many teachers equate good writing with correct English. Too many professors outside of English departments are indifferent to how well a student expresses himself. Witness the junior who said to the English teacher: "Put me straight on the apostrophe again; I haven't used any for a year and a half." And within English departments there could be far more unanimity about the relative seriousness of the dangling participle and the misplaced modifier. The main point, however, is clear. Intelligent, educated people may quarrel violently about the virtues of an experimental novel or an original play; but they do not disagree seriously about the fundamentals of good writing.

These fundamentals will be discussed in detail in various places throughout the book. But the student cannot postpone writing a complete theme until he has traveled over every inch of the ground. The rest of this chapter, therefore, is designed to give him a preliminary bird's-eye view of the land, with some of the main signposts tentatively illuminated.

CONTENT

"Are we graded for what we say or for how well we say it?" This inevitable classroom question can be quickly answered. Content and form are inseparable. On any piece of writing, whatever the subject, the writer should be judged for what he says, not for what he seems to be trying to say—and the difference between the two is measured by how well he says it. A student should not get a good grade in an English course for neatly saying nothing or a good grade in any other kind of course for crudely saying much.

A seasoned familiar essayist—a Charles Lamb or a Max Beer-bohm—may succeed in making a charming literary mountain out of a molehill of thought. But there are few incipient Lambs and Beerbohms in college composition courses. All the resources of rhetoric are useless if the writer has nothing to say to begin with. The student who merely nibbles around the edges of a subject, or tries to whip up a whim into a fluffy idea, or replays for the thousandth time a tired tune that wasn't worth playing in the first place cannot expect a passing grade. The old adage—"If you have nothing to say, don't say it"—may seem severe to a writer with a regular deadline to meet, but if it were taken more seriously, there would be far less drivel in the weekly theme pile. One of the phenomena of our time is the appalling number of books that should never have been written because the author had nothing to say. Another is the number of good books written by people who are not trained professional writers but who do have something interesting to say.

ORIGINALITY

It is not expected, of course, that what the average college freshman has to say will be strikingly original. Originality—in the highest sense of the word, "creativeness"—is not a quality that can be acquired from a textbook or a teacher. A gifted under-graduate in a "creative writing" course may turn out a distinctly original short story. A patient investigator in an advanced course in literature may produce a good piece of original research. But these students are rare. The freshman instructor is not looking for genuinely creative writing, though he is delighted when he finds it, but only for the clear, intelligent, lively writing that should be expected of high school graduates but is far too seldom found.

How original can the average freshman be? If he cannot be strikingly original, he can at least avoid being annoyingly un-original. He can evade the hardy perennials that have flourished since the days of papyrus. Every experienced composition teacher has his own forbidden list. The theme on how hard it is to write a theme, the description of a beautiful woman that turns out in the end to be a portrait of a favorite Pekingese, the short short-story with the then-I-woke-up snapper ending—these are only a few of the hoariest. The student can also try to avoid trite phrases (clichés) and obviously empty banalities. Even on the first theme of the year—usually an autobiography—he does not have to start with "In the beginning, of course, I was born" and go on to record that when he "first saw the light of day," his "proud parents" were delighted to find that their "blessed event" was a "bouncing baby boy."

But the absence of triteness is only a negative virtue. *Any student can take a positive step toward originality if he will draw freely on his own experiences, accurately record his own observations, and do his own thinking.* An "average" college freshman reflecting disconsolately on the campus routine and a humdrum existence of eighteen years may quickly conclude that neither his life nor his view of life is any different from those of thousands of his contemporaries. But this is a craven surrender of his individuality. Strictly speaking, every student's experience is peculiarly his own, and he is the world's leading authority on it. If he will draw on that experience for fresh, authentic illustrations regularly, not merely when the teacher assigns an exercise in autobiography; if he will record what he sees in his own words, not in the handy rubber stamps of the cliché expert; if he will try to do his own thinking, not let columnists and commentators and teachers and fellow students do it for him—the most uninspired undergraduate has a chance to write interesting, moderately original themes.

HONESTY

Sometimes when the instructor asserts that a theme is not original, he is condemning it for something more serious than triteness. *Plagiarism* is a formal word for literary stealing or, to use the campus equivalent, cribbing. It is as immoral to steal from another person's writing as from his wardrobe or his wallet. Moreover, it is a crime that seldom pays, at least in the amateur college league. The chances of detection are good, for most instructors can distinguish readily between a piece of professional writing or an undergraduate classic from the fraternity swipe file and the standard classroom product of the dishonest student. The severe penalties on conviction include expulsion from college. Finally, cribbing is the worst possible way of learning to write.

There are, to be sure, degrees of plagiarism. For every student who commits grand literary larceny—lifting an entire theme word for word—there are a hundred fundamentally honest classmates who indulge in various kinds of petty larceny through ignorance of the laws of literary ethics. The conscientious student can hardly compose an entire semester's themes out of his own head. Sooner or later an assignment will send him to a newspaper, a magazine, or a book, whether or not the teacher has explicitly required a "source theme," a "library report," or a "research paper." The student must not naïvely assume that he can pilfer with impunity until the fatal week of the research paper arrives, at which time he is suddenly compelled by law to steal honestly. Although incidental borrowings in informal papers are not usually accompanied by footnotes, bibliography, and all the other paraphernalia of modern scholarship, all debts should be acknowledged unobtrusively in the text of the theme, or at least in an accompanying headnote.

The details of proper scholarly acknowledgment are discussed in Chapter Twelve. The general principles for all honest writing can be summarized briefly. Acknowledge indebtedness:

1. Whenever you quote another person's actual words.

2. Whenever you use another person's idea, opinion, or theory, *even if it is completely paraphrased in your own words.*

3. Whenever you borrow facts, statistics, or other illustrative material—unless the information is common knowledge.

In addition to plagiarism there is another, more elusive sort of literary dishonesty: insincerity. The English critic George Orwell has called insincerity "the great enemy of clear language." But it is more than an enemy of clarity. The slightest suspicion that a writer does not know what he is talking about or mean what he says helps to destroy the bond of sympathy which must exist between writer and reader.

Here, as with plagiarism, the student is often unaware of his shortcoming. A subconscious desire to make a good impression may cause him to strain, to transcend the limits of his knowledge and vocabulary, to strike a whole series of false notes. As long as the grade is sacred and the teacher is judge, jury, and executioner rolled into one, few students will be entirely free from the temptation to bluff. But when the writer consciously sets out to impress his reader by conjuring up emotions that he does not feel and affecting opinions that he does not hold, when he tries to pawn off an ersatz product as the genuine article—then he is being as intellectually dishonest as the plagiarist.

The tongue-in-the-cheek is, of course, a legitimate pose for the humorist or ironist. The hypocrite's mask is a disguise of a different color. When the teacher asks the class in good faith to write on "Poetry I Like," he may be discouraged by the honest halfback who confesses frankly that no poetry moves him but "Trees" and "The Ballad of Yukon Jake." But he will prefer this sincere Philistine to the effervescent coed who is "simply thrilled" by "L'Allegro" and "Il Penseroso" when it is perfectly obvious on an examination that she can't understand "The Charge of the Light Brigade."

The poet Robinson Jeffers has summarized his own credo of sincerity in words that might well be taken to heart by any writer:

Not to feign any emotion that I did not feel; not to pretend to believe in optimism or pessimism, or unreversible progress; not to say anything because it was popular, or generally accepted, or fashionable in intellectual circles, unless I myself believed it; and not to believe easily.

CLARITY

"I have never had a thought," wrote Poe, "which I could not set down in words with even more distinctness than that with which I conceived it." Above all, good writing is distinct, clear writing. W. Somerset Maugham put "lucidity" first among the requirements of a good prose style. Joseph Conrad implied the same opinion when he wrote: "My task which I am trying to achieve is, by the power of the written word to make you hear, to make you feel—it is, before all to make you *see*." In some kinds of writing—the directions for assembling a Christmas toy, for example—clarity is all that really matters. In all kinds it is supremely important. It isn't enough to "get the general idea across." An experienced reader is willing to meet a writer half-way, but it is too much to expect every reader to be trained in mental telepathy. In page after page of bad writing vagueness is the villain. The good writer strives to be clear at any cost—even if clarity means throwing out his favorite words and fanciest metaphors.

Clumsy sentence structure, faulty punctuation, careless choice of words and figures of speech—all are enemies of clarity that will be discussed in detail later. But two broad aspects of the problem deserve preliminary mention here:

1. Much undergraduate writing is not clear simply because it is not specific. A number of topics expanded elsewhere—the use of details in building paragraphs, illustrations to bolster generalities, concrete instead of abstract words—all add up to one commandment: *Be specific*. This is a time-honored classroom watchword. "I think you understand the point, but I'm not quite sure," says the professor. "Can't you be more specific?" "Be specific," reads the warning at the head of the examination paper; "support your answers with detailed allusion to your reading in the course." "Use more specific detail!" says the comment on the corrected theme. Yet some students retain their affection for lonely, unsupported generalities. The writer who has learned to replace generalities with concrete details has won half the battle for clarity.

2. Many student papers are vague because they are badly organized. A reader should lose himself because he is absorbed in a piece of writing, not because the author's train of thought has suddenly jumped the track. At any given point in explanatory writing, the reader should know exactly where he is and how he got there, and have some notion of where the writer is taking him. In a narrative, mystery and suspense result from conscious craft, not from careless organization. If a good writer doesn't have a clear plan in mind from the start, he will bring order out of

chaos during the revision of his first draft. The parts of a piece of writing must be arranged in a reasonable order; their size must be proportionate to their importance; and the whole must be the sum of all its parts. A composition should be *composed*—literally *put together*. A theme that is merely made up of disconnected tidbits, like the random jottings of a schoolgirl's diary, is not a composition.

ECONOMY

"An army of words escorting a corporal of thought." Ambrose Bierce's definition of *pleonasm* fits many entire student themes. *Pleonasm, tautology, verbosity, prolixity, diffuseness, redundancy, circumlocution, periphrasis*—these words differ slightly in dictionary definition, but they have a common core of meaning. They are all kinds of wordiness. And the variety of terms suggests the prevalence of the disease.

Good writing is economical. The good writer uses no more words than are needed to express his thought and feeling adequately. This does not mean, of course, that the student should be stingy with details, forsaking all adjectives, illustrations, and effective repetition, and paring down his style to the barest bone. It means that, as a general rule, he should not use three words when one will serve. When a beginner is confronted with a minimum word limit, words acquire a statistical value that has no relation to meaning. Instead of trying to compress his phrases, he finds himself attenuating them like taffy at a taffy pull. But no word limit is meant to be taken literally at the expense of economy. The good writer will be concerned not with counting words but with making every word count.

CORRECTNESS

Now that it is evident that correcting themes does not consist entirely of searching for errors, it is time to admit that good writing does involve correct English. What does the term mean?

As used here, correct English is a record of the usage of careful, educated speakers and writers in the middle of the twentieth century. It is not the private jargon of purists and schoolmarms. Dictionary makers collect and codify it; English teachers guard it from abuse; but the people make it.

The laws of correctness are not chiseled for eternity in stone; they are subject to imminent repeal. Yesterday's proper locution is today's error. Today's illiterate expression is standard English tomorrow. No dictionary is ever right up to date.

Because language is a living record, not a series of dead laws, the line between correctness and incorrectness is not easy to draw. A word may have two or three acceptable spellings with little to choose between them. Usage may be so evenly divided between two locutions that neither can be safely designated as "preferred." An expression may be entirely acceptable in one context and unfortunate in another. On the map of correctness there is always a large area of gray between the black and white.

Some violations of the conventions of correct English are obviously more serious than others. It is the common error of the purist to assume or at least imply that all sins of language deserve equal condemnation. Certainly a word that completely misrepresents a writer's meaning is a more serious offense than a neglected apostrophe; a badly misplaced modifier is more misleading than the weak little phrase ending an unemphatic sentence. The student who wrote *physialocial* for *psychological* was making a bigger mistake than the author of this book committed when he scrawled on the outside of a theme: "Your spelling is *attrocious!*" Generally speaking, clumsy sentence structure and careless choice of words are graver crimes than slipshod punctuation and spelling.

This does not mean, of course, that any slips are pardonable. Prevailing undergraduate opinion to the contrary, "slight" typographical errors are not pardonable sins. The reader cannot be expected to distinguish carefully between bad typing and bad spelling or to supply the missing phrase in a hastily copied final draft.

The rules of correctness are not always logical. The reasons for some can be easily given. It should be evident to the most skeptical student, for example, that the omission of an *m* in the word *comma* is likely to lead to misunderstanding. But a student must not expect an equally satisfying explanation of our reluctance to accept the contraction *ain't I* for *am I not* or to condone the spelling *alright* by a logical analogy with *already* and *altogether*. Nor can he expect more than an unconvincing historical justification of our perversity in pronouncing the *ough* in *cough, rough, sough, though,* and *through* five different ways. He must understand that there are conventions in the language as unreasonable as the etiquette of dress; and that, despite the struggles of such eminent simplified spelling advocates as Noah Webster, Theodore Roosevelt, and George Bernard Shaw, English-speaking people continue to retain their irrational spellings for somewhat the same reason that they insist on torturing themselves with wing collars and boiled shirts and strangling neckties. The student must not blame the English teacher for warning him against conducting a one-man revolution against the linguistic traditions of several hundred million people. He must resign himself continually to the argument that this or that expression is incorrect simply because careful, educated twentieth-century writers do not ordinarily use it.

It is true that Gertrude Stein, E. E. Cummings, and James Joyce have ignored conventional grammar and punctuation, and that William Saroyan once wrote in a celebrated preface: "Do not pay any attention to the rules other people make." The student who invokes such celebrities in his own defense is easy to answer, if hard to convince. One rather condescending answer is that the average teacher would gladly lend any potential Joyce or Shakespeare in the class a more generous amount of rope if he would promise to produce a *Ulysses* or a *Hamlet* instead of hanging himself. Another is that print is not sacred, nor any mortal writer infallible. When Maugham wrote of Fanny Price's suicide in *Of Human Bondage*, "The wretched woman was hanging with a rope round her neck, which she had tied to a hook in the ceiling fixed by some previous tenant to hold up the curtains of the bed"—he was introducing an unintentional guffaw into one of his big scenes because of carelessness about an elementary rule of sentence structure. The coauthors of a recent book have collected an impressive anthology of similar passages from well-known writers.[1] But perhaps the best answer to the student is that many contemporary authors are ceaselessly experimenting with language; that when they take liberties with the rules, they usually know what they are doing and why; and that this can seldom be said of the beginner. A Picasso learns the rules of conventional painting before he dabbles in cubism. A tennis player should learn the principles of orthodox footwork before he tries to bring off a shot with both feet facing the net. By the same token the college writer is expected to display some understanding of accepted techniques before he tries too many experiments.

Finally, the student must not be expected to be furnished with a handbook rule, complete with name and number, to support every objection that the instructor makes. Will Rogers' wisecrack about the pedestrian traffic laws—"If you get hit outside the white lines, it doesn't count"—is not applicable here. Any poor writer can create clumsy expressions that the most imaginative handbook writer could not encompass in a thousand rules. That is why one of the most useful theme-correcting symbols in the instructor's armory is a large *K* or a raucous *awk*—meaning, not incorrect, but just plain awkward.

APPROPRIATENESS

"One time," says a writer in the *New Yorker*, "a newspaper sent us to a morgue to get a story on a woman whose body was being held for identification. A man believed to be her husband was brought in. Somebody pulled the sheet back; the man took one agonizing look and cried, 'My God, it's her!' When we reported this grim incident, the editor diligently changed it to 'My God, it's she!' "

In the final reckoning, the key question is not whether a word or phrase is *correct* according to a dogmatic textbook rule, but whether it is *appropriate* in its context. The writer must

[1] R. Graves and A. Hodge, *The Reader over Your Shoulder*, New York, 1943, pp. 207–446.

be constantly aware of (1) the point of view from which he is writing; (2) the reader for whom he is writing; and (3) the purpose he wants to accomplish.

A story written from the point of view of an eight-year-old child or a passage of authentic dialogue between two college freshmen would certainly violate a number of traditional grammatical rules. A scientific monograph prepared for delivery before the American Chemical Society would have a different vocabulary from that of a popular article on soybeans for the *Woman's Home Companion*. "No spitting allowed" is obviously a more effective, if less elegant piece of writing for a New York subway sign than "Expectoration is expressly forbidden." And there are occasions when "My God, it's her" is supremely appropriate.

Usually a college freshman will be writing strictly from his own point of view as of the date of composition. Until he begins experimenting with various methods of storytelling, the only aspect of the problem likely to bother him is what to call himself. In some kinds of writing—a formal report, for example—he may wish to preserve an air of anonymity or objectivity by staying out of the picture entirely. But in others—an autobiographical anecdote or an informal explanation of a personal view—he will be naturally subjective. Though he may choose to write about himself in the third person, he should not be misled by quaint convention or false modesty into dubbing himself "the writer" or "the present writer." He might as well be absent from the picture as wear such an ill-fitting disguise. The "editorial *we*" is a defensible convention in newspapers and magazines, where one writer presumably reflects the sentiments of the entire staff; but in other contexts it usually gives off an unnatural air of dignity and ceremony like the "royal *we*" of monarchy. "An editorial writer," says E. B. White, "refers to himself as 'we,' but is never sure who the other half of the 'we' is. I have yet to encounter the other half of 'we,' but expect to nail him in an alley some day and beat his brains out, to see what sort of stuffing is behind such omniscience." There is, however, no legitimate objection to the "pedagogical *we*" as long as it clearly refers to the writer and his reader, and not at the same time to *we-the-editors, we-meaning-I,*

or *we-the-people-in-general*. It is better in most explanatory writing than the completely impersonal approach because it helps to eliminate the clumsy passive voice. Roundabout expressions such as "now it can be observed that" are guaranteed to increase both the density and the specific gravity of any piece of writing.

Most of the time the easiest way out of the dilemma is for a writer to call himself what he normally and naturally calls himself every day of his life—*I*. It is absurd for a student to fear that this will make him sound either egotistical or repetitious. Almost all writing is partly autobiographical, and autobiography is about the writer himself, not about two other people. A genuine egotist cannot disguise his symptoms under other pronouns. It is monotonous to repeat *I* too often at the beginning of a sentence, or to overwork such expressions as "I believe" and "in my opinion" when the reader hasn't the slightest doubt about whose opinion is being expressed. But a repetitious writer won't cure himself by merely borrowing a new set of pronouns.

Who is the reader going to be? A man writing for publication may occasionally take up the challenge of Sir Philip Sidney and look in his heart and write. He may look only into his wallet. But he usually takes a good look at his audience—or at least at his publisher's conception of that audience. Vague as that composite picture may be, it is easier to visualize than Posterity. A novelist may consider whether the results from his recipe will be caviare to the general or mush for the masses, whether he is aiming at "fit audience, though few" or the fifteen million readers of a prodigiously popular slick magazine. A writer discussing the miracle of atomic fission must decide whether he is preparing a *technical* paper for a select group of Ph.D.'s in physics; a *semitechnical* article for a larger audience of educated laymen, who require elementary definitions but resent too much chocolate coating on the scientific pill; or a *popular* explanation for "the man in the street"—whoever he may be. One authority has based an entire book on the assumption that "nothing but a scientific check can keep you from forgetting your audience while you are speaking or writing."[2] He has devised a "yardstick formula" that

2 Rudolf Flesch, *The Art of Plain Talk,* New York, 1946, p. 6.

enables a writer, with a little simple arithmetic, to find out whether he has set his sights on a seventh-grader or a college graduate. Such a yardstick may be of doubtful value. But the fact remains that a writer doesn't write only for the reflection of his own ego. He writes to convey meaning to somebody else. And he can't keep asking his reader at the end of every sentence: "Do I make myself clear?"

Actually the college freshman in the average composition course has a reading public of one; the occasional theme inflicted on a roommate or read aloud in class is an exception. The student is naturally tempted to adapt his style and ideas to the supposed tastes and prejudices of the only regular member of his audience— to write what the instructor presumably wants. In a sense this is good; for any audience is better than none. On the whole, however, the student will do well to forget, as far as is humanly possible, that he is writing a "theme" for Elwood Perkins, Ph.D., or even for an English teacher. If he can do this, he will avoid the offensive "Dear Teacher" familiarity of too much undergraduate writing ("As you said in class last Saturday, Prof"); and he will escape the evils springing from the common illusion that there is a unique species of jargon appropriate only to English themes. He can hardly adapt every assignment to a different audience (atomic energy for an audience of Rotarians; the meaning of democracy for a class of seventh-graders; how to bunt a baseball, as explained to the members of an English cricket team). The difficulty of addressing only his classmates is that he may never rise far above the level of dormitory gossip. A reasonable compromise is to aim at a hypothetical, well-educated, mid-twentieth century, adult human being.

What kind of writing is appropriate for this hypothetical adult? It will depend, of course, on whether the writer's purpose is to move him to tears or laughter, arouse him with an angry shout or soothe him with a quiet meditation, tell a story, describe a scene, explain an idea, or convince with an argument. But some preliminary generalities may set the student on the right track.

LEVELS OF USAGE

The English language can be roughly divided according to three levels of usage: (1) *formal;* (2) *informal;* and (3) *vulgate.*

The formal level is employed in an appreciable amount of serious writing, but not so much as is commonly supposed. Research papers, technical reports, textbooks, impersonal business letters, sermons, and commencement addresses—these are some of the contexts in which it can be often discerned. Formal writing eschews colloquialisms and slang, adheres strictly to traditional caveats about syntax, and exhibits a propensity toward technical terminology, abstract diction, and rhetorical artifice—a propensity, one might add, which does not always contribute to clarity. By employing longer sentences than are common in informal writing, by making them grammatically complete—including all essential pronouns and connectives—by using words that are infrequent in conversation, and by indulging in such devices as antithesis and allusion, formal writing conveys a bookish, if not always a literary, impression. This paragraph is an approximation of the formal level.

The informal level is used in a great deal of writing among educated Americans today—in friendly letters, newspaper columns, talks, magazine articles, and many serious books. Informal writing is close to the everyday talk of educated men and women. Though it doesn't stoop to the vulgate, it has a good many colloquialisms—or expressions common in conversation but not in formal writing—and a certain amount of slang, handled with care but not with gloves. It sticks close enough to the basic rule-book but doesn't put much stock in worn-out warnings about the difference between *shall* and *will,* the split infinitive, and the preposition at the end of a sentence. It prefers familiar, concrete words to technical and abstract words, likes short sentences in natural word order, and is suspicious of rhetorical tricks. It doesn't mind taking a few short cuts—omitting unnecessary words and using occasional contractions. It's relaxed but not careless. This paragraph is a reasonable facsimile of informal writing.

The vulgate level don't mean just vulgar words that wouldn't get by in polite society. And it don't mean just slang or mistakes in grammar neither, though it's got plenty of both. It's the kind of a lingo a guy'd hear from millions of straight Joes shooting the breeze on the job or over the back fence. Specially people that don't read much and haven't had much chancet at schooling. It's catch-as-catch-can like and there ain't many holds barred. You don't see it much in printed books, except in places like where people are talking, on account of books are mostly wrote by educated people. Between you and I, this vulgate may be okay in the poolroom, but it don't belong in the ballroom. This here is a sample, as if you didn't know it.

Of course, these illustrations oversimplify the problem. The usage level of any piece of writing is determined not only by vocabulary and grammar, but by sentence structure, punctuation, and such intangibles as tone and rhythm. Obviously there is considerable overlapping from level to level. The problem for a writer is not to memorize a pat formula or three separate vocabularies and sets of rules, but, by wide reading and careful listening, to develop an automatic awareness of levels of usage. When a word or expression is common in informal writing, but not in formal, this book will make that distinction. The question of usage will be discussed again in Chapter Eight. A good dictionary distinguishes slang and colloquialisms from "standard English." But a well-developed awareness of usage levels cannot be acquired from any single book, or teacher, or course in composition.

It was once fashionable in freshman English handbooks to stress formal writing. In recent years, however, the pendulum has swung to the middle of the scale. Since the average college graduate has more opportunities for talking than for writing, it is logical to teach the undergraduate the kind of writing closest to educated speech. Moreover, there is a marked tendency toward informality in the best modern American prose, a trend that partly accounts for the almost complete disappearance of the old academic distinction between the formal and the informal or familiar essay. It's a safe guess that nine tenths of the writing the average student will do after leaving college will be informal. Finally, the writer who learns to steer the treacherous middle course of simplicity between the artificial and pretentious, on the one hand, and the illiterate and inaccurate, on the other, is bowing to no temporary fad. English literature has a tradition of informal prose going back at least as far as the fifteenth century, including such celebrated writers as Sir Thomas Malory, Izaak Walton, Addison and Steele, William Hazlitt, and Thomas Henry Huxley.

CONSISTENCY

After a writer has sized up his audience and decided on the appropriate point of view, level of difficulty, and level of usage, he should follow them consistently unless he has good reason to change; and he should not change without carefully preparing the reader. A careless shift in point of view is common:

> "In preparing *my* new book, 'Above All Nations,' which is the record of deeds of humanity and heroism done in wartime to the enemy, *the present writer* was confronted with the question whether this heroism for the humane, of which Goethe would have so much approved, sprang or could emotionally spring from the culture to which Goethe himself adhered." —George Catlin, "T. S. Eliot and the Moral Issue," *Saturday Review of Literature.*

A sudden switch from one level of usage to another, or an unmotivated change in tone can be equally disconcerting. Sir Arthur Quiller-Couch quotes the well-meaning Babu who wrote of his mother's death: "Regret to inform you, the hand that rocked the cradle has kicked the bucket."[3] This line is not only a mixture of usage levels—a ridiculously sudden switch from formal usage to vulgate; it is a bewildering mixture of tones—the impersonal austerity of official jargon ("Regret to inform you"), the trite sentimentality of a Mother's Day cliché ("the hand that rocked the cradle"), and then, capping the anticlimax, the bluntness of street-corner slang ("has kicked the bucket"). Not only are the two figures of speech on different levels of usage—a clear proof that figurative language is not necessarily formal language; they combine to form a bizarre mixed metaphor—inconsistency number three.

[3] *On the Art of Writing*, New York, 1916, p. 102.

NATURALNESS

Informal writing is natural writing, and natural writing has a clear note of speech throughout. When a student is stuck for a word or conscious of an awkward phrase, he should ask himself not "How shall I *write* it?" but "How would I *say* it?" If he has had ample opportunity to listen to the speech of educated people, he should be suspicious of any expression in his writing that doesn't *sound* natural.

Every day in an English class some earnest student perpetrates something like this:

It was with some mental confusion that I set foot on the tossing deck of college education because I had not regained the all-conquering drive of inspiration that leads to lasting intellectual satisfaction. I had, however, a sufficiently inflated ego, which was the balloon tires to cushion my ride in the mental carriage of pseudo-self-sufficiency, so that I believe myself capable of mastering any educational course.

The reader winces, throws a large red lariat around it, and in the adjoining margin scrawls "vague," "forced," "mixed," or just a large red question mark. In a conference he hopefully asks the student:

"What did you mean by that?"

"Why," answers the author with little hesitation, "I meant that when I first came to college, I was confused because I had lost the desire to study. But I had enough self-confidence to know that I would come through all right."

"If you meant just that, why didn't you say just that?"

"I thought that in an English course—"

The wheel has come full circle and the monster portrayed at the beginning of the chapter is looming up again.

But there is hope for this student, more hope than for a student with a smaller vocabulary, a more limited imagination, a less vivid sense of metaphor. He can be taught that the gulf between speech and informal mid-twentieth-century writing is comfortably narrow. And, like the famous character in Molière who woke up in middle age to discover he had been talking prose for forty years, he may learn at eighteen that he has been talking English not far removed from the writing that is appropriate for an English theme.

CHAPTER TWO

Getting Under Way

Mr. Grant always says in comp. class: "Begin at the begin-
ning." Only I don't know quite where the beginning was.
—Chuck Peters in Stephen Vincent Benét, "Too
Early Spring."

⇛⇛⇛⇛⇛⇛⇛⇛⇛⇛⇛⇛⇛⇛⇛⇛⇛⇛⇛⇛⇛⇛⇛⇛⇛⇛

THE ASSIGNMENT FOR NEXT TIME

There are three kinds of theme assignments. The first allows
the student complete freedom in selecting his subject; the second
permits him to choose from a menu of canned "theme topics" the
item that comes closest to tempting his palate; the third pre-
scribes a single topic and, in many instances, a single method of
preparation.

All these assignments have their virtues, but not one of them
solves the problem of the student who habitually has "nothing
to write about." He is revealing symptoms that go far deeper than
the inability to express himself. The only advice for him is this:
Open your eyes and ears to what's going on in the world around
you. Subscribe to a good newspaper and some grown-up magazines. Read some of the books other people are talking about, and
when you read the assignments in your courses, pencil comments
in the margin. If out of all that you have seen and heard and
probably read, you are consistently unable to accumulate five
hundred words' worth of coherent experience, you are sleep-
walking through life. Wake up.

SELECTING A SUBJECT

If you are given carte blanche or allowed to choose from a
varied menu, you should keep one principle in mind: *Select a subject that you are competent to handle adequately at the required
length.* On the whole, especially at the beginning of the course,
stay close to your own experience. You can probably write a bet-

ter story about an insurance agent next door than about a secret
foreign agent in Moldavia, a better description of a dormitory
room at 7 A.M. than of a tropical sunrise, a better explanation of
fraternity combines than of international cartels. This does not
mean, however, that you should confine yourself to those limited
areas of experience in which you presume to be an authority.
Don't permit yourself to be silenced by false humility ("Who am
I, a poor freshman, to be writing on a subject like *World
Peace?*"). The phrase "a subject you are competent to handle"
must not be taken too literally. The most rewarding assignment
is not the one that lets you explain a hobby you have understood
backward and forward for years, but the one that makes you dig
around and learn something you haven't known before.

STAKING OUT A CLAIM

The main trouble is not that students insist on writing about
World Peace when they ought to stick to *Peace in My Family,* but
that they often try singlehanded to solve in five hundred words
a problem that the peoples of the world have not been able to
solve in millions. The most you can possibly do in five hundred
words is throw a sharp pinpoint of light on one infinitesimal
aspect of a major problem. You must divide the vast area and
subdivide it and resubdivide it until you have staked out a small,
unambitious claim. If you don't do this, you can only scratch the
surface with dull generalities.

Few theme assignments are so narrow and explicit that this
limiting process is unnecessary. It works something like this:

Original assignment   *World Peace* (300–500 words)
Steps in limiting   1. Ways of achieving world peace (dis-
armament, world government, the atomic bomb,
bigger-and-better air forces, world-wide Christianity, the United Nations)
2. World peace through the United Nations (Security Council, General Assembly, International Court of Justice, big nations vs.
small nations, the veto)
3. The veto (arguments pro and con)

Final topic	4. Russia's use of the veto at Lake Success yesterday
Title	*Yesterday's Veto*

In most colleges the first assignment in freshman composition is one of the easiest and the hardest: *An Autobiographical Theme*. It is easy because it enables the student to write on the subject he knows and perhaps likes best. It is hard not so much because of false modesty as because it tempts the writer to hurry all the way from birth to college in five hundred words. Here again limiting is compulsory. In Lytton Strachey's metaphor, the student must "lower the little bucket" instead of trying to swallow the vast ocean of material. The development of a special interest, the influence of a particular person, book, or event, the growth of a dominant character trait, a segment of time (life in the fifth grade), or only a pivotal point (high school commencement)—possible approaches are numberless. The lives of few students are so sensational that a mere synopsis of the-story-thus-far is exciting, or so dull that all the flavor can be concentrated into a single biographical sketch.

THE FIRST DRAFT

Having cut the subject down to size, how do you go about writing on it? There are as many answers to that as there are writers.

Undergraduate opinion traditionally divides students into two classes: those who can dash off a passing theme in half an hour and those who have to sit down for hour on frenzied hour enduring an agony that can best be described in the GI idiom—"sweating it out." The history of literature reveals both kinds too: Shakespeare, who "never blotted a line," and Gray, Keats, and Fitzgerald, who wrote, revised, rewrote, revised—and were never satisfied; Anthony Trollope pouring out novels wholesale during off moments on trains and steamboats and Wordsworth sick from struggling at the sheepfold to find an epithet for the cuckoo. Certainly there are more members of the second fraternity than of the first. Or perhaps it would be more accurate to say that most writers fall between two schools. For most people the baffling act of composition is an erratic mixture of smooth and rough going that bears a close resemblance to a duffer's golf: on some days or holes the shots zoom straight to the pin, on others they don't even find the fairway. A. E. Housman is a consoling case in point. Writing about the last lyric in *A Shropshire Lad,* he tells how the first two stanzas came to him out of the blue just as they were finally printed, and the third followed with a little coaxing after tea. The fourth? "I wrote it thirteen times, and it was more than a twelvemonth before I got it right."

It all adds up to one conclusion: *Writing well is hard work.* This rule has a corollary, which Sheridan once put this way: *Easy writing's curst hard reading.* The manufacturers of mass production fiction may have their formulas; the magicians of the how-do-you-know-you-can't-write ads may peddle "tested" recipes; but serious professional writers generally agree that there is no short cut to creation. Some of them still spend as much time typing idle doodles and chewing pencils as the average undergraduate. And most of them learned their craft the hard way through ink, sweat, and tears.

In the absence of foolproof formulas, these suggestions may help:

1. *Don't sell your subconscious short:* Don't fool yourself into supposing that the writing process consists entirely of putting words on paper. That is the final stage. You will naturally set aside a period, perhaps the same evening each week, to write your theme. But there is no law forbidding a little preliminary rumination one or two days before. Shortly after the subject is chosen, turn it over in your mind a few times. Then, if inspiration is going to strike at all—a fresh approach, an arresting beginning, a well-turned phrase—it may pop suddenly into your mind while you are strolling idly across the campus dreaming about the interfraternity ball. If, on the other hand, you assiduously avoid all thought about English until 7:45 the night before the deadline, and then, starting from behind scratch, try desperately to decoy inspiration from a glaring sheet of virgin paper—you will probably have to settle past midnight for a handful of well-used bromides.

2. *Make a few rough notes:*   English teachers disagree about the value of the formal outline. It is certainly useful in studying organization and in planning a long research paper. If you are aware that weak organization is one of your chief faults, turn at once to page 357 and review the principles of outlining. On the whole, however, only the unusually weak organizer or the exceedingly methodical writer needs a formal outline for an informal paper of five hundred words. Detailed outlines can be a nuisance, curbing natural expression and producing firstly-secondly-thirdly themes with the bare bones of the skeleton glaring through the transparent flesh.

On the other hand, it is easier to hang a theme on visible pegs than to try to visualize it in the mind's wavering eye. A few jottings, however scrappy and inconsecutive, will usually help. The student who has reduced *An Autobiographical Theme* to *My Career in the Fifth Grade* might jot down something like this: Grade 5B—second floor left top of the stairs—Miss Heppelthwaite—skidding pince-nez—a visit to the principal—the "P.S. 87 spee-rit"—chalk dust—clapping erasers—carefully drawn alphabet top of blackboard—"alphabetical frieze" (?)—turkeys on the window at Thanksgiving—third place in the city broad jump—Sylvia Schultz—Theodore Roosevelt Cooper—pigtails and inkwells—Palmer method—"Make your ovals round, children"—"All right or one wrong, stand up"—"Take one and pass the others back"—fights at recess—"Never lead with your right, kid"—penny candy . . . .

This is the kind of flotsam and jetsam that turns up in the notebooks of many successful professional writers who never studied formal outlining. In 1911 Arnold Bennett made these jottings after a football game at Princeton:

7:45. Business men—the humanity beneath. A man said, "I'm just going to get a bromo-seltzer." Thus giving the whole show away. Postal Telegraph. Girl coming behind her counter in hat and cloak, and turning on her counter lights and opening up her shop. Luggage men sitting in a group under stairs and discussing their affairs. Princeton. Man conducting the "official yell." Quarterback calling numbers. Adams said there was a Glee Club concert last night that was delightful. Contortions of enthusiasts. Artistic amenity in contrast to this bloody barbarity. Reserve men waiting in pairs under red rugs. Whole crowd rising up and sitting down at points of play. Nassau Club. Confusion. Princeton Inn. Confusion. After freshman game met Booth Tarkington at Nassau Club. Drink in dining-room. He said he had been drinking beer with undergraduates late, and then couldn't sleep owing to men singing Chinese songs all night in corridor. Auto back to club and then to field. Coloured effect of hats on stands, heaps of violet colour. Harvard opposite to us. Cheer-leaders with megaphones. Standing up and sitting down. At high moments standing on seats. Accident at start. Man led off amid cheers. Several minor accidents. Naïve and barbaric! Merely an outlet for enthusiasm. Touch and goal scored. Left at half time. —*The Journal of Arnold Bennett.*

On the same evening, an American undergraduate, knowing far more about football than the English novelist, probably struggled to put his recollections of the same event into five hundred words plucked out of the air and concluded that there was "nothing to write about" except yards gained and lost and the prosaic fact of the final score.

3. *Choose at least one main point:* The traditional textbook regulation that every theme should have a "guiding" or "controlling" purpose is based on two assumptions: (1) that unless the student keeps one goal clearly in mind, he is in grave danger of ending up nowhere, of writing a theme without a theme; and (2) that one main point is all that can be adequately developed in a short paper. The second assumption is open to some question: a five-hundred-word paper might have two well-made points or three. But the danger of aimlessness is obvious. Many a student is confused at the outset because, having no clear goal ahead at the start—no "angle," as a newspaperman might say—he is busily riding off in all directions at once like the gifted horseman in Stephen Leacock's story. There is, of course, the discursive familiar essay, which begins anywhere, goes everywhere, and ends nowhere, and the modern "stream-of-consciousness" narrative technique, which meanders with the whims of the rudderless human mind. But even these methods have an elusive unity that the undergraduate rarely perceives. The student who merely

opens a door in his forehead and pours the miscellaneous contents of his brain onto the paper is almost inevitably doomed to
failure. The beginner would do well to take the guiding purpose
rule literally.

4. *Begin your first draft wherever you like:* The first sentence you write doesn't have to be the first sentence of the final
product. If you assume that it does, you may be so worried about
getting off on the right foot that you will never get started. Begin
with the part that comes easiest to you—it may eventually turn
out to be somewhere in the middle of the third paragraph—and
get that much down. After you have written that, you can write
the rest of your paper around it. The preface to most books is
fashioned on the home stretch. Richard Wright says of his first
novel: "The book was one-half finished, with the opening and
closing scenes unwritten. . . . The entire guilt theme that runs
through *Native Son* was woven in after the first draft was written."

5. *Write your first draft any way you please:* The first draft
is no place to worry about the instructor and the textbook. Don't
interrupt yourself at this stage to juggle phrases, quibble over
grammar, track down the inevitable word. Revision will come
later, and it is easier to twist a poor sentence on paper into a good
one than to pluck a good one out of the air. The white heat of
your creation may be only lukewarm to begin with. Don't let it
cool off completely by stopping for revisions en route.

BEGINNINGS

How should the theme eventually begin? If you are a slave
to the formula that every piece of writing must have Beginning,
Middle, and End (or Introduction, Body, and Conclusion), free
yourself from bondage now. This is a convenient pedagogical
pattern based partly on a misunderstanding of Aristotle, partly
on the natural fear of abrupt beginnings and dangling, inconclusive conclusions, partly on the intelligent assumption that
any organization, however rigid, is better than none. It may be
useful in composing formal arguments or long dissertations. But
in five hundred words of informal writing, the I-am-about-to-
make-this-point, I-am-making-this-point, I-have-made-this-point

structure implies a weakness in your reader's perception and memory that you probably have no right to assume.

Four kinds of beginnings, to name only a few, are likely to elicit an automatic protest from any experienced reader:

1. *The student who feels that he can't approach his simple personal confession without first inditing a high-sounding truism about life-in-general:*

Throughout the history of the world men have had affairs with women. Adam and Eve, Antony and Cleopatra, Napoleon and his Austrian princess, and so throughout the centuries. This ancient tradition is more common in the modern era than ever.

Or this:

Down through history, from Eve to Joan of Arc, from Cleopatra to Eleanor Roosevelt, we find that women have provided inspiration for men and molded their lives, their efforts, and their destinies. For the love of women men have robbed, murdered, pillaged, gained riches, and gained greatness.

After opening cannonades like these, no short theme could be anything but an anticlimactic sputter of grapeshot.

2. *The student who discourses at length on the difficulties of writing a theme on the assigned subject:*

Who am I? This question is quite a difficult problem to analyze, even though it looks quite simple at a glance. To give a complete analysis of yourself it takes quite a considerable length of time, even though you have lived with yourself all your life. Not many students take this viewpoint that I take, so I shall try to give an analysis of myself.

The author of this wordy windup is like the public-speaking nuisance who spends the first five minutes complaining that he can't possibly begin to cover his subject in the fifteen minutes allowed.

3. *The student who begins with a personal apology to the teacher that belongs, if anywhere, in a headnote or a billet-doux clipped to the outside of the theme:*

After searching vainly for a subject on which to write which would be related to the assigned topic, *A Literary Criticism,* I came to the conclusion that everything I considered as a possible theme had already been well "hashed over" in class. Therefore, I gave up and succumbed to a desire I've had since very early in this course—to write about Walter Pater and some of his writings.

4. *The student who begins an expository theme inevitably with a dictionary definition:*

Before entering into a discussion of the wit of Oscar Wilde as displayed in *The Importance of Being Earnest,* it is first necessary to ask ourselves: What do we mean by *wit? Webster's Collegiate Dictionary* defines wit . . . .

This kind of beginning is less objectionable than the others. It is based on the plausible assumption that sooner or later key terms should be defined. The student is to be commended for naming his source instead of vaguely writing: "The dictionary says . . . ." But regardless of the importance of definition, the dictionary definition beginning has become thoroughly hackneyed.

If you have to warm up to your subject on paper, one obvious solution is to cross out the first paragraph and begin the final draft with the second. There is some truth to the stories about novelists who regularly jettison the first hundred pages of every book they write. George Meredith tossed away three of the first four chapters of *The Ordeal of Richard Feverel.* Keats threw out the entire first stanza of his first draft of the "Ode on Melancholy."

The old rule—Begin at the beginning—is sound in principle but not too helpful. Here are a few more tangible suggestions:

1. *Begin with a simple statement of fact:*

I passed all the other courses that I took at my University, but I could never pass botany. This was because all botany students had to spend several hours a week in a laboratory looking through a microscope at plant cells, and I could never see through a microscope. —James Thurber, "University Days," *My Life and Hard Times.*

The armistice came when I was eighteen. —Vincent Sheean, "The Modern Gothic," *Personal History.*

My trouble with doilies dates way back. —E. B. White, "The Doilie Menace," *Quo Vadimus.*

2. *Begin with a sentence that awakens or startles the reader with its bluntness or frankness:*

Education is indeed the dullest of subjects and I intend to say as little about it as I can. —Jacques Barzun, *Teacher in America.*

These are the times that try men's souls. —Thomas Paine, *The Crisis.*

This will never do. —Francis Jeffrey, Review of Wordsworth's "Excursion," *Edinburgh Review.*

3. *Begin with a significant dramatic incident, instead of one that comes first chronologically, and then revert to the steps leading up to that incident:*

A shiver went through Lonnie. He drew his hand away from his sharp chin, remembering what Clem had said. It made him feel now as if he were committing a crime by standing in Arch Gunnard's presence and allowing his face to be seen.

He and Clem had been walking up the road together that afternoon on their way to the filling station when he told Clem how much he needed rations. Clem stopped a moment to kick a rock out of the road, and said that if you worked for Arch Gunnard long enough, your face would be sharp enough to split the boards for your own coffin. —Erskine Caldwell, *Kneel to the Rising Sun.*

4. *Begin with a question or series of questions, the answer to which is the core of your theme:*

"Tell me, Mr. Broun," said the young lady to my right, "how did you happen to become a Red?" —Heywood Broun, "From Spargo to Carver to Speaker," *New Republic.*

5. *Begin with a pertinent quotation—but be sure it is short and fresh:*

"I would like to see Gopher Prairie," says the heroine of Mr. Sinclair Lewis's *Main Street,* and her husband promptly replies: "Trust me. Here she is. Brought some snapshots down to show you." That, in substance, is what Mr. Lewis has done himself. He has brought down some snapshots to show us and posterity. —E. M. Forster, "Sinclair Lewis," *Abinger Harvest.*

However various, these beginnings have one trait in common: they are all simple and direct. In each one the writer not only gets off to a fast start himself but takes the reader right along with him.

ENDINGS

Ending is easier than beginning. *When you have finished what you have to say, stop.* The danger of leaving a reader "up in the air" has been overrated. In a story an inconclusive ending may be a conscious device. In explanation or argument, a point left up in the air is one that has never really been put across in the first place, and no stylish epilogue will save it. Actually more students botch endings by saying, not too little, but too much:

So ends the analysis of myself and the question of who am I has been answered in a brief form.

This ending, by the same student who contributed the beginning under (2) on page 27, is about as necessary as the old-fashioned *Finis.* It is as if the writer were signing off like a radio announcer to clarify matters for a reader who has tuned in in the middle of the fourth paragraph.

The most objectionable ending is that of the student who, having no clear-cut plan from the start, wanders along until he hits a blind alley, counts his words hopefully and finds that he is still below the minimum, and then, gathering his forces for one last struggle, either appends a superfluous summary of what has just been said, or shoots off bravely on a brand new course that he hasn't the slightest notion of pursuing to a logical conclusion.

Even good writers have made the mistake of going a step too far. Joseph Conrad admitted in a letter to H. G. Wells that he should have ended *Youth* with the men sleeping in the boats, exhausted after the exasperating voyage to the East, instead of permitting Marlow to launch once more into a rapture on the resiliency of youthful hearts. It is a common student error to begin discussing a point and abruptly drop it. It is equally common for a student to make a point and then mar it by pointing out the point he has just made.

REVISION

When your first draft is ended, you are ready to revise. Revision is not the simple act of giving the first draft a once-over-lightly for missing commas and occasional misspellings. It is a major step in creation. It demands not only painstaking proof-reading for mechanical errors in grammar, punctuation, and spelling, but recasting awkward sentences, rearranging passages for more effective order, adding details and subtracting others, substituting sharp, concrete words for fuzzy abstractions. For every trained writer who has never blotted a line in revision, there are hundreds whose first copies are almost illegible mazes of insertions and deletions, cobwebs of carets and circles and meandering arrows. Honest revision is often so complete as to require at least one intermediate draft before the final copy.

Here are some general aids in better revision:

1. *Put your first draft aside for some time before attacking it again:* After a reasonable interval—the longer the better—you should be able to approach it with some detachment. The memory of what you meant to write will be dulled, and you will have a clearer perspective on what you actually have written. More than once you will ask yourself: "Did I really write that?" This advice assumes, of course, that you haven't postponed the whole project until the eleventh hour.

2. *Let another student read it:* Obviously, if he makes complete alterations for you, you will learn little. The final product should be yours, not a collaboration. There is no reason, however, moral or otherwise, why you should not invite suggestions from another critic. An ambiguity which has never occurred to you may strike him at once. (Ask any teacher who has tried to make out a set of examination questions that will convey the same meaning to a whole roomful of undergraduates.) Few trained writers would think of writing a book without inflicting an early draft on a dozen or more previewers.

3. *Read it out loud:* Unless you are a trained proofreader, your eyes will play tricks on you—ignoring words and pretending to your brain that you have seem them. The ear will catch many

errors—clumsy, unemphatic sentences, discordant phrases, weakening repetition, careless omissions—that the eye will never see.

4. *Read it at least three times:*   A sound plan, if somewhat arbitrary, is to read once for such broad aspects as logical organization (including intelligent paragraphing); a second time for your favorite errors (You should know after two or three themes are returned whether spelling, punctuation, grammar, or sentence structure is your special weakness and lay your emphasis accordingly); and the third time as a sort of final check for good measure. If this ambitious plan seems to assume that you have nothing to do but write English compositions, remember that you can read five hundred words slowly in less than five minutes and can afford fifteen or twenty minutes to save yourself a lot of woe. Remember also that perhaps half of all freshman errors are due to sheer carelessness. Moreover, the ideal final copy should be nothing but a clean duplicate of your rough draft—with no last-ditch rewriting.

5. *Use reference books freely:*   It doesn't take much longer to consult a dictionary for a correct spelling than to consult your roommate, who may not know how to spell either. Moreover, the book you are now reading is intended to be more than a series of consecutive lessons to be approached only when "pages 212–234" are "assigned for next time." You may not "study" punctuation formally until two months from now, but that is no reason why you should blissfully misuse the semicolon until you get there. Use the Index and Glossary freely.

This advice applies also to the content of your theme. Get direct quotations straight. Replace generalities with specific facts. Don't try to get by with a rough guess about a historical event when five minutes in the library will put the record straight.

THE CLEAN COPY

After you finish revising, make a neat, careful copy in strict accordance with all the local ground rules. These will probably require the following:

1. Write legibly in blue or black ink, or type double-space,

on one side of regulation theme paper (usually 8½ by 11 inches).

2. Use lined paper for handwriting, unlined for typing.

3. On handwritten copy center the title on the top line of the first page and leave a space between title and text. On typed copy center the title about 2 inches from the top of the first page and leave about an inch before beginning the text. Do not underline the title or enclose it in quotes.

4. Leave good-sized margins (1½ inches at the left and 1 inch at top, right, and bottom; half an inch for paragraph indentations).

5. Number the pages in the upper right-hand corner with Arabic numerals.

6. Arrange pages in the proper order and fold them lengthwise so that the theme opens like a book (not a Japanese book). Longer manuscripts such as term papers are often handed in flat, with an additional title page.

7. Endorse the theme at the top of the outside sheet to the right of the fold, giving at least:

> Your name
> The title
> The date

The rules will probably not require that you type, but you are unfortunate if you can't and foolish if you don't learn at the first opportunity. Try as he might to be strictly objective, a teacher can't help preferring a neat, double-spaced manuscript in clear black type to the most punctilious specimen of penmanship. He may be excused for suspecting immaturity in an "immature" hand, assuming misspelling of an illegible word, and refusing to pore over sprawling, slanting hieroglyphics or cultivated hothouse backhand.

In making the clean copy, be careful to avoid all short cuts taken in your first draft merely to save time. Even if you can't wait to reach the final period of the final draft, the manuscript should not betray your haste. A few privileged abbreviations are acceptable in any kind of writing: Dr., Mr., Mrs., and the like before proper names; Jr., Sr., M.D., Ph.D., and the like after proper names; A.D. and B.C., A.M. and P.M., No. and $ when they are used with dates and figures. Many are common in technical papers: btu, cm, ft, rpm, for example. In informal writing it would be absurd to replace abbreviations as simple and common as SPCA and WCTU with such unwieldy titles as *Society for the Prevention of Cruelty to Animals* and *Women's Christian Temperance Union*. It would be tiresome to write an article on the organization of today's federal government without using some abbreviations. But in most nontechnical writing, however informal, abbreviations are used sparingly. The general reader wants to read words, not shorthand symbols; he prefers *Street* to *St., chapter* to *ch.* or *chap., Charles* to *Chas., Wisconsin* to *Wis., for example* to *e.g., and* to &, and so forth (which he prefers to *etc.*).

The general rule for numbers is simpler: Except in technical writing and in a few special instances such as dates and addresses, *spell out all numbers if you can do it in two words* (*twenty-three, forty, 137*); if you can't avoid beginning a sentence with a number, spell it out; if a passage contains one number that can't be spelled out, use numbers consistently throughout the passage.

After you have made your final copy, *give it at least one farewell reading,* scouting particularly for the common errors of copying: the omission of words and punctuation marks. Make all final corrections carefully in ink, erasing errors neatly or deleting them with a single horizontal line. Make additions with a caret. *This final reading is important.* There is only one answer to the student who says: "I had it right on my first draft." The instructor doesn't see your first draft.

THE TITLE

You may have hit on a suitable title long before this stage, but you don't have to. For every book that is written to conform to a bright, prefabricated title, there are a hundred whose labels are not chosen until the last minute just before the manuscript goes to press.

1. *Remember that the subject, whether yours or the teacher's,*

is not a title: An Autobiographical Sketch or *Exposition of a Process* is an insipid label for a theme.

2. *In much explanatory writing the best title is often a sober, factual statement of the ground covered:*   This is true, for example, in research papers, where the reader wants only to know whether the article touches on his field of interest: *The Bearing of Science on the Thought of Arthur Hugh Clough.* Yet even in this kind of writing compression and imagination may help. *The Road to Xanadu* is better than *A Study of the Creative Processes Underlying the Poetry of Coleridge.*

3. *In most kinds of writing, a good title may suggest mood and tone without being explicit about content:*   *Arsenic and Old Lace* evokes the quality of a famous stage hit more subtly than the original title: *Bodies in Our Cellar.* In *My Life and Hard Times* the simple insertion of an adjective changes a conventional, matter-of-fact title into one that suggests some of the comic desperation of James Thurber's modern classic.

4. *A matter-of-fact title is better than one that is too cryptic or clever:*   An apt quotation may make an excellent title, but the modern tradition under which the author chooses his favorite obscure quotation from his favorite obscure poet and challenges the reader to guess its connection with his story is wearing thin. If you are original, an original title may come to you. If you are not, be explicit and concise, and let who will be clever. *Cyrano, Ham, Heel, or Hero?* is on the border line of good taste. The student who entitled the account of his visit to the insane asylum *A Pound of Mixed Nuts* crossed over the border. In writing, as in golf, it is a good rule not to press too hard.

CHAPTER THREE

Organizing and Developing

Some act of national recovery is needed if the English paragraph is to be saved.

—Henry Seidel Canby.

➤➤➤➤➤➤➤➤➤➤➤➤➤➤➤➤➤➤➤➤➤➤➤➤➤➤➤➤➤➤➤

THE PURPOSES
OF PARAGRAPHING

In a great deal of writing, organization is not a major problem. Often it is determined automatically by the subject matter. The storyteller may follow a natural chronological order, setting down events as they occur. The writer of description may use a simple spatial sequence: once he has decided on his point of view—whether to describe things from the outside in or the inside out, from the angle of a bird flying overhead or a mouse in the near corner—his order may be clearly established. A student explaining the orthodox process of starting a 1949 Plymouth knows that one should first step on clutch pedal (A), then turn on ignition (B), step on starter (C), put gear in low (D), and lift foot on clutch pedal (E). But in many kinds of writing, the steps don't fall so neatly into place. Sometimes the raw material presents itself in a bewildering array of little bits that have to be welded together into a single mosaic. Sometimes the parts run frantically together in the mind like beads of mercury and have to be patiently separated. In any event, the writer has to impose a logical order on them from the outside. Organization becomes a serious problem.

These two freshman themes show how serious it can be:

CHARACTER BUILDING IN HIGH SCHOOL

When I first entered high school, I became very much aware of two decided factions consisting of the fraternity and non-fraternity students. The former group was a closely knit crowd of boys and girls who considered themselves superior to the latter. I'm not speaking from a prejudiced point of view, for I was a member of one of these fraternities. Because of the snobbishness of the fraternity members, many non-fraternity students who would otherwise have become well-known and well-liked were forced to take a back seat in school activities. The politics and practically every extra-curricular activity of the school were controlled by the Greek letter organizations. The situation became so bad that a girls' club known as the girls' Hi-Y, a YWCA organization, would admit only girls belonging to sororities. This wasn't a fact known by the club's faculty advisors: it was just "understood" by all the girls. This didn't hurt the feelings of the non-sorority girls too much, for they sensed that they weren't wanted, and very few ever applied for membership. The most deplorable situation resulted every year when prospective members were "rushed." I've seen girls actually crying in the school halls when they realized they were outcasts from this socially "superior" group. Boys have sulked for months over it and even carried hatred in their hearts for certain individuals who in the boys' minds probably "blackballed" them. "Blackball" is an evil term that can turn the staunchest friend of a person into a bitter enemy. A majority vote or even a two-thirds vote would be more desirable than "two blackballs and he's out." It seems a shame that fraternities and sororities had to seep into our high school activities. The immaturity of the members and their inability to have any regard for the personal feelings of their fellow students make them unqualified to belong to any such organization. There is no purpose in them except that you can say when you have graduated, "That's where I learned to drink." As for their standards, a person wanting to become a brother had to be an athlete or a "hell raiser." As one of the presidents of one of the fraternities said when they were going over their list of prospective pledges, "It is imperative that they play football, drink beer, or have been a president or some other officer of their class, school, or club." Never is there any mention of a boy's qualities of being just a nice guy. These false standards and false ideals have done nothing but corrupt the members of this exclusive group and ruin other students' possible chances for a brilliant high school career. The fraternities and sororities should be excluded completely from the high school curriculum. They give an entirely distorted view of college fraternity life. When I entered college my impression of fraternities was one of distaste. Since then I have seen the good that can come from them if conducted in a decent and correct manner. Students in high school are at the stage where a great ideal of character-building takes place, but with the fraternity system now present in my alma mater, many students start college life and vocational life with chips on their shoulders. All this is caused by the cruel snobbishness on the part of some of their fellow students.

CAMP HIAWATHA

A place I liked very much was Camp Hiawatha on the Delaware River. It was not only a place to work with kids, but it had an ideal location with beautiful trees, green grass, crystal clear water, and fresh air.

The camp accommodates nearly four hundred boys each camping season. Each boy has a counselor to look after him and guide him in the camp's activities. The counselor has seven boys to help, and together they form one bunkhouse. This bunkhouse eats, sleeps, works, and plays together.

The boys can learn to play ball, swim, make craft projects, etc. They have an evening entertainment every evening with camper and counselor participation.

The camp helps boys to grow strong both physically and mentally.

With regular mealtimes and regular sleeping periods, the camp remains on a sound schedule all summer. This helps the boys to form good habits and keeps them in good health.

The counselor in each bunkhouse spends much time with his campers. He reads them the Bible every morning, tells them stories at night, plays ball with them when he is free, and attends church with them on Sundays.

The swims are guarded by thirty-five counselor lifeguards in boats, canoes, punts, and standing around the area.

Diving boards, rafts, and other such facilities are used by the more advanced swimmers.

Camp Hiawatha has a great deal of camp spirit, and boys are always glad to be there. Songs, both funny and serious, are sung at campfires every Sunday night. The campers enjoy this, and look forward to it with joy.

The main thought in every leader at Camp Hiawatha is to send the boy home more spiritually deepened.

Camp Hiawatha is a place I liked very much, and it will always hold a warm spot in my heart.

In some respects these efforts are markedly different. The writer of the first is apparently a maturing young man who has done some detached thinking about his high school experience and records the results in a moderately interesting, if awkward, manner. The author of the second is obviously less mature. But the two students have at least one trait in common. Neither betrays the faintest suspicion of what a paragraph is. The first writer has, to be sure, indented his opening sentence. The second student has been eleven times as generous. But the road to good organization is paved with something besides good indentions.

The two writers have clearly revealed the reasons for paragraphing. The fraternity critic has not bothered to *divide* his mass of raw material in accordance with the different aspects of his subject. Fraternities and sororities, control of student affairs, rushing, qualifications for membership, snobbishness of members, the effect of exclusion on nonmembers, high school vs. college fraternities—he discharges them all at the reader in a single volley. The contented camper has made no effort to *combine* the tiny particles into solid segments of thought; he peppers his readers with random sprays of birdshot. Moreover, the unrelieved slab of solid print in the first theme is offensive to both eye and brain. Since the Greeks first began breaking up their solid pages with the familiar symbol (¶), we have become accustomed to the conventional pause between paragraphs.

These then are the three main purposes of paragraphing:
1. To *divide* the whole into parts.
2. To *combine* smaller parts into larger.
3. To give the reader intermittent breathing spaces.

HOW LONG IS A PARAGRAPH?

A good paragraph is exactly as long as the writer needs to make it to serve his purpose. The minimum limit is one word and there is no maximum. A single paragraph in Aldous Huxley's "Wordsworth in the Tropics" runs to 1,257 words, and that is no record. Averages by statisticians reveal about what trained readers would expect: that paragraphs, like sentences, have shrunk in the last century; that paragraphs in narrative are shorter than in exposition; that paragraphs in newspapers are shorter than in books; and that there is a disturbing tendency in mass-production journalism and advertising to "bomb the paragraph" into glittering bits, perhaps eventually into oblivion. Authorities have urged students to think twice about any expository paragraph of more than three hundred words or less than one hundred and to cast a suspicious eye on any page of double-spaced typing without a single indention. These are useful formulas if one allows for the common exceptions. Short paragraphs— often of a single short sentence—are commonly used:

1. *In reporting dialogue:* Ordinarily each new speaker opens a new paragraph:

"Do you know Jordan, plays drums for Jeff?" Rick said.

"Smoke?" Valentine said. "Sure I know him."

"How is he?" Rick said.

"He's all right," Valentine said. "Fact is he's the best drummer in the country."

"I mean how's he getting along?"

Lee Valentine didn't make much of this either. "They're all getting along all right," he said. "They're packing them in at the Old South, and have been all winter."

"Well," Rick said, and gave it up.   —Dorothy Baker, *Young Man with a Horn.*

2. *For transitions:* Sometimes a separate short paragraph is used as a bridge from one paragraph to another:

Whereupon I began to ponder why, when she wants relaxation, she reads what even she considers trash. Why does the cheap, the ephemeral, the highly colored, the falsely romantic, relax and amuse the educated mind instead of boring it? Education, to be sure, has left this mark—it has taught people a sense of shame, so that they know they should have on their tables the great names and books of literature. But these are not what they really read. The threat to literature, the check upon its development is not from the low standards of the many ignorant, but from the low standards of the few intelligent, who more often demand of literature that it shall not be true art rather than that it shall.

There are reasons, of course, for this state of being. Foremost, perhaps is our often boasted youth.

Culture, of course, is after all a matter of time and long, mellowing age. And collectively we are not old and individually we cling to childhood and its enjoyments. We do not want to grow up. And the reason for this is that the average person in America is not yet interested in life. That is, he is not interested in human nature and its true character. Or perhaps it would be truer to say he is interested in the activities of life, but not in its meaning or its philosophy. He is instinctively frightened of anything like a view of himself and why and how he is. And yet that view, of course, is what literature is.

—Pearl Buck, "Literature and Life," *Saturday Review of Literature.*

3. *For emphasis:* Any time a writer wants a single assertion to stand out, he may set it off in a brief paragraph:

You know you have to read "between the lines" to get the most out of anything. I want to persuade you to do something equally important in the course of your reading. I want to persuade you to "write between the lines." Unless you do, you are not likely to do the most efficient kind of reading.

I contend, quite bluntly, that marking up a book is not an act of mutilation but of love.

You shouldn't mark up a book which isn't yours. Librarians (or your friends) who lend you books expect you to keep them clean, and you should. If you decide that I am right about the usefulness of marking books, you will have to buy them. Most of the world's great books are available today, in reprint editions, at less than a dollar.

—Mortimer J. Adler, "How to Mark a Book," *Saturday Review of Literature.*

This device of using short paragraphs for emphasis is especially common for beginnings and endings. Thus Sinclair Lewis begins a dramatic chapter in *Arrowsmith* with a clean-cut one-sentence paragraph: "Professor Max Gottlieb was about to assassinate a guinea pig with anthrax germs, and the bacteriology class was nervous." And Professor Oscar Campbell ends an article on the theories that Shakespeare didn't write Shakespeare with another: "The man thus blessed was William Shakespeare, and he was none other than himself." Of course, if every other sentence is splendidly isolated for emphasis, as in many editorials and advertisements, nothing is emphasized—or organized.

THE STANDARD RECIPE

It should be obvious by now that there is no such animal as *the* paragraph. Any experienced writer with an orderly mind can arrange his material in dozens of different paragraph patterns of all sizes and shapes. A student can learn more by examining this infinite variety in the pages of good writers than by memorizing a synthetic formula derived from a nonexistent average paragraph. But the beginner may also profit from a simple blueprint. The old-fashioned formula, with some additions and corrections, still serves as a handy recipe for concocting a common garden variety of expository paragraph. It can be illustrated this way:

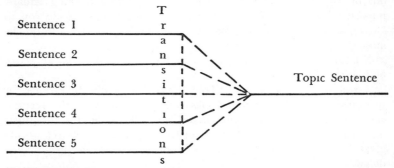

As the diagram reveals, the sentences of this paragraph (1) relate to a single point represented by a *topic sentence (Unity)*, and they (2) follow each other in a logical order and are linked together by *transitions (Coherence)*.

UNITY

Sometimes the topic sentence is actually expressed; sometimes it is merely implied. The orthodox test for unity is whether the whole point of a paragraph can be summarized in a good sentence. Compare these four examples:

1. "Plain Folks" is a device used by politicians, labor leaders,

business men, and even by ministers and educators to win our confidence by appearing to be people like ourselves—"just plain folks among the neighbors." In election years especially do candidates show their devotion to little children and the common, homey things of life. They have front porch campaigns. For the newspaper men they raid the kitchen cupboard, finding there some of the good wife's apple pie. They go to church picnics; they attend service at the old frame church; they pitch hay and go fishing; they show their belief in home and mother. In short, they would win our votes by showing that they're just as common as the rest of us—"just plain folks"—and, therefore, wise and good. Business men often are "plain folks" with the factory hands. Even distillers use the device. "It's our family's whiskey, neighbor; and neighbor, it's your price." —Clyde R. Miller, "How to Detect Propaganda," *Propaganda Analysis*.

2. There's a sixty-mile auto trip that I take about a dozen times a year. About twenty miles from the college campus along that route is an utterly indefensible small-town traffic light. In order to avoid it, I make a hairpin turn about two blocks from the intersection and desert the smooth highway for a miserable little alley, which meanders aimlessly in and out of peoples' cabbage patches and finally rejoins the main road a half a block beyond the light. The alley is a garage man's Shangri-La, pitted with large pocks and generously sprinkled with broken bottles and tenpenny nails. I know it doesn't save me money, and I'm not sure it saves me time. But when I am directing a friend over that highway, I say to him with a knowing glint in my eye: "Now when I get here, I always take a little short cut I discovered. It isn't on the map"; and I beam all over as if I'd just planted the Stars and Stripes on an uncharted iceberg in the Antarctic. There's only one reason why I take that short cut: I'm an American. And we Americans are a nation of incurable short cutters.

3. We debunked too much. During the iconoclastic twenties spirited biographers laid about them with a mighty modern hand. They told us that Lincoln was a small-town politician, Washington a land grabber, Grant a stubborn and conceited mule, and Bryan an amusing idiot. We learned that there was something to be said for Aaron Burr, but not very much for Sam Adams, Longfellow, or Harriet Beecher Stowe. In place of being American vikings, the pioneers turned out to be neurotic, dissatisfied fellows unpopular in their home towns, and Columbia, the gem of the ocean, was described as a sort of kept woman in the pay of millionaires. Apparently the only Americans who ever died to make the world safe for democracy died in 1917–1918, and made

a mistake in doing so. I do not deny either the truth or the necessity of many of these modern biographies. I am no more comfortable than the next man in a room full of plaster saints. But, when the biographers got through, all the heroes had disappeared. —Howard Mumford Jones, "Patriotism—But How?" *Atlantic Monthly*.

4. A man went to Paris for the first time, and observed right off that the carriages of suburban trains had seats on the roof like a tram-car. He was so thrilled by the remarkable discovery that he observed almost nothing else. This enormous fact occupied the whole foreground of his perspective. He returned home and announced that Paris was a place where people rode on the tops of trains. A French-woman came to London for the first time—and no English person would ever guess the phenomenon which vanquished all others in her mind on the opening day. She saw a cat walking across a street. The vision excited her. For in Paris cats do not roam in thoroughfares, because there are practically no houses with gardens or "areas"; the flat system is unfavourable to the enlargement of cats. I remember once, in the days when observation had first presented itself to me as a beautiful pastime, getting up very early and making the circuit of inner London before summer dawn in quest of interesting material. And the one note I gathered was that the ground in front of the all-night coffee-stalls was white with eggshells! What I needed then was an operation for cataract. I also remember taking a man to the opera who had never seen an opera. The work was *Lohengrin*. When we came out he said: "That swan's neck was rather stiff." And it was all he did say. We went and had a drink. He was not mistaken. His observation was most just; but his perspective was that of those literary critics who give ten lines to pointing out three slips of syntax, and three lines to an ungrammatical admission that the novel under survey is not wholly tedious. —Arnold Bennett, "Seeing Life," *The Author's Craft*.

In the first paragraph the opening sentence clearly announces the central theme, and the others accumulate supporting details. In the second the student author reverses the order, using a single illustration to lead up to a simple and arresting topic sentence at the end. Professor Jones—in what might be called a "sandwich paragraph"—begins with one brief topic sentence and reiterates it at the end in more explicit terms. And though no ready-made topic sentence summarizes Arnold Bennett's various examples, the reader can easily devise his own: Many people are shortsighted observers, staring at trivialities and overlooking essentials. Each of these paragraphs is built around a single point, and not a sentence is irrelevant. They are all models of unity.

Now look at these two:

1. During my senior year I had a very nice time at prep school. My marks came up a little and I graduated with an average of about eighty-two. About last December my Dad bought me a little thirty-nine Ford convertible coupe. I have had a great time with this little car even though I could not always afford to buy gasoline. I have worked for my Dad on week ends and during vacations for some years now. My Dad is a funeral director and I have been of some help to him most of the time. Dad has a good business built up and I would like to follow in his footsteps. My grandfather was an undertaker and my mother was the first woman in the county to obtain her undertaker's license. Therefore it seems only natural that I try to get into the business.

2. As a speaker, Franklin Delano Roosevelt was one of the greatest orators of his time. He was a very sincere man and always believed that what he did was for the good of the nation. In reality he did have many enemies, due to the fact that he gave liberal aid to the unemployed all over the country. By rights, labor was given too much power, but labor represented a majority of the country, and therefore he was able to be nominated. Roosevelt was the first President to be chosen for a third time, which he actually was in 1940. On December 8, 1941, he appeared before Congress and asked for a declaration of war against Japan after the sneak attack on Pearl Harbor on December 7, 1941. During these four years of war, Roosevelt and the leaders of the other allied nations had planned an "unconditional surrender" ultimatum. Before he could see the great plan completed, he became stricken with a cerebral hemorrhage while he was staying at Warm Springs, Georgia. On April 12, 1945, he died at the age of sixty-five. The death had come very suddenly. The only witness had been an artist who had been sketching his portrait, who claimed that Roosevelt had complained of a "terrible headache" and had then become unconscious. His body was taken to his father's estate at Hyde Park, New York State.

Try to distil each of those meandering paragraphs into a good sentence and what do you get? (1) I had a good time during my senior year at prep school, and for years I have helped my father in the family undertaking business, which I expect to inherit myself some day. That is a "Siamese Twin" sentence. (2) Roosevelt was a great orator and a sincere man, but he had enemies because of helping the unemployed, but his help for labor put him in office for several terms, during the third of which he had to ask for a declaration of war—but why go on?

As a student progresses beyond the first steps in paragraphing, he can afford to take some liberties with the conventional formula for unity. In actual practice, especially in informal writing, an author may get away with a technical violation of unity— if, unlike the undertaker's son, he is thinking in a straight line and if, unlike the young biographer of Roosevelt, he doesn't throw everything into the paragraph as if it were a tossed salad. Examine the following selection:

> This may seem merely a matter of taste. On such, I have urged, it is vain for critics to debate; the only *general* judgments criticism can even attempt, I think, consist in saying, not "This is good" (good for what?) or "This is beautiful" (beautiful for whom?) but simply "This is true: that is not," or "This looks sane; and this, diseased." It would be a great pity to banish writers like Baudelaire, as Plato would unhesitatingly have done. It is a great loss not to have read them. But it does not seem to me intelligent to ignore that such writers *are* diseased (as a great deal of genius is not) ; to live too much on, and with, them; or to forget that there remain certain advantages in being sane rather than morbid, sound rather than sick. And my complaint against much modern criticism is that it does forget these things; that it cares nothing if a writer is squalid, or brutal, or grovelling, or imbecile, provided he is "interesting" and leaves a new taste, however brassy, in the mouth. Our age is full of budding Baudelaires dyeing their heads green; when there is little enough need, with most of them, for that.
> —F. L. Lucas, *The Decline and Fall of the Romantic Ideal.*

It would be hard to prove that Lucas confines himself strictly to a single point. His argument progresses logically through at least three closely related assertions. Beginning not with a topic sentence but with a simple transition from the previous paragraph, he proceeds to argue (1) that there are only two general judgments criticism can make; (2) that much modern literature fails by one of these standards; and (3) that much modern criticism ignores this failure. Yet a reader, though he might disagree violently with the author's assertions, could hardly find him guilty of poor paragraphing.

Although such a paragraph is not recommended as a model for beginners, there is a lesson here. The conventional picture of a paragraph as a "self-contained unit"—a sort of Lilliputian theme—in which a "single point is made" does not fit all the facts of custom. A trained writer may make one point in a paragraph; he may make more than one; he may continue a point begun in a previous paragraph; or he may merely lead up to one that he intends to clinch in a subsequent paragraph. It matters little as long as he gives his reader a clear indication of where he is going en route. A paragraph is not static but dynamic, not isolated but interwoven with the larger texture of the composition. The doctrine of unity must not be taken too literally.

COHERENCE

It is possible for a paragraph to be unified without being clearly organized. Theoretically the sentences should be not only related to a single point but arranged in a logical order and connected so that the reader can cross from one to another without danger of falling into the chasm between. The most common transitions are:

1. Conjunctions (*and, but, for,* etc.), conjunctive adverbs (*also, however, therefore,* etc.), and directive phrases (*in other words, on the other hand,* etc.)
2. Pronouns
3. Repeated words
4. Synonyms and other substitutes

Here is a short paragraph with the key transitions italicized:

Most undergraduates are under the illusion that they take satisfactory lecture notes. *But* very few know the first principles. Good *note-taking* does not consist of cryptic scrawls among the doodles in the textbook margin. *It* is a minor literary skill, the art of intelligent digesting. Even if a student can read his *marginal hieroglyphics* six weeks later, he seldom has the vaguest notion of their meaning. The professor's pearls on Henry the Eighth, *for example,* are melted down —as in Christopher Morley's epigrammatic example—to: "H 8, self-made widower." Can *this little splinter of knowledge* serve as the foundation for an intelligent discussion on an examination? *Yet* the student insists that he has "taken notes on the lecture."

The transitions are obvious. The conjunction *but* links the second sentence with the first. *Note-taking* in the third repeats *take* and *note* in the first. The pronoun *it* in the fourth sentence refers to *note-taking. Marginal hieroglyphics* in the fifth is substituted for *cryptic scrawls* in the third. *For example* bridges the gulf between sentences five and six. *This little splinter of knowledge* stands for *H 8, self-made widower. Yet,* another conjunction, ties in the final sentence.

But transitions are not always so obvious within the paragraph. As a matter of fact, a formal paragraph cluttered up with *moreover*'s, *furthermore*'s, and *accordingly*'s is like a highway bristling with signboards at every turn. In spite of the long-standing and thoroughly irrational prejudice against beginning sentences with *and* and *but,* the writer soon learns that these simple conjunctions make smoother transitions than their more obtrusive formal cousins among the conjunctive adverbs. Moreover, he also learns that tangible transitions are sometimes redundant. For example, the *as a matter of fact* in sentence two of this paragraph, *moreover* in the fourth sentence, and *for example* at the beginning of this one could all be eliminated without sacrificing clarity. And one of the commonest kinds of wordiness is the labored transition which unnecessarily repeats half of the previous sentence (see pages 67–68).

Since incoherence is a greater evil than occasional wordiness, the beginner can afford to err in the direction of overworking *visible* transitions. But to write with economy as well as clarity, he must eventually learn that in closely knit paragraphs transitions are often *invisible.* When a writer starts with a general assertion, he does not have to begin every subsequent illustration with a *firstly, secondly* or *thirdly.* When he builds a statement in parallel construction with a previous one (as in this sentence), the parallelism is mortar enough. If his argument is firmly constructed the transitions will usually take care of themselves.

PARAGRAPH ANEMIA

Now turn again to the work of the contented camper on page 38. What is the cure for what ails his eleven "paragraphs"? Some combining would help, of course. The duties of the counselors, scattered far and wide in at least five different places, could all be corralled in a single paragraph. The swimming equipment might be confined to one. Mental, physical, and spiritual activities could make a useful, if thoroughly arbitrary, three-paragraph division. But the theme needs something more than a few ligatures; it needs a complete blood transfusion. For the "paragraphs" are not merely short; they are anemic. The most common ailment of undergraduate paragraphing is not disunity or incoherence but pernicious anemia.

This is a problem that goes far beyond paragraphing or organization. A student may be able to construct an orderly outline in which II follows I and B follows A with unerring logic. But as soon as he is faced with the dilemma of putting flesh and blood on the bones and breathing life into them, he throws up his hands in despair. Another student may be fairly comfortable as long as he can record the tangible steps in a process or explain an intricate mechanism that looms up before him in the laboratory; but as soon as he has to discuss an idea, he is lost. A third may traffic blithely in generalities but be totally unable to build one with the materials of sound argument.

The same problem comes crying home to the teacher whenever he gives an examination containing discussion or essay questions. It isn't that many of the answers are wrong. A genuine discussion question cannot be answered right-or-wrong or true-or-false by drawing a thin lead line with a graphite pencil. The trouble is simply that so many of the answers are anemic. Three or four cramped sentences on a half-hour discussion of the causes of the First World War! The reason may be, of course, that the student, having surmised that he wouldn't get a question on the causes of the First World War, doesn't know any more than three or four sentences' worth. But he may know considerably more. Why hasn't he written more? The answers are variously evasive: "Well, what more was there to write?" Or: "You don't measure these answers with a ruler, do you, Prof?" Or: "I thought it wasn't how *much* we said that counted." Or perhaps: "I can't sling it on these discussion questions like my roommate. He's going to be an English major. Me, I just stick to the hard, cold facts."

The last answer is the real giveaway. The implication is that there is no happy medium between the "hard, cold facts" unqualified by reasoning and a voluminous fiction unadulterated by fact. There is, of course: a well-rounded discussion based securely on the evidence.

The chances are, moreover, that the student's hard, cold facts are not facts at all but vapid generalities. "To generalize," said the poet William Blake, "is to be an idiot." A more tolerant view might go something like this: In the hands of a philosopher— a Confucius or a Sir Francis Bacon—an unsupported generality may be an original truth; turned by a wit—an Oscar Wilde or a Bernard Shaw—it may be a classic epigram; to an ordinary mortal it is merely a blunt tool with which he scratches the surface of an idea. A minister doesn't get up in his pulpit, announce his text, and promptly sit down again. An experienced writer seldom lets a generality stand alone and impotent. A well-developed paragraph is a well-supported generality.

There is no magic cure for anemic paragraphing. But one simple suggestion may help: *Do not fall into the habit of beginning every paragraph with a topic sentence.* This is a legitimate device to be sure. Many authorities endorse it with the argument that the beginning and the ending are the traditional spots for emphasis. In many a textbook, paragraph after paragraph opens with a topic sentence, conveniently attired in boldface or *italics* to prevent the lazy reader from having to read any further. But there are two troubles with this kind of writing. One is that it becomes exceedingly monotonous. The other is that when an inexperienced writer launches a paragraph with a generality, his mind is in danger of stalling then and there. He has not come to his conclusion; he has jumped at it. The main point has been stated. A judgment has already been pronounced. Without the evidence, to be sure, but why bother? The mind rests. If, on the other hand, he forms the habit of developing his thought *inductively*—of setting down at least some of the evidence before arriving at a judgment, sometimes letting the reader infer the verdict from the evidence—he is likely to write paragraphs with flesh on their bones.

SELECTED SAMPLES

In the long run, of course, the best way to learn how paragraphs are developed is to examine the paragraphs of those who know how to develop them. Here are some samples grouped to illustrate seven common methods of expansion. Not that experienced writers say consciously to themselves: "I shall develop point B under Roman numeral one in two paragraphs of *comparison-and-contrast.*" But conscious study of these methods should help to combat paragraph anemia.

Read each group first and see what you can discover about the organization before turning to the analysis that follows.

I

A. The average citizen strives hard to attain modest comfort and decency. But having reached that point, he continues to strain himself, often with little regard for mental poise. The Ford becomes a Chevrolet, the Chevrolet a Buick, the Buick a Lincoln, the Lincoln a Rolls Royce. The room becomes a flat, the flat an apartment, the apartment a duplex, the duplex a palatial home. The man becomes older and caustic and tired. Luxuries become necessities. Life loses stability.
—Arthur Garfield Hays, *Democracy Works.*

B. Along 66 the hamburger stands—Al & Susy's Place—Carl's Lunch —Joe & Minnie—Will's Eats. Board-and-bat shacks. Two gasoline pumps in front, a screen door, a long bar, stools, and a foot rail. Near the door three slot machines, showing through glass the wealth in nickels three bars will bring. And beside them, the nickel phonograph with records piled up like pies, ready to swing out to the turntable and play dance music, "Ti-pi-ti-pi-tin," "Thanks for the Memory," Bing Crosby, Benny Goodman. At one end of the counter a covered case; candy cough drops, caffeine sulphate called Sleepless, No-Doze; candy, cigarettes, razor blades, aspirin, Bromo-Seltzer, Alka-Seltzer. The walls decorated with posters, bathing girls, blondes with big breasts and slender hips and waxen faces, in white bathing suits, and holding a bottle of Coca-Cola and smiling—see what you get with a Coca-Cola. Long bar, and salts, peppers, mustard pots, and paper napkins. Beer taps behind the counter, and in back the coffee urns, shiny and steaming, with glass gauges showing the coffee level. And pies in wire cages and oranges in pyramids of four. And little piles of Post Toasties, corn flakes, stacked up in designs. —John Steinbeck, *The Grapes of Wrath*.

C. At that moment the boss noticed that a fly had fallen into his broad inkpot, and was trying feebly but desperately to clamber out again. Help! help! said those struggling legs. But the sides of the inkpot were wet and slippery; it fell back again and began to swim. The boss took up a pen, picked the fly out of the ink, and shook it on to a piece of blotting-paper. For a fraction of a second it lay still on the dark patch that oozed round it. Then the front legs waved, took hold, and, pulling its small sodden body up it began the immense task of cleaning the ink from its wings. Over and under, over and under, went a leg along a wing, as the stone goes over and under the scythe. Then there was a pause, while the fly, seeming to stand on the tip of its toes, tried to expand first one wing and then the other. It succeeded at last, and sitting down, it began, like a minute cat, to clean its face. Now one could imagine that the little front legs rubbed against each other lightly, joyfully. The horrible danger was over; it had escaped; it was ready for life again. —Katherine Mansfield, "The Fly," *The Doves' Nest*.

At first glance those three specimens might appear to have nothing in common. The first is an expository paragraph taken from an essay; it is developed logically and held together partly by parallel sentence structure. The second is a descriptive paragraph from a distinguished novel; the staccato fragments are grouped in a loose spatial pattern—taking the reader from the outside into the center of the room—but the order is not important. The third is a narrative paragraph from a short story, following a chronological order to the climax of a miniature drama. Yet all three share a common technique in paragraph development: the *accumulation of details*. Without the life-giving details, Hays' point shrinks to the tired old cliché about keeping up with the Joneses; Steinbeck's painfully authentic description becomes the mere mention of a typical joint; Mansfield's fascinating fly, so strangely human in its eagerness to live, degenerates into another routine target for the swatter.

These details, of course, have to be observed before they can be recorded. Average people, who, as Arnold Bennett asserts, exist through life with half-shut eyes, can pass an hour in a roadhouse or an idle moment gazing at a fly and never see either with the acute vision of the trained writer. And, of course, the cataloguing of trivial details can reach a saturation point beyond which lies the deadly land of Boredom. Details must be carefully selected to serve a purpose: Steinbeck is setting the scene for one of the most pathetic chapters of his novel; Mansfield realizes the struggling insect with great patience in order to portray more fully her central character, the dominating biped who will eventually send it to an inky doom. But for every beginner who overworks trivialities there are a hundred who are unaware that the patient accumulation of particulars is one of the simple secrets of good writing. Their paragraphs are pallid because they are not pumped full of the lifeblood of detail.

II

A. This brings me to my final argument for freedom of speech. It creates the happiest kind of country. It is the best way to make men and women love their country. Mill says:

> A state which dwarfs its men, in order that they may be more docile instruments in its hands even for beneficial purposes, will find that with small men no great thing can really be accomplished.

And Arthur Garfield Hays tells the story of a liberated slave who met his former master on the street. The master asked, "Are you as well off as before you were free?" The Negro admitted that his clothes were frayed, his house leaked, and his meals were nothing like the food on the old plantation. "Well, wouldn't you rather be a slave again?" "No, massa. There's a sort of a looseness about this here freedom that I likes." —Zechariah Chafee, Jr., *Free Speech in the United States.*

B. Consider, for example, our addiction to the rapid conveyance of our bodies in petrol-propelled mechanisms over the surface of the earth. If two men leave Manchester for Bettws-y-Coed and the one drives so gently that not a single speck of dust on a pedestrian's shoe is disturbed, while the other drives so vigorously that he leaves a trail of frightened humanity along the whole route, what margin separates the pair at their journey's end in Wales? Fifteen minutes! And how does the speed devotee spend that quarter of an hour which he has stolen from the clasp of inexorable Time? He lounges, all liver and no legs, in the bar a little longer before he feeds, consumes an extra cocktail, toys with a few stale magazines, grumbles that his food is not ready, brags a little about his driving. . . . The world suffers through his speed; and it suffers to no noble purpose. If he were a surgeon hastening to a purulent appendix, we could bear with him. If he were a lover fresh home from the Indies yearning to meet his bride, we could bear with him. If he obtained any real or lasting satisfaction from his speed debauch, his conduct, although still intolerable, would be at least excusable. But he does not. He is just a fool in a hurry. He has no possible defense for his folly, and we know it as well as he knows it. —C. E. M. Joad, "Value in the Modern World," *Return to Philosophy*.

Both of those paragraphs are developed by the simple method of *illustration*. Chafee begins with a transitional sentence, announces his main point in the next two (either of which could be considered the topic sentence), and then illustrates it neatly with a pertinent quotation (indented and without quotes, as is customary with longish quotations) and a fresh modern anecdote. Having done this, he has no need of driving the point any further; the illustrations speak for themselves. Joad uses the same technique but resourcefully manufactures his own illustration. Although his liverish speeder is only a hypothetical example, Joad brings him to life with concrete detail, using parallel sentence structure ("If he were" and so forth) to lead up swiftly to his satirical climax ("He is just a fool in a hurry" and so forth). The generalities that freedom makes people happy and speed gets them nowhere fast are common enough in themselves. But they are commonplaces that need constant repetition in the modern world of tyranny and hurry. The illustrations here give them a brave new look.

III

A. It is easier to say what loyalty is not than to say what it is. It is not conformity. It is not passive acquiescence in the status quo. It is not preference for everything American over everything foreign. It is not an ostrich-like ignorance of other countries and other institutions. It is not the indulgence in ceremony—a flag salute, an oath of allegiance, a fervid verbal declaration. It is not a particular creed, a particular version of history, a particular body of economic practices, a particular philosophy.

It is a tradition, an ideal, and a principle. It is a willingness to subordinate every private advantage for the larger good. It is an appreciation of the rich and diverse contributions that can come from the most varied sources. It is an allegiance to the traditions that have guided our greatest statesmen and inspired our most eloquent poets— the traditions of freedom, equality, democracy, tolerance, the tradition of the higher law, of experimentation, co-operation, and pluralism. It is a realization that America was born of revolt, flourished on dissent, became great through experimentation. —Henry Steele Commager, "Who Is Loyal to America?" *Harper's Magazine.*

B. And then in simple justice to the undecorated men of the *Reluctant* it should also be pointed out that heroism—physical heroism —is very much a matter of opportunity. On the physical level heroism is not so much an act, implying volition, as it is a reflex. Apply the rubber hammer to the patella tendon and, commonly, you produce the knee jerk. Apply the situation permitting bravery to one hundred young males with actively functioning adrenal glands and, reasonably, you produce seventy-five instances of clear-cut heroism. Would, that is, but for one thing: that after the fifty-first the word would dissolve into meaninglessness. Like the knee jerk, physical courage is perhaps latent and even implicit in the individual, needing only the application of situation, of opportunity, to reveal it. A case in point: Ensign Pulver. —Thomas Heggen, *Mister Roberts.*

In both examples the writers are concerned with the eternal problem of *definition.* They know, of course, that such sprawling abstractions as *loyalty* and *heroism* can never be defined with scientific accuracy. Definition is a complex riddle that will be discussed further in later chapters (see pages 231–239, 321–323) . But they also know that as long as these abstractions are thrown loosely around to make and break reputations, their meaning cannot be evaded. A beginning writer, if he is aware that defining terms is a necessary evil, will go inevitably to the dictionary. If the term can be scientifically defined, a good dictionary can give him the essential facts: the *genus* or class in which the object belongs; and *differentiae* or features that distinguish it from other objects in the same class. But dictionary definitions are not much help in understanding *loyalty* and *heroism*. The widespread illusion that such intangibles can be easily capsulated is a dangerous enemy to clear thinking. All a thinking writer can do is suggest some limits to their elusive meaning. It can be done not in a scientific definition but only by what is sometimes called *literary definition*. This kind may be reduced to an epigram: "A farm is an irregular patch of nettles bounded by short-term notes, containing a fool and his wife who don't know enough to stay in the city" (S. J. Perelman); "A torch singer is a woman who has lost her voice and insists on bewailing the fact in public" (Deems Taylor). But a serious attempt to limit an abstraction usually requires at least a paragraph.

To define the much abused word *loyalty* is the purpose of Commager's entire essay. But the selection here illustrates two common ways of developing a paragraph by definition: (1) the negative approach, defining what a thing is not; and (2) the affirmative approach, defining what it is. The definition is, of course, not final but partial and tentative. The author of *Mr. Roberts,* in a tentative effort to suggest the nature of heroism, uses one of the time-honored devices of exposition: he draws an analogy between the intangible quality and a tangible experience which is familiar to everyone who has ever taken a complete physical examination. Thus he brings *heroism* out of the clouds of glory and down to earth. Incidentally, the formal rules and regulations about paragraphing might insist that he end on something more emphatic, postponing his transition to the beginning of the next paragraph. But by introducing Ensign Pulver here, he contrives a small amount of suspense that tempts the reader to hurry on.

IV

A. I propose to offer two apologies for our species, the one defensive, the other penitential. The defensive apology in behalf of man pertains to his appearance, physique, and biological habits. The only proper recipients of such an apology would be the anthropoid apes, whom man sometimes claims as his nearest relatives. The second and penitential apology is offered for man's behavior—for his use of the gift of articulate speech, for his attempts to control nature, for his social habits and his systems of ethics. It is owed to man himself, to Nature, and to the universe. —Earnest A. Hooton, *Apes, Men and Morons.*

B. There are three kinds of book owners. The first has all the standard sets and best-sellers—unread, untouched. (This deluded individual owns woodpulp and ink, not books.) The second has a great many books—a few of them read through, most of them dipped into, but all of them as clean and shiny as the day they were bought. (This person would probably like to make books his own, but is restrained by a false respect for their physical appearance.) The third has a few books or many—every one of them dogeared and dilapidated, shaken and loosened by continual use, marked and scribbled in from front to back. (This man owns books.)   —Mortimer J. Adler, "How to Mark a Book," *Saturday Review of Literature.*

Those paragraphs are obviously developed by *division*. This device is especially useful in introducing a subject. A formal introduction is usually superfluous in a five-hundred-word paper. But in a longer expository paper it helps the reader to have a preliminary map showing the main divisions of the territory to be traversed. If this is done clearly in advance, the writer is spared the nuisance of adding long transitions later. Having given a preview of his key points, he doesn't have to reintroduce each one at length when the time comes to expand it. Professor Hooton's paragraph is an example of this sort of introductory division of the material. Each of the two apologies is later developed in detail.

The specimen from Professor Adler's essay represents a somewhat different use of the dividing paragraph. He doesn't introduce the reader to his first two book owners because he is going to discuss them in detail later; he uses them merely as foils for book owner number three, the more deserving subject of the rest of the essay. He uses the device of division to eliminate subjects that do not concern him, thus clearing the decks for action on the one that does. This trick is similar to the negative approach to definition. Like all introductory devices it should be handled with care. There is always the danger that a writer, like an exhausting after-dinner speaker, will talk too long about the things he is not going to talk about. The subject of a short paper should be whittled down to size before the opening paragraph.

v

A. That doctrine may easily be condensed to two chief points—the eternal contest between Hebraism and Hellenism, and the mediating function of culture, of "sweetness and light." The final aim of both Hebraism and Hellenism Arnold found to be the same, man's perfection or salvation, in spite of the fact that they approach the problem by utterly diverse routes. Hebraism lays the whole stress on doing, on the importance of the *act,* on religion, on strictness of conscience. On the other hand, Hellenism stresses knowing rather than doing, the whole rather than a part, spontaneity of consciousness. The "uppermost idea with Hellenism is to see things as they really are: the uppermost idea with Hebraism is conduct and obedience." Ideas of action and conduct fill the space of the Hebraist's mind. "He is zealous to do battle for them and affirm them, for in affirming them he affirms himself, and that is what we all like." The Hellenist, on the other hand, tries to apprehend the whole of life, to let no part of it slip, to stress no part to the exclusion of the others. He insists upon a flexible activity of mind, and so attains to that clearness and radiancy of vision, that intelligence and tolerance, which Arnold called "sweetness and light." Nothing, he states, can do away with the ineffaceable difference between these two approaches to the problems of life. —James Truslow Adams, "Sweetness and Light—Sixty Years After," *Atlantic Monthly.*

B. The natural sciences are primarily concerned with the material world (including living organisms in so far as they are parts of the material world), and their aim is to disclose the structure and behavior of material things in generalized terms (in terms of mathematics so far as possible) which will be true irrespective of variable conditions of time and place. In dealing with his subject matter the work of the natural scientist is greatly facilitated by the fact that he is not emotionally entangled with it: he does not care how his subject matter behaves, his subject matter is indifferent to what he does to it, and ignorant of what he has learned about it. Fortunately for the physicist, the atom cannot acquire a knowledge of physics. The physicist can, therefore, proceed on the assumption that any knowledge he may acquire about the behavior of the atom will not modify its behavior and thereby invalidate conclusions based upon its behavior up to date. The social scientist cannot make this assumption, at least not without important qualifications. For his subject matter is the behavior of men in the world of human relations; and men are not, like the atom, indifferent to what is done to them or ignorant of what is learned about them. On the contrary, the subject matter of the social scientist can find out what he has learned about its behavior in the past, and as a result of that knowledge behave differently in the future. This is the fundamental difference between the natural sciences and the social sciences; whereas the behavior of material things remains the same whatever men learn about it, the behavior of men is always conditioned by what they know about themselves and the world in which they live. —Carl L. Becker, "The Function of the Social Sciences," *Science and Man,* ed. by Ruth N. Anshen.

That kind of development is commonly called *comparison-and-contrast. Comparison* would be label enough, for in its broadest sense, *to compare* is to set two or more things side by side in order to bring out either resemblances or differences between them. But the familiar academic formula is: "Compare and contrast the following." Why is this sort of question so common on examinations? The reason is not that it is a handy way to ferret out ignorance but that it tests a student's powers of thought. A man cannot think for long on any subject without making comparisons. The old proverb "Comparisons are odious" might well be changed to "Comparisons are inevitable." A person with a head stuffed like a ragbag full of miscellaneous tidbits of disconnected information may make a killing on a radio quiz and get slaughtered on one in college. One badge of an educated man is the power to synthesize shreds of knowledge into an intelligible pattern; and this requires the ability to see resemblances between them. Another is the power to evaluate—to assess the relative worth of ideas, or works of art, or other human beings; and this demands the capacity to see differences more subtle than that between black and white. Comparison-and-contrast is more than a textbook formula for developing paragraphs.

As the selections from Adams and Becker show, there are two common ways of developing paragraphs by comparison.

Adams, in paraphrasing Matthew Arnold's famous distinction between Hebraism and Hellenism, makes his comparison point by point en route, weighing the sentences with calculated balance, phrase against phrase, clause against clause. Becker first explains the method of the natural scientist in some detail before turning to the social scientist; then he ties up the contrast in a neat package with a final topic sentence. Either method is legitimate. The careful dovetailing technique of Adams' paragraph is more useful in making subtle detailed comparisons, but it is not easy for the beginner. It requires an acute power of analysis and a sense of symmetry to sustain the balance of both ideas and sentences. The method used by Becker is adequate when comparison is organized around a single point. Since the beginner is not likely to make more than one point in a paragraph, he will use this method more often. (This paragraph, incidentally, is developed by comparison-and-contrast.)

It is possible, of course, to suggest comparisons without explicitly making them. But this device, though common in narrative and descriptive writing, is often ineffective in exposition. The student writer, when asked to compare and contrast A and B, as on an examination, too often discusses them consecutively at great length without either implying or expressing the resemblances or differences between them. This is evading the problem.

VI

A. During the recent decades we built up our cities without giving any particular thought to the social consequences of environments. We permitted economic eagerness to erect factories and skyscrapers, to create high speculative land-and-housing values, to crowd families into quarters too small for decent living. In rural areas we permitted various forms of tenantry to flourish under conditions of the most abject poverty. Without quite realizing what we were doing, we subordinated our democratic interest in human beings to our economic interest in successful ledger balances. The result has been that for equality of environmental opportunity we have substituted a pattern of suburb and slum, of residential area and blighted region, of owners' mansions and tenants' shacks. We have built inequality into the essential living conditions of our existence, and countless numbers of children have been the victims. —H. A. Overstreet, *A Declaration of Interdepend-ence.*

B. Meanwhile, the Army and Navy's victorious inoculation of the anti-linguistic American boy is not hard to account for. It was not a secret; it was mainly Concentration. The men were segregated, put in charge of foreign instructors, drilled morning, noon, and night under conditions of prisonlike rigidity. Standards were high and fail-ures from laziness or incapacity were weeded out as fast as they showed up. A competitive game was set going, which keyed up the good minds to outdo themselves. Outside the class hours, the men would quiz each other, talk, joke, and write in the language they were learning. Two powerful motives were at work: the negative fear of not keeping up and therefore being returned to the ranks, and the positive wish for a commission and the pay that goes with it. —Jacques Barzun, *Teacher in America.*

Those examples are developed by showing the relation be-tween *cause and effect*. The author of the first begins by listing the causes of the national housing dilemma and concludes in the last two sentences with the disastrous results. Professor Barzun begins by mentioning the successful result of the wartime lan-guage program, then catalogues the causes. One paragraph moves from cause to effect, the other from effect to cause. Both represent a method of paragraph development commonly used in argument.

VII

A. Clubs, fraternities, nations—these are the beloved barriers in the way of a workable world, these will have to surrender some of their rights and some of their ribs. A "fraternity" is the antithesis of *frater-nity*. The first (that is, the order or organization) is predicated on the idea of exclusion; the second (that is, the abstract thing) is based on a feeling of total equality. Anyone who remembers back to his fraternity days at college recalls the enthusiasts in his group, the rabid members, both old and young, who were obsessed with the mystical charm of membership in their particular order. They were usually men who were incapable of genuine brotherhood or at least unaware of its impli-cations. Fraternity begins when the exclusion formula is found to be distasteful. The effect of any organization of a social and brotherly nature is to strengthen rather than to diminish the lines which divide people into classes; the effect of states and nations is the same, and eventually these lines will have to be softened, these powers will have to be generalized. It is written on the wall that this is so. I'm not inventing it, I'm just copying it off the wall. —E. B. White, *One Man's Meat.*

B. I remember years ago attending a public dinner to which the Governor of the state was bidden. The chairman explained that His Excellency could not be present for certain "good" reasons; what the "real" reasons were the presiding officer said he would leave us to conjecture. This distinction between "good" and "real" reasons is one of the most clarifying and essential in the whole realm of thought. We can readily give what seem to us "good" reasons for being a Catholic or a Mason, a Republican or a Democrat, an adherent or opponent of the League of Nations. But the "real" reasons are usually on a quite different plane. Of course the importance of this distinction is popularly, if somewhat obscurely, recognized. The Baptist missionary is ready enough to see that the Buddhist is not such because his doctrines would bear careful inspection, but because he happened to be born in a Buddhist family in Tokio. But it would be treason to his faith to acknowledge that his own partiality for certain doctrines is due to the fact that his mother was a member of the First Baptist church of Oak Ridge. A savage can give all sorts of reasons for his belief that it is dangerous to step on a man's shadow, and a newspaper editor can advance plenty of arguments against the Bolsheviki. But neither of them may realize why he happens to be defending his particular opinion. —James Harvey Robinson, *The Mind in the Making.*

Those specimens are included here to demonstrate what may have been evident in other examples: that the methods of paragraph development are not mutually exclusive. A single paragraph may be expanded in several different ways. Thus E. B. White's penetrating comment includes *division* of the material, *definition* of two terms, *comparison-and-contrast* between them, the use of a familiar *illustration* from the fraternity house, a *cause-and-effect* analysis of the influence of "the exclusion formula"—the whole encased in a sweeping comparison between clubs and nations. In the same way it could be argued that Robinson develops his paragraph by *illustration, definition, division,* and *comparison-and-contrast.* It isn't that either writer consciously lays out an intricate blueprint of interlocking techniques in advance. The nature of their material leads them naturally to a combination of methods.

REPETITION—VICE AND DEVICE

There is always the danger that a student, forced by pedagogical pressure to expand his undeveloped paragraphs, will respond by inflating them full of repetitious hot air. Repetition will be discussed again in this book, but the kinds that are directly related to paragraph development deserve special consideration here. A trained writer may repeat a single word or an entire passage. He may repeat a passage word for word, restate the same point in different words, or merely reinforce the same word-pattern in consecutive parallel sentences. All these are legitimate devices, which he uses consciously or unconsciously to make his point clear or emphatic. But the inexperienced writer often repeats himself through inexcusable carelessness. Unnecessary repetition is always confusing and weakening, if not intolerably childish.

The extent to which a modern writer uses repetition for emphasis depends partly on the nature of his material. Fifty years ago it was a familiar device in writing. Today, with the general trend toward conversational ease and away from calculated rhetorical tricks, extensive repetition too often smacks of platform oratory. For this reason it is more common in argument than in other kinds of writing. It should always be handled with care. Like many habit-forming drugs, repetition can be both a stimulant and a soporific, depending on the dosage.

There is no magic answer to the problem of when and how to repeat. But an analysis of the following paragraphs may suggest some guiding principles:

1. We did sleep that night, but we woke up at six A.M. We lay in our beds and debated through the open doors whether to obey till, say, halfpast six. Then we bolted. I don't know who started it, but there was a rush. We all disobeyed; we raced to disobey and get first to the fireplace in the front room downstairs. And there they were, the gifts, all sorts of wonderful things, mixed-up piles of presents; only, as I disentangled the mess, I saw that my stocking was empty; it hung

limp; not a thing in it; and under and around it—nothing. My sisters had knelt down, each by her pile of gifts; they were squealing with delight, till they looked up and saw me standing there in my nightgown with nothing. They left their piles to come to me and look with me at my empty place. Nothing. They felt my stocking: nothing.
—Lincoln Steffens, *Autobiography*.

2. The schools today are full of practical courses: practical storekeeping for little children who can't add or subtract, practical civics for youngsters who know nothing about the historical development of American democracy, practical journalism and business correspondence for adolescents who can't read or write a simple English sentence. And with visiting committees of practical men insisting annually that curricula in the colleges cannot be accredited until further practical courses are added to the already groaning course of study, the old-fashioned ideals of liberal education are being rapidly relegated to the footnotes in the college catalogues.

3. There is great virtue in the independent small college; virtue even in smallness, because that may mean that here a man and a boy may walk and talk and work together, with mutual sympathy. But there is little or no virtue in it if it is small against its own will, and eager to be large, and so is wasting its resources in recruiting campaigns and all sorts of devices to lure more students to its campus. It has little virtue if, though it enable a man and a boy to walk and talk and work together, the man is not worth walking and talking with. It has little virtue if to its physical littleness is added littleness of spirit so that its faculty is broken up into still smaller units by artificial barriers and its student body broken into social cliques which encourage snobbishness and cheap campus politics and leave lonely students without companionship. Its opportunity is greater than that of any other type of college to adventure in the world of scholarship, and to regain a singleness of purpose which would bind campus and classroom together in a strengthening co-operation. It is utterly lacking in virtue if it imitates all the weaknesses of a big university and offers no compensating strengths of its own. —Burges Johnson, *Campus vs. Classroom*.

4. The task education must accomplish, if free societies are to continue to exist, is the re-creation of the sense of individual responsibility—which means the re-establishment of the belief of men in man. Fascism is only another name for the sickness and desperation which overcome a society when it loses its sense of responsibility for its own

life and surrenders its will to a tyrant it, and it alone, has invented. But the sense of responsibility in a nation is a sense of responsibility in the individuals who compose that nation, for the sense of responsibility is always a charge upon the individual conscience and vanishes when many share it. And to re-create the sense of individual responsibility it is necessary to restore the belief of men in man—the belief that man can direct his destiny if he will. —Archibald MacLeish, "Humanism and the Belief in Man," *Atlantic Monthly.*

5. It is indeed true, as the quotation says, that there are marked differences between William Congreve's play, *The Way of the World,* and Sheridan's drama, *The School for Scandal.* In the first place, the two were writing at different times in the history of the English drama. William Congreve's play, *The Way of the World,* was composed many years before Sheridan's *School for Scandal.* The reader would naturally expect that two plays written by different playwrights in different periods would reveal marked differences in style, and this is certainly the case. *The Way of the World* reflects the dramatic tradition of Congreve's time, and *The School for Scandal* "holds up the mirror" to society in its author's period. This is the first important difference between the two plays.

6. I tried to get my whole family interested in snakes, but I couldn't get them to come close enough to see what a snake really looked like. Finally, however, I was given a room in which to keep my snakes. I then began to start a collection of snakes, catching some local species and buying some other species of snakes not so readily obtainable locally until I had a collection of some twenty-two snakes with nine different species of snakes, all harmless.

The first paragraph shows how the calculated repetition of a single motif can be extremely effective in telling a simple story. In one sentence Steffens restates the theme of emptiness four different ways: "I saw that my stocking was empty; it hung limp; not a thing in it; and under and around it—nothing." And then to sustain the pathos of the scene he echoes the word *nothing* three times more, building up the boy's emotion to a climax of desolation.

The student author of the second paragraph consciously repeats the single word *practical* to produce an ironic effect. Burges Johnson reveals how the repetition of a single phrase, with slight variations, can strengthen an argument: "There is great virtue . . . . there is little or no virtue . . . . It has little virtue . . . . It has little virtue . . . . It is utterly lacking in virtue." Coming at the beginning of sentence after sentence, this echoing phrase helps to cement them together in parallel structure. The addition of the strong expression *utterly lacking* adds climactic strength to the final summarizing topic sentence. Of course, if the author were to continue the same device from paragraph to paragraph, it would soon begin to call too much attention to itself, and the law of diminishing returns would take effect.

Archibald MacLeish builds his entire paragraph by *restatement,* repeating the topic idea of the importance of *individual responsibility* four different ways in consecutive sentences. This too is a legitimate device, especially when one considers that the article was originally delivered as a speech during a period of national crisis. But when MacLeish uses the phrase *sense of responsibility* three times in a single sentence, he probably drives his point past home. The student who uses the same device for simple exposition in paragraph five is obviously restating his flimsy material not for emphasis but out of desperation. He is concealing his ignorance on an examination by trying to play an entire symphony on a single string. The result is a ludicrous failure. This use of repetition to conceal ignorance is not restricted to undergraduates; it is the first refuge of spellbinding demagogues and other assorted windbags.

The student snake-fancier is probably unaware of his reptilian redundancy. A quick revision can eliminate much of the unnecessary wordiness:

I tried to interest my whole family in snakes but couldn't get them to come close enough to see what a snake really looked like. Finally, however, I was given a room in which to keep my pets. I then began a collection, catching some local species and buying others not so readily obtainable until I had twenty-two snakes of nine different varieties, all harmless.

Unconscious repetition is one of the most irritating habits of inexperienced writers. There are several simple ways of curing it:

1. *Read the theme out loud:* This practice, already sug-

gested in Chapter Two, is especially important for students with the repetition habit. Wordiness is often heard, not seen.

2. *Delete references to things already referred to:* This may seem like begging the question. But, however obvious, it is a step many students are loath to take. The intelligent reader, unlike the girl in the row behind you at the movies, does not have to be *told* everything; he can infer a great deal. Sooner or later he gets the idea that the student is writing about snakes without being reminded by constant references to snakes that the theme is about snakes.

3. *Use synonyms:* For reasons discussed in detail in Chapter Eight, this cure should be used with discretion. It would be absurd for the pet-lover to open Roget's *Thesaurus* and substitute a synonym for every *snake* after the first. The word *serpent,* for example, conjures up legions of historical and mythological beasts a world away from his modest collection. Moreover, "elegant variation" can become an offensive trick of style. The sports writer who cannot *kick the ball* more than once in a story, who after that must *boot the pigskin, toe the ovate spheroid, propel the leather pellet,* and so on until the reader yearns for the simple statement of a simple fact, is not the ideal model for college writing. On the other hand, there is no reason why the writer could not have referred once or twice to pets.

4. *Use pronouns:* After all, they were devised to take the place of nouns—like the *they* in this sentence. They too should be used with caution; faulty reference is always lurking around the corner (see pages 94–96). But pronouns are handier words than most repeaters know. Their use as transitions, already mentioned, is one of the best ways of achieving economy. Notice, for example, how the author of the following passage rephrases half of the first sentence merely to make a transition at the beginning of the second:

Wordy: Eventually the adults tend to become suspicious of the nature of the affair. Benét illustrates *how the feelings of the adults tend to change during the affair* when Chuck and Helen are seen driving home from the cottage by Miss Eagles, a highly imaginative old schoolteacher, who obviously thinks the children have been making love out in the country.

Rewritten: Eventually the adults become suspicious. Benét illustrates *this* when Chuck and Helen are seen driving home from the cottage by Miss Eagles, a highly imaginative old schoolteacher, who obviously thinks the children have been making love out in the country.

This substitution of the single pronoun *this* makes the transition neatly and clearly; eleven unnecessary words are eliminated. The patterns of progress from sentence to sentence within a paragraph should look like this:

Not like this:

Inchworms don't make much progress.

THE PARTS AND THE WHOLE

By merely expanding the recipe, the student can apply the principles of good paragraphing to the organization of a short theme. The fundamental principle of unity is the same: a writer may make only a single major point in a five-hundred-word paper, but if he makes more than one, they should be closely related. He may announce the main purpose of a theme in a generality at the beginning—taking the same risks which attend starting a paragraph with a topic sentence; he may postpone it until later, perhaps in a concluding summary; or he may, as in a paragraph, let the reader infer it from the evidence. Coherence in the whole theme is as important as in the paragraph. Transitions between paragraphs may be longer than a single word or phrase; an entire sentence is sometimes used and occasionally a transitional paragraph. But visible bridges are no more sacred than those between sentences; if the thought of the theme is closely knit and the order logical, a writer doesn't have to begin each new paragraph with something as obvious as: "I proceed now to my second point." Anemia in paragraphing means anemia throughout the theme. Entire compositions may be developed by use of details, illustration, definition, division, comparison-and-contrast, cause-and-effect —or by a combination of these methods. Similarly, repetition can be both a useful device and a useless vice on the larger scale of the whole theme. The writer may intentionally reiterate in a final summary an important point he has made at the beginning—though this kind of repeating is usually superfluous in a short paper; or he may make the error of unconsciously returning in paragraph four to a point which he has already passed in paragraph two. A student who can organize a unified, coherent, well-developed paragraph should have no serious trouble organizing a short theme.

EXERCISES

I. Analyze each of the following paragraphs to determine (1) the main point or points; (2) the topic sentence, if any; (3) the transitions, both expressed and implied; and (4) the method or methods of development:

1. In Boston the member of a First Family lives in a world of special privilege. For him the minor inconveniences of life are all but by-passed. If he lives on Beacon Hill he will probably have a view of the Common or perhaps a fenced-in park of his own, such as on fashionable Louisburg Square, where the twenty-two so-called proprietors or homeowners have practically no responsibility to their city at all, own the entire square outright, and meet annually to tax themselves for the upkeep of their park and the care of their street. If he lives in Back Bay, he will doubtless be on the "water side" of

Beacon Street or the "sunny side" of Commonwealth Avenue; the other side of these streets would be, for him, the wrong side of the tracks. Outside his home, he may even have a special kind of sidewalk to distinguish his residence. So-called "rich men's sidewalks," they are small areas of glazed brick laid in fancy patterns instead of the ordinary Boston rough brick or cement walks. Ames Corner, located at the north corner of Commonwealth and Dartmouth Streets, is one of these; dangerously slippery as the corner is in wet weather, it has been allowed to remain as a sort of Boston monument to a man who was once officially connected with seventy-five of the country's railroads. If the Proper Bostonian is one of the many who have moved to the suburbs, he will be "protected" by rigid zoning laws of his own making and may not have a numbered street address at all. That is part of the privilege. —Cleveland Amory, *The Proper Bostonians.*

2. Everyone knows the popular conception of Florence Nightingale. The saintly, self-sacrificing woman, the delicate maiden of high degree who threw aside the pleasures of a life of ease to succour the afflicted, the Lady with the Lamp, gliding through the horrors of the hospital at Scutari, and consecrating with the radiance of her goodness the dying soldier's couch—the vision is familiar to all. But the truth was different. The Miss Nightingale of fact was not as facile fancy painted her. She worked in another fashion and towards another end; she moved under the stress of an impetus which finds no place in the popular imagination. A Demon possessed her. Now demons, whatever else they may be, are full of interest. And so it happens that in the real Miss Nightingale there was more that was interesting than in the legendary; there was also less that was agreeable. —Lytton Strachey, "Florence Nightingale," *Eminent Victorians.*

3. I mean, by a civilization, the smallest unit of historical study at which one arrives when one tries to understand the history of one's own country: the United States, say, or the United Kingdom. If you were to try to understand the history of the United States by itself, it would be unintelligible: you could not understand the part played in American life by federal government, representative government, democracy, industrialism, monogamy, Christianity, unless you looked beyond the bounds of the United States—out beyond her frontiers to Western Europe and the other overseas countries founded by West Europeans, and back beyond her local origins to the history of Western Europe in centuries before Columbus or Cabot had crossed the Atlantic.

But, to make American history and institutions intelligible for practical purposes, you need not look beyond Western European civilization to the decline and fall of the Graeco-Roman civilization. These limits of time and space give us the intelligible unit of social life of which the United States or Great Britain or France or Holland is a part: call it Western Christendom, Western Civilization, Western Society, the Western World. Similarly, if you start from Greece or Serbia or Russia, and try to understand their histories, you arrive at an Orthodox Christendom or Byzantine World. If you start from Morocco or Afghanistan, and try to understand their histories, you arrive at an Islamic world. Start from Bengal or Mysore or Rajputana, and you find a Hindu world. Start from China or Japan and you find a Far Eastern world. —Arnold J. Toynbee, *Civilization on Trial.*

4. A surprising number of the people of Hiroshima remained more or less indifferent about the ethics of using the bomb. Possibly they were too terrified by it to want to think about it at all. Not many of them even bothered to find out much about what it was like. Mrs. Nakamura's conception of it—and awe of it—was typical. "The atom bomb," she would say when asked about it, "is the size of a matchbox. The heat of it is six thousand times that of the sun. It exploded in the air. There is some radium in it. I don't know just how it works, but when the radium is put together, it explodes." As for the use of the bomb, she would say, "It was war and we had to expect it." And then she would add, *"Shikata ga nai,"* a Japanese expression as common as, and corresponding to, the Russian word *"nichevo"*: "It can't be helped. Oh, well. Too bad." Dr. Fujii said approximately the same thing about the use of the bomb to Father Kleinsorge one evening, in German: *"Da ist nichts zu machen.* There's nothing to be done about it." —John Hersey, *Hiroshima.*

5. There is another side to this picture of the possibilities of decadence. At the present moment a discussion is raging as to the future of civilization in the novel circumstances of rapid scientific and technological advance. The evils of the future have been diagnosed in various ways: the loss of religious faith, the malignant use of material power, the degradation attending a differential birth-rate favouring the lower types of humanity, the suppression of aesthetic creativeness. Without doubt, these are all evils, dangerous and threatening. But they are not new. From the dawn of history, mankind has always been losing its religious faith, has always suffered from the malignant use of material power, has always suffered from the infertility of its best

intellectual types, has always witnessed the periodical decadence of art. In the reign of the Egyptian king, Tutankhamen, there was raging a desperate religious struggle between Modernists and Fundamentalists; the cave pictures exhibit a phase of delicate aesthetic achievement as superseded by a period of comparative vulgarity; the religious leaders, the great thinkers, the great poets and authors, the whole clerical caste in the Middle Ages, have been notably infertile; finally, if we attend to what actually has happened in the past, and disregard romantic visions of democracies, aristocracies, kings, generals, armies, and merchants, material power has generally been wielded with blindness, obstinacy, and selfishness, often with brutal malignancy. And yet, mankind has progressed. Even if you take a tiny oasis of peculiar excellence, the type of modern man who would have most chance of happiness in ancient Greece at its best period is probably (as now) an average professional heavy-weight boxer, and not an average Greek scholar from Oxford or Germany. Indeed, the main use of the Oxford scholar would have been his capability of writing an ode in glorification of the boxer. Nothing does more harm in unnerving men for their duties in the present than the attention devoted to the points of excellence in the past as compared with the average failure of the present day. —Alfred North Whitehead, *Science and the Modern World.*

II. Select three well-organized paragraphs from your reading and analyze them as in Exercise I.

III. Analyze the paragraphs of one of your own themes as in Exercise I.

IV. Each of the following paragraphs is weakly organized (as far as a reader can tell from a paragraph ripped out of its context). Pick out the flaws in organization.

1. Probably the main reason why I like my home town is that the people there are so friendly. It is not like one of the big cities where a person can drop out of sight and nobody know the difference. Everybody in my town knows everybody else and everybody else's business. This can get awfully annoying, of course. Gossip is one of the worst troubles with small towns, and the women in my town are no different from other women. When the tongues start to wagging, gossip can quickly turn into scandal. Sometimes in my home town you can't call your life your own.

2. I'm not arguing that poetry should be left out of the Freshman

English course. I only maintain that Electrical Engineers should not be made to study it. Take me, for example. Ever since my fifth grade teacher made me stay after school because I wouldn't memorize Wordsworth's "Daffodils," I have hated poetry. Nobody can learn to appreciate anything when it's thrust down his throat no matter how much sweet syrup is poured along with it. Electricity used to be simple in the days of Ben Franklin's kite. But it's getting more complicated every day. Four years is a short enough time to become an Electrical Engineer without having to become a poetry-lover at the same time. Of what practical use will poetry be to me when I apply for a job after I get out? Besides, most of the students I know hate poetry— even the Arts students.

3. If football scholarships were abolished, a lot of deserving young men would be deprived of a college education. These players can pass all the requirements of the Admissions Office. Why should they be penalized in life for failing to pass the requirements of the Bursar's Office? Is there any moral difference between a man working his way through college on the gridiron in the stadium and another earning money for standing over a hot gridiron in the kitchen at the Union? All the colleges I know anything about give football scholarships. Because of "purity" codes some of them won't admit it publicly, but the influential alumni could give anyone the inside story if the President couldn't or wouldn't. Why should the honest colleges be penalized with poor teams year after year, while the top teams in the nation pretend that they can get to the Rose Bowl with a bunch of amateurs pure as lilies? Besides, football is a practical money-making proposition, and we might as well face it honestly. Those who foot the balls must foot the bills. Why shouldn't they get their cut?

4. It doesn't take an expert to see why Boswell's *Life of Johnson* is generally considered the greatest biography in the English language, if not in the world. Boswell was a first-rate reporter with a tireless zest for living, a keen eye for the eccentricities of human nature, and a genuine gift for dramatizing them. Many of the people in his own day had no use for him. Horace Walpole and Fanny Burney both criticized him. In the nineteenth century Macaulay created a monstrous carica- ture of an intolerable "lick-spittle" who was a great biographer only because he was a great fool, and this picture has stuck in the popular imagination down to our own time. It raises the age-old question of whether the morals of the author have anything to do with the criticism of his book. This question has often come up in connection with

Oscar Wilde and has more recently arisen in connection with Ezra Pound. Today, as the result of the amazing discovery of Boswell papers during the last twenty years, we are beginning to realize that Boswell's Life of Boswell is also a masterpiece.

5. I agree heartily with the author that our main economic problem is to find a fair compromise between the chaos of unchecked individualism and the slavery of unbridled state control. In doing this, we must distinguish carefully between the liberty that is necessary for a man or group of men to build an enterprise and the license that may result if it becomes too powerful. We must also distinguish between the necessary government regulations to protect free enterprise from itself and the shackling controls that make every businessman the helpless puppet of an expert in Washington. The power of management must not be allowed to go too far on the one hand, or the power of labor on the other. During the last decades of the nineteenth century management in some industries ran wild, and, as the author says, "Rugged Individualism paid no attention to ragged individuals." But it is also true that the unions got away with a lot during the nineteen-thirties. This is still going on today. Controlling unions is one of our greatest economic problems in 1951.

V. How could the following theme be more intelligently organized? Does it have other shortcomings besides faulty paragraphing? How does the point made in Chapter Two, pages 21–22, bear on this theme and on the general question of adequate paragraph development?

MY AUTOBIOGRAPHY

I was born in eastern Pennsylvania twenty years ago last summer. This makes me a typical Dutchman. At least that is what everyone calls me.

When I was in the sixth grade, my father passed away. This left my mother and me alone, as I didn't have any brothers or sisters.

We lived in a small New Jersey town near Trenton. It has a population of about two hundred and fifty people. The business section contained four stories and a post office. We lived in this town until I was eleven years old.

When I was graduated from elementary school we moved to a larger town near Newark, where I entered high school. At that institution I engaged in several sports.

In 1941 I showed up as a freshman at the small college in my home town. It was here that I made many friends who will remain in my memory as long as I live.

Six months later, I transferred here. I took a straight A.B. course, which also contains English. I did not live on the campus during my first term, but at present I stay at the Sigma Nu house.

Late in March 1942, I was called to the service by Uncle Sam. The Navy was my choice because I figured that one always had a good place to sleep until his ship went down.

There were about one hundred and fifty fellows in our Company when we stepped off the train at the Great Lakes Naval Training Station, Illinois.

We were given another physical examination the first day. Only seventy-five per cent of the fellows passed.

The other twenty-five per cent were sent back home or to base hospital. I was among the latter group. They said I had a bad back. It had never given me trouble previously, however. A week later we were discharged and returned home. They gave a month's pay and traveling expenses. Pretty good for a week's work.

VI. How could the author of "Character Building in High School" (page 37) have organized his material into paragraphs?

VII. The following section from an essay on "The Purpose of Liberal Education" is printed without paragraph indentions. Divide it logically into paragraphs. (It originally contained five, but this number is not sacred.)

Harvard College was founded in 1636 "to advance learning and perpetuate it to posterity: dreading to leave an illiterate Ministry to the Churches when our present Ministers shall lie in the dust." A century and a half later President Clapp of Yale categorically defined a college as "a group of ministers to train young men for the ministry." In those dear dead days the typical American college was a high-minded vocational school. During the course of the nineteenth century, as more and more young men came to the campuses with no intention or preparing for the Church, the faculties were forced to concede that the growing nation needed educated men in the pews as well as in the pulpit; and the purpose of the college broadened to include, not merely the training of ministers, but the "liberal education" of "gentlemen"—many of whom would become, after the specialized instructior of the new graduate schools, leaders in other professions as well. But the time-honored classics remained at the heart of the curriculum. College-educated men in those days had something more in common than a mutual enthusiasm for the victories of the Brooklyn Dodgers. They had shared the same intellectual experience. Through hard-won familiarity with Plato and Aristotle, Horace and Catullus, Homer and Virgil, Aeschylus and Sophocles, they had acquired a common cultural heritage. Towards the end of the century, with the young studies in the physical and social sciences elbowing into the curriculum and a new generation of students of more various backgrounds swarming onto the campus—the hard core of classical learning began to disintegrate. Under the bold leadership of President Eliot, the rigid, old-fashioned curriculum gradually surrendered to the brave new elective system. The strict table-d'hôte diet prescribed by the professor gave way to the entrancing à la carte menu catering to the student. Down the four-year cafeteria line they came with their trays, indiscriminately gathering in a dish of this and a dash of that, while the harried advisers behind the counter tried desperately to persuade them to select *some* solid food to ballast their multifarious desserts. In the best liberal arts colleges, this disintegration of the classical curriculum was a change more in the method of higher education that in its ultimate purpose. Whatever the shortcomings of the elective system, President Eliot's fundamental faith in what he called "the social value of the cultivated man" was not a far cry from Matthew Arnold's stubborn insistence that education should develop "the power of conduct, the power of intellect and knowledge, the power of beauty, and the power of social life and manners." The great threat to American higher education was not the elective system but a more formidable menace: the lion rampant in the field was misguided vocationalism. The evidence of the catalogues is clear. Courses once labeled "Economics" tagged as "Business"; "History" distorted as "History for Sixth-Grade Teachers"; time-tested "English Composition" modernized as "Business English," "Pharmacy English," "Journalism" and "Scenario Writing." The slick catalogues with the bright come-hither looks bore a strange resemblance to the modern drugstore—with the sundries—vocational courses in Radio Announcing, Flower Arranging, and Lip Rouging—lavishly displayed in the front counters, while, in an obscure corner at the rear, the old-fashioned medicine bottles—Latin Poets, Chaucer, Greek Philosophers —gathered dust beneath a sign which read, "We also fill prescriptions."

VIII. Build a well-developed paragraph of at least 150 words on one of these "topic sentences," following any *one* of the methods of development discussed on pages 51–63.

1. "Colleges are places where pebbles are polished and diamonds are dimmed." —R. G. Ingersoll.
2. "To know how to suggest is the great art of teaching." —Amiel.
3. "Patriotism is the last refuge of a scoundrel." —Samuel Johnson.
4. "A poem should not mean but be." —Archibald MacLeish.
5. "A highbrow is the kind of person who looks at a sausage and thinks of Picasso." —A. P. Herbert.
6. "The civilized man has built a coach, but has lost the use of his feet." —Emerson.
7. "The historian is a prophet looking backwards." —Schlegel.
8. "Harmony seldom makes the headlines." —Silas Bent.
9. "Words are the most powerful drug used by mankind." —Kipling.
10. "Athleticism focuses its attention on doing good for the boys who least need it." —Robert M. Hutchins.

IX. Rewrite the following paragraphs, eliminating all unnecessary repetition:

1. With the assistance of a summer school course I managed to scrape together enough credits to be accepted by this college. Two days after I had been accepted by this college the draft law was changed, and I became elegible for the draft. I immediately made up my mind to join the navy directly after graduating from high school. I paid a visit to the local recruiting center in order to obtain some information about the navy; this was as close as I ever got to joining the navy. The officer in charge told me that the navy would not accept me because of my speech defect. In spite of the fact that the navy had rejected me, I still thought that the army would accept me. But I was wrong because the army rejected me too.

2. The Union Pacific Railroad had begun its track-laying about eighteen months after the Central Pacific had begun. The Union Pacific had a much greater distance over which to lay tracks than did the Central Pacific and the fact that the land over which the Union Pacific had to travel was flat made very little difference in the condi-

tions between it and the Central Pacific. The Union Pacific encountered storms, blizzards, buffalo stampedes, and, worst of all, Indian attacks. But in 1868 the Union Pacific was as near to the meeting place with the Central Pacific as was the Central Pacific.

3. The future days of the classroom movies are the ones when the literature course will be the most popular course in high school and college. Instead of many students shying away from advanced literature as they now do, they will instead crowd the literature classes. Interest is what is needed in studying ancient literature and classroom movies are just the thing to supply the added interest. The days when literature will be dramatized in the classroom by movies, and possibly even television, are still many years away, but when that day comes the ideal prescription for supplying interest to a literature course will have been found.

4. I once had an intense hatred for poetry. It all started when I was in the third grade in grammar school and was compelled to recite a poem from memory. The fact that I was made to memorize the poem was probably the reason for my early dislike of poetry. I believe that if I had been allowed to read the poem for pleasure alone I would not have had that prejudice toward poetry. For eight years I had this utter hatred for poetry firmly fixed in my mind.

5. Henry's parents said that he had a mania for driving cars. They had absolutely forbidden him to drive until he was sixteen, and they could not understand why he had this craze to drive cars. Investigation disclosed that Henry's urge to drive a car was largely the result of the refusal of his parents when he asked to drive. Their flat denial made driving seem a very real pleasure to him. He spent hours imagining he was driving, even got road maps and planned long trips. It seemed to him an eternity to wait till he was old enough to drive cars; consequently, driving became a compulsion that he could not resist.

X. Write a paragraph on each: (1) the difference between unity and coherence in paragraphing; and (2) the use and abuse of repetition.

CHAPTER FOUR

Grammar

There are moments when anyone resents gravitation very much, as, say, Mr. Alexander Woollcott resents grammar. But you do not repeal the law of gravity if you step off a cliff into thin air. You only illustrate it.

—Wilson Follett.

Grammatical expressions have been formed in the course of centuries by innumerable generations of illiterate speakers.

—Otto Jesperson.

Alice Brown can write the English language with grammatical precision without being able to tell a noun from a verb. Albert Jones can rattle off declensions and conjugations like catechisms—and even knows what a cognate accusative is—but when he puts fingers to typewriter he turns out the most barbarous English. What price grammar? The answer is that, though grammar has gone through a period of deflation in the schools during recent years, the experts are beginning to set a higher value on it. And the reason is that both Alice Brown and Albert Jones are rare exceptions. Alice may have learned the rules and forgotten them; or perhaps, like many professional writers, she chooses to pretend that she has never learned them. Or possibly she belongs to that even rarer minority of students who, because they have read wisely and widely in good books and associated with careful speakers, have learned to play the language accurately by ear. Although she may protest that she "doesn't know any grammar," her writing belies her protest. Many a touch-typist hasn't the vaguest notion of where the letters are until he puts the fingers to the keys. Albert, on the other hand, does not really know grammar; he has merely memorized the rules and regulations like a well-oiled robot.

There is no virtue in a mechanical man's ability to define a dangling participle if he continues to write sentences like "Being a tough piece of meat, I refused to eat the steak." And if the student can avoid such a pitfall, most teachers will forgive him for not knowing that the grammarians have a word for it. For every Alice and Albert in the college classrooms, however, there are countless undergraduates with neither Alice's habitual accuracy nor Albert's obedient memory. Either they commit errors without knowing it until the red pencil descends, or they are uneasily aware that something is wrong but haven't the vaguest notion of how to set it right. Witch-doctoring will not mend a sick sentence. Accurate diagnosis and cure presume a knowledge of the parts, the jobs they do, their relation to each other, and the common ailments that beset them. Grammar can be roughly defined as a study of the first principles of sentence anatomy.

IS GRAMMAR HARD?

Grammar and *glamour* are historically the same word. Back in the eighteenth century one of the meanings of *grammar* was *magic.* The Scotch let the *r* slip into an *l,* and, despite the efforts of Hollywood and the women's magazines to kill the word with kindness, *glamour* still has the meaning of *magic.* But the point is not that grammar is glamorous in the loose Hollywood sense. As William Cobbett said succinctly over a century ago, "The study is dry . . . it engages not the passions." The point is that people still insist on regarding it as magic—a sort of black magic permeated by taboo. This is absurd. Grammar has been brewed not by Merlins in mortar boards but by "innumerable generations of illiterate speakers." It is by no means as mysterious as the witchery of the chemistry laboratory or the jungle of tubes and pipes under the hood of an automobile or a maze of varicolored macaroni inside the radio set. A citizen may live to a ripe old age without having to reveal an ignorance of these mysteries. But if he is ignorant of grammar, he may betray himself whenever he opens his mouth or puts words on paper.

English grammar, despite its little inconsistencies, is relatively simple. English-speaking people can hardly boast about the mysteries of their spelling or pronunciation, but their grammar deserves praise. A grammar that has almost completely replaced a complex system of declensions with a few simple principles of word order and substituted for an involved scheme of conjugations a set of versatile auxiliaries; a grammar in which parts of speech are virtually interchangeable and gender and sex are comfortably synonymous—in contrast to German or even French this is a thing of streamlined beauty. But it must not be taken for granted.

THE IMPORTANCE OF TERMS

The beginning of wisdom in the study of grammar is the ability to recognize *and name* the grammatical elements. The *and name* is stressed because there is a widespread classroom illusion that a student can understand a subject without benefit of terminology. Up to the point where they degenerate into needless jargon, technical terms are indispensable to understanding. "Every self-respecting mechanic," says John Dewey, "will call the parts of an automobile by their right names because that is the way to distinguish them." The mechanic cannot convey intelligence by resorting to the lazy GI habit of calling everything a *gismo* any more than a biologist can get away with calling an *amoeba* a *wiggly piece of gelatine* or a physicist can define *Archimedes' principle* as *what happens to a body in a bathtub.* The student may forget the terms after accuracy has become habitual. Many seasoned writers have. But as long as he is slipping grammatical cogs, he and the teacher must talk a common language. If he writes "Between you and I, George and Mary is going to the Interfraternity Ball," the teacher can hardly get anywhere by sputtering: "Words like *between, among, in, on,* and so forth, are followed by words like *me, him, her,* and *whom;* and when you have two people who *do* or *are* something, they *do* or *are* it, not *does* or *is.*" He can convey intelligence clearly by saying: "A preposition takes an object in the objective case; a compound subject takes a plural verb."

Nor is identifying grammatical elements valuable only in the study of grammar. The knowledge acquired in a careful reading of this chapter will accumulate by a kind of compound interest and pay dividends in subsequent chapters. Grammar, sentence structure, and punctuation are subtly interrelated; handbooks must draw arbitrary distinctions for teaching purposes. This chapter defines a *clause* (grammar); the next chapter discusses the combination of clauses known as a *compound sentence* (sentence structure); and Chapter Six considers the use of commas and semicolons in the combination of clauses known as a compound sentence (punctuation). This is a house that Jack can build only if he starts by learning to recognize a clause in the first place.

A complete English grammar is a project for a fat book. This chapter aims only to describe those grammatical terms and conventions that may help the student in his writing. It does not define such fifty-cent terms as the *cognate accusative* and the *illative conjunction*. It relegates many "problems" of usage to the GLOSSARY, including such notorious teapot-tempests as *shall-will,* the *split infinitive,* and the *preposition-at-the-end-of-a-sentence.* The problems that bother undergraduates more than any others are starred for emphasis (*). The student who continually makes grammatical errors had better begin with the parts of speech and study the chapter carefully from beginning to end, not parroting the rules but trying to understand how they reflect actual usage. The more advanced student whose grammar may be only a little rusty around the edges can save time and energy in three ways: (1) by turning to the *list of key terms* on pages 115–116 and referring in the chapter only to those that he cannot clearly define or illustrate; (2) by concentrating on the starred sections; and (3) by testing his understanding of grammar-in-action in the exercises on pages 116–125.

DESCRIPTION AND PRESCRIPTION

All students, however, are reminded of the discussion of correctness in Chapter One. They will find that the treatment of grammar here is more a description of current usage than a prescription compounded of one part petrified-rule and one part awful-warning. Mr. Follett's analogy at the head of this chapter must not be taken too literally; the "laws" of grammar are not as immutable as the law of gravity. For example, a hoary law that would insist on changing the first *as* in the previous sentence to a *so* has all but faded from the books, relegated to the same limbo as the quaint convention that would put *an* before *hoary* in this sentence. It is hard to walk through a modern English sentence without stepping on the grave of a dead grammatical rule. Some so-called laws—the distinction between *among* and *between,* for example—not only do not conform to usage now but never did. Some rules that were once violated by literate people are now strictly observed: no educated man today says *he don't,* like his nineteenth-century ancestors. Still other laws—on the use of *who* and *whom,* for example—have reached the point in their evolution where strict observance depends on the level of usage. It would be easy in this chapter to pretend that all that's not white is black, every expression not formally grammatical is vulgate. But that simply isn't so.

THE PARTS OF SPEECH
(See Exercises I and II on pages 116–117)

Examine the following passage:

Poor George trudged slowly through Manhattan. Alas, he felt bitter, for life had been against him.

Classified according to the work they do, the words in those two sentences (like all the other words in the language) fall into five categories:

1. Words that name or designate persons, places, or things (*George, Manhattan, he, life, him*). These are known as *substantives.*

2. Words that assert action, state, or being (*trudged, felt, had been*). These are *verbs,* the most important words in a sentence.

3. Words that describe, limit, or qualify other words (*poor, slowly, bitter*). These are called *modifiers.*

4. Words that tie the parts of the sentence together (*through, for, against*). These are *connectives.*

5. Words that merely exclaim (*alas*). These are *interjections.*

By subdividing three of these categories, grammarians distinguish eight *parts of speech* in English:

Substantives

1. *Noun*—the name of a person, place, or thing:

> *Kilroy, Kokomo, carrot*

2. *Pronoun*—a word used in place of a noun:

> *he, who, that, either, myself*
> *Kilroy* was here. (noun)
> *He* was here. (pronoun)

3. *Verb*—a word used to assert action, state, or being:

> Boy *kisses* girl. (action)
> Boy *feels* happy. (state)
> Boy *is* happy. (being)

Modifiers

4. *Adjective*—a word used to modify a noun or pronoun:

> *red, small, extracurricular, funnier, a, an, the* (The last three are called *articles*.)
> In *a red house* the adjective *red* modifies the noun *house*.

5. *Adverb*—a word used to modify a verb, adjective, or other adverb:

> Alfred ran *slowly*. (The adverb *slowly* modifies the verb *ran*.)
> He was an *incurably* stubborn man. (The adverb *incurably* modifies the adjective *stubborn*.)
> He ran *very* slowly. (The adverb *very* modifies the adverb *slowly*.)

Connectives

6. *Preposition*—a word used to connect a noun or pronoun (its object) with some other word in the sentence and show the relation between them:

> George went *to* the dance. (*To* connects *dance* with *went*.)
> He danced *with* her. (*With* connects *her* with *danced*.)

Connectives \
(cont.)

7. *Conjunction*—a word used to connect words, phrases, or clauses (see pages 113–114):

> ham *and* eggs (connects words)
> of the people, by the people, *and* for the people (connects phrases)
> Daniel Webster was a great statesman, *though* he never became president. (connects clauses)

8. *Interjection*—an expression of emotion, unrelated grammatically to the rest of the sentence:

> *Hurray,* we won!
> *Zowie,* what a ball game!

Many a word cannot be safely classified as a part of speech without considering the part it plays in a sentence. What part of speech is *up* in each of the following sentences?

He climbed *up* a tree.
Whatever goes *up* must come down.
The time is *up*.
He has his *ups* and downs.
Speculators always *up* the price.

The answers are, respectively, preposition, adverb (modifying *goes*), adjective (modifying *time*), noun, and verb. By the same token, *for* can be a preposition (He ran *for* home) or a conjunction (He ran, *for* home was near); *home* can be a noun, adjective, adverb, or verb; *down* can be a noun, adjective, adverb, verb, or preposition. You can ship a man or man a ship, walk a block or block a walk, run a show or show a run, study in a dream or dream in a study—the list is endless. This flexibility is one of the distinctive traits of the English language. It means that the beginner, in identifying a part of speech, must ask himself: What does this word do in the sentence? Does it name or designate a person, place, or thing? Does it assert action, state, or being? Does it modify? Does it connect? Does it merely exclaim?

Interjections, which raise no grammatical problems, can be respectfully left in peace. Prepositions cause no serious trouble for students with an elementary grasp of English idiom. The reader who cannot readily distinguish them from conjunctions on the basis of the definition here (and such definitions are always inadequate) should become more aware of the difference as he sees them used later in the chapter. But nouns and pronouns, verbs, adjectives and adverbs, and—to a lesser extent—conjunctions require further dissection.

NOUNS

Five kinds of nouns are generally recognized.

1. A *proper noun* is the name of a particular person (*Wendell Willkie*), place (*Skaneateles*), or thing (*Coca-Cola*)—and is invariably capitalized.

2. A *common noun* is any other noun.

3. A *collective noun* names a group of persons or things:

> gang, team, family, navy, congregation, flock

4. A *concrete noun* names something that can be seen, heard, touched, smelled, or tasted:

> boat, bell, fur, perfume, caviar

5. An *abstract noun* names a quality or idea that cannot be perceived by the senses:

> happiness, apathy, pessimism, democracy, Communism, Existentialism

Nouns have gender, number, and case.

GENDER

To any American student who has struggled with a foreign language, the facts about sex in English are refreshingly simple. Males are *masculine* (*man, boy*), females *feminine* (*woman, girl*), others *neuter* (*parlor, bedroom, sink*). In a poem the sun may be personified as *he* or a Grecian urn as *she;* in colloquial American almost any neuter object—a favorite jalopy, for example—can become feminine. But these exceptions need not worry the undergraduate writer. Whereas the student of French or German must memorize the article (*le* or *la; der, die* or *das*) with each new noun in his vocabulary, *a, an* (*indefinite* articles), or *the* (*definite* article) will serve in English for all genders. There are only a few borrowed English nouns whose sex is denoted by a special ending (*alumnus, alumna; fiancé, fiancée*). Nor is the student in any real danger of failing to make the gender of the pronoun agree with that of the noun. (The chair is so comfortable I am going to buy *her*). For all practical purposes the gender of English nouns can be forgotten.

NUMBER

The greater importance of number will become apparent in the discussion of agreement on pages 107–113. As every schoolboy should know, a noun referring to one person, place, or thing is *singular* (*boy, lunch, mouse*), to more than one is *plural* (*boys, lunches, mice*). Most English plurals merely add *s* or *es* to the singular; *mice* is an exception. Some of the common exceptions are discussed in the GLOSSARY.

CASE

Grammarians usually recognize only three cases in English: *nominative* (or *subjective*), *possessive* (or *genitive*), and *objective* (or *accusative*). In nouns the possessive is the only case with a distinctive ending, and this is commonly formed by adding '*s* to the singular and merely an apostrophe to the plural ending in *s* (one *horse's* neck, two *horses'* necks). The problem is really not grammar but spelling. Students who need further enlightenment about it should turn to the discussion of the apostrophe on pages 212–213.

USES

In addition to its possessive use, a noun can be used as a *subject*, an *object*, a *subjective complement*, an *objective complement*, an *appositive*, or a word in *direct address*.

1. SUBJECT (*nominative case*)

The subject of a sentence is the person, place, or thing about which an assertion is made or a question asked:

The *horse* ran down the street.
Did the *horse* run fast?
The *horse* and his *rider* were both killed. (compound subject)

2. OBJECT (*objective case*)

Direct object: The direct object is a person, place, or thing directly affected by the action of a transitive verb (see page 96) :

Herbert passed the *butter.*

Indirect object: The indirect object is indirectly affected by the action of a transitive verb. It precedes the direct object and can be considered as the object of a phantom preposition *to:*

Herbert passed [to] *Homer* the butter.

3. SUBJECTIVE COMPLEMENT (*nominative case*)

A subjective complement completes the sense of a linking verb (see page 96) or a passive transitive verb (see page 97) and refers to the subject. It is also called a *predicate nominative,* indicating that it belongs to the part of the sentence that *predicates* or asserts something about the subject—that is, the verb part of the sentence:

Subject   Predicate

You are a *student* of English grammar. (*Student* completes the sense of *are* and refers to *you.*)
Roosevelt was elected *president* four times. (*President* completes the sense of *was elected* and refers to *Roosevelt.*)

4. OBJECTIVE COMPLEMENT (*objective case*)

An objective complement completes the sense of a transitive verb and refers to the direct object:

He called his roommate a *liar.* (*Liar* completes the sense of *called* and refers to *roommate.*)
She considered the dress a *bargain.* (*Bargain* completes the sense of *considered* and refers to *dress.*)

5. APPOSITIVE

A noun that usually comes immediately after another and repeats its meaning is called an *appositive*. An appositive has the same case as the noun with which it is in *apposition:*

George Washington, the *father* of his country, died in 1799. (*Father* is in apposition with *George Washington,* and both are nominative.)

Popular error has confused Frankenstein, Mrs. Shelley's *hero,* with the monster he created. (*Hero* is in apposition with *Frankenstein,* and both are objective.)

6. NOUN IN DIRECT ADDRESS

Children, come here.
Farewell, cruel *world.*

PRONOUNS

Pronouns are classified as follows:

1. PERSONAL PRONOUNS

In addition to having number, gender, and case, personal pronouns are classified by person. They are declined as follows:

	Singular	*Plural*
	First Person (All Genders)	
NOMINATIVE:	I	we
POSSESSIVE:	my, mine	our, ours
OBJECTIVE:	me	us
	Second Person (All Genders)	
NOMINATIVE:	you	you
POSSESSIVE:	your, yours	your, yours
OBJECTIVE:	you	you

Third Person

	Masc.	*Fem.*	*Neuter*	*All Genders*
NOMINATIVE:	he	she	it	they
POSSESSIVE:	his	her	hers, its	their, theirs
OBJECTIVE:	him	her	it	them

2. RELATIVE PRONOUNS

The relative pronouns are *who, which, that, what* (meaning *that which*) and, rarely, *whoever, whichever,* and *whatever.*

Of these the declension of *who* is important because it has a different form for all three cases:

Singular and Plural

NOMINATIVE:	who
POSSESSIVE:	whose
OBJECTIVE:	whom

* Notice carefully now that the possessive case of both personal and relative pronouns has no apostrophe.

Who commonly refers only to persons and animals, *which* to animals and inanimate things, and *that* to any of the three. In informal writing, *which* often has the possessive form *whose* instead of the more formal *of which:*

This was the generation *whose* girls dramatized themselves as flappers. —F. Scott Fitzgerald, *The Crack-up.*

Many careful writers use *that* and *which* indiscriminately; some argue that *which* is more formal; others use whichever sounds better in the sentence. Statistics indicate that restrictive clauses are more often introduced by *that,* nonrestrictive clauses by *which* (see page 176): This sentence is one *that* illustrates the difference, *which* is not of world-shaking importance.

3. INTERROGATIVE PRONOUNS

Interrogative pronouns are used to introduce questions: *who, which, what, whoever, whichever, whatever.* The interrogative *who* is declined like the relative *who.*

4. INDEFINITE PRONOUNS

The long list of indefinite pronouns includes *any, anybody, anyone, anything, each, either, everybody, everyone, everything, neither, nobody, none, one, somebody, someone,* and *something.* The main problem with these pronouns is number; it is treated under AGREEMENT on pages 108–109.

5. DEMONSTRATIVE PRONOUNS

Demonstrative pronouns are used to demonstrate or point out: *this,* plural *these; that,* plural *those.*

6. REFLEXIVE PRONOUNS

A reflexive pronoun is usually used as the direct object of a verb and refers back to the subject. (The plagiarist fools only *himself.*) Such pronouns are formed by adding *self* or *selves* to certain of the personal pronouns: *myself, yourself, himself, herself, itself, ourselves, yourselves, themselves.*

7. INTENSIVE PRONOUNS

Intensive pronouns have the same forms as reflexives but are used for emphasis:

I'll marry her *myself.*
You did it *yourself.*

8. RECIPROCAL PRONOUNS

The reciprocal pronouns are *each other* and *one another.* They may be used interchangeably whether referring to only two or more than two.

* CASE
(See Exercise III on page 117)

Although the case of nouns presents no problem to the student who understands the use of the apostrophe, the case of personal, relative, and interrogative pronouns can be a nuisance. *Me want dinner* and *Does her love me?* are baby talk. *Johnny hit I* and *Don't say that about she* would hardly get by in the nursery. An educated person might not consciously consider that the objective form *me* or *her* should not be the subject of a sentence, or the nominative form *I* the direct object of a verb; but he would instinctively avoid the error. Yet when the sentences are only slightly altered—with compound subjects and objects introduced— many a half-educated person who ought to know better will make exactly the same grammatical errors:

You and *me* want dinner. (objective case for subject)
Do Mary and *her* both love me? (same error)
Johnny hit Bob and *I*. (nominative case for object of verb)
Don't say that about Harold and *she*. (nominative case for object of preposition)

Often the most elegant hostess will launch her pet rumor with "Just between you and I"—apparently under the illusion that she is avoiding the "vulgar error" in *It is me*. Ironically, while *between you and I* (using the nominative case as the object of a preposition) is still regarded as vulgate, *It is me* (using the objective case as the predicate nominative) has won general acceptance in informal English. In fact the formally correct form has become such a joke that the best advice to a student might be: When you say, "It is I," smile. It is one of the quirks of usage that violations of the same grammatical principle (It is *us*, It is *her* and so on) are more generally frowned upon.

To sum up, the student may permit himself some leeway with the use of the first person of the personal pronoun as a predicate nominative. (After all is said and done, the occasion doesn't arise often in written English anyhow.) But for the other uses of personal pronouns he should stick close to the cases of the regular declension on page 89, using the nominative case as the subject of a sentence and the objective case as the object of a verb or preposition:

The river lay between *him* and *me*. (formal and informal)
The river lay between *he* and *I*. (vulgate)

That amused Throckmorton and *me*. (formal and informal)
That amused Throckmorton and *I*. (vulgate)

It is *I* who tapped the wires. (formal)
It is *me* who tapped the wires. (informal)
I am the one who tapped the wires. (acceptable and most natural)

A similar nuisance is the choice between *who* and *whom*. The labors of generations of English teachers to persuade students to distinguish properly between them have brought forth a comic legend of the same family as the *It is I* gag. In one recent cartoon the well-educated owl on the limb outside the English building is hooting "Who-o-o-m!" And the well-meaning hostess with her *between you and I* is matched by James Thurber's caricature of correctness *Whom are you anyways?* When the who-and-whom dilemma pricks a student's conscience without penetrating his brain, it is a safe bet that he will respond by peppering his writing full of inexplicable *whoms.*

This problem too has been exaggerated, for in informal speech and writing, the dilemma is normally evaded simply by omitting the annoying pronoun. Whereas formal writing might have: *Dr. Livingston was the surgeon to whom my father sent me,* the informal version would probably be: *Dr. Livingston was the surgeon my father sent me to.* Even the best-educated gag man doesn't say: "Who was that lady with whom I saw you last night?"

In *formal* writing:

1. *Use* who *as the subject.*

Who owns the house with the pink roof? (subject of *owns*)

I know a man *who* sleeps only four hours a night. (subject of *sleeps*)

General Eisenhower, *who* many people thought was the best candidate, refused to enter the lists. (*Who* is the subject of *was*, not the object of *thought; many people thought* is parenthetical.)

It is not easy to decide *who* will make the best president. (*Who* is the subject of *will make,* not the object of *decide;* the object of *decide* is *who will make the best president.*)

2. *Use* whom *as the object of a verb or preposition.*

Whom did the speaker mean when he mentioned the termites feasting on the ship of state? (object of *mean*)

I know the man *whom* he condemned. (object of *condemned*)

Did you see the girl to *whom* the President of the Deke House gave his pin? (object of preposition *to*)

For students who have trouble with the formal use of *who* and *whom,* it is sometimes helpful to substitute *he* for *who* and *him* for *whom.* Tested this way, *It is not easy to decide whom will make the best president* becomes *It is not easy to decide him will make the best president*—obviously incorrect.

In *informal* writing and speech *who* is acceptable as an object:

Who did the speaker mean? (informal)

I knew the girl *who* the President of the Deke House gave his pin to. (informal)

* REFERENCE
(See Exercise IV on page 118)

The word or group of words to which a pronoun refers is called its *antecedent*. Be sure that there is no doubt about the antecedent of any pronoun. Careful reference is less a question of grammatical etiquette than of common sense.

There are four common kinds of faulty reference:

1. NO REFERENCE (*a pronoun has no antecedent*)

My Last Duchess is so obscure that I don't know whether *he* is talking about *his* unlamented wife to the middleman in a dowry deal or trying to unload some canvas on an art dealer. (What is the antecedent of *he* and *his?* The poet? Or the duke? Neither is mentioned. The antecedent could, of course, be in a previous sentence.)

2. REMOTE REFERENCE (*the antecedent of a pronoun is buried too far back for the reader to exhume it handily*)

Shakespeare wrote for a theater which was appreciably different from ours. Today we are accustomed to realistic settings with their elaborate scenic and lighting effects. We wait patiently between the acts while stagehands trundle heavy flats into place. In Elizabethan times *it* had a simple platform stage with no proscenium arch. (*It* refers to *theater,* which is buried three sentences back.)

3. WRONG REFERENCE (*a pronoun apparently refers to the wrong antecedent*)

I clenched the arms of my chair until *they* turned red. (*They* refers to the arms [of his chair]. Presumably his hands turned red.)

4. SQUINTING REFERENCE (*a pronoun is cross-eyed from referring to two antecedents at once, only one of which is correct*)

Older people believe that eighteen-year-olds are not fully developed socially and intellectually. *They* pay very little attention to political problems. (*They* might conceivably refer either to *older people* or to *eighteen-year-olds*. To assume that it refers automatically to the nearer antecedent is misleading here, because a reader tends to infer that the subject of one sentence will be the subject of the next unless he is explicitly told otherwise.)

The conventions of strict usage also forbid *loose reference*—in which the antecedent is implied but not explicitly stated—and *broad reference*—in which the pronoun refers to the whole idea embodied in the previous clause or phrase. But these common constructions are acceptable in informal writing if they do not mislead the reader:

Loose	*Strict*
When Christmas was at hand I had given up all hope of a pony, and on Christmas Eve I hung up my stocking along with my sisters', of *whom,* by the way, I now had *three.* —Lincoln Steffens, *Autobiography.* (According to strict grammar, *whom* refers to sisters' [stockings], though there is no doubt about its intended antecedent.)	When Christmas was at hand I had given up all hope of a pony, and on Christmas Eve I hung up my stocking along with those of my sisters, of whom, by the way, I now had three.

Broad	*Strict*
At the same time these crops are seasonal, *which* means that they are largely handled by migratory workers. —John Steinbeck, "Dubious Battle in California," *Nation.* (*Which* refers broadly to the whole statement of the previous clause.)	At the same time these crops are seasonal, a fact which means that they are largely handled by migratory workers.

Faulty reference can usually be cured—but not always—by rearranging the words in the sentence so that the pronoun is as near as possible to its antecedent. Do not repeat the antecedent after the pronoun:

Clear but awkward	*Improved*
Through his use of picturesque words he plays upon the reader's imagination so eloquently that he (the reader) feels exactly what the writer feels.	Through his use of picturesque words he plays upon the reader's imagination so eloquently that the reader feels exactly what the writer feels.

No pronoun is worth saving at the expense of clarity. If, after a reasonable effort to recast a sentence, you are still requiring the reader to track down the antecedent, throw out the pronoun and repeat the noun.

VERBS
(See Exercise V on page 119)

There are three kinds of verbs.

1. *A transitive verb* needs a direct object to complete its meaning:

I *opened* the shutters quickly.

2. *An intransitive verb* does not require a direct object:

When the door *opened,* the murderer *lay* still in a corner.

Most verbs, like *open* in these illustrations, can be either transitive or intransitive. The verb *lie,* from which we get the past tense *lay,* is intransitive only. When in doubt about whether a verb takes a direct object, consult a dictionary, where the abbreviations *v.t.* and *v.i.* are commonly used.

3. A *linking verb* is an intransitive verb which connects the subject with a predicate nominative (see page 88) or predicate adjective (see page 106) :

Truman *became* President in 1945.
Many people *felt* sorry for him.

Among the commonest linking verbs are *appear, be, become, feel, look, smell, sound,* and *taste.*

Verbs have number, person, mood, voice, and tense. Number and person have already been considered with nouns and pronouns and will be discussed again under AGREEMENT (see pages 107–113) . Mood and voice can be disposed of quickly:

MOOD

There are three moods in English:

Indicative—to state something as a fact

Cold *makes* people shiver.

Imperative—to command

Come and *get* it.

Subjunctive—to express wishes, doubt, or condition contrary to fact

I wish I *were* rich.
He wondered if he *were* going blind.
If I *were* you, I could get away with it.

Notice that the last three examples all involve the past subjunctive of the verb *to be,* which is *were* in all three persons and both numbers. One form of one verb—that is the only subjunctive of much importance in current English; and in informal writing, the indicative *was* would be acceptable in all three of those illustrations. Most of the other uses of the subjunctive are stiffly formal (If that *be* treason, make the most of it) or embalmed in stereotyped expressions. (I move that this *be* stricken from the record; *Come* what may; *Be* that as it may; Resolved that Mrs. Fewsmith *be* given a rising vote of thanks for supplying the peonies). Use of the subjunctive in such expressions is automatic. Despite its importance in many foreign languages, the subjunctive is apparently dying in English, at least on the informal level. It will have few mourners.

VOICE

A verb is in the *active voice* when the subject does the acting, in the *passive voice* when the subject is acted upon:

Active: Abbott *threw* Costello.
Passive: Costello *was thrown* by Abbott.

Where a logical choice exists between the two, use the active voice because it is more direct. *John threw the football* is obvi-

ously more natural than *The football was thrown by John.*
Undue affection for the passive is one of the surest symptoms of
a heavy, plodding style (see pages 150, 295–296).

Do not confuse active and passive with present and past tense.

TENSE

English has six tenses:

First person singular,
indicative, active voice

PRESENT: I *study* today
PAST: I *studied* yesterday
PRESENT PERFECT: I *have studied* since yesterday
PAST PERFECT: I *had studied* hard the day before yesterday,
                  but yesterday I studied harder
FUTURE: I *shall (will) study* again tomorrow
FUTURE PERFECT: I *shall (will) have studied* by tomorrow night
                  for three straight days

Notice especially the three "past forms," which colloquial
usage tends to lump under a single tense. The past represents
past time not continuing to the present; the present perfect
stands for past time continuing to the present; and the past
perfect signifies the "past before the past."

Of course, this brief picture hardly begins to indicate the
versatility of English verb forms. For example, the present tense
may be used for future time (I *take* my final examinations tomorrow); past time (the *historical present:* It *is* early morning of
December 7, 1941, and all *is* peaceful at Pearl Harbor); or to make
a statement that is presumably true at any time (Birds of a
feather *flock* together).

With the use of *auxiliaries*—assistant verbs such as *be, have,
do, shall, will, can, may, might, must, should,* and *would*—a vast
number of verb forms can be made. For instance, we use the
forms of the auxiliary *be* to express progressive action (I *am* eating, I *was* eating, I *have been* eating, and so on) and the auxiliary
do for emphasis (I *do* love you, I *did* say it). Some of the distinctions between auxiliaries (*shall* and *will, should* and *would, can*

and *may*) are breaking down in informal English (see the GLOSSARY).

The problem of consistency in tenses can get complicated, but the following general principles include the commonest errors:

1. If the verb in the main clause is past tense or past perfect, make the verb in a subordinate clause past tense or past perfect:

Wrong: I knew that war *is* coming.
Right: I knew that war *was* coming.

Wrong: I had known for some time that war *is* coming.
Right: I had known for some time that war *was* coming.

2. Use the present perfect tense, not the past tense, to indicate past time continuing to the present:

Wrong: I *was* here since eight o'clock.
Right: I *have been* here since eight o'clock.

3. Use the past perfect tense whenever it is necessary to distinguish between two times in the past:

Wrong: Now that peace *came,* Germany was in disgrace for the destruction she *brought* on the world.
Right: Now that peace *had come,* Germany was in disgrace for the destruction she *had brought* on the world.

4. Avoid all unnecessary shifts in tense:

Wrong: Major Rathbone *attempted* to intercept him, but Booth *slashes* him in the arm with a knife.
Wrong: He *does* not characterize the boy or his father by saying, "The old man was short and fat and had bushy hair." Instead, he *presented* the man in action. He *shows* him puffing as he *jogged* along the road.

This continual shifting between past and present is especially common in literary criticism, where the writer is discussing a work written in the past but being analyzed in the present. He can avoid confusion by using the past for facts directly concerned with literary biography (When Shakespeare *wrote* "The Rape of Lucrece," the theaters *were* closed) and resorting to the present for his own critical comments (The poem *is* full of sensuous detail).

* VERBALS
(See Exercise VI on page 120)

Any verb limited to a specific person and number (He *drinks*—third person singular) is called a *finite verb*. *Verbals* are not limited by person and number. They are parts of verbs that do the work of nouns, adjectives, and adverbs well but do not ordinarily carry the entire verb load in a sentence. The student who can readily distinguish between a finite verb and a verbal is not likely to write careless fragmentary sentences.

There are three verbals: *infinitives, participles,* and *gerunds*.

1. INFINITIVES

Most versatile of the verbals, the infinitive may be used as a noun, an adjective, an adverb, or as part of a finite verb. Its forms are:

	Active	Passive
PRESENT:	(to) try	(to) be tried
PERFECT:	(to) have tried	(to) have been tried

As a noun, it may be:

Subject: *To write* for a living is not easy.

Object of a verb: Soon after the war, the nations began *to fight* again.

Object of a preposition: His roommate did nothing but *sleep* and *eat.* (The *to* is often omitted.)

Predicate nominative: His only ambition was *to get* a degree.

As an adjective:

He had a speech *to make.* (modifying *speech*)

As an adverb:

I come *to bury* Caesar, not *to praise* him. (modifying *come*)

With an auxiliary as part of a finite verb:

You can't *go* home again.

2. PARTICIPLES

The participle may be used as an adjective, as part of a finite verb, and in an absolute construction. Its forms are:

	Active	*Passive*
PRESENT:	singing	being sung, sung
PAST:	having sung	having been sung, sung

As an adjective:

> Pascal called man a *thinking* reed. (modifying *reed*)
> Carlyle called him a *forked* radish. (modifying *radish*)

As part of a finite verb:

> I am *dying,* Egypt, *dying.*
> I have *been* faithful to thee, Cynara, in my fashion.

In an absolute construction (a phrase independent grammatically of any other part of the sentence):

> The Dodgers *having lost,* Flatbush was dejected.

3. GERUNDS

The gerund has the same form as the present participle (ending in *ing*), but is used as a noun:

> *Subject (active and passive)* : *Rowing* is good exercise, but *being rowed* is more fun.
> *Object of a verb:* I prefer *walking.*
> *Object of a preposition:* Huxley devoted his life to *popularizing* science.
> *Predicate nominative:* His favorite indoor sport was *making* money.

The old rule that the subject of a gerund should be in the possessive case has been belied by usage. Generally speaking, the possessive is more common in formal English (I could see no reason for *Tom's* acting that way), the objective more common in informal English (I could see no reason for *Tom* acting that way). Formal usage clings more zealously to the possessive case when the subject is a pronoun than when it is a noun (I could see no reason for *his* acting that way). Sometimes the choice of case with the gerund appears to make a difference in emphasis:

I never thought of *Sylvia* winning a beauty contest.
(Of all persons!)
I never thought of *Sylvia's* winning a beauty contest.
(Slightly more charitable)

PRINCIPAL PARTS

The complete *conjugation* of a verb consists of naming its *principal parts* (present infinitive; past tense—first person singular; and past participle) and of supplying all the forms of the three persons, six tenses, two voices, and three moods. Most English verbs are *regular,* forming the past tense and past participle by merely adding *ed* or *d* to the infinitive (*jump, jumped, jumped; blame, blamed, blamed*). The complete conjugation of such verbs requires no special drill; the omission of a verb ending from a regular verb is almost always due to carelessness. (The horse *gallop* down the street). Some *irregular* verbs, which change a vowel rather than adding an ending, make trouble. A few of these are discussed in the GLOSSARY.

* LIE *AND* LAY

Also considered in the GLOSSARY are several pairs of verbs, both regular and irregular, which are often interchanged (*leave* and *let, rise* and *raise, sit* and *set*). Of these the most notorious pair deserves special mention here. According to standard usage:
Lie is an intransitive verb meaning to *recline*

I *lie* (am *lying*) down now. I *lay* down yesterday. I have *lain* down before.

Lay is usually a transitive verb meaning to *place*

I *lay* (am *laying*) the book down now. I *laid* the book down yesterday. I have *laid* the book down there before.

The commonest deviations are the substitution of the present participle and past tense of *lay* for those of *lie:*

Wrong: The football player was *laying* out on the field.
Wrong: He *laid* there unconscious.
Right: The football player was *lying* out on the field.
Right: He *lay* there unconscious.

Despite the long-standing confusion of these verbs, even in some educated speech, misuse of *lie* and *lay* is still widely regarded as an offensive grammatical error.

* ADJECTIVES AND ADVERBS
(See Exercise VII on page 121)

HOW TO TELL THEM APART

The only safe way to tell adjectives from adverbs is to find out what they modify. By definition an adjective modifies a noun or pronoun; an adverb modifies a verb, adjective, or other adverb. For students who can't readily distinguish them, the old-fashioned schoolboy test is useful:

Adjectives answer these questions:

1. How many? (*nine* muses)
2. What kind? (a *snap* course)
3. Which one? (*That* boy stole *your* dog.)

The third example illustrates the pronoun used as an adjective, or *pronominal adjective.*

Adverbs usually answer these questions:

1. How? (Please drive *carefully.*)
2. When? (The circus is coming *tomorrow.*)
3. Where? (The bride went *home* to mother.)
4. How much? (The world is *less* peaceful than in 1900.)

Not included in this list are *conjunctive adverbs* (*however, moreover, nevertheless, therefore*); and *adverbs of assertion and concession* (*yes, no, not, maybe, probably*).

Many adverbs end in *ly,* and many of these are formed by adding *ly* to the adjective or, if the adjective ends in *y,* by changing the *y* to *i* before adding *ly: early, sweetly, gaily, happily.* But the *ly* ending is not a safe recognition feature for these reasons:

1. Some adjectives also end in *ly:*

    heavenly, holy, ungodly, unearthly

2. Some adverbs have no *ly* form:

    now, there, then, up, down, far (the last four of which can also be adjectives)

3. Some adverbs have two forms, one with *ly* and the other without:

loud, loudly	soft, softly
quick, quickly	tight, tightly
slow, slowly	wrong, wrongly

With some adverbs in this group (*late, lately; low, lowly; hard, hardly*) there is a clear difference in meaning between the two forms. With the others the choice depends on sound and on level of usage. The *ly* ending is more common in formal writing; it is the usual form when the adverb precedes the verb. (*Slowly* he ambled down the street.) The form without *ly* appears frequently after short verbs in informal English, especially in commands. (Come *quick,* drive *slow,* hold on *tight.*)

COMPARISON

FORMS

Adjectives and adverbs have no inflection for person, number, or case. Instead they are compared in three degrees:

ADJECTIVES

Positive	*Comparative*	*Superlative*
strong	stronger	strongest
glum	glummer	glummest
lovely	lovelier, more lovely	loveliest, most lovely
beautiful	more (less) beautiful	most (least) beautiful
good	better	best

ADVERBS

far	farther	farthest
quickly	more (less) quickly	most (least) quickly
beautifully	more (less) beautifully	most (least) beautifully
well	better	best

Words of one syllable are usually compared by adding *er* for the comparative, *est* for the superlative. Words of two syllables often have these forms as well as the forms with *more* and *most;* the choice is determined by rhythm and emphasis. Words of three or more syllables are compared only with *more* (*less*) and *most* (*least*).

USE

In strict formal writing the comparative degree is used in comparing two things, the superlative with three or more:

John is the *faster* of the two
He is the *handsomest* of seven children.

In speech and informal writing the superlative is often used for two:

May the *best* team win.
Put your *best* foot forward.

But prejudice against the use of the superlative-for-two in writing is still widespread.

So-called *absolutes* cannot, strictly speaking, be compared. Logically, there is only one degree for *dead, possible, perfect,* or *unique.* But here usage has all but conquered logic, and the purists are fighting a losing rear-guard action. In informal writing such words are often compared. This is partly for emphasis (*deader* than a college campus on Sunday), partly because some of these words have virtually lost their absolute meaning. In *a most unique occasion, unique* has become a loose synonym for *rare.* The damage has come not from comparing *unique* but from overworking the word until it is drained of its uniqueness. If everything is perfect, as in the excited chatter of delighted schoolgirls, we must either have a *more perfect* and a *most perfect* or abolish perfection from the language.

POSITION OF ADJECTIVES

When the *thirsty* traveler saw the stream, *cool, clear,* and *inviting,* he did not know that it would taste *salty.*

In that sentence the adjective *thirsty* precedes the noun *traveler,* which it modifies. On the other hand, *cool, clear,* and *inviting* follow their noun, *stream.* This order is less common but entirely acceptable.

Salty is a *predicate adjective* following the linking verb *taste,* modifying the pronoun *it.* Thus an adjective, like a noun, can serve as a subjective complement after a linking verb. This is not true of an adverb. It is incorrect to say: "It tastes *saltily,*" "This smells *sweetly,*" or "The house looks *shabbily.*" Though it violates the same rule, "I feel *badly*" is now accepted by some authorities. Since both *good* and *well* are adjectives, the difference between "I feel good" and "I feel well" is one of meaning, not grammar (see the GLOSSARY).

CONJUNCTIONS

There are four kinds of conjunctions:

1. COORDINATING CONJUNCTIONS

    and, but, for, or, nor (*These should be memorized.*)

2. SUBORDINATING CONJUNCTIONS

    although, as, because, if, since, unless, while, *and others*

3. CORRELATIVE CONJUNCTIONS (*used in pairs*)

    both . . . and, either . . . or, neither . . . nor, not only . . . but also, *and others*

4. ADVERBIAL CONJUNCTIONS (*conjunctive adverbs*)

    however, moreover, nevertheless, therefore, *and others*

The differences among these four kinds should become clearer when their uses are discussed later in connection with sentence structure and punctuation.

* AGREEMENT
(See Exercise VIII on page 121)

Statistics have indicated that mistakes in agreement are the commonest *grammatical* errors in undergraduate writing. The general formal rules for agreement can be briefly stated:

1. A verb agrees with its subject in number and person.

2. A pronoun agrees with its antecedent in number, gender, and person.

3. A demonstrative adjective (formed from a demonstrative pronoun) agrees with its noun in number.

Mary *takes her* lamb to *this* school.

The verb *takes* agrees with *Mary* in number (both are singular) and person (both are third person). The pronoun *her* agrees with its antecedent, *Mary,* in number (singular), gender (feminine), and person (third). The demonstrative adjective *this* agrees with *school* in number (singular). This much is simple.

But there are numerous agreement problems, several of them presenting borderline instances of divided usage. In these the writer is usually confronted with a conflict between grammar and meaning, correctness and logic. His choice is often determined by the level of usage on which he is writing.

1. Two or more subjects joined by *and* (*compound subject*) take a plural verb:

Beaumont and Fletcher *were* successful collaborators.

Exception: when they refer to the same person or thing:

My lord and master *is* coming.

2. When two or more subjects are joined by *or* or *nor,* the number of the verb is determined by the nearer subject:

Either you or he *has* to lose.
Neither the girls nor the boys *were* able to answer the question.

I wonder if John or his friends *are* going.

I doubt if the professors or the president *insists* on that kind of education.

3. A singular subject followed by a phrase beginning with *as well as, in addition to, together with,* or *with* takes a singular verb in formal writing, but often appears with a plural verb in informal English. At best such an expression is often awkward:

> *Formal:* Stanley as well as the American people *was* overjoyed.
> *Informal:* The thief with his confederates *were* given twenty years.

4. a. The following indefinite pronouns take a singular verb: *anybody, anyone, each, every, everybody, everyone, nobody, no one, somebody, someone:*

> I wonder if anybody *is* home; everyone *seems* to be gone away.

b. In formal writing a pronoun referring to any of those words is also singular:

> The scoutmaster expects everyone to do *his* duty.
> When the lieutenant asked for volunteers, everybody made *himself* inconspicuous.
> The teacher went around the class giving individual help to anyone having trouble with *his* work.

c. In informal writing the pronoun referring to *anybody, anyone, each, every, everybody,* or *everyone* is often plural:

> *Informal:* Each of the voters decided according to *their* attitudes.
> *Informal:* Now is the time for everybody to come to the aid of *their* party.

d. Formal usage treats *either* and *neither* as singular pronouns, but they often appear as plural in informal writing:

> *Formal:* I do not know if either of them *is* going to throw *his* hat into the ring.
> *Informal:* Neither of the girls *intend* to continue *their* studies.

There are two reasons for the divided usage of some of these pronouns. One is that, though grammatically singular, they often convey a distinct plural meaning. *Everybody* may refer grammatically to only *onebody,* but to a reader it conveys the notion of *manybodies.* The other reason is that the English language possesses no singular pronouns which serve equally well for both sexes—pronouns which are neutral without being neuter. Sentences like "If every man and woman does his or her best to consult his or her conscience before casting his or her ballot" are obviously absurd. Since new pronouns cannot be established by emergency legislation, the choice still lies between insisting on *his* as the bisexual possessive—accepting a masculine prerogative that may be outmoded—or falling back on the plural *their,* a form which many educated people, trained in traditional grammar, are still reluctant to use. Students who do not wish to be suspended between the horns of a grammatical dilemma are always safe in treating these indefinite pronouns as singular.

e. *Any* and *none* may be treated as either singular or plural according to the writer's intention:

Are any of them going to the picnic?
None of them but George *has* signed up yet.

5. When a collective noun (*class, group, family, mob, number, team*) is considered as a whole, it takes a singular verb and pronoun; when the individuals are considered separately it takes a plural verb and pronoun:

The Lackawanna football team *overwhelms its* traditional rival annually.

The squad *receive their* letters for playing in this game.

The class matriculating in 1940 *call* out in *their* infant breath, "Rah! Rah! Forty-four." —Stephen Leacock, *Education Eating Up Life.*

Its crew never *refer* to it by name: to *them* it is always "this bucket." —Thomas Heggen, *Mr. Roberts.*

Down in the armory a group of six men *sits* tensely around a wooden box. —Thomas Heggen, *Mr. Roberts.*

6. a. In formal writing a pronoun takes a verb of the same number and person as its antecedent:

"It is I who *am* the law in this community!" shouted the educated dictator. (The antecedent of *who* is *I;* hence the verb *am* is first person singular.)

He was one of *those* patriots who are always shouting about the American Way out of one corner of *their* mouths and spewing *their* odious prejudices out of the other. (The antecedent of *who* is patriots; hence the verb *are shouting* and the pronoun *their* are third person plural. Notice also that *mouths* and *prejudices* are plural for the sake of consistency.)

b. In informal writing the *one of those who* construction often takes a singular verb and pronoun:

Being one of those musical illiterates who *is* overcome with a surge of pride when able to distinguish "Fair Harvard" from "Boola-Boola," I will not presume to have an opinion about Richard Rodgers's score. —John Mason Brown, *Saturday Review of Literature.*

c. Remember that, though the number, gender, and person of a pronoun are determined by its antecedent, the case of a pronoun is determined by its use in the sentence:

Landon was the man *whom* Roosevelt defeated in 1936. (The antecedent of *whom, man,* is predicate nominative, but *whom* is objective because it is the direct object of *defeated.*)

Thousands cheered the punch-drunk boxer, *who* was lying prostrate on the bloody canvas. (The antecedent of *who, boxer,* is objective, but who is nominative because it is the subject of *was lying.*)

(7.) A verb agrees in number with the subject, not with the predicate nominative:

A complete game *is* four quarters of fifteen minutes each.
Twelve lectures *are* a week's teaching for anybody.

(8.) a.   Ordinarily *there is* and *there was* are used when the subject is singular, *there are* and *there were* when it is plural:

There *is* many a slip 'twixt the cup and the lip.
There *are* smiles that make us happy.

b. When the first part of a compound subject is singular, though other parts are plural, *there is* and *there was* are permissible:

There *is* an aardvark, a wapiti, and two platypuses in the local zoo.

In the sentences in (a) and (b) *there* is not the real subject out an anticipatory subject or *expletive*. The word *it* (*It* is time for a change) often serves the same purpose.

9. The expressions *these* kind, *those* kind, *these* sort, and *those* sort, followed by a plural noun, are common even in educated speech. But most careful writers still follow the law for demonstrative adjectives, keeping the singular throughout:

Formal and informal: Despite his faith in liberal education, he did not like *that* kind of course.

Colloquial: The coach said: "*Those* sort of players are no asset to the team."

10. For words that are plural in form but often singular in meaning (*athletics, mathematics, politics*), see the GLOSSARY.

11. Do not be misled in applying any of these conventions by the intrusion of other words between subject and verb, pronoun and antecedent. This is one of the commonest causes of errors in agreement. Notice the following student sentences:

Wrong: The rhythm of the words *sound* like music to the ear. (The subject is *rhythm,* not *words.*)

Right: The rhythm of the words *sounds* like music to the ear.

Wrong: Each of these items *are* checked as the system is traced. (The subject is *each,* not *items.*)

Right: Each of these items *is* checked as the system is traced.

Wrong: Only the high spots and important background of each game *is* at the disposal of the writer. (The compound subject is *high spots and background,* not *game.*)

Right: Only the high spots and important background of each game *are* at the disposal of the writer.

Wrong: Everybody from the highest ranking officer down to the private *are* briefed on the method to be used in taking the town. (The student would not write *everybody are briefed,* but a whole army has squeezed in between subject and verb, and he is carelessly thinking of all the soldiers as the subject.)

Right: Everybody from the highest ranking officer down to the private *is* briefed . . . .

12. a. Even in a situation where the choice of number is optional, be consistent throughout. Beware of unnecessary shifts

in number and person. Notice the inconsistent use of pronouns in the following student sentences:

No state would be able to lay up *their* own store of atom bombs and then on some dark night go out and conquer all of *its* neighboring nations. (shift in number)

I have learned never to trust them behind *your* back. (shift in person)

The majority *was* treated unjustly because *they* lacked the power to vote. (Shift in number. Either singular or plural is permissible with the collective noun *majority*, but not both.)

To be able to speak what *you* want is something that makes *a person* feel more at ease than anything else. (shift in person)

The *individuals* described above are completely lacking in insight, more so than any other type of mental disorder except possibly the lowest grade of mental deficiency. *He* is incapable of love in even the most primitive sense of the word. However, there is something about the hidden immaturity of *these people* that women seem to be attracted to. *He* is often a very attractive person superficially and ofen makes a strong impression when one first meets him. (shift from plural to singular to plural to singular in four sentences)

b. Slavish consistency in the use of the impersonal pronoun *one* is an awkward concession to formality:

When *one* speaks of *one's* old teachers, it is generally to *one's* college teachers that *one* refers. For it is then, if *one* is lucky, that *one* comes in contact with men who communicate and articulate the things and ideas which become the seeds of *one's* later intellectual and imaginative life. —Irwin Edman, *Philosopher's Holiday.*

One gets weary of that sort of thing, doesn't one? It is not only permissible but preferable to refer to the impersonal *one* with the personal pronouns *he, his, him, she,* and *her:*

Without some modicum of thinking *one* cannot write at all, and it is emphatically true that *one* cannot ever write any better than *he* can think. —O. J. Campbell, "The Failure of Freshman English," *English Journal.*

In informal writing the impersonal *you* is more natural than *one:*

The advantage of "teaching" is that in using it *you* must recognize —if *you* are in your sober senses—that practical limits exist. *You* know by instinct that it is impossible to "teach" democracy, or citizenship or a happy married life. —Jacques Barzun, *Teacher in America*.

PHRASES AND CLAUSES
(See Exercise IX on page 123)

Although the discussion of grammar so far has concentrated on the analysis of individual words, it has not been entirely possible to avoid mentioning two grammatical terms for groups of words: *phrase* and *clause*. The student who knows the parts of speech should have little trouble with phrases and clauses, for they usually do the same jobs as nouns, verbs, adjectives, and adverbs.

A phrase is any group of related words without a subject and finite verb. Phrases can be classified in two ways:

According to form:

PREPOSITIONAL:	to the house at the game
INFINITIVE:	He played *to win,* not *to be beaten.*
PARTICIPIAL:	an old city *sleeping in the sun*
	a game *halted by darkness*
GERUND:	*Crossing the street* is dangerous.
	I liked his *doing that.*
VERB:	am coming, have arrived

According to function:

NOUNS: *Tossing the javelin* takes coordination. (A gerund phrase is used as the subject. It is just as if the writer were saying merely: "Track takes coordination.")

Many people have tried *swimming the channel.* (gerund phrase used as the object of the verb)

He was jailed for *stealing a car.* (gerund phrase used as the object of a preposition)

To tell the truth is not always easy. (infinitive phrase used as the subject)

He managed *to open the safe.* (infinitive phrase used as the object of the verb)

VERBS: I *am coming* in a minute. He *has done* it again.

ADJECTIVES: The woman *in the black dress* is a secret agent.
                    (prepositional phrase modifying *woman*)
                    The man *running the store* is my uncle Murad
                    (participial phrase modifying *man*)
                    He is a man *to admire.* (infinitive phrase modify-
                    ing *man*)

ADVERBS: The horse jumped *over the barrier.* (preposi-
                    tional phrase modifying *jumped*)
                    He swerved *to miss* the child. (infinitive phrase
                    modifying *swerved*)

A clause is a group of related words which usually contains a subject and a finite verb:

An *independent* (*main, principal*) clause is one that can stand alone as a complete sentence; a *dependent* (*subordinate*) clause is incapable of standing alone. (For exceptions see pages 129–130.)

DEPENDENT CLAUSE: Although a dependent clause may grow
                      like this one to a considerable size, adding
                      phrase after phrase like the branching
                      twigs of a tree,
INDEPENDENT CLAUSE: it still needs a main trunk like this to
                      support it.

A *dependent* clause may serve as a noun, an adjective, or an adverb:

That he would eventually return to his black-eyed Bess was the highwayman's bold promise. (noun clause, subject)

Nobody knows *what enormous loads of wood a woodchuck can chuck.* (noun clause, object of the verb)

On the fifth page of his paper he came to *what was obviously his key point.* (noun clause, object of the preposition *to*)

A man *who has no music in his heart* may be merely tone deaf. (adjective clause modifying *man*)

Where many had failed before him, the great Unus alone suc-ceeded in standing on a single digit. (adverbial clause modifying *suc-ceeded*)

To distinguish easily between dependent and independent clauses is to solve the most elementary problem of sentence structure. But that is a subject for the next chapter.

A LIST OF GRAMMATICAL TERMS
(With Page References to This Chapter)

absolute, 105–106
absolute phrase, 101
abstract noun, 86
accusative case, 87–94
active voice, 97–98
adjective, 84, 103–106
adjective clause, 114
adjective phrase, 114
adverb, 84, 103–106
adverbial clause, 114
adverbial conjunction, 106
adverbial phrase, 114
agreement, 107–113
antecedent, 94–96
apposition, appositive, 89
article, 84
auxiliary verb, 98–99

case, 87–94, 110
clause, 114–115
collective noun, 86, 109
common noun, 86
comparative degree, 104–105
comparison, 104–106
complement, 88, 106
compound subject, 107
concrete noun, 86
conjugation, 102
conjunction, 85, 106–107
conjunctive adverb, 103, 106
connective, 83–85
coordinating conjunction, 106
correlative conjunction, 106

definite article, 87
demonstrative adjective, 107, 111
demonstrative pronoun, 91
dependent clause, 114–115
direct address, 89
direct object, 88, 91–94

expletive, 110–111

finite verb, 100
future perfect tense, 98
future tense, 98

gender, 86–87, 89, 107, 109
genitive case, 87, 89–90, 101–102
gerund, 101–102
gerund phrase, 113

historical present, 98

imperative mood, 97
indefinite article, 87
indefinite pronoun, 90, 108–109
independent clause, 114–115
indicative mood, 97
indirect object, 88
infinitive, 100
infinitive phrase, 113–114
intensive pronoun, 91
interjection, 83, 85
interrogative pronoun, 90
intransitive verb, 96
irregular verb, 102

EXERCISES

I. Name the part of speech of each word in the following sentences. If it is a noun, pronoun, adjective, or adverb, explain its function in the sentence. (*Example:* He fails lazy students regularly. *He* is a pronoun, subject of the sentence; *lazy* is an adjective modifying the noun *students; students* is a noun, direct object of the verb *fails; regularly* is an adverb modifying the verb *fails.*)

1. I never saw a more beautiful morning for sleeping through class.

2. All students of elementary government should understand the fundamental difference between a democracy and a republic.

3. In this era of strutting majorettes, many spectators whom the music once thrilled now look at the band without hearing it.

4. Nobody who has not been in Hiroshima or Nagasaki can fully understand the devastation that a single atomic bomb can bring to a populous industrial area.

5. Oh, how he suffered over weekly themes!

6. If the dawn did come up like thunder, it would never wake Shorty.

7. He turned on me like a prosecuting attorney and asked bitterly if I understood the difference between *like* and *as.*

8. Although I drove slower than Murgatroyd, my wife always shouted louder at me from the back seat.

9. It had some effect on his disposition, but it did not permanently affect his constitution.

10. Apparently there is an old Chinese proverb for every situation in life.

II. Each of the following words may be used as more than one part of speech. The number of different classifications, according to *Webster's New Collegiate Dictionary,* follows in parentheses. Name all the classifications you can and write a sentence to illustrate each.

but (5)	empty (3)
check (3)	head (3)
down (5)	out (6)
dry (3)	round (5)
effect (2)	true (4)

III. In accordance with the conventions of *formal* writing, choose the correct case of the pronoun in each of the following sentences and defend your choice:

1. I picture him as an innocent adolescent (who, whom) life had taught nothing.

2. Between the house and (whoever, whomever) was hiding be-hind the tree, stood a policeman.

3. Moses, (who, whom) the principal had chosen to represent the school, went to bed with the mumps on the day of the contest.

4. Her mother is more intelligent than (her, she).

5. The mayor, (who, whom) the voters had decided was dishonest, did not run for another term.

6. If it came to a choice between (her, she) and (I, me), I would bow out gracefully.

7. He saw John and (me, I) standing on the corner waiting for a trolley.

8. Three-fingered Pete, (who, whom) they thought had done it, was still at large.

9. I didn't like (him, his) saying that about (her, she) and (I, me).

10. Coach Anthrax, (who's, whose) finishing his first year at Princemouth, has brought the college (its, it's) first intercollegiate chess championship.

IV. Rewrite the following sentences, correcting faulty or questionable reference of pronouns:

1. He had a taste of what a dictator was like, and he was willing to die to protect his home from it.

2. I started college in the summer term, which was unfortunate because the summer is the most agreeable season for loafing.

3. Boswell considered Dr. Johnson one of the greatest literary men of his century, and it is an accepted fact that he was, and that consequently he continually sought Johnson's company.

4. He soon learned the second and more practical use of the hair brush; in fact, he learned it so well that he would run upstairs and throw it out of the window whenever he could find it.

5. My personal problems I have always kept to myself, consulting nobody for advice until I have tried to do it to the best of my ability.

6. Galsworthy describes Ashurst's feelings so well that he makes you sympathize with Ashurst when he later realizes with anguish that he was in love with Megan.

7. Through his use of picturesque words and phrases he plays on the reader's imagination so powerfully that he feels the depth of the writer's emotion.

8. Robert W. Service does not wander aimlessly, which I believe Whitman tends to do in many of his poems.

9. Poetry is nothing but a conglomeration of beautiful phrases put together in such a manner that I seldom know what he is talking about.

10. When my father came back into the house, he said that the man was standing where he (my father) could not see him clearly.

11. This pain was alleviated in my junior year when the doctor said I could participate in track, which led to my winning a letter.

12. Her wedding dress has been carefully stitched together and hung in the closet for over a week. This is also true of her bridesmaids.

13. Some teachers treat students as if they don't care how much they get out of the course as long as they get promoted.

14. He had several feet of black friction tape wound around his sprained ankle, which was all he was able to find at the country store.

15. Although he is not an educated man, he seldom shows the lack of it.

16. Mabel stood at the window and watched the horse trudging slowly along the road. It was broken, and the cold wind whistled through.

17. When the coach told him to turn in his uniform, he was more angry than I have ever seen him.

18. She could dimly discern a man's face who was peering at her across the smoke-filled room.

19. They have taken advantage of their friends until they no longer have any use for them.

20. He brought home four juicy steaks in a package, which he broiled for dinner.

V. Rewrite the following sentences, correcting any errors in verb forms:

1. It all started when I was playing with some boys whom my mother previously told me not to visit.

2. I wasn't playing very long before she came and dragged me home.

3. During the two years in which I attended Lackawanna College, there is some irresistible force which compels me to repeat English 1.

4. When it became apparent to me that my wishes will come true, I began to ask my father questions about the medical profession.

5. You may not believe me when I say that I was waiting here since ten-thirty this morning.

6. I looked out of the window and saw Junior laying full length on the sidewalk where the men had just laid the fresh concrete.

7. He lay in the same bunk where he had laid ever since we left Saipan.

8. If my rich Uncle Toby didn't stake me, I never could have started the business.

9. Although they are married for seven years, they never had a second honeymoon.

10. The money was not laying where I had laid it only an hour earlier.

VI. In the following sentences, classify all finite verbs as transitive or intransitive and give number, person, mood, voice, and tense. Pick out all linking verbs. Classify all verbals as infinitive, participle, or gerund.

1. Many students reading the life of Chaucer are surprised to learn that he was an outstanding man of affairs to whom poetry was an avocation.

2. Although playing one of the hardest schedules in the country, Notre Dame will probably have won most of its games before the season is over and be national champion again.

3. William Carlos Williams, a physician as well as a poet, has drawn inspiration from his patients.

4. If it were not for the common illusion that a major in economics guarantees success in business, many students would never have decided to enter that crowded department.

5. Not having lived in New York for more than ten years, I feel strange on Times Square even on New Year's Eve.

6. I wish I were able to recall the facts from memory, but I shall look them up at the earliest opportunity.

7. In a year and a half he had been converted from a wide-eyed young man, eagerly looking ahead to a college education, into a typical member of the fraternity, existing only for the next week end.

8. He tried so hard to be one of the boys that all the sharp edges of his individuality were quickly worn away.

9. When the leaders of all the nations are as tired of wars as the men who have to fight them, peace may come to the world.

10. Only yesterday he looked hale and hearty, striding down the street as if he were going to live forever.

VII. Choose the correct form of the two in parentheses and identify it as an adverb or an adjective. If both forms are permissible in writing, distinguish them according to levels of usage.

1. As I look back to my high school days, I am aware that most of my time was spent rather (foolish, foolishly).

2. Because I was always listening to the radio, I seldom did an algebra problem (correct, correctly), but this didn't make me feel (stupid, stupidly).

3. A soldier must be able to do his job (good, well) if he wishes to be promoted (quick, quickly) in the army.

4. He sang more (loud, loudly) than his sister but not so (beautiful, beautifully).

5. Dempsey was the (strongest, stronger) of the two heavyweights, but Tunney was the (best, better) boxer.

6. He drove (slow, slowly), holding (tight, tightly) to the wheel with one hand.

7. The orchestra played so (good, well) that nobody in the audience suspected that the conductor had felt (miserable, miserably) all day long.

8. This drink doesn't taste as (sweet, sweetly), but it is the (more expensive, most expensive) of the two.

9. The theory sounds (credible, credibly) to me though I think (different, differently) from him on most subjects.

10. The second ballad, sung (soft, softly) and (slow, slowly), was (considerable, considerably) more appealing than the other numbers on the program.

VIII. Correct the errors in agreement in the following sentences. In instances of divided usage, distinguish between the formal and the informal level.

1. Those sort of values are worth much more to me than a fraternity pin.

2. History books state that as early as 1750 talk and writing about independence was circulating in the colonies.

3. Although there has been many objections to the short ballot, most of them boil down to one point.

4. The bathing suits in 1890 were more voluminous than that of today.

5. One of the things that has changed greatly in the past fifty years are military tactics.

6. Although many of these requirements have been abolished, there has arisen other abuses.

7. Unless we do away with these evils, which affects thousands of our citizens, we cannot consider America fully democratic.

8. The results of a survey taken by the Army in recent years shows that the two main things demanded of an officer and leader is competence and interest in the welfare of the men.

9. He is one of those people who speaks such good English that everyone turns their heads to see who is talking.

10. For anyone to raise their voice to Miss Smith was a great mistake, for she merely screamed back, making the student's eardrums throb before sending them to the principal.

11. The only significant conclusions that I have drawn from this experience is that the whole class is collectively responsible and none of the students are entirely innocent.

12. Since neither George nor Michael is going this week end, I wonder if either of them intend to go at all.

13. It looked as if every man was suspicious of the rest and would not trust him.

14. A large body requires less air than a smaller one; therefore, Ayvad's Water Wings are made purposely porous so that it should leak a little to adjust itself properly.

15. The strongest superstition of the young is that everybody but themselves prefer to live by make-believe.

16. Finally, the gambling scene, where he completely ignores the probable results of his behavior, illustrate the deficient judgment of a typical psychopath.

17. The main reason is that Ibsen looked favorably on woman, whereas Strindberg found them revolting.

18. With our greetings go a word of thanks from the Continental Motors Company for the consideration you have shown them in waiting so patiently for a new Lincoln or Mercury.

19. Under this plan no state would be able to lay up their own store of atom bombs and then on some dark night launch a surprise attack on all of its neighbors.

20. Each one of the members of the Phillipsburg Hunting and

Fishing Club are going to try their luck in the annual fly-casting contest.

IX. In the following sentences, identify all phrases and dependent clauses and explain the function of each. (*Example:* That is a horse of a different color. *Of a different color* is a prepositional phrase used as an adjective modifying *horse*.)

1. Although rapid reading can be useful for undergraduates, it should not replace slow, meditative reading.
2. Tired of studying, he went to the movies at the foot of the hill.
3. Starting down the trail, he found soon that his skis had no intention of remaining parallel.
4. The Philadelphia Athletics are in no danger of winning this year, even if the manager tries all the tricks in the book.
5. As soon as he had discovered the atom bomb, man immediately forgot that science is an international language.
6. He jumped into the lake with all his clothes on to save the carefree youth who had fallen through the ice.
7. Few lovers of Joyce Kilmer's "Trees" consider that the same God who makes the trees makes the fools who make the poems.
8. Now that pediatricians have finally discovered that a baby knows when he's hungry better than an alarm clock, the two o'clock bottle is rapidly becoming extinct.
9. The game of bridge is all that stands between some women and a life of continuous boredom.
10. After the game ended, every loyal alumnus stood at embarrassed attention faithfully trying to improvise the Alma Mater.

X. Consult the GLOSSARY for information on the following points of grammar not discussed in this chapter:

ain't	can, may
alumnus, alumna	considerable
amount, number	data
anybody's else	different from, than
born, borne	double negative
boughten	due to
broke	fewer, less
burst, bust	foot, feet

former, latter	plenty
formulas, formulae	politics
freshman, freshmen	preposition at the end of a
get, got, gotten	sentence
good, well	proved, proven
had ought, hadn't ought	raise, rise
in, into	real
is when, is where	reason is because
kind of, sort of	self
later, latter	shall, will
learn	should, would
leave, let	sit, set
lighted, lit	split infinitive
like, as	sure
loan	suspicion
locate	type
mathematics	very
most	want

XI. (General review) Rewrite the following sentences, correcting all errors in grammar and explaining your corrections. In instances of divided usage, distinguish between the formal and the informal levels.

1. The man who's not aware of his own shortcomings is often very angry when anyone accuses them of making mistakes.

2. There was a difference of opinion between David and she on the question of whether to overlook him going out three nights a week.

3. After questioning Mrs. O'Halloran and whomever it was that wouldn't give his name, the police decided that the victim was dead since midnight.

4. When the class heard it's commencement address, they listened more attentive than to the average classroom lecture.

5. If I was you, I wouldn't care what anyone said about their own feelings on the question, for neither your mother nor your sister know all the facts.

6. Senator Jones can hardly believe that it is patriotic to accuse everyone with who he doesn't agree regardless of whether he has any grounds for uttering them.

7. While the corpse was still laying in the room, Inspector O'Toole calmly announced that one of the servants obviously committed the murder, which was a premature decision for one who experience should have taught otherwise.

8. Although Higgins is the least democratic of the two candidates, every one of his many supporters argue that he will uphold it against all enemies.

9. The radio is blaring so loud that I wish it was down at the bottom of the ocean telling Neptune who's soap flakes will make black things white quicker than a magic wand.

10. It is me who is always going with my relatives on picnics, even though they bore me to death.

$\mathscr{S}$entences

If a sentence puzzles you, pull it to pieces. If it is good writing, then the harder you pull, the more tightly you will discover it to be woven together, and the more closely you examine it, the more meaning it will yield.

—Dorothy Sayers.

"A sentence," writes Professor Curme, "is an expression of a thought or feeling by means of a word or words used in such form and manner as to convey the meaning intended." According to this comprehensive definition, when the baby in the play pen says, "Up," when the wild fan at the football game yells, "Yowie," when Tarzan of the movies grunts, "Me friend"—all are speaking sentences, for all are clearly conveying the meaning intended. To be sure, the test of meaning is fundamental. Many of the bad sentences discussed later in this chapter fail because, for one reason or another, they don't convey the intended meaning, or at least because they don't convey it in the smoothest, most emphatic way. But many others, even if they get the point across clearly enough, are unsatisfactory for a different reason: they disregard conventions of sentence structure that careful, educated writers normally follow.

A telegram may convey its meaning with clarity and economy: ARRIVE SEVEN THIRTY. DINNER ON TRAIN. WILL TAKE CAB FROM STATION. LOVE ALBERT. But the conventions of etiquette require a letter writer to address his hostess in a more finished fashion. A telegrammatical examination answer may contain clear, accurate information: *"The Way of the World*—Congreve's last play— comedy of manners marking highest achievement of type in Restoration—famous for scintillating dialogue between Mirabell, Millamant." But the conventions in answering discussion questions demand that the student unburden his brain more systematically. "Sighted sub sank same" was an admirable dispatch, custom-tailored for the headlines; but the reader of an official report on the incident would naturally expect subjects for the verbs, articles with the nouns, and conjunctions to tether the clauses. In its broadest sense, a sentence may be any statement that conveys meaning. But in most contexts readers expect sentences that are *grammatically complete*. What is a grammatically complete sentence?

COMPLETE SENTENCES
(See Exercise I on page 157)

Reduced to its lowest terms, a complete sentence consists of a *subject* and a *predicate:* <u>Students</u> <u>study</u>. This statement (with subject underlined once, predicate twice) may be expanded in numerous ways:

By making the subject compound:

<u>Students</u> and <u>teachers</u> <u>study</u>.

By making the predicate compound:

<u>Students</u> <u>study</u> and <u>play</u>.

By giving the verb a complement:

<u>Students</u> <u>study</u> books.

By adding modifiers to either subject or predicate:

In their spare time good <u>students</u> <u>study</u> books for general enlightenment.

But whatever is added, the solid foundation of subject and predicate remains. This is true if the *declarative sentence* is changed to an *interrogative sentence* (Do <u>students</u> <u>study</u>?); an *exclamatory sentence* (How seldom <u>students</u> <u>study</u>!); or an *imperative sentence* (<u>Study</u>, students!—in which the subject is *you* understood).

If, on the other hand, the basic sentence is changed to *students studying* or *although students study*, it becomes incomplete. The first illustration contains a *verbal* instead of a *finite verb*. The second, introduced by a *subordinating conjunction*, is a *subordinate* or *dependent clause.* To complete the first asser-tion, the writer must add a finite verb: <u>Students</u> studying <u>groan</u>. To complete the second, he must supply an *independent clause:* Although students study, <u>they</u> sometimes <u>fail</u>.

To summarize, *a complete sentence must contain a subject and a finite verb, and every dependent clause must be supported by an independent clause.*

The incomplete sentences written by most undergraduates are the accidents of ignorance or indifference. Usually they serve no purpose that could not be better served by completing them. This error is commonly known as the *sentence fragment* or *period fault.* Notice how the following student specimens are improved either by completing fragments or incorporating them into com-plete sentences:

Passage with fragment	*Improved*
The second week the coach called the squad together and broke them into two groups. *The linemen comprising one group and the backfield the other.* (*Comprising* is a present participle, not a finite verb.)	The second week the coach called the squad together and broke them into two groups, line-men and backfield men.
The principal kinds of trans-portation were trains and horses. *The automobile having not yet come into the picture.* (*Having come* is a participle, not a finite verb.)	The principal kinds of trans-portation were trains and horses. The automobile had not yet come into the picture.
I came to college not only to study English but to get a broad liberal education. *To prepare my-self for the great struggle that lies ahead.* (*To prepare* is an infini-tive, not a finite verb.)	I came to college not only to study English but to get a broad liberal education and prepare my-self for life.
I am glad this college is not filled with coeds. *Although I like the girls well enough.* (Dependent clause standing alone.)	Although I like the girls well enough, I am glad this college is not filled with coeds.

I was born in Jersey City in 1932. *Lived in Weehawken until the age of eight, then moved to Newark, where I still live. Started school in Weehawken.* Then I went to Newark to complete my schooling. (Omission of subjects —"telegrammar.")

Thus ended the tragic life of Julius Caesar. *The greatest man that Rome ever produced.* (A phrase *in apposition with Caesar,* an *appositive.*)

I was born in Jersey City in 1932 and lived in Weehawken until the age of eight. Then I moved to Newark, where I am still living. I started school in Weehawken and finished in Newark.

Thus ended the tragic life of Julius Caesar, the greatest man Rome ever produced.

Of course, many incomplete sentences are legitimate and effective. Some of the most common are:

1. *In dialogue:*

Where you been, boys? he said.
Swimming, Joe said.
Swimming? he said.
Sure, Joe said. We showed that river.
Well, I'll be harrowed, the grocer said. How was it?
Not three feet deep, Joe said.
Cold?
Ice-cold.
Well, I'll be cultivated, the grocer said. Did you have fun?
Did we? Joe asked my cousin Murad. —William Saroyan, "The Three Swimmers and the Grocer from Yale," *My Name Is Aram.*

2. *In description:*

I wish I could tell you about the South Pacific. *The way it actually was. The endless ocean. The infinite specks of coral we called islands. Coconut palms nodding gracefully toward the ocean. Reefs upon which waves broke into spray, and inner lagoons, lovely beyond description.* I wish I could tell you about the sweating jungle, the full moon rising behind the volcanoes, and the waiting. *The waiting. The timeless, repetitive waiting.* —James Michener, *Tales of the South Pacific.*

3. *For transitions:*

Now to my next point. One final observation.

4. *Exclamations, questions, and answers:*

Remarkable! What price glory? The exorbitant price of war, the price of death and devastation.

5. *When a phrase or clause that would normally be tied to a previous sentence is segregated for emphasis:*

Eileen and I thought that little tale was almost as good as *Chickie. But not quite.* Nobody had a baby.   —Ruth McKenney, *My Sister Eileen.*

Segregation for emphasis is especially common when several phrases or clauses are in parallel structure and repetition of subject and verb would be superfluous:

A government exists when it governs, when it makes laws and administers them. *When it levies taxes and collects them. When it recruits armies that fight under its orders.* By this test there is today a French government.   —Walter Lippmann, New York *Herald Tribune.*

However useful such sentences may be to experienced writers, many English teachers expect a student to avoid most of these practices until he has at least proved conclusively that he knows a complete sentence when he sees one.

RUN-TOGETHER SENTENCES

One other elementary error raises the question of whether the writer can recognize a complete sentence. The *run-together* or *run-on sentence* contains two or more complete sentences rolled into one without adequate punctuation to separate them. Occasionally there is no punctuation whatever between them:

My mother was very fond of the song "My Buddy" therefore I became Buddy and it has stuck to me ever since.

But this glaring error is relatively rare in college writing. It is a far more common practice—and not always a mistake—to separate two complete sentences with only a comma. Since this "comma fault" represents confusion about conventional punctuation as well as ignorance of sentence structure, it is discussed in detail in the next chapter (see pages 173–175).

COMBINING CLAUSES
(See Exercises II and III on pages 158–160)

By the age of three the average child is lisping in complete sentences. But they are usually *simple sentences;* that is, sentences with only a single clause: "We went to the zoo. We saw three tigers. They were big ones too. One of them made a great big noise. I was scared. Mother bought me an ice-cream cone." Before long he begins tying them together with a few common conjunctions, not because he has been taught any formal grammar, but because he is unconsciously aware of connections between them. Partly through juvenile breathlessness and partly because he cannot distinguish clearly among these relationships, he is likely to pour out an indiscriminate torrent like this: "We went to the zoo and we saw three tigers and they were big ones too but one of them made a great big noise so I was scared and Mother bought me an ice-cream cone." From the standpoint of sentence structure this eager prattle is little different from what comes out of the mouths of some adults: the garrulous woman whose tiresome anecdotes fall into marathon sentences thinly cemented together with "and I says to her . . . and she says to me . . . so I says to her, I says"; the after-dinner speaker who ties clauses together with *and-er* and *so-er* like endless strings of sausages. Children have no monopoly on immature sentence patterns.

A writer cannot achieve maturity until he has learned to avoid the infinite monotony of simple sentences. He must not abolish them all; the simple sentence is the backbone of twentieth-century prose. Nor should he string clauses together indiscriminately like a breathless child merely for the sake of making short sentences longer. He must learn to apply two simple and logical rules of sentence organization:

1. If two or more related elements are of equal importance, put them in a *coordinate* construction.

2. If one element is more important than the others, put it in an independent clause and *subordinate* the others.

Since in talking few people have the foresight to distinguish important elements from unimportant, these rules may not be strictly followed in informal writing that reflects the loose structure of conversation. But all trained writers tend to follow them. That is why mature writing naturally contains, in addition to simple sentences, three other kinds

1. *Compound sentences* contain two or more coordinate independent clauses but no dependent clause:

Frank threw the winning pass, and Kelley caught it.

(Sometimes the comma and conjunction are replaced by a semicolon.)

2. *Complex sentences* contain one independent clause and one or more dependent clauses:

Although Frank's pass was high, Kelley caught it.

3. *Compound-complex sentences* contain two or more independent clauses and one or more dependent clauses:

Although Frank's pass was high, Kelley caught it, and Jones erased the safety man.

These distinctions were not devised by grammarians to make simple writing difficult. They are necessary to enable an adult to express relationships more subtle than those a child perceives.

Failure to understand coordination and subordination results in the following common faults:

1. PRIMER PROSE (*inadequate coordination and subordination*)

Faulty	*Improved*
I was seized by a wanderlust every summer. I also wanted to see what the rest of the country was like. Several summers were occupied in this. I hitchhiked from place to place. I usually had no plan. I just went the same place the driver was going. I went	Every summer I was seized by a wanderlust and a desire to see what the rest of the country was like. During several vacations I hitchhiked aimlessly from place to place. Wandering without an itinerary, going wherever the driver was heading, I went across

across the country and back this way three times. Now I won't be able to do it any more. I'll have to work summers to get through college.

the country and back three times. Now that I shall have to work in the summer to get through college, my hitchhiking days are over.

2. FALSE COORDINATION (*"Siamese twin sentences," in which elements are unnaturally joined*)

Faulty	*Improved*
Mildred was an adopted child, and she was having her teeth straightened with shining braces.	An adopted child whose real parents had neglected her teeth, Mildred was having them straightened with shining braces.
The class of which I was a member had four exciting dances, and we were rewarded at the end of the school term by receiving diplomas. (Here it is implied that the diplomas were awards for social activity.)	Although the members of my class had four exciting dances, not a single student failed to study hard enough to get his diploma.
He hid on the dock, and there was a large mountain looming up behind him.	He hid on the dock in the shadow of a large mountain that loomed up behind him.
Their faces and white uniforms stood out in the gathering darkness, and between them sat an oiler just off duty.	Their faces and white uniforms stood out in the gathering darkness. Between them sat an oiler just off duty.

3. EXCESSIVE COORDINATION (*in which all clauses are made coequal—with* and—but—so—*emphasizing everything, and nothing*)

Faulty	*Improved*
The trip was very interesting, but I sometimes wonder about its value, for it practically set me back a year scholastically, for in the Florida schools I could not finish German and chemistry, so upon graduation from high school I had to attend prep school.	Although the trip was very interesting, I sometimes wonder about its value, for it practically set me back a year scholastically. Because I could not finish German and chemistry in Florida, I had to attend prep school on my graduation from high school.

In my freshman year I came out for goalie on the soccer team, and for my efforts I received a regular position on the first team, but because of my dislike of the goalie position, I tried out for a halfback position, but because of the fact that these positions were held by juniors and seniors I could not avail myself of a position on the soccer team here.

In my freshman year I came out for goalie in soccer and earned a regular position on the first team. Because I disliked playing goalie, I later tried out for halfback. Since the halfback positions were held by juniors and seniors, I could not make the grade.

4. UPSIDE-DOWN SUBORDINATION *(in which the main idea is put in the subordinate clause or phrase)*

Faulty

He was strolling calmly on the deck when a large wave washed him overboard.

He fell seven stories and broke eight ribs, puncturing a lung and living to tell the tale.

Improved

As he was strolling calmly on the deck, a large wave washed him overboard.

Although a fall of seven stories gave him eight broken ribs and a punctured lung, he lived to tell the tale.

5. CARELESS USE OF CONNECTIVES

Faulty

Although these people have a point, but I feel that my point is better. (The writer starts with a subordinate clause, then carelessly makes the main clause coordinate by inserting *but*.)

Politics is a strenuous game and which often corrupts honest men. (By inserting *and,* the writer makes the second clause into an impossible coordinate-subordinate hybrid.)

You have no doubt heard that since eighteen-year-olds can

Improved

Although these people have a point, I feel that mine is better.

Politics is a strenuous game which often corrupts honest men.

You have no doubt heard that since eighteen-year-olds can

fight a war that they should be given the privilege of voting. (The superfluous *that* is common in careless writing.)

fight a war they should be given the vote.

He tried five times to be elected President, and he never succeeded. (The wrong connective expresses an inaccurate relationship between the clauses. For other connectives which are sometimes weak or ambiguous, see *as* and *while* in the GLOSSARY.)

He tried five times to be elected President, but he never succeeded.

MODIFIERS
(See Exercise IV on page 160)

Once a student has learned to write complete sentences and to combine clauses intelligently, he has gone a long way toward writing acceptable sentences. But careless use of modifiers, even in simple sentences, may still spell his downfall.

Adjectives usually come immediately before the noun they modify (He wore an *old, battered* hat on his head). Sometimes they follow immediately after (He wore a hat, *old* and *battered,* on his head). But in the absence of inflectional endings to link them with their noun, the writer who places them anywhere else may be in trouble. If he writes, "He wore a hat on his head, *old* and *battered,*" his meaning is slightly ambiguous. If he writes, *"Old* and *battered,* he wore a hat on his head," it is radically changed.

With adverbs there is more leeway:

Slowly he slouched down the street with his hands in his pockets.
He *slowly* slouched down the street with his hands in his pockets.
He slouched *slowly* down the street with his hands in his pockets.
He slouched down the street *slowly* with his hands in his pockets.

All these mean essentially the same, though the placing of the adverb makes differences in emphasis and rhythm. But if the sentence is changed to "He slouched down the street with his hands in his pockets *slowly,*" the reader may easily be misled.

Except with special nuisances such as *only,* few students

have real trouble with one-word modifiers. But when adjectives and adverbs are expanded into phrases and clauses, the trouble begins. Whether a modifier has one word or twenty, the same elementary principle applies: A good sentence leaves no doubt about the words to which the modifiers refer. Although it over-simplifies the problem, this is a useful rule for beginners: *Place every modifier as near as possible to the word it modifies.*

Because they present different problems in revision, it is convenient to summarize the various kinds of misrelated modifiers under two main classes: (1) *dangling modifiers,* which have nothing in the sentence that they can logically modify; and (2) *misplaced modifiers,* which can be corrected in a first draft by merely changing their position in the sentence with a loop and an arrow.

1. DANGLING MODIFIERS

Faulty	*Improved*
1. *Being rushed* through the registrar's office on the way to the dean, the well-kept records impressed me. (dangling participle)	1. As I was rushed through the registrar's office on the way to the dean, the well-kept records impressed me. *Or:* Being rushed through the registrar's office . . . I was impressed by the well-kept records.
2. *Walking* out on the stage, my music blew off the stand. (dangling participle)	2. When I walked out on the stage, my music blew off the stand. *Or:* Walking out on the stage, I saw my music blow off the stand.
3. Sometimes, *wiping* the damp cloth back and forth on the counter, her dream-widened eyes centered on the screen door, her pale eyes flexed and then closed for a moment. —John Steinbeck, *The Wayward Bus.* (dangling participle)	3. Sometimes, as she wiped the damp cloth back and forth on the counter, her dream-widened eyes centered on the screen door, her pale eyes flexed and then closed for a moment.
4. My ego was further boosted by *being elected* to the	4. My ego was further boosted when I was elected to the

student council. (dangling gerund)

student council. *Or:* . . . by my being elected to the student council.

5. *To be* really literate, books should be read thoroughly. (dangling infinitive)

5. To be really literate, a student should read books thoroughly.

6. *When only one year old,* my family moved to Ashtabula. (dangling elliptical clause—that is, a clause with words omitted)

6. When I was only one year old, my family moved to Ashtabula. *Or:* When only one year old, I moved with my family to Ashtabula.

7. *At the age of six* my parents sent me to a private school in York. (dangling phrase)

7. At the age of six I was sent to a private school in York. *Or:* When I was six, my parents sent me to a private school in York.

(Do not confuse such danglers as these with the legitimate absolute construction, where the participle really modifies the entire sentence: *Confidentially speaking,* the participle in this sentence is innocent of dangling.)

As the examples show, the best argument against dangling modifiers is not that they are grammatically indefensible, but that they are liable to be either (1) *ambiguous* or (2) *unintentionally humorous.* Sentences 1 and 5 are ambiguous: What is being rushed through the registrar's office, the student or the records? What is to be really literate, the student or the books? The reader of Sentence 1 can never be sure of the meaning. Sentence 5 may derail the reader only for a moment, but even a momentary ambiguity should be abolished. Although the actual meaning of the other sentences is clear, they all run the risk of provoking unsolicited laughter. The reader knows that the music did not walk out on the stage, the dream-widened eyes did not function as a dishcloth, the student's ego did not appear on the ballot, and nobody's parents are six years old—but such bizarre conceptions can still be distracting.

When a dangling modifier provokes neither misunderstanding nor mirth, it is unobjectionable. Such harmless danglers as these appear frequently in the most reputable writing:

Settled down at last at Amorbach, the time hung heavily on the Duke's hands. —Lytton Strachey, *Queen Victoria.*

While *thinking* about Mr. Chase's book, the opening lines of a poem by e. e. cummings kept up a running bass in my mind. —Willard Thorp, New York *Herald Tribune.*

But until a writer has reached the age of sentence discretion, he would do well to examine all danglers, especially *ing* verbals, with a suspicious eye.

2. MISPLACED MODIFIERS

Ambiguous or Humorous

He studied the woman who sat in his chair *secretly.* (Here the adverb *secretly* appears to modify *sat.*)

Judith Henry was killed while lying in bed by a bullet which entered her house. (Here the phrase *by a bullet* appears to modify *lying.*)

She had a new Easter bonnet on her blonde head, *which had been bought at a bargain basement but was really very attractive.* (Here the entire clause appears to modify *head.*)

I asked him *after the year was over* to lend me the book. (This squinting modifier could modify either *asked* or *lend.*)

God can *only* make a tree.

Clear

He secretly studied the woman who sat in his chair.

Judith Henry was killed by a bullet which entered her house while she was lying in bed.

On her blonde head she had a new Easter bonnet, which had been bought at a bargain basement but was really very attractive.

After the year was over I asked him to lend me the book. *Or:* I asked him to lend me the book after the year was over. (depending on the writer's meaning)

Only God can make a tree.

When a misplaced *only* leads to absurdity, as in the last illustration, it should be put in its place. The same is true of *almost, also, even,* and *merely.* But informal writing is not strict about the position of the ubiquitous *only.* When E. M. Forster writes, "Freedom in England is *only* enjoyed by people who are fairly well off," he is following a common tendency to place *only* before the verb. A more formal writer might be expected to say: "Freedom in England is enjoyed *only* by people who are fairly well off."

Other misplaced modifiers, though they may not result in ambiguity, are awkward because they interrupt the flow of the sentence by splitting parts that normally come close together:

Awkward	*Improved*
Professor Thorndike, always eager to keep his students awake regardless of their obvious lack of interest in either the subject or the course, *puts* on a three-ring circus. (long interrupter between subject and verb)	Always eager to keep his students awake regardless of their obvious lack of interest in either the subject or the course, Professor Thorndike puts on a three-ring circus.
I did not *know,* in spite of the hours I spent in reviewing, the *answers* to more than half the questions. (interrupter between verb and object)	In spite of the hours I spent in reviewing, I did not know the answers to more than half the questions.
I stood in lonely isolation where I *had,* only four short years before, *participated* in the greatest invasion in history. (interrupter between parts of the verb)	I stood in lonely isolation where, only four short years before, I had participated in the greatest invasion in history.
Smithfield Cobb, played by Melvyn Douglas, is able *to,* through the mind of Janet Ames, played by Rosalind Russell, *show* her the reasons why five people should be alive and not her husband.	Smithfield Cobb, played by Melvyn Douglas is able, through the mind of Janet Ames, played by Rosalind Russell, to show her the reasons why five people should be alive and not her husband.

Used sparingly, such split constructions can be a conscious trick of style for the sake of suspense and variety.

The last illustration is awkward because it sunders two parts of a verbal with a ten-word modifier. It happens to be a *split infinitive,* but reasonable students of the language no longer consider all split infinitives as heinous crimes or even awkward expressions. Further discussion of this construction is relegated to the GLOSSARY.

REQUIRED PARALLELISM
(See Exercise V on page 161)

"The world will little note, nor long remember, what we say here, but what was done by them can never be forgotten." This misquotation should jar the most insensitive American ear. For it does violence not only to history but also to the prose style of a great writer. A glance at the original should quickly reveal the difference: "The world will little note, nor long remember, what we say here, but it can never forget what they did here." The basic meaning is the same in the misquoted version. Nothing really new has been added. Two verbs have been changed from active to passive voice, and that is all. But the whole sentence is tilted off balance and falls flat. Notice the difference in a diagram:

The world will	little note,	nor
	long remember	what we say here,
but it can	never forget	what they did here.

| The world will | little note, | nor |
| | long remember | what we say here, |

but what was done by them can never be forgotten.

The awkward paraphrase of Lincoln's famous sentence dis-regards an important principle of sentence structure: *Put parallel elements in parallel form.* Three common violations of this principle are (1) *shifted constructions;* (2) *careless use of correlatives;* and (3) *false comparisons.*

1. SHIFTED CONSTRUCTIONS

Not parallel	*Parallel*
I felt that the activities were dull, and the pampering of the pupils annoyed me. (shift of subject)	I found the activities dull and the pampering of the pupils annoying.
If he has a plain gray suit, then a tie should be bought that	If he has a plain gray suit, then he should buy a matching tie.

will match it. (shift of subject and voice)

He is honest, hard-working, patriotic, and has a firm nature. (from adjectives to a clause)

He is honest, hard-working, patriotic, and firm.

One summer I found a job which seemed to be different and an easy way of making money. (from adjective to a phrase)

One summer I found a job which seemed to be different and lucrative. *Or:* One summer I found a job which seemed to be a different and easy way of making money.

During five years in the laboratory I advanced from bottle-washing to a chemist. (from job to jobholder)

During five years in the laboratory I advanced from bottle-washer to chemist. *Or:* . . . from bottle-washing to chemistry.

For other illustrations of the same principle, shifts in tense and in the number and person of pronouns, see pages 99, 111–112.

2. CARELESS USE OF CORRELATIVES

Such correlative conjunctions as *both . . . and, either . . . or, neither . . . nor,* and *not only . . . but also* require parallel construction. The construction is like a simple lever: a misplaced correlative or changed construction on either side of the fulcrum destroys the balance.

Not parallel

He failed *either* to come to class *or* came unprepared. (*either* verbal *or* verb)

Parallel

He *either* failed to come to class *or* came unprepared. (*either* verb *or* verb) *Either* he failed to come to class *or* he came unprepared. (*either* pronoun *or* pronoun)

I voted for Jones *both* because he was honest *and* intelligent. (*both* conjunction *and* adjective)

I voted for Jones because he was *both* honest *and* intelligent. (*both* adjective *and* adjective)

Clarence Day's father *not only* was eccentric *but also* lov-

Clarence Day's father was *not only* eccentric *but also* lovable. (*not only* verb *but also* adjective)

3. FALSE COMPARISONS

<table>
<tr><td>Not parallel</td><td>Parallel</td></tr>
</table>

Not parallel

I can notice that my opinions are not always the same as my parents. (*opinions* compared with *parents*)

When I left Germany in 1945 the effectiveness of the nonfraternization policy was compared with the old prohibition law in the United States. (*effectiveness* compared with *law*)

Jazz brings me as much personal enjoyment as those people who enjoy reading Byron, Shelley, and Keats. (*Jazz* compared with *people,* implying that the people bring him enjoyment)

He studies less than any member of the class. (*He* is compared with *any member,* including himself.)

able. (*not only* adjective *but also* adjective)

Parallel

I can notice that my opinions are not always the same as those of my parents.

When I left Germany in 1945, the effectiveness of the nonfraternization policy was compared with that of the old prohibition law in the United States.

Jazz brings me as much personal enjoyment as the poems of Byron, Shelley, and Keats bring to others.

He studies less than any other member of the class.

In formal writing prepositions, articles, auxiliary verbs, and conjunctions are commonly repeated before parallel elements. This repetition is unnecessary unless the sentence is ambiguous without it:

Formal

He asked for permission *to* call the doctor, *to* visit the hospital, and *to* bring food to the patient.

Ambiguous

The critics praised him for having the courage of his convictions and his honesty in presenting the material.

Less Formal

He asked for permission to call the doctor, visit the hospital, and bring food to the patient.

Clear

The critics praised him *for* having the courage of his conviction and *for* his honesty in presenting the material.

LENGTH
(See Exercise VI on page 162)

Thomas De Quincey once complained that the German philosopher Kant wrote sentences which had been measured by a carpenter and that some of them ran to two feet six inches. Most readers of Kant will sympathize with his English critic's point of view. But De Quincey must have known that even a three-foot sentence may be a good sentence if it does its job, for he wrote some remarkable three-foot sentences himself. Theoretically it is meaningless to say only that a sentence is too long. When the critic adds a qualifying phrase—too long for a loosely constructed compound sentence; too long for the concluding sentence of a chapter; too long for readers with twelve-year-old minds; too long considering all the long sentences in the same paragraph—he is measuring sentence length with a more accurate instrument than a carpenter's rule. A good sentence, like a good paragraph, should be exactly as long as the writer needs to make it to serve his purpose. The famous shortest sentence in the Bible is only two words long: "Jesus wept." But another successful sentence, equally effective in a different way, might run to two hundred and two.

The long and the short of it can be illustrated by two passages from modern storytellers:

She was an old woman and lived on a farm near the town in which I lived. All country and small-town people have seen such old women, but no one knows much about them. Such an old woman comes into town driving an old worn-out horse or she comes afoot carrying a basket. She may own a few hens and have eggs to sell. She brings them in a basket and takes them to a grocer. There she trades them in. She gets some salt pork and some beans. Then she gets a pound or two of sugar and some flour.

Afterwards she goes to the butcher's and asks for some dog-meat. She may spend ten or fifteen cents, but when she does she asks for something. Formerly, the butchers gave liver to anyone who wanted to carry it away. In our family we were always having it. Once one of my brothers got a whole cow's liver at the slaughter-house near the fairgrounds in our town. We had it until we were sick of it. It never cost a cent. I have hated the thought of it ever since.

The old woman got some liver and a soupbone. She never visited with any one, and as soon as she got what she wanted she lit out for home. It made quite a load for such an old body. No one gave her a lift. People drive right down a road and never notice an old woman like that. —Sherwood Anderson, *Death in the Woods.*

A battle exists on many different levels. There is the purely moral level, at the Supreme Headquarters perhaps eighty miles away from the sound of the guns, where the filing cabinets have been dusted in the morning, where there is a sense of quiet and efficiency, where soldiers who never fire a gun and never have a shot fired at them, the high Generals, sit in their pressed uniforms and prepare statements to the effect that all has been done that is humanly possible, the rest being left to the judgment of God, Who has risen early, ostensibly, for this day's work, and is partially and critically regarding the ships, the men drowning in the water, the flight of high explosive, the accuracy of bombardiers, the skill of naval officers, the bodies being thrown into the air by mines, the swirl of tides against steel spikes at the water's edge, the loading of cannon in gun emplacements, and the building far back from the small violent fringe between the two armies, where the files have also been dusted that morning and the enemy Generals sit in different pressed uniforms, looking at very similar maps, reading very similar reports, matching their moral strength and intellectual ingenuity with their colleagues and antagonists a hundred miles away. —Irwin Shaw, *The Young Lions.*

No statistician is necessary to point out the obvious difference in sentence length. Anderson's sentences average 12.5 words, about the same as those of an average sixth-grader. Shaw's second sentence unrolls to 207 words, almost half the length of an entire freshman theme. Neither passage is recommended as a model for beginners, but both can be justified from the standpoint of sentence length. Anderson is telling a simple story of the tragic death of a simple woman in the simplest sentences and words he can find. The absence of variety in both sentence length and vocabulary captures the monotony of her existence. Shaw, in illustrating the vastness of war, has tried to paint an extensive panorama— the chaos of the fighting, the relative calm of both General Staffs, even an ironic picture of a Heavenly High Command—in a single sweeping sentence. By this method he contrives, not only to pile irony swiftly on irony but to preserve a sense of contemporaneity which the usual sentence techniques of consecutive narrative often fail to capture.

In short, the problem of sentence length—like the problems considered in the rest of this chapter: economy, variety, and emphasis—is more a question of literary style than of elementary structure. It cannot readily be reduced to rules.

It makes some sense, however, to speak of a sentence as "too long for the middle of the twentieth century." In the days of crinolines and sideburns, when the pace of life was still geared to the first rickety iron horse, when women had time to spend tedious months on patchwork quilts, when even men found time to read three-volume novels and walk to the office, when ornate architecture was more fashionable in prose style, especially in the earnest perorations of parliamentary debate, a writer was more likely to construct sentences as synthetic as this one, balancing word against word, phrase against phrase, clause against clause, carefully building up the suspense until the final climax—or anti-climax. But the pace of modern life is different. Laborsaving devices have given us more leisure than our ancestors dreamed of. But we have not time to enjoy it. We are too busy being busy. We run up escalators to save three useless seconds. We read digests of digests. Radio commentators give us all the news in fifteen hectic minutes. Newspapers and magazines shoot the straight dope at us like machine guns. So we are more likely to write sentences like these. Short, snappy, staccato sentences, or half sentences.

The dangers of both extremes should be apparent; they are equally artificial, equally tedious. But for better or worse, sentences are shorter than they used to be, and this generation of readers is accustomed to the staccato style. Despite the over-all gain in literacy, few people today have the patience to thread the maze of an elaborate sentence. The studies of Rudolf Flesch indicate that an average reader will have no trouble with a sentence average of seventeen words, but that as soon as the average reaches twenty-one, the level is "fairly difficult," and when it gets to twenty-nine, reading is "very difficult." An artist can hardly be expected to take such statistics seriously. Even in the machine age, a man cannot be required to type with one hand and work a comptometer with the other. But the bare figures should be sobering to a writer of simple exposition, whose chief aim is to get his point across to a reader with the least possible misunderstanding. Two British experts, Robert Graves and Alan Hodge, reduce the problem to a simple rule: "Sentences should not be so long that the reader loses his way in them." This might have been an insult to our Victorian ancestors, but today it has some practical value.

The writer of monotonous primer sentences does not have to be told to err on the side of brevity in order to be fashionable. Nothing said here is meant to condone his bad habit or encourage anyone who has burst the bonds of primer slavery to return happily to bondage. But when a student finds himself tangled in a long construction, and all the rules of coordination, subordination, modification, and parallelism avail him nothing, he need not be ashamed to take the easiest way out: breaking up the long sentence into two or more short ones. Notice how the following exhausting sentences can be effectively broken up:

Nonstop	*Easy stages*
The project of giving each school in the vicinity where there is a class of instrumental music two tickets to be used at each concert by the student making the most progress in his musical studies between concert dates, which was announced in our last program, has been well received.	The project announced in our last program has been well received. Under this plan we distribute two tickets for each concert to every school in the vicinity with a class in instrumental music. They are awarded to the student making the most progress in his musical studies between concert dates.
The embedded ambition to become a surgical doctor, which was aroused by the sudden death of his mother, was retarded by a temporary illness of blindness initiated by an extensive reading	The death of his mother fired him with the ambition to become a surgeon. For two years his studies were interrupted. Physical neglect had undermined his health, and the long hours of

of books late at night and by a poor condition of health due to neglect of his body, but after two years of illness the normal condition of health was restored by a rigid procedure prescribed by the physician.

night reading had brought on temporary blindness. But by following a rigid procedure prescribed by his doctor, he completely recovered.

Confirming our telephone conversation, I would like to say that I think it was very nice of you to agree to purchase one of the tickets which we are now offering for sale for our annual Police Benefit Ball, and in addition I would very much like to express my own personal gratitude for your very excellent cooperation in making a financial contribution to our efforts, which are principally directed toward raising a sufficient amount of money to keep twelve retired police officers on our pension list and also make it possible for twelve more, who have reached retirement age and are eligible to retire at any time from active police duties to have their names placed on the inactive roster.

Confirming our telephone conversation, I want to thank you, both personally and on behalf of the department, for your kindness in agreeing to buy a ticket for the annual Police Benefit Ball. Your cooperation will help us raise enough money to achieve two goals: (1) to keep twelve retired police officers on our present pension list; (2) to enable twelve more, who are now eligible for pensions, to retire at any time.

Of course, length is not the only culprit in these sentences. All three of them illustrate the general principle that nonstop sentences usually violate more fundamental rules of structure. The first sentence has a modifier (*which was announced* . . .) that is sundered by thirty-seven words from the noun it modifies (*project*). The last two are inexcusably wordy. The writers are not only saying more in one sentence than they can handle; they are taking too many words to say it. This brings up the inevitable problem of economy.

ECONOMY
(See Exercise VII on page 163)

Any wordy sentence is too long no matter how short it is. Repetition has already been discussed in connection with paragraphing (see pages 63–68), and the lessons there are equally applicable within the sentence. But unnecessary repetition of the same words is only one brand of wordiness. Others are (1) *needless repetition of the same thought in different words;* (2) *coordinate synonyms;* (3) *unemployed words;* (4) *circumlocutions;* and (5) *overweight constructions.*

1. SAME THOUGHT REPEATED IN DIFFERENT WORDS

Wordy	*Economical*
Against this was the argument that slaves could neither read nor write, were considered illiterate, and were from a race far inferior to white men.	Against this was the argument that slaves were illiterate and inferior to white men.
The undersigned men whose signatures appear below are authorized to carry secret and confidential dispatches addressed to this ship.	The undersigned men are authorized to carry secret and confidential dispatches addressed to this ship.
All team matches must begin punctually on time.	All team matches must begin on time.

2. COORDINATE SYNONYMS

Wordy	*Economical*
The two most important qualities of good leadership are *ability* and *competence.*	The most important quality of good leadership is ability,
It is well that they have learned to recognize this source of *advice* and *counsel.*	It is well that they have learned to recognize this source of advice.
They had a *marriage based on deceit* and *deceptiveness* rather than a *union founded on trust*	Their marriage was based on deceit rather than trust.

and mutual *faith*. (Notice how overlapping synonyms sometimes result from trying too hard for parallelism.)

My favorite hobbies are *athletics, football* and *baseball*. (In this common construction the whole overlaps the parts.)

My favorite hobbies are football and baseball.

Though no two synonyms have identical meanings, if they overlap too much, the second is usually superfluous. This principle does not apply, however, when the writer makes the distinction clear, however slight it may be: This book is both *learned* and *scholarly:* the author's prodigious knowledge has been assimilated and used to enlighten mankind.

3. UNEMPLOYED WORDS

Words, phrases, and clauses which do no work in the sentence can be summarily dismissed without changing its essential meaning.

Wordy	*Economical*
[There are] three problems [which] are paramount in this discussion.	Three problems are paramount in this discussion.
I can help the government in war because [of the fact that] I hold a radio license.	I can help the government in war because I hold a radio license.
The plot of the story was [a] very exciting [one].	The plot of the story was very exciting.
Since most of my father's customers [consist of those who] are Polish and Russian, I acquired a knowledge of both languages.	Since most of my father's customers are Polish and Russian, I acquired a knowledge of both languages.

4. CIRCUMLOCUTIONS

Don't go around the circumference of a verbal circle when you can cut across the diameter.

Wordy	*Economical*
In comparison with the writing of compositions, the reading of literature was not as trying.	Reading literature was not as trying as writing compositions.
On more than one occasion during my basic training, the whole group was called together by the commanding officer for the purpose of giving us an opportunity to ask him questions pertaining to our problems.	More than once during my basic training the commanding officer called the whole group together to give us an opportunity to ask questions about our problems.
Several times during the term he was asked by the professor whether the lesson had been prepared.	Several times during the term the professor asked him whether he had prepared his lesson.

Notice how the shift from passive to active voice improves the last two illustrations. Most wordy writers are in love with the passive voice.

5. OVERWEIGHT CONSTRUCTIONS

Many a construction, though not exactly a circumlocution, is too heavy for the light load of thought that it carries. *Infinite predication*—the use of phrases with verbals instead of clauses with finite verbs—is one of the handiest aids to economy in the language. Flabby, overweight sentences can be reduced by converting clauses to phrases and phrases to single words.

Wordy	*Economical*
The first entrant *who solves the puzzle* will receive a pencil *which has four kinds of lead.*	The first entrant solving the puzzle will receive a pencil with four kinds of lead.
While I was playing tennis, I decided *that I would go for a swim in the lake.*	While playing tennis, I decided to go for a swim in the lake.
The next week *it was reported that Russia had an atomic bomb which was more powerful* than those *which had been dropped on Hiroshima and Nagasaki.*	The next week Russia was reported to have an atomic bomb more powerful than those dropped on Hiroshima and Nagasaki.

In the long run, of course, whether a word is preferable to a phrase or a phrase to a clause depends not only on the weight of the thought but also on the level of usage and the rhythm of the passage. Even in informal writing, a writer must not take so many short cuts that his style degenerates into shorthand.

VARIETY
(See Exercise VIII on page 164)

The problem of sentence variety has already been indirectly treated. The passage on page 132 clearly shows the need for it. If a student can learn to avoid the monotony of primer prose by intelligently combining clauses, and to eliminate unnecessary repetition, he should write with a decent minimum of variety. But only by reading widely and becoming aware of the great flexibility of sentence patterns can he hope to achieve a sentence variety that is more than the mere absence of monotony. Take, for example, this paragraph from the work of a distinguished modern novelist and critic:

(1) Before such power as this we are made to feel that the ordinary tests which we apply to fiction are futile enough. (2) Do we insist that a great novelist shall be a master of melodious prose? (3) Hardy was no such thing. (4) He feels his way by dint of sagacity and uncompromising sincerity to the phrase he wants, and it is often of unforgettable pungency. (5) Failing it, he will make do with any homely or clumsy or old-fashioned turn of speech, now of the utmost angularity, now of a bookish elaboration. (6) No style in literature, save Scott's, is so difficult to analyse; it is on the face of it so bad, yet it achieves its aim so unmistakably. (7) As well might one attempt to rationalize the charm of a muddy country road, or of a plain field of roots in winter. (8) And then, like Dorsetshire itself, out of these very elements of stiffness and angularity his prose will put on greatness; will roll with a Latin sonority; will shape itself in a massive and monumental symmetry like that of his own bare downs. (9) Then again, do we require that a novelist shall observe the probabilities and keep close to reality? (10) To find anything approaching the violence and convolution of Hardy's plots one must go back to the Elizabethan drama. (11) Yet we accept his story completely as we read it; more than that, it becomes obvious that his violence and his melodrama,

when they are not due to a curious peasant-like love of the monstrous for its own sake, are part of that wild spirit of poetry which saw with intense irony and grimness that no reading of life can possibly outdo the strangeness of life itself, no symbol of caprice and unreason be too extreme to represent the astonishing circumstances of our existence.
—Virginia Woolf, "The Novels of Thomas Hardy," *The Common Reader, Second Series.*

Although that passage, with an average sentence length of about twenty-seven words, is somewhat more formal and involved than most modern American prose, it amply illustrates the value of variety. The sentences range in length from the strikingly direct five-word third sentence to the relatively intricate final sentence of eighty-four words. The passage contains five simple sentences (numbers 3, 5, 7, 8, and 10), but these vary in structure from the third, with its simple subject and predicate, to the eighth, with its carefully balanced compound predicate. Further variety is achieved by the use of the rhetorical question (sentences 2 and 9), an effective device if employed sparingly to support meaning, not indiscriminately, as in windy oratory, to evade it. Finally, notice that in four of the declarative sentences (1, 5, 8, and 10) the subject is preceded by one or more introductory phrases. Experienced writers understand the value of *putting something before the subject*—a phrase or a clause—in order to avoid sentence monotony.

It isn't that this is all conscious craftsmanship. But such analysis reveals one of the traits that make good writing good. In contrast to primer prose, in which the simple sentences march jerkily down the page—subject-verb-object-period, subject-verb-object-period—like mechanical soldiers, Mrs. Woolf's paragraph is a delight to read.

EMPHASIS
(See Exercise IX on page 167)

In ordinary conversation the common methods of emphasis are obvious. We hit a word harder, pronounce it more carefully, underline it with a facial grimace or a manual gesture. In trying to carry over these devices into the silent speech of writing, beginners often rely too heavily on the artificial aids of punctuation, spraying the page with underlinings and exclamation points (see pages 185, 193). But there are more subtle ways of achieving emphasis in sentences. The four most common are (1) *segregation;* (2) *position;* (3) *repetition;* and (4) *parallelism.*

1. SEGREGATION

If a main point is occasionally segregated from more elaborate constructions, it stands out. Hence, the short sentence is especially useful in the most important positions in the paragraph, the beginning and the end. Notice how the writers of the following passages have achieved emphasis by segregating significant statements in short, wiry sentences:

> Apparently there were additional words, but if so he never sang them. The only *Märchen* in his repertoire had to do with a man who built a tin bridge. I recall nothing of this tale save the fact that the bridge was of tin, which astonished my brother and me all over again every time we heard of it. We tried to figure out how such a thing was possible, for the mention of tin made us think of tomato-cans. *But we never learned.* —H. L. Mencken, *Happy Days.*
>
> H. G. Wells is the great exemplar, with his sociological studies wrapped in description and tied with a plot. In a sense, such stories are certainly to be regarded as a protest against truth-dodging, against cheap optimism, against "slacking," whether in literature or in life. But it would be equally just to call them another result of suppressed idealism, and to regard their popularity in America as proof of the argument which I have advanced in this essay. Excessively didactic literature is always a little unhealthy. In fresh periods, when life runs strong and both ideals and passions find ready issue into life, literature has no burdensome moral to carry. *It digests its moral. Homer digested his morals. They transfuse his epics. So did Shakespeare.* —Henry Seidel Canby, "Sentimental America," *Definitions.*

2. POSITION

Greater emphasis can often be attained by placing important words either at the beginning or the end of the sentence. Of the two positions, the end is usually the more important.

Weak	*More Emphatic*

Weak

Such qualities as strong legs and a good arm will open the eyes of a big league scout.

The history of English words is the history of our civilization in many ways.

There were several curious false dawns of the English novel before the eighteenth century.

Use Listerine Antiseptic, the *extra-careful* precaution which instantly sweetens and freshens the breath . . . helps keep it that way, too . . . not for seconds . . . not for minutes . . . but for hours, usually. —Advertisement in *Redbook.*

More Emphatic

Strong legs and a good arm will open the eyes of a big league scout.

The history of English words is, in many ways, the history of our civilization.

Of the English novel before the eighteenth century, there were several curious false dawns —Elizabeth Bowen, *English Novelists.*

Use Listerine Antiseptic, the extra-careful precaution which instantly sweetens and freshens the breath and helps keep it that way, not for seconds, not for minutes, but usually for hours.

After building up emphasis in several obvious ways—italicizing *extra-careful,* and separating phrases with fancy dots, and calculated parallelism—the copywriter lets the whole sentence peter out in a ludicrous anticlimax.

Of course, anticlimax may be used purposely for satiric or comic effect:

She was just seventeen; and deep was the impression left upon that budding organism by the young man's charm and goodness and accomplishments, and his large blue eyes and beautiful nose, and his sweet mouth and fine teeth. —Lytton Strachey, *Queen Victoria.*

It's the women who have made our college life the bright, happy thing it is—too bright, too happy. —Stephen Leacock, *Model Memoirs.*

The importance of final position must not be pushed too far. Inversions can be extremely awkward in English. Since we do not normally anticipate the end of sentences in conversation, the natural tendency is to put the main clause first. Sentences using this natural order, known technically as *loose sentences,* appear regularly in the best writing side by side with *periodic sentences,* which put the main clause last. Occasionally a long periodic sentence is effective. The writer of the following, well aware of the importance of final position, carefully builds up his suspense to a quietly understated climax:

> If we look at the buildings of the Cotswolds, at an Essex Village, at a Queen Anne country house, or at Chartres Cathedral, and then compare them with the typical products of this age and the last, petrol pumps and garages, bungalows and railway stations, miners' cottages and national schools, gas works and power stations and rich men's "follies," we must, I think, concede that ours is not an age that expresses itself easily in visual beauty. —C. E. M. Joad, "Value in the Modern World," *Return to Philosophy*.

But this kind of sentence must be handled with extreme care. Like other elaborate rhetorical devices, it too often suggests the synthetic bombast of old-fashioned oratory.

3. REPETITION

Used sparingly, conscious repetition can add emphasis within the sentence:

> I didn't like the swimming pool, I didn't like swimming, and I didn't like the swimming instructor, and after all these years I still don't. —James Thurber, "University Days," *My Life and Hard Times*.
>
> I had reported the Manchurian incident and the Shanghai incident and I had been in Peking to watch Japan provoke the Lukouchiao incident which enlarged into the final ironic euphemism, the China "incident." —Edgar Snow, *People on Our Side*.
>
> No race or religion or group or nationality can be permitted to assume that it has a monopoly of American history, and no race or religion or group or nationality can be permitted to feel that it is excluded, if political democracy is to survive. —Howard Mumford Jones, "Patriotism—But How?" *Atlantic Monthly*.

4. OPTIONAL PARALLELISM

Parallelism, which is sometimes required to avoid awkward shifts, can also be used for emphasis. But like repetition and the periodic sentence, it is a dangerous weapon in the hands of a novice. The day is past when words were weighed so carefully that a noun with three adjectives on one side of a conjunction could not possibly be balanced by a noun with only two on the other, and today's reader, more accustomed to the natural rhythms of easy conversation than to the contrived phrasing of formal rhetoric, is likely to be irritated by the pithy parallelism of Bacon's essays, the sonorous symmetry of Johnson's criticism, and the obvious balance of this sentence. But parallelism can give an epigrammatic finish to a short sentence:

> We believe that teachers should be fired
> ‖ not in blocks of three for political wrongness
> ‖ but in blocks of one for unfitness.
>
> —"The Talk of the Town," *New Yorker.*

It can be genuinely effective in a long sentence:

> All this— ‖ the disillusionment,
> the braggadocio,
> the ‖ advertised and
> ‖ cultivated emancipation from the ‖ ideas and
> ‖ conventions
> of the
> nineteenth
> century,
> ‖ the half-hearted hankering after strange foreign gods—
> was an indication that the spokesmen for the people of the United States
> ‖ were losing some of the old instinctive confidence in themselves,
> ‖ were no longer altogether sure ‖ of the high significance of
> the nation's history
> of the superiority of its
> institutions, or
> ‖ of the essential rightness
> of what the nation
> ‖ had done,
> ‖ was doing, or
> ‖ would in the future
> be doing.
>
> —Carl L. Becker, "What We Didn't Know Hurt Us a Lot," *Yale Review.*

But such an intricate balanced sentence is rare in informal writing today.

SUMMARY

The essential doctrine of this long chapter can be briefly summarized:

1. Write grammatically complete sentences unless the context justifies incomplete ones.

2. Combine clauses logically in accordance with the principles of coordination and subordination.

3. Relate each modifier clearly to the word it modifies.

4. Put parallel elements in parallel form.

5. Adjust the length of sentences to fit your purpose, avoiding primer prose and nonstop sentences.

6. Be economical, avoiding all unnecessary repetition.

7. Aim at variety in sentence length and form.

8. Aim at emphasis without sacrificing naturalness.

EXERCISES

I. Rewrite the following passage, eliminating all ineffective, incomplete sentences. If an incomplete sentence is acceptable, give your reason for retaining it:

A college dean once wrote that students come to college for one of three reasons. Culture, contacts, and careers. The student who comes for culture not knowing exactly what the word means. Although his conscience tells him that, whatever it is, it is a good thing to get. During the four-year course some culture-seekers learn something about the meaning of a liberal education. But not many. Most seniors in the liberal arts curriculum being as aimless as the freshmen. The student who comes to college for contacts has a clearer aim. To meet the fellow students who may be useful to him after graduation. His policy is based on the assumption that college friendships usually last forever. Whereas experience has proved that a large percentage do not survive beyond the first reunion. Few business executives caring if a man was a Rho Rho Rho at State unless he can produce. The career-minded student talks like this: "What price culture in a materialistic society conceived in competition and dedicated to the proposition that success is measured in dollars and cents? Can Shakespeare get you a job? A job teaching Shakespeare. Can poetry pay you a salary? Not unless you write singing commercials. Culture indeed!" So he assiduously avoids all courses without the ring of the cash register. Except perhaps one course in Turkish architecture. The most notorious snap course on the campus. And a year after graduation, he is embarrassed to discover that all his practical knowledge is already out of date. His boss becoming at the same time increasingly aware of his inability to read and write.

II.   (1) In each clause in the following sentences, pick out the subject and the verb.   (2) Classify each clause as dependent or independent.   (3) Classify each sentence as simple, compound, complex, or compound-complex.

1. Our generation is characterized by a tendency to exalt knowhow and ignore know-where and know-why.

2. One aim of a liberal education is to learn to distinguish between thinking and throbbing.

3. The Levites of the sacred ark of culture have failed to convince the average young American that three thousand years of human wisdom are at least as important in his life as three decades of technical progress.

4. Although pageantry may be one of the ingredients of drama, even Cecil B. De Mille should admit that performing elephants have a limited emotional gamut.

5. Americans being so fond of short cuts, few people were surprised when a state legislator suggested that pi be reduced to three flat to make geometry easier for school children.

6. Some educators argue that a coed should specialize in domestic science to prepare for marriage and motherhood, but others contend that, if she is given a broad education, she can meet and solve these problems successfully without academic training.

7. Many people would never notice the heat unless they were bothered constantly by neighbors asking if it is hot enough for them.

8. Part of the American equipment went across the Pacific to Korea, and the other part went across the Atlantic to arm Western Europe.

9. William James once argued that war could not be stopped until man had found a moral equivalent for it.

10. William Faulkner, considered by some to be the greatest living

American storyteller, writes sentences that make others unable to read him.

III. The following passages illustrate the errors in sentence structure discussed on pages 132–135: primer prose, false coordination, excessive coordination, upside-down subordination, and careless use of connectives. Rewrite them in accordance with the principles for effectively combining clauses.

1. Why was it that now that he had accomplished a thing he had always wanted to do that he wasn't enjoying it?

2. He dropped the needle in the meantime and couldn't find it, so his wife threaded another needle for him, and then he continued, but he was still cursing when I last saw him, and I wouldn't be surprised if he is cursing still.

3. He spent three years as a left fielder in the International League, and he has amassed a fortune of a hundred thousand dollars selling novelty items.

4. My name is George Curtis. I was born in Ashtabula, a city in northern Ohio. I was born on October 28, 1931. At the present time I am nineteen years of age. I am the last one of thirteen children born to my parents.

In my childhood only two happenings were interesting. Both of these happenings were tragedies. The first occurred to me when I was about three years of age. I almost lost the sight in one eye. It happened while a man was repairing our stairway. I was toddling up and down bothering him. All of a sudden I stepped on one end of a loose board. The other end had a nail in it. The nail struck my eye. The other happening occurred when I was ten years old. My father was killed by a railroad train. He was driving a truckload of stones across the tracks. I shall never forget that day. A neighbor brought the news to mother. She was standing over a washtub in the kitchen. She turned white as a sheet.

5. She was walking along the street when the gas tank exploded half a block away, crushing her against the wall.

6. Although he didn't paint very well, but he understood the technical fundamentals.

7. Mr. Truman met each problem and tried to settle it, but he had little success, for strikes started to spread, first in the coal industry, then in the steel industry, and finally a railroad strike was about to

break, and this was a little too much, for our country's industry was slowly coming to a standstill.

8. Marion joined a sorority in her sophomore year, and she studied hard, graduating with highest honors.

9. He has never read a book or taught a class, so that he is hardly a fit candidate for the presidency of the college.

10. There are already a number of boys and girls from Mauch Chunk in the orchestra, and the invitation for members is still out, and not only does this mean Mauch Chunk but all the communities in the area we are trying to serve, but everyone must be signed up at least a month before the first concert.

IV. Rewrite the following sentences, eliminating all dangling and misplaced modifiers:

1. Having lived seventeen years in a small Pennsylvania town, looking back to write an autobiography seems like reviewing the life of Henry Aldrich.

2. After being there for a while, mathematics and I became very close friends.

3. A point in favor of this philosophy is that you can put the men who have the welfare of the public in mind and who can better understand the people's problems into office.

4. Being a class officer several times, as well as captain of the basketball team, life in school was far from dull.

5. Homer Rich married the girl to whom he had been engaged for two years on Saturday night.

6. Here I worked in the drill press department, and after talking with some of the men and seeing a few accidents, the job quickly lost its glamour.

7. High-principled, good-natured, equipped with a brilliant mind, always trying to improve his teaching, I remember Mr. Horne as the best teacher in the school.

8. The lost jewelry was not valuable, a woman's necklace, and a two-headed man's snake ring with rubies for eyes, but it had a sentimental value.

9. Reading the essay on leadership, a good many experiences with army officers came to my mind.

10. I have often caught a bat while flying to and fro in our garden making an evening meal of insects.

11. While affixing a two-cent decalcomania tax stamp to cigarettes

for a tobacco wholesaler on Wednesday, the ring dropped into a carton and was swallowed in the channels of trade.

12. When only nine years old my father took me to Asbury Park to introduce me to the tawdry atmosphere of the Jersey shore.

13. He scowled at the man who had come into the room fiercely and coldly and told him to get out at once.

14. No one questions the authenticity of his account of Isadora Duncan, being the close friend of hers that he was.

15. Disguised as a popular song, I can enjoy a classical theme that I would scorn in its original setting.

16. The scene is pathetic because Cyrano is in love with Roxane, and, though posing as Christian, the words come from his heart.

17. I received first prize at an Atlantic City hotel for dressing up as Winston Churchill at a New Year's party when only seven years old.

18. He ran eagerly to where his aunt, a wizened old woman with a face like a rusty hatchet, stood.

19. Her favorite daughter was gored while picking daisies in a field by a bull.

20. First fed through an eye dropper, the nurses said that the baby was now out of danger.

V. Rewrite the following sentences, correcting all violations of parallelism:

1. For this exploit the people gratefully elected Napoleon first consul for life, and later he was proclaimed emperor by the Senate.

2. Without having to pass out too many cigars, I was elected to the presidency of four clubs, secretaryship of two others, class vice-president in my sophomore year, and president of the student council in my last academic year.

3. My decision was based both on the fact that the country was still at war, and also his record was better than his predecessor in office.

4. A young man may believe he is in love with a girl but actually be only infatuated or maybe his affections are based entirely on physical desire.

5. If anything is unsatisfactory, please notify the head waiter at once so that he can not only replace your order but also to make it possible for us to get at the source of the trouble in our kitchen.

6. I enjoyed playing football, running around the track, and was especially fond of tennis.

7. He said that either we must continue the war or negotiate an honorable peace.

8. I not only disagreed with him when he said my face was exactly like my father but also when he ascribed my success in school entirely to heredity.

9. If an engineer has no conception of the world in which he builds his bridges, distinction in the profession will probably not be attained.

10. Hitler succeeded for a time partly because of appeasement by other nations but also the Weimar Republic had been a failure.

VI. Break up the following passages into shorter sentences without omitting essential details or lapsing into primer prose:

1. At half-past nine on the morning of July 2, 1881, as President Garfield walked through the Baltimore and Potomac Railway Station on his way to take a train for Elberon, New Jersey, where his family had already gone, an assassin slipped up behind him and fired two shots from a forty-four caliber Navy revolver into his back, then turned to flee, leaving him fatally wounded and shocking a nation which only sixteen years before had been rocked to its foundation when a bullet from the gun of John Wilkes Booth killed Abraham Lincoln.

2. I am left-handed, which is not an unusual phenomenon, nor is is necessarily a handicap, but it has brought me more trouble than any other physical peculiarity I possess, and yet it helps in many different ways, so if I had the choice I would find it difficult to make up my mind whether to be left-handed or not, considering all my experiences as a southpaw.

3. He left on Monday, the sixteenth of September, shortly after I had received an old car from my mother in order to go back and forth to college, for my parents could not afford to have me live there, and I had resigned myself to four years of commuting, which sets me apart from the average student who lives in the fraternity and spends most of his spare time hanging around the college bookstore.

4. I was interested in soccer and competed for a place on the team, but because of nearsightedness without my glasses was unable to make the grade, though I did play in many of the interclass games, and our class won the intramural championship, but in spite of the fact that the members of the team received numerals, I was always jealous of the wearers of varsity letters, wondering constantly if I could have made the varsity if I hadn't inherited my father's vision.

5. The playwright's characters cannot be perfectly portrayed by words, neither can their speech be interpreted completely by actors, because they are complete only in the mind of the author, and his only method of conveying them is through the medium of words, which are elusive and unreliable, and in summary it may be said that no artist, whether in words, music, or painting, can exactly convey his conception of a character to another person.

VII. Rewrite the following sentences, making them as economical as possible without omitting essential details:

1. He died the next morning, April 15, 1865, at about seven A.M. in the morning.

2. I certainly agree with Gerald W. Johnson's essay on that point which he makes when he points out that the average person does not study the country's problems.

3. In my opinion I think no person should be allowed to vote until he is twenty-one years old.

4. Between the years 1932 and 1940 the national debt rose faster than it had ever risen before in the history of the nation.

5. The military training which I received was not of a sufficiently strict enough character to make me object strenuously or rebel.

6. In the following days my fellow classmates and I learned that there are three kinds of freshmen who are considered objectionable by sophomores.

7. Although I have lived a happy life in the eighteen years that I have been alive, in the case of my roommate the situation has been entirely different.

8. When you sail with the wind more speed can be had by the raising of the centerboard unless your boat is of the keel-type variety.

9. The main reason for the lack of observation on my part concerning the unusual use of atmosphere is that, though the story is not written by the author in the first person, it is told from the point of view of Frank Ashurst, who is the hero of the story.

10. This type of individual is more adequately described by the term "semantic dementia," for though the verbal use of words is possessed by the individual, the meaning and significance of language as such are completely ignored and overlooked.

11. In the characters we meet in *The Lower Depths* we can find no evidence of this disorder in any of the characters.

12. Miss Adelaide Pennyfeather, daughter of the Reverend and Mrs. Charles H. Pennyfeather, is at Camp Okachobee, Tomahawk, Wisconsin, where she is an instructor in the camp there for instruction in Sunday school work for girls.

13. I have been waiting in expectation for the sequel to that book to appear so that I could obtain a copy of that particular volume to continue on where the previous story left off.

14. Due to the fact that I had walked past her house three times without daring to ring the doorbell, I finally came to the realization that I was completely lacking in the self-assurance that was had by my competitor.

15. There are three factors which must be considered by the thinking citizens in the case of the Korean War.

VIII. Analyze the sentence structure in each of the following passages by answering these questions: (1) What is the average sentence length in each? (2) How many simple, compound, complex, and compound-complex sentences does each passage contain? (3) In which sentences does the writer use a phrase or subordinate clause before the subject? (4) What devices are used for emphasis? (5) To what extent are the differences in sentence structure among the passages justified by the context or the writer's apparent aim?

1. It is not too much to say, I think, that the language of the English Bible owes its distinctive qualities, and that perhaps in no unequal measure, on the one hand to the vast desert spaces and wide skies of the hither Orient, and on the other to the open seas and rock-bound coasts of England. Nor do I mean that in the least as a mere figure of speech. For at the beginning of the long chain of development which makes the very language of the English Bible what it is are the men who, beside the rivers of Babylon and Egypt, or among the hills and pasture lands of Israel and Judah, or in the wide stillness of Arabia, brooded and wondered and dreamed, and left a language simple and sensuous and steeped in the picturesque imagery of what they saw and felt. At the end of this same chain of causes are the theatres of Shakespeare's London and the ships of the Elizabethan voyagers—of men whose language was as virile and vivid as their lives. And between are the seventy at Alexandria and Jerome in his desert—Greece and Rome between Mesopotamia and England. How did the elements

fuse?   —John Livingston Lowes, "The Noblest Monument of English Prose," *Essays in Appreciation.*

2. When the life has entirely gone out of a work of art come down to us from the past, when we read it without any emotional comprehension whatsoever and can no longer even imagine why the people for whom it was intended found it absorbing and satisfying, then, of course, it has ceased to be a work of art at all and has dwindled into one of those deceptive "documents" from which we get a false sense of comprehending through the intellect things which cannot be comprehended at all except by means of a kinship of feeling. And though all works from a past age have begun in this way to fade there are some, like the great Greek or Elizabethan tragedies, which are still halfway between the work of art and the document. They no longer can have for us the immediacy which they had for those to whom they originally belonged, but they have not yet eluded us entirely. We no longer live in the world which they represent, but we can half imagine it and we can measure the distance which we have moved away. We write no tragedies today, but we can still talk about the tragic spirit of which we would, perhaps, have no conception were it not for the works in question.   —Joseph Wood Krutch, "The Tragic Fallacy," *The Modern Temper.*

3. Babbitt moaned, turned over, struggled back toward his dream. He could see only her face now, beyond misty waters. The furnace-man slammed the basement door. A dog barked in the next yard. As Babbitt sank blissfully into a dim warm tide, the paper-carrier went by whistling, and the rolled-up *Advocate* thumped the front door. Babbitt roused, his stomach constricted with alarm. As he relaxed, he was pierced by the familiar and irritating rattle of some one cranking a Ford: snap-ah-ah, snap-ah-ah, snap-ah-ah. Himself a pious motorist, Babbitt cranked with the unseen driver, with him waited through taut hours for the roar of the starting engine, with him agonized as the roar ceased and again began the infernal patient snap-ah-ah—a round, flat sound, a shivering cold-morning sound, a sound infuriating and inescapable. Not til the rising voice of the motor told him that the Ford was moving was he released from the panting tension. He glanced once at his favorite tree, elm twigs against the gold patina of sky, and fumbled for sleep as for a drug. He who had been a boy very credulous of life was no longer greatly interested in the possible and improbable adventures of each new day.   —Sinclair Lewis, *Babbitt.*

4. One of the most fabulous characters in that war theatre was

Lieutenant Rudolf Charles von Ripper. He was so fabulous, a man might have been justified in thinking him a phony until he got to know him. I had known him since the previous summer in Algeria. Most of the other correspondents knew him. One whole fighting infantry division knew him. He was no phony.

Von Ripper was the kind they write books about. He was born in Austria. His father was a general in the Imperial Austrian Army, his mother a baroness. They had money. He could have had a rich, formal, royal type of existence. Instead he ran away from home at fifteen, worked in the sawmills, collected garbage, was a coal miner for a while, and then a clown in a small travelling circus. At nineteen he went into the French Foreign Legion, served two years, and was wounded in action. After that he went back to Europe and studied art. He was first of all an artist.

He travelled continuously. He lived in London and Paris. He lived in Shanghai during 1928. Then he returned to Berlin, joined liberal groups, and did occasional cartoons. Because he helped friends hiding from the Nazis, he was arrested in 1933, accused of high treason and sent to a concentration camp. Dollfuss of Austria got him out after seven months. Then he went to the Balearic Islands off the coast of Spain and hibernated for a year, doing political, satiric drawing.
—Ernie Pyle, *Brave Men.*

5. It was about one o'clock when Paul's mother and father drove up to their house. All was still. Paul's mother went to her room and slipped off her white fur coat. She had told her maid not to wait up for her. She heard her husband downstairs, mixing a whiskey and soda.

And then, because of the strange anxiety at her heart, she stole upstairs to her son's room. Noiselessly she went along the upper corridor. Was there a faint noise? What was it?

She stood, with arrested muscles, outside his door, listening. There was a strange, heavy, and yet not loud noise. Her heart stood still. It was a soundless noise, yet rushing and powerful. Something huge, in violent, hushed motion. What was it? What in God's name was it? She felt that she knew the noise. She knew what it was.

Yet she could not place it. She couldn't say what it was. And on and on it went, like a madness.

Softly, frozen with anxiety and fear, she turned the door-handle.

The room was dark. Yet in the space near the window, she heard and saw something plunging to and fro. She gazed in fear and amazement.

Then suddenly she switched on the light, and saw her son, in his green pyjamas, madly surging on the rocking-horse. The blaze of light suddenly lit him up, as he urged the wooden horse, and lit her up, as she stood, blonde, in her dress of pale green and crystal, in the doorway.

"Paul!" she cried. "Whatever are you doing?"

"It's Malabar!" he screamed, in a powerful, strange voice. "It's Malabar!" —D. H. Lawrence, "The Rocking-horse Winner," *The Portable D. H. Lawrence.*

IX. Rewrite the following sentences to make them more emphatic:

1. I hope that the great ship comes home safely after the war with all our boys from foreign soil and that she once again becomes the luxury liner of the seas and has all her beautiful ornaments replaced.

2. Little did the leaders of the temperance drive know that during the meeting that week there was a half case of the honey-flavored beer in the back closet of their clubhouse as I found to my surprise.

3. The Atlantic Charter is one of the most significant documents of the twentieth century for a number of reasons.

4. Communism is a religion, not merely an economic theory, to many of its followers.

5. I was so excited that I started to tremble when the colonel announced that our outfit would probably move up to the front lines in two weeks or thereabouts.

6. I saw three spotted fawns two nights ago under the tree across the road.

7. They finally decided on a separation after seven years of continual bickering over issues that were trivial to say the least.

8. I didn't expect to win first prize and hear my name read over the radio by the Governor himself, though I felt I had done reasonably well for a beginner, considering the odds, law of averages, etc.

9. Communism cannot be abolished from the globe as long as poverty exists, according to the speaker.

10. He argued that the people of the United States are obligated to help in Asia's fight against death, disease, and squalor.

X. (General review) Rewrite the following sentences, correcting each mistake in sentence structure and giving a reason for your correction:

1. Having played magnificently through four strenuous sets, two foot faults called at the beginning of the fifth threw him off his game.

2. The speaker maintained that either we had to fight for liberty as our forefathers had done or bow the knee to a foreign conqueror.

3. Although he had never taken a course in economics, but he was always throwing around such terms as *unearned increment* and *marginal utility* as if he had invented them.

4. Having successfully completed a four-year course in business administration, I started looking for a job, but I found that employers in general were less interested in the labels of the courses I had taken and the kind of degree I had after my name than in my general record, which, I must admit, left something to be desired, and I was discouraged when some of them hired classmates of mine who had taken the straight liberal arts course which I had considered so useless, so my philosophy of education has changed now that my formal education is all finished.

5. His uncle was a vice-president of a plastic corporation, and he played golf in the low seventies.

6. It was maintained by the chairman of the committee that on account of the fact that there were several factors of importance meetings should be held once a week during the year.

7. The mayor asked the critics of his administration what they had done during the months when they had been complaining so violently to help the city.

8. Out in the marshes, standing on one slender leg, I like to watch the stately blue herons.

9. He said that you couldn't win an election without building a good organization, writing an ambiguous platform, and unless you wandered up and down the state talking to all the little people.

10. The instructor said that until I could learn to solve problems in elementary arithmetic accurately without mistakes, calculus could not be passed.

11. One morning my father was shaving when the news was brought by my mother that Fred had been killed by a truck during an overnight hike at the camp he was attending.

12. The coroner decided that, though a large dose of sleeping pills had been taken by the victim before retiring, that death could not have been caused by that alone.

13. While sitting on the porch at the club, the finalists in the tournament made their approach shots to the eighteenth green.

14. Not only was the play a box office success but also an artistic triumph.

15. The stock market crash in 1929 wiped my father out practically.

16. Never having seen a play until he was over twenty-one, it was a miracle that at the age of twenty-five he should write *Torrents of Flame,* which was acclaimed by the critics as the best new play of the season and put him in the front rank of the younger playwrights, and even though his subsequent plays, *Tides of Destiny* and *Westward the Course,* have not lived up to this early promise, the first triumph cannot be ignored in any final assessment of his contribution to the theater.

17. Although football is supposed to build men, there are few players who survive four years of college ball without acquiring a trick knee, a bad shoulder, or maybe they become the victims of an even more serious handicap as a lifetime souvenir.

18. Shakespeare willed his "second-best bed" to his wife, to whom he had been married for thirty-four years, according to the biographers.

19. He gave three reasons for his stand as follows: (1) that the law violated the spirit if not the letter of the First Amendment to the Constitution; (2) its being unenforceable; (3) the likelihood that it would be used by many as an excuse for promoting hysteria.

20. Balked by the school board in his efforts to expel Mr. Lake, his next move was to begin a campaign of slanderous rumors.

CHAPTER SIX

Punctuation

> An ideal punctuation system . . . should indicate much more clearly than our own the attitude, the mood, even the tone of voice, of the writer.
>
> —Isaac Goldberg.

> The comma was just a nuisance. If you got the thing as a whole, the comma kept irritating you all along the line.
>
> —Gertrude Stein.

Punctuation is a delicate art that has defied the best-laid plans of grammarians to convert it into an exact science. In the two centuries since man's first attempts to domesticate the elusive comma in a rule book, he has devised innumerable systems of punctuation, but the best are only rough facsimiles of actual usage. Personal preference still plays a large role. Many authorities feel that the modern tendency toward *open* punctuation is a distinct gain over the cautious *close* punctuation which peppered the pages of our ancestors with commas and semicolons; others are afraid that too strict an economy may plunge the language into chaos. One writer is fascinated by the power of the comma to convey the most subtle nuances of rhythm and feeling; another treats the comma as a routine signpost whose main virtue is to keep the reader from making a wrong turn; a third (and the third is not necessarily Gertrude Stein) disdains it as an irritating nuisance.

To concede these differences in the theory and practice of experts is not to give the college undergraduate a free ticket of admission to the Confetti School of Punctuation. The student of this popular school handles punctuation marks by the gross. Having scrawled a first draft in blissful disregard of the rule book, he becomes uneasily aware that he "has not put in enough commas." Whereupon he takes a random handful, with an occasional colon or semicolon intermixed, and throws them like confetti at the paper, letting them fall almost where they may. The *almost* means that he may have one or two false principles to misguide him—such as always to toss in one comma before *and* and to bracket *however* with a pair. When the teacher points out that this comma is superfluous and that one downright confusing, he admits humbly that he "has put in too many commas." It is all vaguely quantitative and thoroughly unreasonable.

RULES AND REASONS

Despite the variety in practice, there are reasons for punctuation. Some of the conventions, to be sure, are hard to defend without falling back on tradition. There is probably no good reason, for example, why we should still put a comma between *St. Louis* and *Missouri* when every mature reader knows where the city ends and the state begins. On the other hand, most of the important "rules" have evolved from man's honest efforts *to make reading easier.*

According to some teachers, punctuation is merely grammar-made-graphic. Others contend that it can be reduced to a table of pauses and stresses like the rests and crescendos in music. Does a period mean, "This is the end of a sentence" or "Come to a full stop, please"? Does an exclamation mark mean, "You have reached the end of an exclamatory sentence" or "Please register surprise here"? Or both? Such academic questions can be evaded by admitting that the average experienced writer does nine tenths of his punctuating automatically without minding the why and wherefore. The exceptional undergraduate who has read widely and wisely may punctuate well by ear. But the average student's grasp of the unmysterious mysteries of commas and semicolons is in direct proportion to his understanding of grammar and sentence structure. It is not very helpful to tell a student to "put in commas where the natural pauses come" if he pauses naturally in the middle of every strange new polysyllabic word. Moreover, the trained reader with the keenest ear for prose rhythms does not necessarily pause when he sees a comma or come to a full stop when confronted by a period. He may speed right through a comma and acknowledge the stop sign by merely shifting swiftly into second or tapping lightly on the brake pedal. The schoolboy formula that a comma is a green light, a semicolon an amber light, and a period a red light is too neat to be more than half true. A thorough understanding of a handful of more explicit rules is better for the beginner.

Remember, however, that the rules here are conventions based on usage. Remember also that understanding is not memorizing or unthinking obedience. Understand the *reasons behind the rules,* and you will begin to feel the distinction between the illiterate violations that cause confusion and sensible deviations that may herald progress.

THE COMMA

The comma has five main uses: (1) to separate main clauses; (2) to set off introductory clauses and phrases; (3) to set off nonessential elements; (4) to separate parts of a series; (5) to avoid ambiguity.

1. TO SEPARATE MAIN CLAUSES

a. A comma is ordinarily used in a compound sentence before the coordinating conjunction (*and, but, for, or,* and *nor*):

It is well known that shipboard food is several cuts above shore-based food, and this consideration was perhaps a factor in Miss Williamson's ready acceptance.   —Thomas Heggen, *Mister Roberts.*

b. The comma is often omitted in this construction, especially if the sentence is short:

There is but one thing more red-blooded than poetry and that is life itself.   —Gordon Keith Chalmers, "Poetry and General Education," *College English Association Chapbook.*

She lived over by Reading and probably her folks had to tie her to get shoes on her.   —William Allen White, Emporia *Gazette.*

Beware, however, of omitting the comma before *but* and *for* in a compound sentence. The reader is entitled to a warning that the connective is a conjunction introducing a clause, not a preposition introducing a phrase:

> He did not go, for George was already on his way home. (conjunction)
> He did not go for George. (preposition)

c. If the conjunction is omitted from a compound sentence or replaced by a conjunctive adverb or transitional phrase (*however, moreover, nevertheless, therefore, in fact, as a matter fact, on the other hand,* and so on), the comma is ordinarily replaced by a semicolon:

> John loved Mary, but she loved a non-Greek named Homer.
> John loved Mary; she loved a non-Greek named Homer.
> John loved Mary; however, she loved a non-Greek named Homer.

The Comma Fault

If the writer had used a comma instead of the semicolon in either of the last two samples, he would have been guilty of the *comma fault* (or *comma splice* or *comma blunder*). Student themes are crawling with comma faults:

> In the Victorian age a woman was expected to stay in the home, cooking, cleaning, dusting, and looking after the children were her solemn duties.
> The device of separate ballots is being used in some states, however, it is time we decided what officials are to be elected and what ones are to be appointed.

But reputable professional writers offer similar deviations:

> I do not desire to drive Europe out of the colleges, I merely insist upon the necessity of putting America in. —Howard Mumford Jones, "The American Scholar Once More," *Atlantic Monthly*.
> Trade journals delight in them, public speakers and political hacks would be helpless without them. —Bernard De Voto, "The Easy Chair," *Harper's Magazine*.

The question is: When is a comma fault a fault? And the harassed student's answer might be: When it is committed by a student in a composition course. Obviously the problem cannot be solved honestly by a single dogmatic rule. The choice of a comma depends on these intangibles: (1) the relation of the clauses; (2) the length and rhythm of the sentence; (3) the subject matter (for the reader needs less punctuation in a rapid-fire narrative than in a closely knit argument). Rule or no rule, the reader must not be misled.

Now look again at the samples. Either of the first two sentences might throw anybody for a loss. The reader of the first might logically assume that *cooking, cleaning, dusting* and *looking* are participles modifying woman, and that the sentence ended with *children*. When he came to the second verb, *were,* he would be naturally confused. The simple substitution of a semicolon after *home* would make the unbalanced construction clear. The trouble in the second sentence is with the word *however.* When the trained reader sees this squinting connective bracketed by commas, he instinctively regards it as a parenthetical word looking back at a previous sentence. For it is commonly used this way as a transition between sentences. Omitting the comma after *however* may help. But a semicolon (or even a period) before *however* makes it immediately clear that this word actually introduces the second independent clause of a compound sentence. Notice the same difference in these illustrations:

Clear: The circus is coming to town. I am not excited, however, about educated pachyderms.

Clear: The circus is coming to town. I am not excited; however, I shall probably go.

Confusing: The circus is coming to town. I am not excited, however, I shall probably go.

The two samples from Jones and De Voto are chosen to make it clear that the letter of the strict comma fault rule can be violated without ambiguity, especially in a crisp, balanced construction. Here the relation of the two clauses is close *both in thought and structure.* These sentences, containing so-called *contact clauses,* are as lucid as the other two are confusing.

Experienced writers often use a comma where the brevity and symmetry of the sentence are not so obvious:

His image was simply always present in more or less degree, he was sometimes nearer the surface of her thoughts, the pleasantest, the only really pleasant thought she had.   —Katherine Anne Porter, *Pale Horse, Pale Rider.*

The disaster left the Nazis strategically bankrupt, from then on men who never believed in victory by defensive operations were obliged to improvise a means of salvation.   —Edgar Snow, *People on Our Side.*

I thought of all the men who had lived here and left the visible traces of their spirit and conceived extraordinary things, I thought of the dead child.   —Aldous Huxley, *Young Archimedes.*

If one of them writes a note it is rounded with a graceful phrase, their most extempore speeches are turned with a flourish of rotund rhetoric.   —Lord David Cecil, *The Young Melbourne.*

But this freedom is not recommended for the unseasoned writer. When a comma fault makes trouble, it still makes real trouble. This is a safe general rule:

When two main clauses in a compound sentence are not joined by a coordinating conjunction (and, but, for, or, nor), do not separate them with only a comma unless they are brief and balanced. When in doubt, play safe and use a semicolon.

2. TO SET OFF INTRODUCTORY CLAUSES AND PHRASES

a. A comma is frequently used to set off introductory clauses and phrases preceding the main clause. This comma is essential to avoid confusion when it is not clear where the introductory element ends; it is welcome when the introductory expression is long:

Confusing: A short while after I visited the school and decided Peddie was the place for me. (Without the comma following *after,* the reader might be misled into assuming that a subordinate clause ends with *school.*)

Confusing: The planes having passed over George lay in the ditch cursing his luck. (Without the comma after *over,* the *absolute phrase* would probably be read: The planes having passed over George.)

Clear: But whenever I start to talk about the South Pacific, people intervene.   —James Michener, *Tales of the South Pacific.* (The omission of the comma might imply, if only momentarily, that he is going to talk about the South Pacific people.)

Clear: With the women who hadn't been sensible and had taken love too seriously, John Bidlake had been ruthlessly cruel. —Aldous Huxley, *Point Counter Point.* (a long phrase)

b. After a short introductory clause or phrase, where there is no danger of ambiguity, the comma is often omitted:

When his first wife called for Lucy's banquet he had pulled a long face. —Glenway Wescott, *The Pilgrim Hawk.*

Apart from a few plays of Shakespeare nobody gave me anything good to read until I was a sophomore in college. —Robert Maynard Hutchins, "Education for Freedom," *Harper's Magazine.*

3. TO SET OFF NONESSENTIAL ELEMENTS

The term *nonessential* is a general adjective applied here to words or groups of words which interrupt the flow of the sentence or are not closely related to its central thought. The list includes nonrestrictive modifiers, transitional words and phrases, mild interjections, words in direct address, interrupters in dialogue, and other interrupters. If one of these elements comes in mid-sentence, it is isolated with *two* commas.

a. *Nonrestrictive vs. Restrictive Modifiers*

A nonrestrictive modifier (clause, phrase, or word) is set off by commas; a restrictive modifier is not:

Nonrestrictive: John B. Throckmorton III, *who does not understand the principles of punctuation,* will not recognize the nonrestrictive clause in this sentence.

Restrictive: A student *who understands the principles of punctuation* will recognize the restrictive clause in this sentence.

Notice the difference. In the first sentence the subject has already been restricted on being named (there is presumably only one John B. Throckmorton III), and the clause that follows merely supplies additional information. It can restrict him no further; it is nonrestrictive. In the second sentence, the clause *who understands the principles of punctuation* is needed to restrict the general subject *a student* to a special kind of student. Take another pair of examples:

Nonrestrictive: He ran toward Wilbur, *who had observed the flight.*

Restrictive: A college professor is not usually a man *with more than one car.*

Observe that the nonrestrictive clause in the first sentence can be deleted without appreciably altering the meaning (*He ran toward Wilbur*). The removal of the restrictive phrase in the second completely changes the writer's point (*A college professor is not usually a man*). In other words, a nonrestrictive modifier is *nonessential;* a restrictive modifier is *essential.* A student may see the difference more clearly by applying these less technical terms.

To put it another way, a restrictive modifier limits the scope of the word it modifies. The name *Wilbur* identifies a specific person and is therefore not further limited by the nonrestrictive clause which follows. On the other hand, *man* is specifically limited to a particular group of men (those with more than one car) by the restrictive phrase which modifies it.

Often the choice of punctuation involves a choice of radically different meanings:

Restrictive: Women who can't keep secrets should never be told about their husbands' business affairs.

Nonrestrictive: Women, who can't keep secrets, should never be told about their husbands' business affairs.

The same sentence, but two commas make the difference between caution and woman-hating.

An *appositive* can also be classed as restrictive or nonrestrictive:

Restrictive: Charles *the First* was executed in 1649.

Restrictive: The fact *that punctuation cannot completely cure a sick sentence* is overlooked by many students.

Nonrestrictive: Joe Louis, *the fabulous brown bomber,* had passed his peak.

Nonrestrictive: Even in this, *the most pessimistic of his books,* Orwell does not run away into otherworldliness. —V. S. Pritchett, New York *Times Book Review.*

Students are more likely to set off restrictive modifiers than to omit the commas from around nonrestrictive ones. Many students will settle for a single comma when the construction demands two. Remember always that *when a clause or phrase comes in mid-sentence the choice is between two commas and none.*

b. *Other Nonessential Elements*

Transitional expressions: The doctor said, *however,* that the patient would recover. *As a matter of fact,* he predicted that Sam would be back at work on Monday. The fever, *nevertheless,* continued unabated. *Also* strange new symptoms appeared. (As in the last sentence, the punctuation is often omitted if the expression does not appreciably interrupt the flow.)

Mild interjections: Well, let me try it just once. *Oh,* I don't think I need your help. *Why,* it's really easy.

Words in direct address: Gentlemen, you come along with me. *George,* you stay here. As for you, *Joe,* suit yourself.

Interrupters in dialogue: "After all," *he said bitterly,* "we can't achieve peace if we assume that war is inevitable."

Other interrupters: This is not, *if I understand the gentleman's argument,* the most logical defense of his position.

Undergraduates are, *on the whole,* eager to be taught how to write but slow to learn.

The elder, *banished to a village parsonage while his brother entered Parliament and laid claim to the lapsed d'Eyncourt barony by way of maternal descent,* transferred his ambition to his sons. Emery Neff, New York *Times Book Review.*

4. TO SEPARATE PARTS OF A SERIES

a. Commas are used to set off words, phrases, and clauses in a series. (When the parts of a series are long, semicolons are often used—see page 182.):

The room was dark, damp, and dreary. (words)

Lincoln was not the first to speak of government of the people, by the people, and for the people. (phrases)

But American men still ate too much meat, ate it too often, and did not balance it with sufficient fruit and vegetables.   —D. W. Brogan, *The American Character.* (clauses)

b. Although the traditional formula retains the comma before *and* in a series, many writers do without it:

He suggested to his listeners the cry of the wildcat, the falling of trees in the forest and the thunderous tread of the buffalo herd on the prairie.   —Van Wyck Brooks, *The World of Washington Irving.*

Sometimes authorities argue that the omission of the comma before the conjunction suggests a closer relation between the last two items than between other parts of the series. Obviously the comma should be omitted if the final pair is as inseparable as *ham and eggs* or *Gilbert and Sullivan.* In other contexts the choice makes no real difference as long as the writer is consistent.

c. When more than one conjunction appears in a series, commas are usually omitted before conjunctions:

Before the dawn of progressive education students learned reading and writing and 'rithmetic.

From time to time they made up packages to Jefferson, antelope skins and skeletons, plants and roots, wolf skeletons, deer-horns, weasel skins and buffalo robes, a foxskin, bows and arrows and painted Indian robes and pottery.   —Van Wyck Brooks, *The World of Washington Irving.*

d. Like other words in a series, coordinate adjectives are usually set off by commas:

Coordinate: She wore a *long, sheer, glittering* gown.
Not coordinate: A *good big* man is better than a *good little* man.

In the first example *long, sheer,* and *glittering* receive equal emphasis as modifiers of *gown.* In the second sentence *big man* and *little man* are treated as two-word nouns. Thus the difference between a *smelly old pipe* and a *smelly, old pipe* is one of emphasis; in the first the emphasis is largely on its odor, in the second, it is equally distributed between odor and age.

There is a tendency in modern writing to omit commas even between coordinate adjectives:

Yesterday there had been two pairs of legs dangling, on either side of her typewriter, both pairs stuffed thickly into funnels of *dark expensive-looking material.* —Katherine Anne Porter, *Pale Horse, Pale Rider.*

5. TO AVOID AMBIGUITY

Regardless of the other rules, use a comma wherever it is necessary to avoid ambiguity. Notice how a comma can come to the assistance of the reader in each of the following:

Confusing: In the days that followed George and Mary saw a lot of each other. (The days are following George and Mary.)
Clear: In the days that followed, George and Mary saw a lot of each other.
Confusing: Inside the horses were eagerly awaiting the big day. (We are taken inside the horses.)
Clear: Inside, the horses were eagerly awaiting the big day.
Confusing: He told the student to come now and again the following week. (To come now and again?)
Clear: He told the student to come now, and again the following week.

6. SOME MISCELLANEOUS USES

Commas are also used conventionally in the following ways:

a. *To separate day and year in dates:*

December 7, 1941

But the comma is optional when no day is given:

December, 1941, or December 1941

b. *To separate places in addresses:*

Ottumwa, Iowa   Moscow, Russia

c. *To separate names from titles or degrees:*

George V. Denny, Jr.   George Lyman Kittredge, A.B.
Alexander Throttlebottom, Vice President

d. *To set off quotations, especially short ones:*

It was Mr. Cobb who remarked, upon hearing that his city editor was ill, "Nothing trivial, I hope." —Heywood Broun, *It Seems to Me.*

e. *After salutations in friendly letters:*

Dear Harry,

and after complimentary closes in all letters:

Sincerely yours,
Douglas

THE SEMICOLON

There are two common uses of the semicolon, both of them already mentioned in the discussion of the comma:

1. Between main clauses
2. Between parts of a series

1. BETWEEN MAIN CLAUSES

a. A semicolon is used to separate main clauses in a compound sentence when the conjunction is omitted or replaced by a conjunctive adverb (see page 173):

The face was black, smooth, impenetrable; the eyes had seen too much. —William Faulkner, *Go Down Moses.*

He wrote for the public, not for the learned journals; hence he was spared the necessity of becoming a pedant. —Theodore Morrison, "Dover Beach Revisited," *Harper's Magazine.*

b. A semicolon is used in a compound sentence before the coordinating conjunctions (*and, but, for, or,* and *nor*) when the clauses are unusually long or the writer wishes to emphasize the pause between them:

In the next chapter of history, China will be open all around, from the land as well as from the sea; for the times in which we are now living no longer respect the isolation of China or of any other country. —O. and E. Lattimore, *The Making of Modern China.*

I watch with fascinated surprise the baby, finger in mouth, grow into the politician, tongue in cheek; but I find nothing either fascinating or surprising in the discovery that the cynicism of the politician has matured into the pomposity of the Cabinet Minister. —A. A. Milne, *Autobiography*.

2. BETWEEN PARTS OF A SERIES

A semicolon is used to separate parts of a series, especially when the parts are long and contain commas within them:

> The important thing is that I got through my head at an early age a few simple truths: that the proper reading of a good writer requires energy and application; that reading is not mere "diversion"; that it is impossible to admire writing you do not understand; that understanding it does not destroy but rather enhances its beauty; that unless a writer's mind is superior to, more complicated than, your own, it is a bore to read him. —Clifton Fadiman, "My Life Is an Open Book," *Reading I've Liked*.

> To name a few that I can think of as I write, there was the Pig Woman, witness in the Hall-Mills murder inquest; the Woman in Red, who betrayed Dillinger to the Law; the Bobbed-Hair Bandit, a lady stickup man of the twenties; the Broadway Butterfly, who was strangled to death in 1924; and the Black Dahlia, a young woman unpleasantly done in about a year ago in Los Angeles. —A. J. Liebling, "Horsefeathers Swathed in Mink," *New Yorker*.

A student must avoid treating the semicolon with the special affection of a child for a new toy. To the conscious stylist whose prose reveals subtle cadences and delicate balancing feats the semicolon may be indispensable. But its indiscriminate use tends to blot out useful distinctions:

> Pessimism is at best an emotional half-holiday; joy is the uproarious labour by which all things live . . . . The explanation is simple; he is standing on his head; which is a very weak pedestal to stand on . . . . Christianity satisfies suddenly and perfectly man's ancestral instinct for being the right way up; satisfies it supremely in this; that by its creed joy becomes something gigantic and sadness something special and small. —G. K. Chesterton, *Autobiography*.

Orthodox editing would probably allow Chesterton his first semicolon and replace the others respectively with a colon, a comma, a comma, and a colon. The famous master of the paradox is not the only writer to use the semicolon with such carefree abandon.

On the other hand, Anatole France viewed it disdainfully as a "bastard period." The inexperienced student would do well to strike a happy medium by limiting himself to the two main uses discussed here.

THE COLON

A single rule summarizes all the important uses of the colon: A colon is used to anticipate something that immediately follows. It may introduce

1. A formal series—with or without *as follows* or *the following:*

He used the following arguments: that big-time football did more harm than good to the players; that it did not support the rest of the athletic program; and that it was intended primarily to appease the alumni, entertain the trustees, and provide a spectacle for the general public.

2. An illustration or explanation:

He was a brilliant entrepreneur, the little man: he used to point with pride to the ceilings of the skyscraper in which he had his office, saying, "That ceiling is a good six inches shallower than the law allows." —Vincent Sheean, *Personal History.*

Teaching in America is a twenty-four hour job, twelve months in the year: sabbatical leaves are provided so you can have your coronary thrombosis off the campus. —Jacques Barzun, *Teacher in America.*

3. A quotation, often long or rather formal:

There is a certain American magazine which sends out slips for its contributors' guidance, stating: "Humor, tragedy and pathos are acceptable, but not stories that are morbid or that leave the reader uncomfortable." —Elizabeth Drew, *The Modern Novel.* (Longer quotations are indented in a separate paragraph—see page 360.)

4. The body of a business letter:

Dear Sir:
    We have received your order for four jumbo self-lathering windshield wipers.

Except in beginning a business letter or introducing a quotation of one or more complete sentences, a colon may be followed by either a small letter or a capital. The capital is more common when a complete sentence follows the colon. It is superfluous to supplement the colon with a dash (:—).

THE PERIOD

1. A period is used at the end of a sentence that is neither a direct question nor a strong exclamation:

This use of the period after a complete sentence need hardly be illustrated.

A period is also used after an incomplete sentence. This one, for example.

He asked when the St. Louis Browns were going to stop losing ball games. (No question mark after an *indirect* question.)

2. A period is used after abbreviations:

A.B. M.A. Ph.D. C.O.D. Mr.

But others, names of government bureaus, institutions, and common technical terms, for example, often do without it: FBI, OPA, USC, rpm

3. A period is sometimes used after a request in the form of a question, as in a business letter:

Will you kindly send a check with your reply. (A question mark here would be considered slightly more formal.)

4. Three periods are used to indicate an omission from a quotation; when the omission comes at the end of a sentence, a fourth period (or question mark or exclamation point) is added:

"Fourscore and seven years ago our fathers brought forth . . . a new nation . . . ."

THE QUESTION MARK

1. A question mark is used after a direct question or to show that a statement of fact is open to question:

Where were you on the night of March 14, 1937?
That was a close call, wasn't it?
Thomas Dekker's dates are 1570?–1632.

2. A question mark is not used after an indirect question:

Indirect question: I asked why he insisted on dating my girl.
Direct question: I asked: "Why do you insist on dating my girl?"

3. It is juvenile to use a question mark in parentheses to label irony or wit:

Juvenile: When it comes to giving out with the French I am the brightest (?) *garçon* in the whole class.

THE EXCLAMATION POINT

The exclamation point (or mark) is used to emphasize an emotion—wonder, surprise, admiration—or put starch into a command:

Ah! What a beautiful beverage!
He gazed out incredulously. "No trees, just nothingness! It's like going through an endless cloud. Imagine living here! Imagine wanting to conquer this place! Imagine *trying* to conquer this place!" —Edgar Snow, *People On Our Side.*
"Blow this joint or I'll drill you!" exclaimed Lefty.

An exclamation often identifies itself without a label: an *ah* may be open-mouthed enough when followed by an unassuming comma. Like the boy in the fable who cried wolf, the effervescent fashion editor or the movie ad man can shriek *exclamation* once too often. This sort of shouting punctuation, in which the exclamation point is often accompanied by other artificial aids to emphasis, can quickly bludgeon a mature reader into apathy:

No wonder the Literary Guild Book Club is the world's largest, with almost a million members!
Including the free Bonus Books, a Guild membership saves you up to 50% of your book dollars—and you get the *new books you don't want to miss!* Why not join *now* while you can get the TWO exciting bestsellers shown here FREE with membership—plus your copy of "Let Love Come Last" as your first selection! Mail the coupon now! —Advertisement in *Redbook.*

And, of course, the familiar device of exploding a single sentence with exclamation points in duplicate or triplicate (Zowie!!!) should be confined to the comic books.

QUOTATION MARKS
(See pages 359–361)

1. Quotation marks are used to enclose words quoted directly from either speech or writing:

"How did you come to college this year, Mr. Bolenciecwcz?" asked the professor. "*Chuff*a chuffa, *chuff*a chuffa."

"M' father sent me," said the football player.

"What on?" asked Bassum.

"I git an 'lowance," said the tackle, in a low, husky voice, obviously embarrassed. —James Thurber, "University Days," *My Life and Hard Times.*

In a recent speech before the New England College English Association, Ludwig Lewisohn paid tribute to America's "half-pathetic faith in education." Although he admitted that many of the two million students in our colleges have "slipped into college through the too large meshes of a fraudulent net," he asserted hopefully: "Enough and more than enough remain to be persuaded to some measure of disinterestedness, some not wholly superficial sense of the meaning of value, some freedom from the servitude to materialistic superstition, some feeling of responsibility for the culture of their country, some aspiration beyond the collection of fees and the multiplication of vain devices."

If the final quotation in the preceding paragraph were any longer—that is, longer than about five lines—it would be indented and single-spaced in a separate paragraph *without* quotation marks (see page 360).

2. Quotation marks are *not* used around an indirect quotation:

Direct quotation: He said: "I don't go to the movies more than twice a year."

Indirect quotation: He said that he didn't go to the movies more than twice a year.

3. Quotation marks are used to enclose a title when it is necessary to distinguish the title of a selection from that of the book or periodical in which it appears:

In "The Art of Biography," published in the *Atlantic Monthly* for April 1939, Virginia Woolf argued that biography is a craft, not an art.

Most magazines and newspapers still use quotation marks for all titles. Some writers limit their use of quotes to titles of chapters, short stories, short poems, and magazine articles, whether or not the book or periodical title actually appears in the text. But many writers today are using italics (underlining) for all titles—unless the part and the whole appear together. Whatever choice a student makes, he should be consistent.

4. Quotation marks are also used (a) to distinguish words-as-words; (b) to call attention to irony; and (c) to label unfamiliar terms or slang:

a. He would ask what "independent" meant and when he was told the meaning he lay awake nights thinking about the meaning of the meaning of "independent." Other words bothered him, such as "predestination." —Carl Sandburg, *Abraham Lincoln: The Prairie Years.* (But italics are often used—as throughout this book—for the same purpose.)

b. On her part Japan announced plans to "emancipate" the Europeans' former colonies but remained mum on the subject of Korea. This omission did not greatly weaken her propaganda against "white domination" however. She actually set up "self-government" in several areas. —Edgar Snow, *People on Our Side.* (Here the quotes are the equivalent of an ironic *so-called.*)

c. Each man has two rooms to himself, a "bedder" and a "sitter," not too handsomely furnished . . . . —R. M. Carson, "Oxford through American Eyes."

In the third illustration the author is using quotes legitimately to label unfamiliar Oxford slang for American readers. But this device should be used sparingly. Many teachers of English require students to label slang as an aid in learning usage levels. But the truth is that modern American writers seldom segregate slang in apologetic quotes. Informal writing includes a certain amount of slang (see page 237), and labeling it is like inviting a guest to a party at an exclusive club on condition that he wear a yellow tag saying "Nonmember." Modern American usage can be pretty well summarized in this blunt rule of thumb: *If an expression belongs, admit it without quotes; if it doesn't, leave it out.*

Beware especially of the common habit of spreading quotation marks around indiscriminately like measles, enclosing not only slang but respectable colloquial idioms, trite expressions, and commonplace metaphors:

> Applying the principles of research he took 150 executives "apart" . . . . And in his fascinating book "How to Develop Your Executive Ability," he shows what makes them "tick." (The quotes are used around *apart* and *tick* presumably because the words are not to be taken literally, but any reader knows that the executives have not swallowed watches and are not being drawn and quartered.)

> I remember the first test "as if it were only yesterday." (The student might defend these quotes on the ground that the phrase is a quotation from thousands of other speakers and writers. But so are all hackneyed phrases, and encasing them in quotes merely calls attention to their triteness.)

> At this point I find that like the proverbial "sore thumb" it is standing out again. (Here the student has already apologized unnecessarily for borrowing from proverbial wisdom without adding excuse to apology by using quotes.)

SINGLE QUOTES

Single quotes are used for material quoted within quotations:

> "I did not," he said, "call you a liar. I merely said, 'You are laboring under a misapprehension of the truth.' "

POSITION OF QUOTES

It has already been said that both the comma and the colon are used to introduce quotations and that interrupters in quotations are usually set off by commas. Most style books prescribe the following order for quotes and other punctuation marks:

Put quotes

1. Always outside the comma and period:

> "Hello, Tom," he said, "it's good to see you."
> He threw what the experts called a "blooper ball."

2. Always inside the semicolon and colon:

He lived in what he optimistically called "luxury"; he died in real poverty.

3. Outside or inside the question mark and exclamation point, depending on the context:

a. If only the quoted matter is a question or exclamation, put the quotes outside:

He said, "Where are you going, my pretty maid?"
She shouted, "None of your fool business!"

b. If the entire sentence is a question or exclamation put the quotes inside unless the quoted matter is also a question:

What do you mean by saying, "I won't do that"?
What a story from a man who still says, "I am innocent"!
Did you ask this young woman, "Where are you going?"

Notice that only one question mark or exclamation point is used.

THE DASH
(On the typewriter, two hyphens)

The dash is a strong comma usually used to convey an abrupt break in the sentence. It may be used:

1. To break off an unfinished sentence:

"Awfully sorry. The fact is, I am unusually busy at this moment, and besides—" —Norman Douglas, *Looking Back.*

2. To prepare the reader for a climax or anticlimax:

Away with all this talk; let's have action—now. —Zechariah Chafee, Jr., *Free Speech in the United States.*
He [Hitler] believes absolutely in what he says—at the moment. —John Gunther, *Inside Europe.*
The average woman, long eclipsed, realized that now was her chance to come into her stride with a new and practical kind of beauty, the product of intelligent care, which could be hers for the asking—and the paying. —Margaret Case Harriman, "Glamour, Inc.," *New Yorker.*

3. To gather up the parts of a long introductory series:

> The short-vamp shoe, the decline of the American custom of eating peas with a knife, elegant feminine underthings, the popularity of Scotch and soda, and smoking by adolescents and women—all may be traced in some measure to Hollywood's persuasive power. —Leo C. Rosten, *Hollywood.*

4. Or to set off a clause, phrase, or even a single word which is more parenthetical or emphatic than those usually enclosed by commas:

> I am not really competent to judge them, but I like to read them, perhaps primarily because for me—I am a scientific illiterate—they present challenging difficulties. —Clifton Fadiman, "My Life Is an Open Book," *Reading I've Liked.*
>
> When Mr. Landon was elected president—and the *Literary Digest* poll showed he was sure to be—everything would be safe and sound again. —Stuart Chase, *The Proper Study of Mankind.*
>
> I relaxed—completely—drew a deep breath of relief and let a big grin spread over my face. —Beirne Lay, Jr., *I Wanted Wings.* (Notice how in this illustration, isolating the word *completely* tends to emphasize it instead of sidetracking it as an incidental aside.)

The dash is also used as an all-purpose gadget by people dashing off letters and notes in too much of a hurry to punctuate. This promiscuous use of the dash can become an irritating nuisance when it occurs in writing more serious than chitchat between pen pals.

The colon-dash and comma-dash combinations are apparently dying a well-earned death.

PARENTHESES

1. Parentheses or curves are used to enclose parenthetical matter. Like two dashes they normally imply a stronger interruption than commas used for the same purpose. Although some writers use two dashes and parentheses interchangeably, dashes often emphasize the interrupter, whereas curves tend to isolate it as an aside. The difference is illustrated in the first of the following samples:

In the modern president's life the centrifugal pull away from education is so strong—into finance, public relations, endowment drives, civic works, innumerable speeches on subjects like "Forestry Faces the Future" or "The Challenge of Nursing in the Atomic Age," (all generally ghost-written) —that unless his roots go deep into the educational subsoil he will find himself becoming everything but an educator. —Dixon Wecter, "Prowling for Campus Presidents," *Saturday Review of Literature.*

It was a special trick, and, until you learned it (usually from another Ford owner, but sometimes by a period of appalling experimentation) you might as well have been winding up an awning. The trick was to leave the ignition switch off, proceed to the animal's head, pull the choke (which was a little wire protruding through the radiator), and give the crank two or three nonchalant upward lifts. —E. B. White and Richard Lee Strout, "Farewell, My Lovely!" *New Yorker.*

If the material in parentheses is a complete and separate sentence, a period (question mark, or exclamation point) is supplied inside the second curve; if the parenthetical element is part of another sentence, both capital and end-punctuation may be omitted:

It is by no means easy to discover what *exactly* are the aims of Fascists, on the one hand, and of Communists on the other. (The emphasis, be it noted, is on the word *exactly.*) —L. Susan Stebbing, *Thinking to Some Purpose.*

A cow wandered by morosely (cows in India are rude and insolent as camels) and scrawny chickens strutted about the yard. —Edgar Snow, *People on Our Side.*

Marks of punctuation that belong to the sentence as a whole come outside the second parenthesis:

He was a scholar (if slightly pedantic), a gentleman, and a good teacher (he told me himself).

2. Parentheses are also used for enclosing dates and for numbers introducing parts of a series:

In the year which is traditionally set as the end of the Romantic Period (1832), three important events occurred: (1) the death of England's robust storyteller Sir Walter Scott; (2) the death of the great

German sage Goethe; and (3) the first Reform Bill, which extended the franchise to thousands of new voters.

BRACKETS

Brackets are used when the writer wishes to insert a comment of his own inside a quotation:

> What he actually wrote was: "These arguments [referring presumably to the assertions in the *Times*] are entirely irrevelant [*sic*] to the present question."

Here *sic* means: *Thus* it was in my source; don't blame me for the mistakes.

UNDERLINING

Underlining means to a printer: Set this in italics. It is used:

1. To distinguish titles from the rest of the text (see page 186):

> When Ellen in *The Male Animal* observes that Tommy has had several articles in *Harper's* and the *Atlantic Monthly,* and Joe replies that the *Reader's Digest* is a great little magazine, Tommy quietly asks, "Do you like bullion cubes?"

The article *the* of a periodical title and the name of a city in the title of a newspaper are now usually not italicized even if part of the masthead: the New York *Times* instead of *The New York Times.*

2. To distinguish words from the things to which they refer:

> As for *surplus* and *deficit,* they are less exciting as words than as facts. —Isaac Goldberg, *The Wonder of Words.*

Quotation marks are also used for this purpose (see page 187).

3. To mark foreign words and phrases which have not yet been assimilated into English:

> This disability no doubt makes them tend, when they assume the pince-nez of the *juge d'instruction* and open Dossier D, to lean more towards drama than reality. —D. B. Wyndham Lewis, *The Hooded*

Hawk. (Here *pince-nez* and *dossier* are treated as assimilated English words. A good dictionary makes such distinctions.)

4. Occasionally for emphasis:

There is no doubt that the A-bomb is an *effective* weapon, but it is not a *decisive* weapon. —R. E. Lapp, New York *Times Book Review.*

But chronic underlining, like exclamation-pointing, is better left to shrieking hucksters and excited women. Notice how the young Queen Victoria's breathless italics make everything in plain Roman type seem strangely trivial:

A great event and a great compliment *his* visit certainly is, and the people *here* are extremely flattered at it. He is certainly a *very striking* man; still very handsome. His profile is *beautiful,* and his manners *most* dignified and graceful; extremely civil—quite alarmingly so, as he is so full of attentions and *politeness.* But the expression of the *eyes* is *formidable,* and unlike anything I ever saw before.

PUNCTUATION AS AN ART

So much for the conventions of punctuation. (Other matters sometimes discussed as punctuation—the apostrophe, capitalization, and the hyphen—are considered in the chapter on spelling— see pages 210–214.) Building on this foundation, a sensitive writer can use punctuation marks with a subtlety that goes far beyond these simple principles. According to Fowler the difference between "The master beat the scholar with a strap" and "The master beat the scholar, with a strap" is the gulf between matter-of-factness and indignation. Look at the following passages:

For sometimes, instead of riding off on his horse to inspect his crops or bargain with his tenants, Sir John would sit, in broad daylight, reading. —Virginia Woolf, "The Pastons and Chaucer," *The Common Reader.*

Like most British colonials, they look, and act, more English than the English. —Stewart Alsop, New York *Herald Tribune.*

I try to tell somebody what the steaming Hebrides were like, and first thing you know I'm telling about the old Tonkinese woman who used to sell human heads. As souvenirs. For fifty dollars! —James Michener, *Tales of the South Pacific.*

There is no rule requiring Virginia Woolf to set off *in broad daylight* in commas. But by doing so, she manages to inject a note of astonishment and suspense into what might otherwise have been a dead-pan statement of fact. An exclamation point at the end would capture only the astonishment, and that in a more obvious way. It isn't simply that Sir John would sit in broad daylight reading. He would sit, mind you, in broad daylight, believe it or not, reading, of all things. A similar effect is produced by the commas around *and act* in the Alsops' newspaper column. Without them *look-and-act* would be run together as a cliché. With them, it is surprising enough that these British colonials should *look* more English than the English, even more surprising that they should *act* it. And if Michener had merely written about the old Tonkinese woman who used to sell human heads as souvenirs for fifty dollars, the reader might take it in stride and hurry on to something more exciting. But the unorthodox use of the two full stops gives each of the three macabre details a moment to sink in and take separate effect.

Perhaps this is breaking a comma on a wheel. But it is meant as a closing reminder that punctuation can be something more than a slavish salaaming to rules and regulations.

EXERCISES

I. In accordance with the first rule for the comma (pages 172–175), make all necessary changes in the following sentences, and give a reason for each:

1. They had to write well if their work was to endure for time is a severe test of any piece of literature.

2. The result of my careless driving was that I almost fractured my skull, to be exact, there was a margin of only one eighth of an inch between life and death.

3. This is democracy at its height but, it is a little unfair to the man who is earning his own living and paying taxes.

4. I was unluckily tall for my age, being tall got me into all sorts of trouble with my teachers, every time a teacher sensed trouble, she would automatically call my name.

5. He was born in poverty, he lived in luxury, he died completely penniless.

6. My first-grade teacher developed an intense interest in my welfare, in fact, this interest was so intense that she decided to keep me back for another year.

7. I played left field for the rest of the season, and batted a respectable .286, however, I didn't turn out to be much of an all-round ball player.

8. The feeling appears to be prevalent among Arts students that this office is partial, on the contrary, we would greatly welcome the opportunity to place our services at the disposal of all students.

9. He wasn't a scholar, he was only a lover of trivial details.

10. Booth arrived at the theater a little after ten and stopped in the lobby to note where the President was sitting, he then proceeded upstairs to the President's box.

II. In accordance with the rule for restrictive and nonrestrictive modifiers (pages 176–178), make all necessary changes in the following sentences, and give a reason for each:

1. Much to my surprise, when the day came for the instruments to be passed out, I was given the French horn which is played very much like the cornet.

2. During the later stages of the ship's construction, Captain Molnar who went down with her had admitted her lack of lifesaving equipment.

3. He argued that there were many Russians who didn't want to fight a war with the United States and some others, who had been misled by propaganda into wanting war.

4. A man, with as much ability as Professor Morgan, should not be condemned to a life of poverty.

5. A river crossing is usually made first by the officers who never give their men an order they would not carry out themselves.

6. People who are trained from childhood to fight and die for their country are not easy to overcome in war.

7. The brick latrines which had nicely stained wood ceilings, were the only well-constructed buildings in the camp.

8. He explained that the Darwin who wrote *The Origin of Species* was not the same man as the Darwin who wrote *The Loves of the Plants.*

9. I don't think that anybody, in his right mind, will contend that learning depends entirely on teaching.

10. Much to the children's dismay, the animal, that they saw yesterday in the zoo, was a rhinoceros, not a unicorn.

III. In accordance with the conventions of orthodox punctuation, make all necessary changes in the following sentences, and give a reason for each:

1. Although he learned nothing new, social interests made his freshman year exciting.

2. George is the kind of wit, who thinks that the funniest thing in the world is to refer to the world's fashion capital as Paris France.

3. If a man understands the platforms of all parties can distinguish a statesman from a politician and can vote according to his own conscience, not the prejudices of his favorite commentator; he is an unusual citizen.

4. When I first saw him, he was comfortably settled in a large, red, leather, chair reading an article in "The Saturday Evening Post" entitled Faye Emerson—Blonde Bombshell of TV.

5. He regularly used the following excuses for not coming to class; a broken-down car, a mild case of migraine, an archaic alarm clock, and a dead uncle in Metuchen.

6. It is important however to leave the receiver on at all times; so that the desired frequency can be monitored.

7. Where yesterday's novelist would write "I do not understand you" rejoined Joseph with a look of bewilderment, deftly dispatching a cigarette ash into a convenient cuspidor, today's would probably settle for "Whaddaya mean" said Joe.

8. Such words as case, factor, activate, and implement are common in directives, which come from federal bureaus.

9. Outside the house was in excellent shape for the new owners had spent many hours painting it, however, it was still not worth the outrageous price they asked.

10. I asked him, if there was going to be any collateral reading in such difficult books as Veblen's Theory of the Leisure Class or whether Economics 14 was what the students called a "pipe" or "gut" course.

IV. Explain in your own words the rule illustrated by every mark of punctuation in the following passages (excluding capitals, hyphens, and apostrophes), and give the number of the pertinent page in this chapter:

1. It is this latter interpretation of history which is generally identified with *The Decline of the West,* but Spengler's far more valuable and original analysis is that of contrasting configurations in Western civilization. He distingushes two great destiny ideas: the Apollonian of the classical world and the Faustian of the modern world. —Ruth Benedict, *Patterns of Culture.*

2. How those old Victorian battles had raged about the Prampton table when he was a boy! How the names of Arnold, Huxley, Darwin, Carlyle, Morris, Ruskin had been pelted back and forth by the excited disputants! *Literature and Dogma, God and the Bible, Culture and Anarchy.* —Theodore Morrison, "Dover Beach Revisited," *Harper's Magazine.*

3. Among them are the idea of the ecclesiastical or papal supremacy over temporal powers; the idea of the divine right of kings; the idea of nationalism; the idea of toleration; the idea of self-determination, which ruled events so potently during and after the World War; the idea of rugged individualism; the idea of State Socialism; and the idea of collectivism or the abolition of private property. —Allan Nevins, *The Gateway to History.*

4. The first butterfly and at least two of those mentioned by Gifford were the cloudless sulphur, *Callidryas eubele,* almost identical with our northern form, and the reddish one was the fritillery, *Agraulis vanillae,* which I have already mentioned. —William Beebe, *Galápagos.*

5. "Never say *people* when you mean *persons;*" old man Gibbons had instructed Miranda, "and never say *practically,* say *virtually,* and don't for God's sake ever so long as I am at this desk use the barbarism *inasmuch* . . . . Now you're educated, you may go." —Katharine Anne Porter, *Pale Horse, Pale Rider.*

6. With this for their beginning, their ending is inevitable; all man's qualitative life—his disinterested love of truth, beauty, and goodness—is purely subjective. —Harry Emerson Fosdick, *As I See Religion.*

7. When he writes for the magazine himself (or for another "little" magazine) it is usually criticism or criticism *of* criticism. —Russell Lynes, "Highbrow, Lowbrow, Middlebrow," *Harper's Magazine.*

8. John Skelton, the most gifted English poet at the beginning of the sixteenth century, is one of the happiest innovators in verse form. He has of late become, as he remained for a century after his death,

a notable force in English poetry. New editions and biographies have appeared; his works have been freely anthologized and criticized. —Henry W. Wells, *New Poets from Old.*

9. The demand for teachers had suddenly become enormous, and one of these universities set up a large college designed, as one famous but bewildered Danish visitor put it, "to teach teachers to teach teachers to teach." —Paul B. Sears, *Charles Darwin.*

10. Sir Robert, she believed in her fury, had tried to outwit her, to take her friends from her, to impose his will upon her own; but that was not all: she had suddenly perceived, while the poor man was moving so uneasily before her, the one thing that she was desperately longing for—a loophole of escape. —Lytton Strachey, *Queen Victoria.*

V. Read the following passages aloud at a normal pace to see how much sense they make with punctuation omitted. Then copy them down, supplying all necessary punctuation marks.

1. Lunchtime I went out and had a roll and coffee I used a nickel to call Dolly This is Jay Freling Matton I said counselor-at-law We have just received word that you are the beneficiary of a large estate left by a Mr Dubelo of Kansas China If you will meet us in front of the lions at the Public Library we will be happy to further discuss the matter with you Willie said Dolly Is that you Willie You'll come I said I didn't say that Remember it is to your benefit The Public Library No I said remembering the nickel I had left I'll pick you up at home I heard Dolly say Willie just as I hung up Why do you lie to me Dolly said Why do you make up all those stories It isn't lying I said Why can't you have an uncle in Kansas or in China I haven't That's all I haven't Dolly you're wonderful You're beautiful Your eyes are like stars Your mouth is a red red ruby Your hair is like spun gold Your hands are like pale pieces of jade Jade is green There's white jade too Well my hands aren't like jade Dolly said I say they are You read it in a book Willie No I didn't It was in a movie The girl was in Malay and the fellow who told it to her was an international thief It was a wonderful wonderful scene I don't like it Dolly said All right you make up something better I don't want to make up anything I want you to tell the truth —Zachary Gold, "Spring over Brooklyn," *Saturday Evening Post.*

2. It could be argued that what the audience demands of a hero is only conformity to race morality to the code which seems to the spectators most likely to make for race survival In many cases especially

in comedy and obviously in the comedy of Molière this is true But in the majority of ancient and modern plays it seems to me that what the audience wants to believe is that men have a desire to break the molds of earth which encase them and claim a kinship with a higher morality than that which hems them in The rebellion of Antigone who breaks the laws of men through adherence to a higher law of affection the rebellion of Prometheus who breaks the law of the gods to bring fire to men the rebellion of God in The Green Pastures against the rigid doctrine of the Old Testament the rebellion of Tony in They Knew What They Wanted against the convention that called on him to repudiate his cuckold child the rebellion of Liliom against the heavenly law which asked him to betray his own integrity and make a hypocrisy of his affection even the repudiation of the old forms and the affirmation of new by the heroes of Ibsen and Shaw these are all instances to me of the groping of men toward an excellence dimly apprehended seldom possible of definition They are evidence to me that the theater at its best is a religious affirmation an age-old rite restating and reassuring man's belief in his own destiny and his ultimate hope The theater is much older than the doctrine of evolution but its one faith asseverated again and again for every age and every year is a faith in evolution in the reaching and the climb of men toward distant goals glimpsed but never seen perhaps never achieved or achieved only to be passed impatiently on the way to a more distant horizon —Maxwell Anderson, "The Essence of Tragedy," *Off Broadway; Essays about the Theater.*

VI. The following passages are printed exactly as they were published. Analyze each passage in detail, distinguishing between conventional and unconventional punctuation. Are the departures from convention effective or confusing?

1. What are the ideas that are important I asked him. Here said he is the list of them I took the list and looked it over. Ah I said I notice that none of the books read at any time by them were originally written in English, was that intentional I asked him. No he said but in English there have really been no ideas expressed. Then I gather that to you there are no ideas which are not sociological or governmental ideas. Well are there he said, well yes I said. Government is the least interesting thing in human life, creation and the expression of that creation is a damn sight more interesting, yes I know and I began to get excited yes I know, naturally you are teachers and teaching is your occupation and naturally what you call ideas are easy to teach and

so you are convinced that they are the only ideas but the real ideas are not the relation of human beings as groups but a human being to himself inside him and that is an idea that is more interesting than humanity in groups, after all the minute that there are a lot of them they do not do it for themselves but somebody does it for them and that is a darn sight less interesting. —Gertrude Stein, "Your United States," *Atlantic Monthly.*

2. Mr. Wylie, I said, I got a beautiful Harley-Davidson downstairs and if you'd like to for a ride, I'd be more than glad to let you set behind me. It's a big seat and if I move up toward the front, you'll be comfortable.

I don't want to ride no motorcycle, he said.

I thought maybe you would, I said.

I went out of the office, and then I went back.

Well, would you care to *see* it? I said.

No, he said.

All right, I said, and I went on downstairs and got on the motorcycle and drove away. It was a beautiful job. The motor was great. I got out on the Great Highway at the beach and then I remembered Monterey and I figured maybe I ought to let her out and tear down to Monterey and then tear back, and then give them back their motorcycle and start looking for another job. They'd maybe give me back some of the money, and maybe not, but even if they didn't, I figured it would be worth it, so I let her out. It was the real thing. April. And the Harley-Davidson under me, and the Pacific Ocean beside me. And the world. And the towns. And the people. And the trees. And I roared down to Monterey in no time. —William Saroyan, "Where I Come From People Are Polite," *Little Children.*

3. Walking round downtown Chicago, crossing and recrossing the bridges over the Chicago River in the jingle and clatter of traffic, the rattle of vans and loaded wagons and the stamping of big drayhorses and the hooting of towboats with barges and the rumbling whistle of lakesteamers waiting for the draw,

he thought of the great continent stretching a thousand miles east and south and north, three thousand miles west, and everywhere, at mineheads, on the shores of newlydredged harbors, along watercourses, at the intersections of railroads, sprouting

shacks roundhouses tipples grainelevators stores warehouses tenements, great houses for the wealthy set in broad treeshaded lawns, domed statehouses on hills, hotel churches operahouses auditoriums.

He walked with long eager steps

toward the untrammeled future opening in every direction for a young man who'd keep his hands to his work and his wits sharp to invent.

The same day he landed a job in an architect's office. —John Dos Passos, *U.S.A.*

CHAPTER SEVEN

Spelling

> Forskor and sevn yeerz agoe our faadherz braut forth on
> dhis kontinent a nue naeshun, konseeved in liberti, and
> dedikaeted to dhe propoezishun dhat aul men ar kreeaeted
> eekwal.
>
> —Suggested "Simplified Spelling"
> by Dr. Godfrey Dewey.
>
> In college good spelling should be taken for granite.
> —Student theme.

If the inconsistencies of English spelling were consistent, any second-grade child would be able to recognize the word *psoloquoise*. His heart would leap with joy at the mere sight of it. For a *psoloquoise* is obviously a circus. As its inventor points out, the initial soft *c* is represented by the *ps* in *psychology,* *ir* by the *olo* in *colonel,* hard *c* by *qu* in *bouquet,* and *us* by the *oise* in *tortoise.*[1] What could be simpler?

To students of the English language, this phonetic puzzle is anchored firmly in the logic of history. The four key words are among the thousands of *loan words* that have become naturalized in English through the centuries without losing their foreign dress. *Psychology* is from the Greek, *colonel* (originally the same word as *column*) from Latin by way of French. Nor are such foreign borrowings the only reason for spelling inconsistency. In 1477, when William Caxton turned out the first book printed in England, English spelling—derived from a wondrous mixture of Middle English dialects with the Norman French of the conqueror—was still a rich chaos. Since then, through the heroic efforts of printers and lexicographers, the steadying effect of a great literature, and the gradual growth of literacy, it has become relatively reasonable. But spelling changes have not kept pace

[1] From a report of the investigations of Falk Johnson in the New York *Times,* September 26, 1948.

with changes in pronunciation. *Knight* was a logical spelling in Chaucer's day (1340–1400) when both the *k* and the *gh* were pronounced. In Milton's time (1608–1674) *colonel* was pronounced with all three syllables, as in the opening line of one of his sonnets:

Captain or Col-o-nel or Knight in Arms.

Not only these two words but about two thirds of the 604,000 entries in Webster's unabridged dictionary are still haunted by the little ghosts of silent letters.[2]

Why doesn't somebody do something about it? The answer to the inevitable impatient question is that somebody has been trying to do something about it since at least as long ago as 1200, when an Augustinian monk named Orm wrote a book with his own private spelling and warned the scribes who followed him to copy his words correctly. Among his spiritual descendants have been such zealous spelling reformers as Benjamin Franklin, Noah Webster, Theodore Roosevelt, and George Bernard Shaw. In 1949 a certain Doctor Follick introduced into the House of Commons a bill to legislate phonetic spelling for England. When it lost by the thin margin of 87 to 74, the *Daily Press* sang a relieved requiem:

Doctor Folic, the member of Lufboro, wants Parliment to alter the Inglish langwij so that it will luk sumthing lyk this. He thincs that foriners wil lurn fonetic Inglish much cwicer than they do now, so Inglish mite becum a wurld tung. Foriners ar welcum to Docter Folic's nu Inglish; we prefer it as it is.

Confronted with a choice between our inconsistent spelling and an alien phonetic doubletalk such as the distortion of Lincoln at the head of this chapter, most educated Americans would promptly answer: "We prefer it as it is." Through the years the suggestions of less radical reformers have borne some fruit. Noah Webster started us on our merry way by dropping the superfluous *k*'s from *musick, logick,* and *tragick.* We are a step ahead

2 *Ibid*

of the English in omitting the *u*'s from *honour, humour,* and *parlour* and the extra *l*'s from *conselling* and *travelling. Alright, tho,* and *thru* are gaining respectability, and whether we like it or not, *nite* and *lite* may eventually filter into standard English through advertising. But such changes are gradual, and it is doubtful if a Secretary of Spelling with cabinet rank could make them come much faster. A dictator might, but the price of uniformity would be exorbitant.

GOOD AND BAD SPELLERS

Students who can't spell by the time they get to college are usually full of excuses. Some bitterly reproach the eccentricities of the language. Some blame their unfortunate heritage: "My father couldn't spell either, and neither could my grandfather. Nobody in my family can spell." One gets a ludicrous picture of thousands of six-year-olds spelling *cat c-a-t-t* and *dog d-o-g-e* on the very first day in the first grade. Others, with more justification, blame a misguided school system that tried to teach them to spell long words by taking a running jump into the middle instead of breaking them up logically into syllables. Still others, even closer to the truth, admit that they can't spell because they don't read. But every one of them has cheerfully diagnosed his own case as both rare and hopeless.

It is doubtful if any college misspeller of normal intelligence is a hopeless case. Some, to be sure, need special clinical help, either physical or psychological. The student who said to his teacher, "All I see when I look at a page of print is some tall thin letters and some short fat ones," could not be helped merely by burying his nose in a spelling book. But most poor spellers are the victims of nothing more mysterious than carelessness and indifference. With a little help and a lot of self-discipline, they can become good spellers.

What is a good speller? According to the tradition of the old-fashioned American spelling bee, a good speller is a freckled genius of twelve who, through a combination of punishing drill, phonetic awareness, and sheer luck, can rattle off the spelling of hundreds of words that he never uses, including the ultimate demon that wins him the cup, an exotic, eccentric monstrosity such as *syzygy*. According to the philosophy of this chapter, a good speller is a human being with enough sense to learn and apply the few useful spelling rules, to memorize a few hundred common words that don't follow useful rules, and to look up all others in a good dictionary. Good spelling is a mechanical virtue at best, far less important in good writing than organization, sentence structure, diction, or even punctuation. Most college English teachers would rather have a student who can write and can't spell than one who can spell and can't write. But the world at large closely associates spelling ability with intelligence and education. For example, the *Saturday Evening Post* periodically collects manuscript misspellings in a box under the caption "Can You Spell Down Our Authors?"—and with many readers this is unquestionably a challenge to intelligence. An executive will shamelessly dictate the most meaningless gobbledygook to his secretary and hit the ceiling when she types it with an extra *c* in *recommendation*. Nor will anything convince him that the brand-new college graduate who ends his letter of application "Hopping to hear from you soon" may possibly be guilty of nothing more monstrous than an unfortunate typographical error. A good speller may not deserve any loving cups after he outgrows his freckles, but a bad speller goes through life with a handicap. In a college-educated man or woman, society takes good spelling for granted.

SPELLING AIDS

The following suggestions should help any poor speller who is willing to meet them more than half way:

1. *Read your first draft out loud slowly:*   There is little relation in English between correct spelling and careful pronunciation. Good spelling is largely based on eye-memory. If a student doesn't know how to spell a word, it will do him no good to linger lovingly over the syllables pronouncing it in his most fastidious manner. But in slow oral reading the eye is less likely to overlook misspellings resulting from hasty writing or typing. Transposing letters and adding or omitting entire syllables are often errors of

indolence, not ignorance. A thorough oral reading would probably have caught the following student slips:

competion for *competition*	*mechism* for *mechanism*
convient for *convenient*	*motony* for *monotony*
critize for *criticize*	*proganda* for *propaganda*
extracurcular for *extracurricular*	*realtion* for *relation*
graudate for *graduate*	*rember* for *remember*

2. *When in doubt consult a dictionary:*   When reading over your first draft, circle all doubtful words. When you have finished, look them all up in a good dictionary and copy them carefully letter for letter. (Many careless students look a word up, close the dictionary, and calmly misspell it again.) Don't guess. Don't ask your roommate.

At first, if you are a very poor speller, you may have to count nearly every word you write as doubtful. After a few weeks of reasonable effort, you should know whether you are more likely to misspell short words or long words, whether you have trouble with doubling consonants or with *ie* vs. *ei,* whether you are addicted to omitting syllables indiscriminately or have a special affection for ignoring *ed* in the past tense of weak verbs. But whatever your personal idiosyncrasies, you should view the following with particular suspicion:

(1) All words ending in *ance* or *ence, ant* or *ent, able* or *ible.* Such words are annoyingly common in English. They follow no useful rule, and many English teachers have to look them up regularly.

(2) All words with *slurred vowels.* For example, the pronunciation of *definitely, hypocrisy,* and *repetition* gives no clue to the choice of the vowels in boldface. An ingenious student may spell them correctly by analogy with *definition, hypocritical,* and *repeat,* but the average poor speller is likely to come up with *definately, hypocracy* (by a false analogy with *democracy*), and *repitition* unless he gets into the habit of looking them up.

(3) All possessives and contractions—because the omission of apostrophes is one of the most unnecessary oversights in modern undergraduate writing (see pages 212–213).

(4) All words that are pronounced or spelled like other words (see pages 214–217).

(5) All words that you rarely use or see in print.

(6) All recent arrivals in your vocabulary.

When you come across a new word in a textbook or look up a strange one in a dictionary, kill two birds with one stone by examining its spelling at the same time that you familiarize yourself with its meaning. It is ridiculous to stay long in a course in biology without learning the difference between *species* and *specie,* or linger in a class in literature without learning to spell *heroes, villain, playwright* (not *playwrite*), *metaphor,* and *rhythm.* The same logic goes for spelling proper names, a problem which college students traditionally approach with sublime indifference. When three hundred freshman examinations on *Othello* contain twenty-seven different misspellings of *Desdemona*—including such combinations and permutations as *Desmonia, Desmondia, Dexdenomia, Desdomnia, Demonia, Desdoma,* and *Desmando*—it is high time students took the spelling of proper names more seriously.

By reading the explanatory notes in the front of your dictionary, you can learn its methods of designating which of two or more spellings of a word is preferred. The distinction is sometimes between American and British English, sometimes between a long, older form and a short, newer form. With some words the short form (*tho* for *though, thru* for *through*) is distinctly informal; with others (*alright*), it may be listed as questionable usage. An inexperienced writer should usually bow to the dictionary on such matters, but if you wish to cast an occasional vote for the reform ticket by using a simplified spelling that is acceptable but not preferred, be consistent. Avoid such incongruities as: "*Tho* the *prolog* to the *catalogue* is not yet finished, we hope to be *through* by November."

3. *Learn and apply the following useful spelling rules:*

(1) *ie* vs. *ei*

I before *e*	(believe, piece, relieve, siege)
Except after *c*	(conceive, deceive, perceive, receive)

Or when sounded like *a* (eight, freight, reign, sleigh)
As in *neighbor* or *weigh*.

The common exceptions are *either, neither, leisure, seize,* and *weird.*

(2) Doubling

In words of one syllable and in accented final syllables, double a single consonant after a single vowel when adding a suffix beginning with a vowel:

brag doubles the single consonant *g* after the single vowel *a* before adding a suffix beginning with a vowel, *ed* or *ing*: bragged, bragging.

net doubles the single consonant *t* after the single vowel *e* before adding a suffix beginning with a vowel, *ed* or *ing*: netted, netting.

occur doubles the single consonant *r* after the single vowel *u* before a suffix beginning with a vowel, *ence, ed, ing*: occurrence, occurred, occurring.

On the other hand, if a word is *not* accented on the final syllable, the general tendency in American English is not to double: benefited, totaled, traveling.

This complete rule may be too complex for handy use by misspellers with a poor ear for accents. The following simpler rule will apply to most one-syllable words, except those ending in *l* and *r: Double the consonant, shorten the vowel.* This should help a student make the important elementary distinctions between *gắpping* (double consonant, short vowel) and *gāping; dĭnned* (double consonant, short vowel) and *dīned; cŏpping* (double consonant, short vowel) and *cōping.* "Mother was busily *moping* the floor" and "The trainer *tapped* all the players' ankles"—such are the ludicrous results of violating the rule for doubling.

(3) Final silent *e*

Drop final silent *e* before a suffix beginning with a vowel; keep it before a suffix beginning with a consonant:

hate	drops the *e* before *ed* and *ing:*	hated, hating
	keeps it before *ful:*	hateful
state	drops the *e* before *ed* and *ing:*	stated, stating
	keeps it before *ment, ly:*	statement, stately

complete	drops the *e* before *ed, ion, ing:*	completed, completion, completing
	keeps it before *ly, ness:*	completely, completeness

The common exceptions to this rule are *argument, awful, duly, truly,* and *ninth;* and words in *ce* and *ge,* where the *e* is kept before *a* and *o:* irreplaceable, noticeable, courageous, manageable.

(4) Final *y*

When a word ends in *y* after a consonant, change the *y* to *i* before all suffixes except *ing:*

try	tries, tried	trying
rely	reliable, reliance, relied	relying
happy	happiness, happiest, happily	
pity	pitiful, pitied, pitiless	pitying

But keep the *y* after a vowel:

employ	employable, employer, employed, employment
relay	relayed

Common exceptions are *laid, paid,* and *said.*

(5) Final *al* and *ly*

When an adjective ends in *al,* form the adverb by adding *ly:*

accidental	accidentally
incidental	incidentally
musical	musically
practical	practically

Adjectives ending in *ic* usually add *ally* to form the adverb:

automatic	automatically
drastic	drastically
chronic	chronically
frantic	frantically (or franticly)

The natural tendency to hurry through the *ally* in pronouncing all these words results in such misspellings as *accidently* and *incidently,* and foretells the time when we shall probably drop the extra syllable throughout the group.

4. *Make your own mnemonics:* Mnemonic devices are

named for the Greek goddess of memory, Mnemosyne. Handy gadgets in all kinds of studying, they can be especially useful in spelling. One student, with a constitutional aversion to learning even four lines of doggerel about *i* before *e*, puts his faith in *Celia*. Another calls the *police*. A third remembers that a principal is a pal, a princip (le) a ru (le). A fourth remembers that *lose* loses an *o*. And so it goes. The field is wide open.

5. *Learn and apply the following conventions for capitals:* Capitalize:

(1) The personal pronoun *I* and the first words of sentences, quotations, and lines of traditional poetry:

I shouted at him: "Quote the passage exactly! It goes:

> Water, water, everywhere,
> And all the boards did shrink;
> Water, water, everywhere,
> Nor any drop to drink."

Fragmentary quotations are not capitalized: He did not speak of "unconditional surrender." Some modern poets have abandoned the convention of capitalizing the first word of every line. In quoting, follow carefully the author's own punctuation.

(2) Persons, titles, and personifications:

John Hancock, Westbrook Pegler

Titles, when used before names of persons or referring to them specifically:

President Truman, General MacArthur, Mother Machree.
He found the President in.

But:

It is not easy to be a five-star *general* or the *president* of a great nation or the *mother* of nine.

Personification:

Do not let Conscience make you a coward.

(3) References to the Deity:

God, Jesus Christ, Our Lord and Master, He

(4) Calendar words: days, months, holidays and holy days:

This year Labor Day comes on Monday, September 4, Yom Kippur on Thursday, September 21.

But not usually seasons of the year:

spring, summer, fall, winter

(5) Geographical words: cities, countries, lakes, rivers, languages, people, races, regions, and so on:

In the United States many people of Oriental extraction live in the Northwest and speak Chinese or Japanese as well as English.

But not points of the compass:

He went *west*.

Usage varies between Amazon River and Amazon river, Hamilton Street and Hamilton street. The practice of beginning the second word with a small letter is uncommon, except in newspapers.

(6) Specific courses in school or college, but not subjects in general.

He took History 31 and Economics 12 because of his interest in history, government, and economics.

(7) Important words in titles of books, articles, plays, poems, and so on. This usually includes the first and last words and all others except articles, conjunctions, and prepositions:

A Handful of Dust
Science and the Modern World
Studies in the Literary Relationships of England and Germany in the Sixteenth Century
You Can't Take It with You

(8) Names of clubs, fraternities, and other institutions:

Kiwanis, Rotary, Modern Language Association, Phi Beta Kappa, Dartmouth College, Northampton Country Club

This list is far from complete. An experienced writer may capitalize for stylistic reasons—emphasis, for example—in the absence of any specific convention. But there has been a marked tendency in recent writing to reduce capitals to a minimum. Students are more likely to over- than undercapitalize.

6. *Use the apostrophe carefully in accordance with the following rules:*

(1) To denote possession. Unless a word ends in *s*, form the possessive of both singular and plural by adding *'s:*

a man's man	men's shorts
Mary's book	women's dresses
someone's hat	children's day
anybody's coat	people's faith

If a singular noun ends in *s,* add either *'s* or the apostrophe only, depending on the pronunciation:

the bass's singing	Venus' or Venus's son
Charles' or Charles's reign	Xerxes' wrath

If a plural noun ends in *s,* add the apostrophe only:

the Joneses' standard of living	the boys' coats
the horses' stable	the girls' behavior

(2) To indicate the omissions in contractions:

aren't	o'clock (literally *of the clock*)
isn't	It's a great life
doesn't	who's who and what's what

(3) To form the plural of letters, figures, and words-as-words: Italicize and add *'s* (which is not italicized):

He knew neither his *p*'s and *q*'s nor his *abc*'s.
He was always rolling *7*'s and *11*'s.
She used too many *and*'s and *so*'s in her sentences.

Do not use an apostrophe in ordinary plurals:

Wrong: Officer's wishing checks for pay day's please notify the disbursing office at least two day's before pay day's.

Do not use the apostrophe to form the possessive of personal pronouns (his, hers, its, ours, yours, theirs) *or the relative or interrogative pronoun* whose (see pages 89–90). Distinguish carefully between:

> *It's* a nice day. (contraction) *and* The dog lost *its* head. (possessive)
> *Who's* afraid? (contraction) *and Whose* book is that? (possessive)

7. *Use the hyphen in accordance with the following principles:*

(1) To divide a word at the end of a line:

Words are divided by syllables. *A one-syllable word should never be divided, even if it ends in ed. (Wrong: fish-ed, crown-ed.)* Syllable divisions can usually be determined by careful pronunciation. Double consonants are almost invariably split (*nap-ping, af-fection, mil-lion*). But when in doubt, consult the dictionary. With a little foresight and discreet use of the margin release, a good typist can avoid dividing a word after a single letter (*e-rupt*) or giving a hyphenated word a compound fracture (*red-head-ed*).

(2) To separate compound numbers and fractions:

The hyphen is regularly used in all compound numbers from *twenty-one* to *ninety-nine.* It is commonly employed in fractions used as *adjectives,* but not in fractions used as nouns or when either the numerator or the denominator is hyphenated.

> seventy-seven   twenty-seven   two hundred (and) forty-three
> a two-thirds majority   two thirds of the people   twenty-five twenty-sixths

(3) To separate prefixes from roots if two vowels or a small letter and a capital will otherwise run together:

> pre-existent   re-election   semi-independent   un-American

A *diaeresis* is also used over the second vowel: *preëminent, reëxamine.* In some common compounds the modern tendency is to let the reader make his own instinctive separation: *cooperate, coordinate.*

(4) To combine words functioning as a compound adjective before a noun:

well-known authorities
hard-working student
end-over-end kick

But omit the hyphen when the expression follows the noun (The authority was *well known*) or when one of the words is an adverb in *ly* (a *beautifully played* shot).

It is vain to compose or remember rules to cover the thousands of possible compounds in English; for many of them are traveling from two words to one via the hyphen route, and even the lexicographers have trouble deciding how fast each is moving and what territory it has reached. Despite the general modern tendency to dispense with superfluous hyphens (*today* and *tomorrow* were regularly hyphenated yesterday), many expressions are still widely represented in contemporary writing at all three stages (*war monger, war-monger, warmonger*).

8. *Study the following lists of commonly misspelled words:*

(1) Words often confused because of similarity in spelling or pronunciation (Even a good speller will continue to have trouble with some of these twins and triplets until he carefully understands the differences in meaning. Some of them are explained in the GLOSSARY.)

accept	all ready	alumna,
except	already	alumnae
		alumnus,
adapt	all together	alumni
adopt	altogether	
		angel
advice	alley, alleys	angle
advise	ally, allies	
		ascent
affect	allusion	assent
effect	illusion	
aisle	altar	bare
isle	alter	bear

baring
barring
bearing

berth
birth

born
borne

bough
bow

breath
breathe

bridal
bridle

Britain
Briton

buy
by

canvas
canvass

censor
censure

capital
capitol

cite
sight
site

clothes
cloths

coarse
course

complement
compliment

conscience
conscious

corps
corpse

costume
custom

consul
council
counsel

dairy
diary

decent
descent
dissent

desert
dessert

device
devise

die, dying
dye, dyeing

discussed
disgust

dining
dinning

dual
duel

elicit
illicit

emigrant
immigrant

fair
fare

formally
formerly

forth, forty
fourth,
    fourteen

hear
here

heard
herd

hoard
horde

holly
holy
wholly

human
humane

idle
idol

ingenious
ingenuous

instance	ordinance	rain
instants	ordnance	reign
		rein
its		
it's	passed	
	past	respectably
later		respectfully
latter	peace	respectively
	piece	
		right
lead (verb		rite
present)	personal	write
lead (metal)	personnel	
led (verb		road
past)	plain	rode
	plane, planed	rowed
lessen	plan, planned	
lesson		seams
	pore	seems
loath	pour	
loathe		shone
	precede,	shown
lose, losing	preceding	
loose (adj.)	proceed,	sole
loose, loosing	proceeding	soul
(verb)	procedure	
		speak
mantel	precedence	speech
mantle	precedents	
		specie
marital		species
martial	presence	
	presents	stationary
metal		stationery
mettle	principal	
	principle	statue
moral		stature
morale	prophecy	statute
	prophesy	
nineteen		steal
ninety	quiet	steel
ninth	quite	

straight	therefor	weak
strait	therefore	week
suit	threw	weather
suite	through	whether
tale	till	which
tail	until	witch
		who's
than	to	whose
then	too	
	two	woman
their		women
there	waist	
they're	waste	your
		you're

(2) Other commonly misspelled words:
(The numbers in parentheses designate words that follow the rules under section 3 on pages 207–209.)

absence	(5) additionally	apologize
absorption	address	apology
accelerate	adequate	apparatus
acceptable	aggravate	apparent
accessible	aggressive	appearance
(5) accidentally	alcohol	appreciate
accommodate	all right	approach
(4) accompanying	allege	appropriate
accomplish	almost	arctic
accumulate	although	(3) arguing
accustom	always	argument
(3) achievement	amateur	(3) arising
acknowledg-	among	arithmetic
ment or	analysis	around
acknowl-	analyze or	arouse
edgement	analyse	(3) arrangement
acquaintance	annual	article
acquire	answer	artillery
(2) acquitted	apartment	assistant
across	(1) apiece	association

(3) athletics
attacked
attendance
audience
auxiliary
awful
awkward

bachelor
balance
balloon
banana
barbarous
battalion
(4) beautiful
(3) becoming
before
beggar
(2) beginning
(1) believe
beneficial
(2) benefited
biscuit
boundary
brilliant
bureau
burglar
bus
(4) business

calendar
candidate
career
(3) careless
carriage
category
(1) ceiling
cemetery
certain
changeable

chauffeur
choice
choose
chosen
college
(3) collegiate
colonel
column
comedy
(3) coming
commission
(2) committed
(2) committee
(3) comparatively
(2) compelled
competent
competition
(3) completely
concede
(1, 3) conceivable
(1) conceive
concrete
condemn
(2) conferred
confidently
conqueror
conscientious
consciousness
consistent
continuously
(2) controlled
convenient
corner
counterfeit
courteous
(4) cries
criticism
criticize or
criticise
curiosity

curriculum
cylinder

dealt
debater
(1) deceive
decide
decision
defendant
definite
(3) definitely
(3) definition
democracy
dependent
descendant
describe
description
(3) desirable
despair
desperate
destroy
develop or
develope
development
or devel-
opement
different
disagree
disappearance
disappoint
disastrous
discipline
discussion
dissatisfaction
dissipation
divide
divine
doctor
dormitory
drunkenness

duly

(4) easily
ecstasy
efficient
eighth
eligible
eliminate
embarrass
emphasize
(3) encouraging
enemy
engineer
enthusiastic
(3) entirely
environment
equipment
(2) equipped
equivalent
erroneous
(5) especially
etc.
evidently
exaggerate
excellent
exhausted
exhilarate
existence
expense
experience
(3) extremely

familiar
fascinate
February
fiery
(5) finally
(5) financially
foreign
forward

(4) fraternities
freshman
(adj.)
friend
(5) fundamentally

(5) generally
goddess
ghost
government
(3) governor
grammar
(3) grievous
group
guarantee
guard
(3) guidance

(1) handkerchief
(4) happiness
harass
height
heroes
hindrance
(2) hoping
huge
humorous
hurriedly
(4) hurrying
hypocrisy

image
(3) imaginary
(3) imagination
(3) immediately
(3) immensely
impossible
impromptu
(5) incidentally
incredible

independent
indispensable
inevitable
instead
intellectual
intelligent
(5) intentionally
interest
intramural
irrelevant
irresistible

judgment or
    judgement

khaki
know
knowledge

laboratory
laborer
laid
legitimate
leisure
library
lightning
(3) likely
(3, 4) loneliness
(3, 4) loveliness
lying

maintenance
manual
manufacturer
(4) marriage
mathematics
mattress
meant
medicine
medieval

Mediter-
ranean
(3) merely
millionaire
miniature
minute
(1) mischievous
misspell
mortgage
murmur

(5) naturally
neither
nickel
(1) niece
noticeable
nowadays

oblige
obstacle
occasion
(5) occasionally
(2) occurred
(2) occurrence
off
omission
(2) omitted
opinion
opportunity
optimist
(5) originally

paid
pamphlet
parallel
paralysis
parliament
particularly
pastime
peaceable

perceive
perform
perhaps
permanent
permissible
(3) perseverance
perspiration
persuade
pertain
(5) physically
picnicking
poisonous
politician
portray
possess
possession
possibly
(5) practically
predominant
preference
(2) preferred
prejudice
preparation
prevalent
prisoner
privilege
probably
professor
prominent
pronunciation
propaganda
prove
psychology
purpose
pursue
(3) pursuing
pursuit

quantity
(2) quizzes

(5) really
recede
(1) receipt
(1) receive
recipe
recognize
recollect
recommend
refer
reference
(2) referred
regard
(1) relieve
religious
remembrance
repetition
representative
reservoir
resistance
restaurant
rhythm
ridiculous
roommate

sacrifice
(3) sacrilegious
(3) safety
schedule
secretary
seize
sentence
separate
sergeant
(3) severely
shepherd
(2) shining
(1) shriek
(1) siege
significant
similar

simultaneous	(3) surely	unnecessary
(3) sincerely	surprise	(3) used
skis	syllable	(3) using
smooth	symmetry	(5) usually
sophomore		
source	temperament	vacuum
specimen	temperature	(3) valuable
sponsor	tendency	vegetable
(2) stopping	thought	vengeance
strenuous	through	view
stretch	together	village
strictly	toward	villain
(4) studying	tragedy	
succeed	(4) tries	(2) warring
successful	truly	Wednesday
sufficient	typical	weird
superintend-	tyrannical	welfare
ent	tyranny	(2) writing
supersede		written
(4) supplies	unanimous	
suppress	undoubtedly	yours

9. *Keep your own list:* Many words listed in this chapter you never misspell. Some of your favorites are missing. The best list for you is tailor-made by the only expert who has struggled continually with your spelling problem since the first grade: yourself. Delete from the foregoing lists all of the words that cause you no trouble. Copy the rest into a large notebook reserved for spelling. Add others that you misspell on themes and examinations, carefully copying the correct spelling from the dictionary. Put a fresh black mark beside a word every time you misspell it. This is old-fashioned schoolmarmish discipline. But it is the only kind for a student who can't spell by the time he gets to college.

CHAPTER EIGHT

What's in a Word?

Those words which you have worked to get will almost certainly come when you need them again.
—Edward Weeks.

->>>

"The way to acquire a good vocabulary is to look up in the dictionary every word you don't understand and find out exactly what it means." At first glance this student sentence appears as foolproof as an axiom from mathematics. But the more it is examined by a critical reader, the more questions it raises. What is a good vocabulary? Is using the dictionary the only way to acquire one? What is "the dictionary"? What does it mean to "look up a word in the dictionary"? Can any dictionary tell you "exactly" what a word means? What does it mean to talk about what a word means? Although these questions bear a family resemblance to the annoying quibbles in which the classroom prosecutor often indulges, they are fundamental to an understanding of words. To answer them in much detail would require a long excursion into the tangled jungle of *semantics,* the intricate study of the meaning of meaning. To answer them briefly is the purpose of this chapter.

BUILDING A VOCABULARY

To begin with, it would be more accurate to speak, not of a person's vocabulary, but of his vocabularies. The most obvious distinction is between the *recognition vocabulary*—made up of words that he more or less understands on seeing or hearing them—and the *active vocabulary*—those that he uses with reasonable frequency and precision. The relative size of the two has never been accurately determined; nor is it easy to fix the exact point at which any single word is transferred from one to the other. But a writer's vocabulary is only as large as the number of words he can use readily, naturally, and intelligently. As Cyril Connolly says, "The vocabulary of a writer is his currency, but it is a paper currency and its value depends on the reserves of mind and heart which back it." A vast word hoard is valueless unless the owner's assets are readily negotiable and intelligently spent.

This does not mean, of course, that it is not important to acquire as large a vocabulary as possible. Assuming equal endowments of intelligence, tact, talent, language sense, and experience in speaking and writing, a person with a recognition vocabulary of a hundred thousand words will certainly express himself more effectively than one with only fifty thousand. For those who insist on more tangible rewards, statistics have indicated that he is also more likely to become a top business executive.

There are two ways of building a vocabulary, the quick way and the slow way. The quick way at its quickest is illustrated by a familiar magazine feature or advertisement: DO YOU KNOW WHAT THESE WORDS MEAN? Increase your mental power! Increase your earning power! Surprise your friends! (All by painlessly "learning the meanings" of a magic list of words neatly arrayed in a multiple-choice examination. *Urbane* means: *suburban, poisonous, polished, botanical, South African.* Underline one.) Like most short cuts this method of vocabulary building has obvious shortcomings. It involves at least four false assumptions: (1) that a word has only one meaning; (2) that the meaning can be clearly established when the word is isolated from its context; (3) that the meaning can be adequately expressed in a single synonym; and (4) that by learning that synonym the reader has necessarily made a useful addition to his vocabulary. The flaws in this reasoning will become clearer later in the chapter. But it should be obvious at once that an earnest list-learner—patiently memorizing his ten words-of-the-week, including such esoteric words as *esoteric*, solemnly vowing that he will use them all on his friends and his boss at the earliest opportunity, impatiently waiting for a chance to parade them in the dinner-table conversation, whether it turns to Plato or potatoes—presents a ludicrous reversal of the natural process. He is in the position of the child in the old-fashioned schoolroom who was asked to memorize the vocabulary for each chapter in the Latin reader before turning to the story. He is like a man with ten assorted buttons looking vainly for a shirt on which to sew them.

This is not to say that a student can't learn something about the meaning of words from well-chosen vocabulary lists, especially if he looks the words up conscientiously in a good dictionary. He can also learn something by memorizing lists of prefixes, suffixes, and common stems: the difference, for example, between *ante* and *anti, hyper* and *hypo, pre* and *pro, phobe* and *phile;* or the fact that English words containing *cede, ceed,* or *cess (precede, proceed, intercession)* are built from the Latin verb *cedo,* meaning *to go.* But after all is said and done, there is only one method of acquiring a large, versatile, useful vocabulary. That is the slow way—the long, patient, natural process of learning what words mean, not in isolated lists, but in their natural habitat of speech and writing. This requires attentive listening and thorough, wide-ranging reading. Anybody who proposes to improve his vocabulary much without being willing to pay this price is only fooling himself.

DICTIONARIES

"Dictionaries," said Dr. Johnson, "are like watches; the worst is better than none, and the best cannot be expected to go quite true." The analogy is sound. But many people who would never think of using a sundial when five dollars will buy a reasonably dependable watch will foolishly rely on an inaccurate, inadequate heirloom of a dictionary. A student may speak loosely about "the dictionary" or "Webster," but he should know that there are dictionaries and dictionaries. And if he has come to college equipped with none at all, or at best with a pocket-sized collection of words-of-one-syllable that was given him as a prize for graduating from the sixth grade, he should go at once to the bookstore and buy an adult model.

There are, of course, several kinds that he may have occasion to use in the library (see pages 349–350): dictionaries specializing in spelling, pronunciation, synonyms, clichés, dialects, slang, and the vocabularies of special fields; great unabridged dictionaries such as the one-volume *Webster's New International* (second edition, 1934), and the twelve-volume *Oxford English Dictionary* (the OED or NED). But as a constant companion for continual reference a student might choose one of the following desk dictionaries:

The American College Dictionary (text edition, New York, Harper, 1948) —hereafter referred to as the ACD.

Thorndike-Barnhart Dictionary (New York, Doubleday, 1951).

Webster's New Collegiate Dictionary (Springfield, Mass., Merriam, 1949) —hereafter referred to as WNC.

A good desk dictionary is a one-book reference library. It may contain biographical entries, with dates; geographical entries, with useful maps; rules for spelling and punctuation; common abbreviations; foreign phrases; instructions for preparing bibliographies and footnotes; proofreaders' marks; signs and symbols used in science; data on colleges and universities; the meanings of common given names; or even a vocabulary of rhymes. But it should be judged primarily for its completeness, clarity, accuracy, and reliability as a book on words.

WHAT WORDS TO LOOK UP

The number of words a student looks up in a dictionary during the course of an evening's study will depend not only on the size of his vocabulary and the difficulty of the reading assignments, but also on the aims of the course. One teacher may expect him to read a hundred pages to get the author's main arguments; another may require him to read only ten but capture the full flavor of every phrase. Most students are quickly overwhelmed if they take too literally the familiar advice about looking up every strange word. A more sensible rule is this: In extensive reading look up any word if your ignorance of its meaning makes it impossible to understand a main point; in intensive reading look up every word whose meaning is not immediately clear from the context.

Inexperienced readers do not take full advantage of the extent to which the meaning of strange words is often implied or even defined in the context. For example, when Harry Emerson Fosdick writes in a sermon about "a *Micawberish* faith that something will turn up," an alert reader naturally associates the adjective with a quality of improvident optimism, even if he has never heard of Wilkins Micawber, Esquire. Later, when the author asserts that true religion "does not use God as a *deus ex machina* which in an emergency will do our bidding," the restrictive clause partly explains the meaning of the Latin phrase. Looking up any word in a good dictionary will give a reader information that he cannot infer from the context. But a more discriminating selection will enable him to devote more time to studying the evidence on the words he does look up.

HOW TO LOOK UP A WORD

The act of looking up a word should be more than a split-second glimpse; it should be a miniature problem in research. Too often a hasty student will look up the meaning of a word and misspell it, look up the spelling and misuse it, look up the meaning and spelling and ignore the grammatical function, jump at the first meaning he sees, pay no attention to the italic labels on any of the meanings, or skip impatiently over the small-print paragraph that makes the delicate distinctions between synonyms. Only by reading the whole story can he avoid these mistakes. Moreover the words studied in this way are the ones most likely to become his own for life.

Take, for example, the word *curious* as it appears in WNC:[1]

cu′ri·ous (kū′rĭ·ŭs), *adj.* [OF. *curios, curius,* fr. L. *curiosus* careful, inquisitive, fr. *cura* care.] **1.** *Obs.* Taking pains; markedly careful. **2.** Exhibiting care or nicety; — now restricted to actions, inquiries, etc., but formerly of anything regarded as exquisite or choice, as food, clothing, etc. **3.** Careful or anxious to learn; also, habitually inquisitive; prying. **4.** Exciting attention or inquiry; strange; rare. **5.** *Colloq.* Extraordinary or eccentric; odd. — **cu′ri·ous·ly,** *adv.* — **cu′-ri·ous·ness,** *n.*

Syn. Curious, inquisitive, prying mean interested in ascertaining facts or conditions. Curious may or may not suggest obtrusiveness, but it always implies eagerness to learn; inquisitive implies habitual, impertinent curiosity and, usually, the asking of many questions about something secret or unrevealed; prying stresses a busy meddling and officiousness. — **Ant.** Incurious.

[1] By permission. From *Webster's New Collegiate Dictionary,* copyright 1949, 1951, by G. & C. Merriam Co.

Carefully analyzed, this entry gives six different kinds of information:

1. *Spelling:* This also includes the correct division into three syllables (see page 213).

2. *Pronunciation:* The word is respelled in parentheses in accordance with the pronunciation key printed on the inside of the front and back covers. (In other dictionaries, the key is often at the bottom of the page.) A check shows that the *u* in *curious* is long as in *cube,* the *i* short as in *ill,* and the *ous* pronounced like the *us* in *circus.* The only accent comes on the first syllable. (Another word might have a heavy accent and one or more secondary accents.)

3. *Grammar: Curious* is classified only as an adjective (adj.). The entry also lists the adverb *curiously* and the noun *curiousness.* (The usual noun, *curiosity,* is considered in a previous entry.)

4. *Etymology (origin* or *derivation):* The word is derived from the Old French (OF) *curios* or *curius,* which comes from the Latin (L) *curiosus* (meaning *careful* or *inquisitive*), which comes in turn from *cura* (meaning *care*).

5. *Definitions:* WNC lists five meanings of *curious* in the probable order of their entering the language. No longer in use, the first meaning is labeled *Obs.* or *obsolete.* The other meanings are still current, but the fifth (Extraordinary or eccentric; odd) is classed as *colloquial* (*Colloq.*), meaning that it is common in conversation but not in formal English.

6. *Synonyms and antonyms:* As synonyms or words of similar meaning to *curious,* the entry lists *inquisitive* and *prying* and gives a brief discussion of the differences among the three. It records one antonym, or word opposite in meaning: *incurious.*

Until a student familiarizes himself with the common symbols and abbreviations in his own dictionary by checking them a few times, this sort of investigation may seem somewhat tedious. But after a while it will become second nature to him and will pay increasing dividends.

Obviously some dictionary entries are briefer than the story of *curious,* others much longer. Not every entry includes all six kinds of information, and the importance of the information in each category varies with the word. A more detailed analysis will indicate the relative importance of the different parts of the story.

PRONUNCIATION

Spelling is discussed in Chapter Seven (pages 202–221). The allied problem of pronunciation is only indirectly related to good writing, but it cannot be entirely ignored in any rounded discussion of the use of the dictionary. A student should bear the following points in mind:

1. To speak of a general standard of "correct pronunciation" for the United States is wrong; to propose it for the whole English-speaking world is foolhardy. Some students of American speech still distinguish three general dialects: New England, Southern, and General American; but travel, movies, and radio are rapidly erasing these distinctions. Moreover, there are appreciable differences between educated speakers in a single locality and even between the pronunciations used by the same speaker on different occasions.

2. The pronunciation given in most dictionaries is more precise than the relaxed speech of educated people on informal occasions and if followed too closely may appear affected. The most accurate guide to pronunciation is J. S. Kenyon and T. A. Knott, *A Pronouncing Dictionary of American English* (Springfield, Mass., 1944).

3. As with spelling, society will often attach more importance to "correct pronunciation" than to intelligent communication. The United States has been called "the only civilized country where social and intellectual standing cannot be told by the voice quality of the speaker." But a pronunciation like *the-ay-ter* or *ve-hĭ'-cle* will be evidence enough to many listeners that the speaker is uneducated.

4. In many heated arguments about "correct pronunciation" (*ad-ver'tise-ment* vs. *ad-ver-tise'ment*, *pā-tron-ize* vs. *pă-tron-ize*, *ră-tion* vs. *rā-tion*, *re-search'* vs. *re'search*, *re-source'* vs. *re'source*, *to-mā-to* vs. *to-mä-to*) the combatants are wasting their breath. A good dictionary records both, and though the first is usually

listed as preferable, either (which may be pronounced *īther*) is correct.

5. Anyone who struggles too hard to shift from one dialect to another over night is likely to end up speaking a strange, unnatural mixture of the two.

6. Short of taking a special course with a sensible expert, a student can best improve his pronunciation by listening attentively to the natural speech of educated people in his community and by checking all strange words and doubtful pronunciations in a good dictionary. In this way he should gradually eliminate the more obvious local and illiterate pronunciations from his speaking vocabulary.

GRAMMAR AND IDIOM

A good dictionary will solve many problems in grammar and idiom:

1. *Parts of speech:* A student who looks up the word *affect* in WNC will find ten different meanings listed. On looking further, he will discover that eight of these uses are verbs and only two are nouns. Of the two nouns, the first is obsolete, the second is a technical term restricted to psychology. There is no general use of *affect* as a noun. Yet many students use *affect* and *effect* interchangeably as nouns meaning *result*. The italic abbreviations for the parts of speech (*adj., adv., n., prep., pron., conj., interj., v.i.,* and *v.t.*) must be carefully observed. Is *beside* a preposition or an adverb? Is *like* a preposition or a conjunction? When is the verb *set* intransitive? When is *lay* intransitive? Is *rise* ever transitive? Similar examples could be multiplied endlessly.

2. *Inflectional endings:* A good dictionary supplies irregular plurals of nouns, the comparison of irregular adjectives and adverbs, and the principal parts of irregular verbs. What are the plurals of *alumnus, analysis, formula,* and *phenomenon?* Is *worser* acceptable as the comparative of *bad?* What are the principal parts of *lie* and *lay?* What is the past tense of *swim?* Is there any difference between *dived* and *dove, hanged* and *hung, lighted* and *lit, proved* and *proven, sang* and *sung, waked* and *woke?*

3. *Problems of number:* When are *athletics, mathematics,* and *politics* singular? When are they plural? Can *data* be used with a singular pronoun or verb? Is *none* singular or plural?

4. *Idioms:* Idioms are the commonplace phrases in a language which often violate conventional grammar or logic. When a student's ear will not supply the proper idiom, a good dictionary will often come to the rescue. Is there any difference between *all the farther* and *as far as, blame it on her* and *blame her for it, doubt if* and *doubt whether?* Prepositions present a special problem in English. What is the difference between *agree to* and *agree with, compare to* and *compare with, in* and *into?* Is *different than* interchangeable with *different from?* Some dictionary entries contain lists of idioms. For example, the entry on the verb *hold* in WNC includes definitions of *hold forth, hold in, hold off, hold one's own, hold one's peace, hold one's tongue, hold out, hold over, hold up,* and *hold water.*

ETYMOLOGY

A half century ago, when the study of literature in many colleges consisted largely of tracing the ancestry of words, the importance of etymology for undergraduates was probably exaggerated. Today, when most students possess no Latin and less Greek, the pendulum has swung to the other extreme. It is pedantic to argue that a reader cannot understand the meaning of any word without knowing its origin. With some words, which have forgotten their ancestry, derivation may be actually misleading: *buxom* from the middle English *buxum* meaning *pliable;* or *candidate* from the Latin *candidatus* meaning *clothed in white.* With others it may be ambiguous at best: *radical* from the Latin *radix* meaning *root* (Is a political radical one who gets down to the roots—a fundamentalist—or one who tears things up by the roots?) But word origins are nearly always interesting to anyone with a minimum of intellectual curiosity: it is intriguing if not exactly useful to know that *ticket* and *etiquette* have the same ancestor and that *island* and *isle* have two different ones. A knowledge of some derivations will both clarify meaning and guard against error. *Liberal arts* will mean more to a student if he knows the Latin significance of *artes liberales,* and an understanding of the Greek words *sophos* (*wise*) and *moros* (*fool*) should be a sobering influence during the second year of college. A student who once looks up the origin of *hyperbole* (Greek *hyper—over* and *ballein—to throw*) should recognize the prefix again when he sees it in *hyperactive, hypersensitive, hypertension,* or *hyperthyroid.* A freshman who knows the Greek *autos* (*self*), *bios* (*life*), *biblia* (*books*), and *graphein* (*to write*) can hardly make the familiar mistake of calling a theme *An Autobiography of My Life* or ending a research paper with *A Bibliography of Books.* And if he knows the Latin *et* (*and*) and *cetera* (*other things*) he will probably not write *and etc.* or fall into the common freshman misspelling *ect.*

Nor is the etymology of all English words confined to tracing them back for centuries to ancient languages. Many familiar expressions owe their origins to historical celebrities and nonentities (*bowie knife, boycott, chauvinism, Chesterfield, gerrymander, nicotine*), to scientists or inventors (*ampere, guillotine, macadam, ohm, shrapnel, volt*), or to characters in literature (*Babbitt, Lothario, malapropism, Mrs. Grundy, Pollyanna, simon-pure*). *Goon* and *jeep* are from the comic strips; *bazooka* is from radio; *cellophane, linoleum, Dictaphone, Kodak, Victrola,* and scores of others are trademarked words that have drifted into general use, those that are properly capitalized being still protected by copyright. The student who forms the habit of examining the origin of words when he looks them up in a dictionary not only takes out extra insurance against forgetting them but opens up new vistas of knowledge.

DEFINITIONS

In 1755 Dr. Johnson wrote that the purpose of his famous dictionary was "to settle the orthography, display the analogy, regulate the structures, and ascertain the signification of English words." Today no scientific dictionary maker would be as ambitious. A modern lexicographer does not attempt to fix the language or sit in stern judgment on it. He is a recorder, not a regulator; he describes usage, he does not prescribe. The people who speak and write the language, who use and abuse it, who give birth to new words and let old words die—they are both the lawmakers and the judges.

The false assumption that any dictionary is an infallible rule book gives rise to two common illusions about definitions: (1) that there is a "right" meaning for every word (the "one-word, one-meaning fallacy"); and (2) that if a word is "in the dictionary" it is "correct" regardless of the restricting labels, the context in which it is used, or the intelligence of the person using it.

Thousands of words in a desk dictionary have more than one meaning. The semanticists Ogden and Richards list 16 main meanings of the word *meaning*. The ACD gives 59 meanings for *roll*, 63 for *pass*, 76 for *take*, 83 for *round*, 93 for *turn*, and 104 for *run*. Notice the differences when a dozen assorted meanings of *run* are put into sentences:

> The track man *runs* the mile.
> The train *runs* into the station.
> I shall *run* up to New York on the train.
> Will Dewey *run* for President again?
> The river *runs* into the ocean.
> A tune kept *running* through his head.
> The spendthrift quickly *runs* into debt.
> The ships are planning to *run* the blockade.
> The play had a long *run*.
> The children were given the *run* of the house.
> He played a fast *run* on his violin.
> Ted Williams made a home *run*.

Such an exercise illustrates the absurdity of the one-word, one-meaning fallacy and the impossibility of defining words accurately out of their context.

It also illustrates the importance of choosing carefully among different meanings of the same word. In the ACD the meanings are listed, according to a scientific word count, in the order of frequency in actual use. WNC attempts to list them in the order in which they entered the language. In either event a student will come to grief if he habitually reads only the first definition listed or the first one that happens to strike his eye. A college freshman once read an essay called "Fliers Are Inarticulate," in which the author makes the point that an experienced aviator acts so instinctively in the air that he is unable to explain articulately the exact process of flying a plane. Stumped by the title, the student promptly consulted a dictionary and hastily read the first definition he saw: "not jointed; having no joints." He had heard of fliers without nerves, but the picture of thousands without joints so confused him that he never did get onto the track of the author's argument.

LABELS AND LEVELS

Among other things, this student had overlooked the *label* before the definition, *Zool.*, which should have warned him that *inarticulate* in the sense of *not jointed* is a technical term from zoology. The subject of labels requires further discussion. They are widely employed in dictionaries—with varying abbreviations—to restrict the use of a word in accordance with (1) subject, (2) time, (3) place, and (4) level of usage.

1. Because an expert will often use a term in a sense entirely foreign to the layman, *subject labels* cannot be ignored. For example, the definitions of the noun *base* in the ACD include special meanings from architecture, botany and zoology, baseball, military science, mathematics, surveying, chemistry, grammar, and heraldry. A writer, especially in an informal context, may occasionally borrow a technical term for general use: he may write of "not getting to first base" in other realms than baseball or call a nonmilitary residence his "base of operations." But usually such terms are confined to technical contexts.

2. If a word, or a particular use of a word, is no longer "current," it will probably be restricted by one of two labels:

obsolete—no longer in use. *Examples: affection* (meaning *affectation*); *dearth* (meaning *costliness*); *dowsabel* (*sweetheart*); *enchant* (meaning *delude*); *fondness* (meaning *foolishness*).

archaic—"obsolete in ordinary language but retained in special contexts, as in Biblical and legal expressions, in poetry, etc." *Examples: eftsoons* (*again, soon*); *methinks* (*It seems to me*); *y-clept* (*called*); *ye* (*you*).

The exact point at which an archaic word becomes obsolete is impossible to fix. For example, the ACD classifies *fere* (*companion*) as obsolete; WNC calls it archaic. The important point for the general writer is that he shouldn't use either obsolete or archaic words unless he intends to convey a distinctly antique flavor. Since most students have few in their vocabularies anyhow, the warning is largely academic.

3. If a word or expression is restricted in place, it may be preceded by a specific *geographical label,* reminding the reader, for example, that it is common in the United States but not in Great Britain, or common in New England but not in other sections of the country. Less exact labels classify a word as *dialectal* or *local,* implying that, though it is not used everywhere, it cannot be accurately restricted to a particular region. Examples of *localisms* are *anywheres* (for *anywhere*); *boughten* (for *bought*); *poke* (for *bag* or *sack*); *reckon* (for *think* or *suppose*). The local or dialectal label does not necessarily condemn a word as incorrect; it means merely that the word may be misunderstood or obscure in a locality where it is not widely used. For this reason, localisms should be omitted from writing intended for a wide audience.

4. Levels of usage have already been briefly discussed in the first chapter (see pages 16–17), and the three general levels—formal, informal, and vulgate—have been alluded to throughout the book. By labeling a word or expression *vulgate* or *illiterate,* a dictionary means that it is largely confined to people without much conventional education. At least, when a well-educated person uses the vulgate, he knows what he is doing. Common illiteracies are *ain't, he done it, I seen it, in regards to, irregardless, that there, theirselves,* and *them potatoes.* Any word or expression so labeled should not be used in polite speech or serious writing, either formal or informal—except, of course, in dialogue or when the writer is assuming a particular point of view.

Dictionaries don't attempt to draw the thin line between informal and formal English. For one thing there are too many words that are common on both levels. They do, however, use two other labels that are widely misunderstood: *colloquial* and *slang*.

The word *colloquial* is too often regarded as synonymous with *incorrect* or *illiterate*. Actually, a *colloquialism* (from the Latin *loqui, to speak*) is merely a word or expression that is more common in speech than in writing. The label *colloq.* is used in the ACD "to mark those words and constructions whose range of use is primarily that of the polite conversation of cultivated people, of their familiar letters and informal speeches, as distinct from those words and constructions which are common also in formal writing."—C. C. Fries. In an age in which informal writing closely reflects natural conversation, it is neither possible nor advisable to restrict colloquialisms to the spoken language. As a result, many expressions that were once flatly labeled *wrong* in handbooks are now more accurately called colloquial. A random selection from the many colloquialisms discussed in the GLOSSARY will show how broadly the term is applied: *ad* (for *advertisement*), *at about, alibi* (for any sort of *excuse), complected, dumb* (for *stupid*), *enthuse, fix* (a *predicament*), *just* (meaning *very*), *over with, rarely ever, right away.* Even *ain't* is sometimes classed as "broad" or "low" colloquial. Colloquialisms are out of place in formal writing. Their appropriateness in informal writing depends on the context. The colloquial label is a warning, not a condemnation. It cannot save the writer the trouble of using his own discretion.

Contractions offer a neat illustration of the present status of many colloquialisms. A textbook published in 1905 prohibited their use even in public speaking, "unless of set purpose, to give a markedly colloquial tinge to what we have to say."[2] Until recently many handbooks dogmatically forbade them in writing on the ground that they are the short cuts of speech. But such common contractions as *it's, I'll, I'm, can't, don't,* and *isn't* turn up everywhere in informal writing and occasionally appear in contexts decidedly formal. A blanket prohibition is unrealistic. Persistent use of such expressions as *does it not* and *is it not* can

---

[2] J. B. Greenough and G. L. Kittredge, *Words and Their Ways in English Speech*, New York, 1905, p. 28.

make writing not only formal but wooden and affected. On the other hand, indiscriminate use of contractions not only gives the impression of rapid, casual talk but implies that the writer's taking as many short cuts as possible because he's in a hurry to finish what he's saying. The following passage, for example, was written by the kind of student who uses &'s for *and*'s:

> A decent arts course can help us to form a good idea of what to do in our spare time (or full time, if *we're* lucky enough) after *we've* left college. *We'll* be able to have fun even if *we're* faced with doing wilder pleasures than reading, and *we'll* find a life *that's* full because *we'll* not only enjoy a fresh smell, a delicious taste, or a pleasant feeling, but *we'll* also understand it.

Generally speaking, the more contractions a writer uses, the more informal his style will be. But a careful writer doesn't measure contractions by the gross. Instinctively or consciously, he chooses each one in accordance with such intangibles as rhythm and emphasis. The question of whether to include the *o* in *not* or substitute an apostrophe often depends on how emphatic he wants to make the negative. The writer of the following passage was following no blanket rule:

> *It is* best to have strong curiosity, weak affiliations. But although *it's* easy to dismiss a professor or make him sign an affidavit, *it is not* so easy to dismiss the issue of academic freedom. —"The Talk of the Town," *New Yorker.*

Do not confuse colloquialisms with localisms. Though many colloquialisms are also localisms and most localisms are colloquial, the terms are not interchangeable. One of the commonest colloquialisms in English—*O.K.*—is international.

The ACD classifies *highbrow* as *colloquial* and *lowbrow* as *slang.* The line between colloquialisms and slang is so hard to draw that *The New College Standard Dictionary* packages both in one term: *popular.* Though most dictionaries try to distinguish them, slang is certainly colloquial in the sense that it is more common in the spoken language. *The Oxford English Dictionary* calls it "highly colloquial," the ACD "markedly colloquial." The difference is an elusive flavor that is easier to taste than define. WNC characterizes slang as having "a forced, fantastic, or grotesque meaning, or exhibiting eccentric humor or fancy." One British expert, H. W. Fowler, calls it "the diction that results from the favorite game among the young and lively of playing with words and renaming things and actions." Another, Eric Partridge, lists thirteen different reasons for slang making, including humor, novelty, picturesqueness, surprise, intimacy, fashion, and sheer high spirits.

At its best, slang is concrete, direct, fresh, and lively. In informal writing a carefully chosen slang expression can be effective:

> It may be that I was more susceptible than my fellow students, for I must report that I *hit the sawdust trail* at each and every lecture in the creation of a united front against the capitalist system. —Heywood Broun, "From Spargo to Carver to Speaker," *New Republic.*

> The future was *one devil of a fine place,* but it was a long while on the way. —E. B. White, "A Boy I Knew," *Reader's Digest.*

> If the intellectual thinks of himself as a man apart, it is probably because so many Americans have been accustomed to distrust doctrine and preferred to operate *off the* pragmatic *cuff.* —Russell Lynes, "Intellectuals vs. Philistines," New York *Times Book Review.*

> He had his uniforms made by the best tailor he could find, he confided to Miranda on days when she told him how *squish* he was looking in his new soldier suit. —Katharine Anne Porter, *Pale Horse, Pale Rider.*

Where slang is appropriate, it should be used without apologetic quotes unless a teacher requires them as a means of distinguishing levels of usage (see pages 187–188).

A beginning writer with an undeveloped instinct for usage levels should use slang with care, even in informal writing. The trouble with slang is not, as many undergraduates assume, that it is always "vulgar" or "bad English." The trouble is that much of it is (1) forced, (2) local, (3) overworked when alive, and (4) soon dead.

1. The very quality that makes some slang appealing in speech makes it irritating in writing. Good writing doesn't call too much attention to itself; many slang expressions are as flashy

as red neon signs on a dark street. Though some slang fills a real need, much of it results from overexuberance or adolescent exhibitionism.

2. A slang expression is likely to be a localism. A popular word in one place may have an entirely different meaning in another. Today's favorite in Chicago may never get to New York. The slang on one campus is so different from that on another that old friends find it hard to communicate when they go home for Thanksgiving vacation. Many slang words are restricted to occupational groups, both within and without the law. Gangsters, baseball players, jazz musicians, mechanics, radio broadcasters, and sailors have their own private jargon, and though a term will occasionally stray into standard English, much of it is doubletalk to the general public. This does not mean, of course, that all occupational *shoptalk* is slang.

3. Most slang expressions are fads. Like flagpole sitting and channel swimming, mah-jongg and canasta, they are wildly overdone for a day or a season. For a time everybody's using an expression merely because everybody's hearing it. This unthinking imitation is stressed in Ambrose Bierce's satirical definition of slang: "The speech of one who utters with his tongue what he thinks with his ear, and feels the pride of a creator in accomplishing the feat of a parrot." Not only do slang expressions become hackneyed overnight. While they do range about in the vocabulary, they often are versatile words-of-all-trades, words that mean everything and therefore nothing, verbicides freely murdering other words that might be more accurately used in their place. One of the surest ways of not building a vocabulary is to give too much houseroom to favorite slang expressions. The country is full of people to whom everything good is *swell,* anything bad is *lousy.* In the armed forces during World War II the stock expression for anything hard, difficult, annoying, laborious, tedious, or grueling was *rugged;* the inevitable slang noun for any tool, utensil, implement, or machine was *gismo.* In San Francisco during March, 1947, according to *Time,* "the word *boodles* was used both as a noun and a verb—and could mean anything under the sun." In Chicago during that confused decade a newspaper

man tried to find out from a group of adolescents why they wore zoot suits, and every member of the group parroted the same answer: "They're *sharp.*"

4. Some slang expressions live to become respectable: *mob* was slang in the eighteenth century, *carpetbagger* in the nineteenth. Other words stay on the slang level for years or even centuries. *Bunk,* which goes back to 1820, bids fair to outlast its more respectable relations *buncombe* and *bunkum,* and will probably still be going strong when such diluted formal expressions as *balderdash* and *poppycock* have long since died; but it is still classified as slang. *Bones* was slang for *dice* in the fourteenth century and still is. But most of yesterday's slang (*spoon, sheik, the bee's knees, the cat's pajamas, says you, so's your old man, twenty-three skidoo*) is dead and unmourned.

The main purpose of considering usage labels carefully is not to prevent an occasional expression from sneaking in where it is not ordinarily invited, but to build up an immunity to this kind of writing:

> If I may be permitted to digress and mingle misogyny with criticism, I'd like to say a word concerning the feminine protagonists of the two plays. If it were a matter of dog eat dog in this existence, I would rather be condemned to death by marrying Laura than endure a living Inferno with Hedda Gabbler. In other words, I'd rather be pushing up daisies than sitting pie-eyed in a corner saloon. But it's a tough choice. It's not that I don't like women. I just think that the female vultures should be relegated to their normal role of subordination to man! (Pity me if my ball-and-chain ever latches onto this paper because she is still blissfully unaware of my pronounced anti-feminist proclivities.)

This offensive passage from a student paper runs the gamut from rather formal language (*misogyny, protagonists, inferno, relegated, subordination, anti-feminist proclivities*) through natural informal language (*I'd like to say a word, It's not that I don't like women*) down to street-corner slang (*pushing up daisies, pie-eyed, ball-and-chain, latches onto this theme*). An orchestra suddenly breaking into hot jazz in the middle of Beethoven's Fifth Symphony could hardly be more disconcerting.

SYNONYMS AND ANTONYMS

When a character in Somerset Maugham's comedy *The Circle* says, "There are no synonyms in the English language," he obviously means "no exact duplicates." In everyday use, of course, when we say that two words "mean the same thing," we mean "nearly the same thing in most contexts." That is what the dictionaries mean by *synonym*. *Antonyms* can be roughly defined as words that are nearly opposite in meaning.

Sometimes a dictionary entry will merely list synonyms without discriminating between them. Sometimes it will contain a special paragraph distinguishing carefully between words of similar meaning; sometimes it will refer the reader to such a paragraph under another entry. The important point to remember is that a writer invites trouble if he merely goes eeny-meeny-miney-mo among the synonyms. Do *importance, consequence, moment, weight,* and *significance* mean the same thing? In a loose way, yes. According to WNC, they all mean "the quality or character of that which impresses one as of great worth, influence, or the like." But the following distinctions in the synonym entry are significant, if not momentous:

Importance implies a judgment of the mind which ascribes superiority of this sort to a person or thing; *consequence* may imply importance in rank or station but it usually implies importance because of possible or probable effects or results; *moment* implies conspicuous or self-evident consequence; *weight* implies a judgment of the relative importance of a thing; *significance* implies a quality or character in a person or thing which ought to mark it as of importance or consequence.

Often a writer will have a word in the back of his mind that stubbornly refuses to come to the front or a general meaning with no word to carry it. Since synonym lists in dictionaries are necessarily limited, he may find help in a thesaurus. But such a thesaurus as Roget's must be used with special care. The words in a single entry range all the way from twins to second or third cousins, and no attempt is made to explain the difference. Formed on a different principle, *Webster's Dictionary of Synonyms* attempts to discriminate carefully among meanings.

DENOTATION AND CONNOTATION

The problem of discriminating among synonyms is complicated by the obvious fact that all words have connotation as well as denotation. Denotation can be roughly defined as the basic, literal meaning of a word, connotation as its overtones. *Stout, portly, plump, rotund, chubby, fat, corpulent, obese*—all have the same essential denotation: "thick in body because of the presence of superfluous flesh or adipose tissue." But they are by no means interchangeable. *Stout* suggests or connotes robust health; *portly,* slow-motion dignity; *plump,* a pleasing fullness of figure; *rotund,* a spherical shape; *chubby,* the bouncy roundness of a cherub or a well-fed baby. *Fat,* the most neutral and general of them all, often carries an uncomplimentary connotation; *corpulent* suggests an unbecoming bulkiness; and *obese* implies an unhealthy excess of fat. Connotation makes all the difference between a compliment and an insult.

It is an inaccurate commonplace to say that a dictionary gives only the denotation of a word. A dictionary may define horse as "a large, solid-hoofed quadruped, Equus caballus." But in distinguishing *horse* from *jade, nag, palfrey, plug, steed,* and *charger,* it must invade the misty region of connotation. It cannot, however, give the complete connotation of any word—all the infinitely various images, associations, and emotions that it may possibly suggest. To one reader the word *steed* may conjure up a favorite scene from *Ivanhoe,* to another a Tennysonian vision of Sir Galahad. To one the word *plug* may suggest a sway-backed farm horse out of his childhood; to another the equine hero of an old-fashioned comic strip called *Barney Google;* to a third the smell of a glue factory. Even the neutral word *horse* can come alive with connotation. When Richard the Third cries desperately, "A horse! a horse! my kingdom for a horse!" no imaginative reader conceives a picture as prosaic as "a large, solid-hoofed quadruped, Equus caballus."

THE LIMITATIONS OF A DICTIONARY

For all its remarkable virtues, then, even the best dictionary has limitations that are fixed by the nature of language. From *aardvark* to *zymurgy* not a single word in the English language can be perfectly defined. The best dictionary definition is merely an attempt to express in other words the approximate picture in the minds of most people when a word is used in a representative context. In or out of context, a simple "concrete" word like *table* will not conjure up identical images in any two minds. A person's own name never "means the same thing twice" for the obvious reason that the mortal to whom it refers changes with the passing seconds. The best way to define *dog* is to go to a kennel and point to one, and that defines only *a dog*, or as the semanticists would put it, dog_1 at a given moment in time. This is not the discovery of twentieth-century semantics. The learned scientists of Lagado in *Gulliver's Travels* (1726) decided "that since words are only names for *things*, it would be more convenient for all men to carry about them such *things* as were necessary to express the particular business they are to discourse on . . . . I have often beheld," continues Gulliver, "two of those sages almost sinking under the weight of their packs, like pedlars among us; who, when they met in the streets would lay down their loads, open their sacks, and hold conversation for an hour together; then put up their implements, help each other to resume their burthens, and take their leave." Since such semantically pure conversation is obviously impractical, we still have to carry on with elusive words, using them as accurately as possible with the help of a good dictionary.

EXERCISES

I. According to your dictionary, what is the etymology of each of the following words:

ack-ack	ballot	cadaver	caterpillar
acrobat	bazooka	calculate	chortle
aftermath	belfry	canopy	dachshund
alcove	cabbage	caprice	eliminate

enemy	iconoclast	plagiarism	succotash
euthanasia	jeopardy	rhapsody	suffocate
flak	mortgage	sabotage	supercilious
GI	muscle	sonar	taxicab
gopher	parapet	spider	torpedo
halibut	pedagogue	squirrel	trapezoid

II. Some of the following words are slang, some colloquial, some unrestricted. Test your own judgment first before consulting your dictionary to see if it agrees with you. For your consolation, WNC and the ACD disagree on *bamboozle, debunk, nitwit, pal, skedaddle,* and *soap opera.*

ballyhoo	high-muck-a-muck	nitwit	skedaddle
bamboozle	hobnob	numskull	squeamish
daffy	hoity-toity	pal	slip-up
dead-pan	hokum	peeve	smashup
debunk	hooch	pep	soap opera
gimmick	hooey	pernickety	softy
gyp (verb)	letup	pooh-pooh	
highfalutin	lollipop	rambunctious	

III. Consult your dictionary to see whether the following words (or meanings) are classified as obsolete, archaic, or current:

abandon (banish)	aim (guess)	certes
abominable	alarum	eke (adverb)
absorb (swallow up)	albeit	quoth
abuse (deception)		

IV. To what walks of life are the following words largely restricted?

abaft	joy stick	pizzicato	skivvies
hash mark	Kinescope	rand	snapback
hepcat			Texas leaguer

V. How are the following words pronounced? When more than one pronunciation is given, is there any difference in usage?

acoustic	anemone	Caribbean	quay
address	baton	imbroglio	sirup
aged	bouquet	leeward	vagaries
almond	cacophony	phthisic	

VI. Consult your dictionary for answers to the following questions on grammar:

1. What parts of speech are *advise, censure, prophesy?*
2. Is *invite* ever a noun?
3. What is the singular of *insignia, species?*
4. What is the plural of *cactus, medium, mongoose, mother-in-law, phenomenon, stadium?*
5. Are *measles, mumps,* and *phonetics* singular or plural?
6. What is the present tense of *wrought?*
7. What does your dictionary say about: *It is me; He drove slow?*

VII. Who are the people whose names survive in the following words, and what, if anything, does your dictionary tell you about them?

dahlia	forsythia	Geiger counter	namby-pamby
diesel	galvanize	mesmerize	pasteurize
farad			sandwich

VIII. With the help of your dictionary, distinguish among the synonyms in each of the following groups:

achieve, attain, gain, reach
admire, esteem, regard, respect
amenable, docile, obedient, tractable
belittle, decry, depreciate, disparage
bizarre, fantastic, grotesque
capricious, fickle, inconstant, unstable
enormous, huge, immense, mammoth, vast
exceed, excel, outdo, surpass, transcend
fool, idiot, imbecile, moron, simpleton
stalwart, stout, strong, sturdy

IX. The words in each of the following pairs are more or less alike in meaning. What is the difference between them? With some pairs the difference is no longer carefully observed except in the most formal writing. Which ones? Some of these words are discussed in the GLOSSARY. Does the account given there agree with the evidence from your dictionary?

agnostic, atheist

apparent, evident

common, mutual

continual, continuous

cynical, skeptical

disinterested, uninterested

economic, economical

egotist, egoist

famous, notorious

farther, further

healthy, healthful

historic, historical

ill, sick

imply, infer

luxuriant, luxurious

oral, verbal

practical, practicable

provocative, provoking

sanatorium, sanitarium

sensual, sensuous

soliloquy, monologue

stimulant, stimulus

tubercular, tuberculous

verse, stanza

X. Distinguish among the expressions in each of the following groups. Label them vulgate, slang, colloquial, informal, or formal, and explain the differences in connotation:

actor, Thespian, trouper

ain't I, aren't I, am I not

all in, exhausted, fatigued, pooped, tired, weary

angry, burned up, irate, mad, sore

at home, home, to home

automobile, car, crate, motorcar

boxer, fighter, leather pusher, prize fighter, pug, pugilist

child, kid, offspring, youngster

chow, food, eats, grub, sustenance, viands, victuals, vittles

cinema, flickers, motion pictures, movies, pictures

cracked, insane, mad, off his trolley, psychotic

dirt, gossip

drunk, intoxicated, plastered, tight

festive occasion, party, shindig

gam, leg, limb, pin

get out, make off, scram, vamoose

job, position, situation

kid, jest, joke

pants, trousers

shut-eye, sleep, slumber

CHAPTER NINE

Words in Action

The perfect use of language is that in which every word
carries the meaning that it is intended to, no less and no more.
—Cyril Connolly.

RIGHT AND WRONG WORDS

Mrs. Malaprop, in Sheridan's comedy *The Rivals,* took special pride in her use of the King's English: "Sure, if I reprehend
anything in this world, it is the use of my oracular tongue, and
a nice derangement of epitaphs!" Such speeches have earned her
a personal memorial in the dictionary, the word *malapropism.*
It is an insult to the memory of that "old weather-beaten she-
dragon" to define *malapropism* as simply an inappropriate or
malapropos word. It belongs to a comic tradition centuries older
than Mrs. Malaprop and as new as Archy of the radio program
Duffy's Tavern: the tradition of words that come close to others
in spelling but miss by a mile in meaning.

Except for the moss-grown favorites from the books of boners,
malapropisms make fascinating reading. They can be ludicrous
(The referee penalized the team for unnecessary *roughage*);
charming (To do this will take more than *wistful* thinking); in-
formative (Many writers who possess an *infirmary* make the most
of it); or macabre (I arrived home safely, greeted the rest of my
family, and after consuming some of my mother's *vitals,* went
happily to bed). Sometimes a malapropism will hit uncomfort-
ably near the truth (The automobile has had a *beneficiary* effect
on many American families). Most weary theme readers would
hate to see them completely abolished. Yet they remain the
most illiterate, though not the most dangerous, of all errors in
diction.

But few errors in diction miss by as much as a mile. Usually when a teacher scrawls the symbols for faulty diction in the margin (WW or D), he doesn't mean "This word is entirely wrong" but "Couldn't you have used a more appropriate word in this context?" The discord may not be as astounding as Mrs. Malaprop's; the word may be closely related in meaning as well as in spelling. But to a careful writer, a near relative is not enough. "Use the right word," wrote Mark Twain on one occasion, "not its second cousin"; and on another, "The difference between the right word and the almost right word is the difference between lightning and the lightning bug."

FRESH AND TIRED WORDS

Some words are not exactly wrong; they are merely worn out from overwork. The previous chapter asserts that most slang is overworked while it lives. But many tired words are more respectable. They may be new words or meanings that have become suddenly famous: *statism, know-how*. They may be relatively old words that have become fashionable overnight: *bureaucrat, integration, personnel*. Some are technical words made currently popular by events: *atomic, matériel*. But many are simply ordinary, everyday, unpretentious words that have slowly grown pale and weak and vague through the years. They are the victims of their own versatility.

Many such *counterwords,* as they are called, are adjectives-of-all-work to express approval: *fine, grand, lovely, nice, perfect, unique, wonderful*. Some are used unthinkingly to express disapproval: *awful, frightful, horrible, terrible*. Others have been bludgeoned lifeless by advertising: *colossal, exclusive, glamorous, smart, thrilling*. Still others have been weakened by social and intellectual pretentiousness: *culture, creative, lady, refined*. A few, such as *very* and *so,* are overworked in an honest effort at emphasis. Others, such as *thing,* often betray intellectual laziness.

When a word is overworked in one sense, its other meanings gradually die of neglect. *Awful* is hardly awe-inspiring in any context or *terrible* terrifying. Notice these differences between discriminating and indiscriminate use of counterwords:

Discriminating	*Indiscriminate*	
a *fine* wire mesh	a *fine*	day, girl, football team, young man, drink, book, meal, baby boy, idea, game of canasta
a *nice* distinction	a *nice*	"
a *grand* view of the canyon	a *grand*	"
a *dreadful* monster	a *dreadful*	"
colossal Mount Everest	This film is the most stupendous, epic-making, *colossal* production of this year or any other year! (until next week)	
culture: a knowledge of "the best that has been thought and said in the world."	The clientele of this establishment is restricted to persons of *culture* and refinement.	

It would be pedantic to expect anybody to exclude such handy counters as *fine* and *nice* from his conversation. Small talk cannot be abolished: a polite guest must still tell her hostess that it's very *nice* of her to have her over to see such a *grand* view of the Bushkill Creek and walk in such a *lovely* garden on such a *fine* day. But in writing, counterwords should be used more sparingly. Ernest Hemingway has proved to most readers that they can be effective in colloquial narrative—at least when it is written by Ernest Hemingway: "The town was very nice and our house was very fine." But less gifted writers would be safer in substituting more precise expressions, saving the counterwords for contexts in which they carry an exact meaning.

NEOLOGISMS

In his search for fresh words, a student may not resist the temptation to coin new ones to suit the occasion. In doing this, he is exercising a legitimate right that thousands have exercised before him. Without wordmakers the language would stagnate. Thomas Henry Huxley coined the useful word *agnostic,* and President Harding gave the nation *normalcy* if not the condition that it presumably represents. But most *neologisms* appeal only to the person who enjoys the thrill of creating them. Some are ingenious: G. M. Young's *bonified,* suggested as a past participle of a verb *bonify* by analogy with *bona fide;* Max Beerbohm's *narrow-casts;* E. M. Forster's disturbing *Armadillo-Armageddon;* the GI's indispensable *snafu;* or even Ring Lardner's *blute* (a smoker who doesn't inhale). Others are required by science, technology, war, or business: *blackout, blockbuster, H-Bomb, aureomycin, cortisone, television.* But many are neither original nor necessary. In these days of flashy journalism and advertising, *portmanteau words* have been minted too freely (*biografiction, cinemactress, cinemaddict, globaloney, histroddity, slanguage, shammateur, Timestyle*). Most English teachers will gladly permit a student to coin a new word if he can prove that it fits the context and fills a genuine need. But useful coinages are uncommon. Even Keats could hardly be forgiven for thinking that *purplue* made an excellent name for a color halfway between purple and blue.

CLICHÉS

Most words, of course, do not occur to a writer as isolated units; they come embedded in phrases. These phrases may be tailored to fit the context or they may be ready-made. Many ready-made phrases are the unavoidable idioms no writer can do without. But others are combinations which, however original they may have been at birth, have become thoroughly trite from overuse. The technical term for them, *cliché,* is taken from a French verb meaning *stereotype.* It is also related to a German noun meaning *a doughy mass.*

A random selection of clichés, grouped to show how they tend to conform to common patterns, will give some indication of their extent:

1. TRITE COMPARISONS

brown as a berry	fit as a fiddle
brave as a lion	pretty as a picture
cold as ice	red as a rose
cool as a cucumber	sober as a judge
drunk as a lord	white as snow

2. CANNED ADJECTIVE-NOUN COMBINATIONS

acid test	clinging vine
budding genius	feverish energy
bitter end	hasty retreat
briny deep	ominous silence
blushing bride	watery grave

3. OVERWORKED PROVERBS AND FRAGMENTS FROM LITERATURE

It's better late than never
A rolling stone gathers no moss
Absence makes the heart grow fonder
All work and no play make Jack a dull boy
All is not gold that glitters
Birds of a feather flock together
Blood is thicker than water
Hope springs eternal in the human breast
In the spring a young man's fancy lightly turns to thoughts of love
Variety is the spice of life

4. PSEUDO-POETIC PERSONIFICATION

arms of Morpheus	Mother Nature
Dame Fortune	the fickle finger of Fate
Father Time	the Grim Reaper
Fortune's Wheel	the irony of Fate

5. MISCELLANEOUS

bolt from the blue	rears its ugly head
calm before the storm	shadow of a doubt
chip off the old block	shot in the dark
cynosure of all eyes	time of your life
little the worse for wear	tired but happy

Since originality is a relative term at best, it is not easy to draw the line between an accepted idiom and a trite phrase, an effective allusion and a hackneyed quotation. Nor is it possible to devise a system by which a student who neither reads widely nor listens carefully can be sure to recognize a cliché when he sees one. But a few further hints should help:

1. *Be wary of quotations from traditional literature.* If

you are not widely read, you are probably familiar with only hackneyed proverbs and overquoted purple passages from the schoolboy canon.

2. *If you use a familiar quotation because of its aptness, introduce it smoothly and unobtrusively.* Do not telegraph it pretentiously in advance:

> This point is clearly illustrated by a quotation from the celebrated Bard of Avon, William Shakespeare, who has well said: "The quality of mercy is not strained."

Do not emphasize its triteness:

> An oft-repeated phrase that has been in use a long time is: "Necessity is the Mother of Invention." I found this out when I went camping.
>
> *Better:* When I went camping, I really found out that necessity is the mother of invention.
>
> *Best:* When I went camping, I took a required course in resourcefulness.

Familiar allusions can be successful if they are woven naturally into the sentence or slightly adapted for the occasion:

> Where an Adams scrupled to tread, it is not for a stranger to rush in. —John Buchan, *Pilgrim's Way.*
>
> There is nothing new in heaven or earth not dreamt of in our laboratories; and we should be amazed indeed if tomorrow and tomorrow failed to offer us something new to challenge our capacity for readjustment. —Carl L. Becker, *The Heavenly City of the Eighteenth Century Philosophers.*

3. *If you do use a trite phrase, don't label it with quotation marks* (see page 188) *or apologize for it in humble or facetious words:*

> *If I may be forgiven the cliché,* I must admit that I never yet felt "as fit as a fiddle" after physical training class.
>
> It slid like water off a duck's back, *to coin a phrase.*

4. *Relax and write as naturally as possible.* This advice may seem strange if you are a natural cliché expert. But with beginners more triteness probably results from struggling for effect than

from indifference to good diction. Often a student's favorite phrases are innocently purloined from the dictionary of clichés.

5. *Don't be eccentric in an effort to avoid triteness.* *Briny deep* may be a cliché, but it is better than *saline depths*. Remember that, even if you could match the great poets ("the unplumbed, salt, estranging sea," "the burden of the desert of the deep," "the rising world of waters dark and deep"), such a phrase would probably be inappropriate in a piece of twentieth-century prose. Possibly *ocean* or *sea* alone would do the job admirably.

Of course, the problem of avoiding clichés is infinitely more complex than examining a representative list and reading a few general hints. Anyone who has followed the career of Frank Sullivan's "cliché expert" in the *New Yorker* and elsewhere should be able to testify to that. Just as Mrs. Malaprop is more than an accomplished murderess of the King's English, Sullivan's Magnus Arbuthnot is more than a gifted parrot of the people's clichés. Whether he is testifying on things-in-general, the Roosevelt administration, football, politics, or atomic energy, he is a disturbing caricature of the unthinking citizen who is willing not only to adopt the ready-made "ideas" of others but to accept their very phrases neatly packaged for rapid delivery as his own. For many of the clichés with which we pretend to express ideas are not the timeworn examples of the handbooks. They are today's slogans and catch phrases, stale almost as fast as they are manufactured. A seasoned cliché expert, whether he is found in a magazine, on a political platform, in the columns of a newspaper, or at either end of a college classroom, is not merely a master of trite diction. He is a victim of something that goes much deeper. The British logician L. Susan Stebbing has aptly called it "potted thinking." The best advice to a cliché expert is this: Think for yourself.

LONG AND SHORT WORDS

Our American tendency toward monetary metaphors (*million-dollar smile, sixty-four-dollar question*) sometimes shows up when we are talking about words. When we speak of fifty-cent words as opposed to ten-cent words, we are usually distinguishing them roughly according to size. The distinction is, of course, a distortion of values. A man with a large vocabulary will "know a lot of big words" and probably be more successful than a man with a small vocabulary composed almost entirely of small words. An educated man will naturally use more long words than an uneducated man, not necessarily to parade his learning—though he may be a pedant and an exhibitionist—but because he will more often make distinctions that cannot be adequately conveyed without resorting to them. But it must not be inferred from this that long words necessarily carry more meaning or that a long word in any context is more valuable than a short one. Sometimes a fifty-cent word is not worth a nickel.

The objection to long words is not new. In the first century B.C., Horace spoke of "sesquipedalia verba"—"words a foot-and-a-half long." Oliver Goldsmith predicted that if Dr. Johnson made little fishes talk, they would talk like whales. A nineteenth-century critic complained of characters in fiction who "express the very weather with a sententious association of polysyllabic ratiocination." But the reaction in our time has been especially strong. During the twenties it was the first rule of style for some writers to reject long words and embrace short words fondly. In more recent years the literary novelty appears to have worn off, but widespread indignation against the interminable terms of government employees, sociologists, educationists, psychologists, literary critics, and others addicted to "gobbledygook" (see pages 294–300) has led to a spasmodic public campaign for shorter words. On the whole, this propaganda for plain talk is sound. Every generation needs to deflate its windbags and cut its pedants down to size. But when the love of short words is combined, as in many undergraduates, with an undiscriminating distrust of long ones, the reason is often not a genuine affection for simple language but mental laziness.

The old classroom rule—"Never use a Latin word when an Anglo-Saxon word will do just as well"—is of little use. It not only assumes some knowledge of Latin and Old English, but it tends to ignore the large number of indispensable short words from the Latin: *act, air, brief, cent, clear, date, face, long, move, peace, state,* and *trade*—to name only a few without which we would all be tongue-tied. A related rule—"Never use a long word when a short word will do just as well"—is a safer guide—if a student doesn't interpret it as an excuse for refusing to enlarge his own vocabulary and automatically suspecting every speaker or writer who uses words that lie beyond its narrow boundaries. The rule is in key with the modern tendency to say simple things in natural, informal language. It can be an effective antidote against the big-word disease. Notice how the following fuzzy passages are clarified and simplified by substituting short words: (Notice also that big-word writing is usually wordy writing as well.)

Long words	*Short words*
The specialization in which the Marquis Company has consistently concentrated is principally directed towards the compilative methodism of searching out those actually or more likely to be subject to reference interest.	The Marquis Company has always tried to choose names which the general reader is most likely to look up.
—Quoted from *Who's Who in America* in a review by Hubert Herring, New York *Times Book Review.*	
In order to substantiate our desire to accommodate our guests we would appreciate your co-operation to anticipate your credit requirements before departure.	If you wish to cash a check, please let us know before leaving
—Sign in a Washington hotel, cited by Charles Morton in the *Atlantic Monthly.*	

It might be argued with some logic that the second translation gains in directness and simplicity but loses in politeness There is a difference in levels of usage as well as in length of words. "Your presence is requested" is on one level; "please come to my party" is on another. The same difference exists between "Trespassing on these premises is expressly forbidden" and "Keep out of this yard." This raises again the inevitable question of appropriateness. After all, an experienced writer doesn't ask himself: "Is this word too long?" or "Will that short word do just as well as this long one?" He instinctively asks: "Is this the best word to convey my meaning? Is it appropriate in this context?" Once these questions are answered, the question of whether a word is short, long, or medium no longer matters. The notorious OCD directive ordering "termination of the illumination" during blackouts should have been simplified, not just because the words in "put out the lights" are shorter, but because that is the natural way to describe the simple act of pushing a button. Just before the murder of Desdemona, Othello says: "Put out the light, and then put out the light." If he said, "Terminate the illumination, and then terminate the illumination," the direct dramatic impact would be killed by false elegance. In another context both *terminate* and *illumination* might be preferred for equally valid reasons. Short words are not always the most direct: *polysyllabic* is more direct than *of more than one syllable; circumlocution* is more direct than *roundabout expression.* Nor are short words always the most familiar or the most exact. Length is only one consideration. The choice between a short and a long word often requires an intelligent compromise based on rhythm, connotation, and a knowledge of the capacities of the reader.

The last consideration is especially important when the choice lies between a long technical word and a short popular word. If the technical word fills a genuine need and isn't merely the secret abracadabra of a cult, it is usually more accurate than a popular synonym and would naturally be used between experts. But obviously the doctor who tells an uneducated woman that she has a *contusion of the tibia* will convey less information than if he calls it a *bruised shin.*

CONCRETE AND ABSTRACT WORDS

The trouble with many long words is that they are too abstract. The chapter on grammar contains a distinction between a concrete noun—naming "something that can be seen, heard, touched, smelled, or tasted"—and an abstract noun—naming a quality or idea that cannot be perceived by the senses. This is an oversimplification. Just as all words have connotation as well as denotation, all words have some abstractness. *Boat* stands for something that can be touched and sometimes heard and smelled, but it also stands for the *boatiness* of boats in general. *Concrete* may have a "concrete" meaning in one sentence (a *concrete* sidewalk) and an "abstract" meaning in another (a *concrete* idea). The same is true of the word *abstract*. However arbitrary, the distinction between concrete and abstract words is still apparent. *My dog Rover,* which has a specific *referent,* presumably in a specific kennel, is obviously more concrete than *dog,* just as *dog* is more concrete than *quadruped.* By the same token, *disease, vehicle,* and *educational institution* are more abstract than *mumps, Cadillac,* and *junior high school.* In short, *abstract words are general; concrete words are specific.* Good writing is specific.

Obviously a person can't spend all his time writing on such tangible subjects as "My Dog Rover." It is easier for a short-story writer to use concrete words than a philosopher. But much vague writing is vague because it is unnecessarily abstract. Look at this sentence from a program note at a concert:

This is perhaps the only fine work in the operatic repertory which one can have a child hear with the definite certainty of desired results.

The writer obviously was trying to hit a main point hard. But the whole sentence falls apart with the final abstraction. What are *desired* results? Does it mean that a child will give up television and become an opera lover for life, go into ecstasies over it, enjoy it, understand it, appreciate it, tolerate it, or merely sit quietly for a change so that his mother can listen? It's anybody's guess.

See how the concrete words make the following paragraph come alive:

And one summer I worked nights in the Post Office, that great gray building wherein are many stories. I sweated with the others, tossed mail hour on hour, my body swaying, my arms moving, my mind going dead, my eyes reading the addresses. We were supposed to sort fifty letters a minute. Figure that out, folks. I must have tossed a few billion while I was there, and where those letters went I did not care, and if the letters had black borders, if they carried sad news, I didn't care either; I kept on tossing them into the small squares. It was some job, and it taught me plenty. It taught me how to stand on one spot until the bell rang. There were long lines of mail-cases and a thousand men on the floor, and the hard chatter of over a hundred canceling machines went on all night. Who knows big business? Who knows all the big mail-order firms, those houses that dump loads and loads of mail into the Post Office? The belts rumbled on, carrying the mail away, and merchandise rattled down the chutes. Some music, folks, a symphony in the blues: the Negroes humming as they tossed the mail, the sweat rolling down their faces, the dust whirling under the lights. Can a man dance standing still? He can. He can if he's a Negro, if he's throwing mail down at the Post Office. He stands at the case, hums and sways, and pretty soon it's dancing. —Albert Halper, *On the Shore*.

Take out most of the concrete words and what is left? Something like this:

One summer I was employed nights in the Post Office, a large, tall building. I became terribly tired of sorting so much mail. We were supposed to sort a certain number of letters in a certain length of time. I don't know how many I sorted in all; I just continued working without caring what the letters contained. I certainly didn't learn much from that job about big business. But who does understand big business? All I remember is a lot of mail and machinery and noise and confusion. The only ones who seemed to be enjoying it were the Negroes.

The sharp outlines of the picture are gone. The motion, the heat and sweat and noise and music, the bitter irony—all are gone. Nothing is left but a frame and a blurred excuse for a picture. The writer has *told* the reader something, but has *shown* him nothing.

Notice how much clearer the following passages are when translated into concrete English:

Abstract	*Concrete*
In this study, as in all others, accessibility of books was a potent	Like all other studies, this proves that the easier it is for a

factor in determining the effectiveness with which the objectives of the program in reading were achieved.

The utilization of any intellectual endowment in cases of retardation among children is dependent on parental reaction toward them in the domestic environment.

Facility of comprehension in a literary situation is not readily effected by indifferent ˮ interpersonal communication.

student to get his hands on books, the sooner he will learn to read.

How much a backward child uses his intelligence depends on how his parents treat him at home.

It is not easy to understand a writer who does not try to be clear.

Often, when the layers of abstractions are peeled off, there is nothing at the core but an empty truism. The high-sounding abstract words are merely a disguise for an intellectual vacuum. Sometimes this disguise is unconscious. Sometimes it is a conscious effort to dress up nothing and make it look like something. Then the sin is not only bad writing but insincerity.

Every field of discussion has its favorite abstractions: economics (*property, inflation, deflation, value, depression, repression, prosperity, employment, capitalism, free enterprise, monopoly*); literary criticism (*romanticism, realism, naturalism, expressionism, impressionism, art, beauty, truth, masterpiece, genius, poetry, major poetry, minor poetry*); education (*culture, integration, orientation, activation, implementation, correlation*); politics (*democracy, communist, socialist, fascist, imperialist, patriotic, liberal, radical, conservative*). A reputable expert will use these terms discreetly with some conception of their meaning for other experts. A propagandist will use them craftily to conceal his distortions of the truth. A layman—and most laymen pose as experts at times on almost any subject—will often use them carelessly without the vaguest notion of what he means by them.

It is vain to argue that such words should be abolished from a person's vocabulary because they mean all things to all people. It is absurd to insist that abstractions should always be used with "their right meaning"; the right meaning is usually my meaning, the wrong meaning yours. It is utopian to assume seriously that any authority, whether it is a dictionary or a committee of the United Nations, can make all people agree on the same meaning for each word—though a powerful propaganda agency can come close to this dubious ideal. But a conscientious writer can observe these two principles:

1. *Whenever possible, write about concrete realities, not about words or abstract phenomena:* A detailed description of a political program in action is worth more than an eloquent hymn in praise of "liberalism" or "conservatism." As soon as the discussion of a political regime no longer refers directly to the individuals who run it, the acts they perform, and the human beings it presumably serves, it loses contact with reality. As soon as human beings become *personnel,* they become impersonal and expendable. When a political discussion becomes a comparison of *isms,* it is likely to degenerate into an argument about words, not realities. By the same reasoning, a clear analysis of a single romantic poet is more valuable than an interminable discussion of *romanticism* without concrete illustrations. A brief explanation of how one curriculum works is better than thousands of glowing words about *integration* or *the humanities.* Because he chose to write about the concrete reality of *teaching,* Jacques Barzun's *Teacher in America* is a better book than a hundred that mull over the abstraction called *education.* See how concretely he states his aim:

> Both political and educational theory are for the rare genius to grapple with, once in a century. The business of the citizen and the statesman is not political theory but politics. The business of the parent and the teacher is not education but Teaching. Teaching is something that can be provided for, changed, or stopped. It is good or bad, brilliant or stupid, plentiful or scarce. Beset as it is with difficulties and armed with devices, teaching has a theory too, but it is one that can be talked about simply and directly, for it concerns the many matters that affect our lives, from the three R's to electronics. To deal with it in that fashion is in fact what I am going to do in this book: very simply and literally I am going to tell tales out of school.

2. *When an inevitable abstract word has a key position in a passage, make your meaning clear by definition or illustration:* Notice how key terms are defined in the following passages:

Money is the cause of athleticism in the American colleges. Athleticism is not athletics. Athletics is physical education, a proper function of the college if carried on for the welfare of the students. Athleticism is not physical education but sports promotion, and it is carried on for the monetary profit of the colleges through the entertainment of the public. This article deals with athleticism, its cause, its symptoms and its cure. —Robert Maynard Hutchins, "Gate Receipts and Glory," *Saturday Evening Post.*

What makes human history such an uncertain and fascinating story is that man lives in two worlds—the world within and the world without—and the world within men's heads has undergone transformations which have disintegrated material things with the power and rapidity of radium. I shall take the liberty of calling this inner world our *ido'lum* (ido-lum) or world of ideas. The word "ideas" is not used here precisely in the ordinary sense. I use it rather to stand for what the philosophers would call the subjective world, what the theologians would perhaps call the spiritual world; and I mean to include in it all the philosophies, fantasies, rationalizations, projections, images, and opinions in terms of which people pattern their behavior. This world of ideas, in the case of scientific truths, for example, sometimes has a rough correspondence with what people call the world; but it is important to note that it has contours of its own which are quite independent of the material environment. —Lewis Mumford, *Story of Utopias.*

These passages are written on two different levels of abstractness. The abstract nature of his subject makes it difficult for Mumford to be as concrete as Hutchins. But both passages are more specific than they would be without careful definitions of *athleticism* and *ideas.*

No definition of an abstract term is of much use unless it is in more concrete language than the term defined. Dr. Johnson's celebrated definition of *network* as "anything reticulated or decussated at equal distances. with interstices between the intersections" is a neat example of a definition that chases the reader in the wrong direction. It is equally futile to define a word in terms of the word itself. Shakespeare's Bardolph unconsciously illustrates this: "Accommodated, that is, when a man is, as they say, accommodated; or when a man is, being, whereby a' may be thought to be accommodated; which is an excellent thing." A more common practice is to define a word in terms of synonyms that are equally abstract. To define *democracy* as "a system guaranteeing liberty and justice" or *culture* as "an appreciation of the humanities" doesn't get a reader much nearer the tangible truth.

If a writer finds himself trapped in such a circular definition, he might remember that the best way to define *dog* is to go to a kennel and point to one. A simple precept follows from this: *The best definition of an abstract term is a good illustration:*

Perhaps I can make clear this matter of the *unconscious* by a simple analogy. Let us say that a man leaves his home to attend a lecture at Cooper Union. He gets in the subway several miles from the hall in which the lecture is to be given. He may probably during that time read a paper or a book or talk to someone. He may not once during the entire journey consciously think of the lecture or his purpose of attending it. It is as if he had made a connection between the purpose of attending the lecture and the Astor Place station in the subway and then, having made such a connection, he drops the matter out of his mind until the subway guard calls "Astor Place." Then he suddenly gets up almost automatically and steps out on the platform. I have often seen people step out on the platform in a rather dazed condition as if for a moment they could not consciously recall how they happened to be there. Now, during the time that our traveler is on his way to the lecture, he is not thinking about the lecture or Astor Place station. Nevertheless, unconsciously, he has for the time so organized himself that the calling of the station automatically discharges him into activity. That is, the purpose to attend the lecture becomes an impulse to act when the fact in the environment with which it is associated is present. —Everett Dean Martin, *Psychology.*

That sort of clear, concrete illustration of an abstract meaning is especially important in explaining a technical subject to a lay reader.

EUPHEMISMS

A special example of the tendency to escape from concrete reality into abstractions is the *euphemism*. A euphemism is the substitution of a presumably inoffensive word for one that might give offense. They are common among people who pride themselves on their gentility (*perspiration* for *sweat, odor* for *smell, paying guest* for *roomer*), in newspapers (*social disease* for *syphilis, criminal assault* for *rape*), and in the business world (*heating engineer* for *plumber, tonsorial artist* for *barber, adjuster of delinquent obligations* for *bill collector*). When they reflect prudery or hypocrisy, they are more offensive to genuinely decent people than the blunt words they replace. Some political euphemisms are a criminal abuse of language; George Orwell illustrates them this way:

> Defenseless villages are bombarded from the air, the inhabitants driven out into the countryside, the cattle machine-gunned, the huts set on fire with incendiary bullets: this is called *pacification*. Millions of peasants are robbed of their farms and sent trudging along the roads with no more than they can carry: this is called *transfer of population* or *rectification of frontiers*. People are imprisoned for years without trial, or shot in the back of the neck or sent to die of scurvy in Arctic lumber camps: this is called *elimination of unreliable elements.*
> —George Orwell, "Politics and the English Language," *New Republic.*

In daily living euphemisms are occasionally necessary out of common decency. There is no point in insisting that a man has *died* if his widow prefers *passed away*. But now that Victoria has been dead half a century, it is sound practice for a writer to call a spade a spade provided he isn't going to use it to dig up dirt for its own sake.

CHARGED AND NEUTRAL WORDS

Gertrude Stein once made this characteristic comment on her own writing:

> I didn't want, when I said "water," to have you think of running water. Therefore I began limiting my vocabulary, because I wanted to

get rid of everything except the picture within the frame. While I was writing, I didn't want, when I used one word, to make it carry with it too many associations. I wanted as far as possible to make it exact, as exact as mathematics; that is to say, for example, if one and one make two, I wanted words to have as much exactness as that. When I put them down they were to have this quality. —Gertrude Stein, "How Writing Is Written."

This is one writer's statement of her effort to solve a problem that sooner or later confronts all writers. Scientists have yearned for a language without a hint of emotional flavor—a perfect, detached, denotative language, an ideal scientific instrument. Not content with the restricted symbols of mathematics, some of them have dreamt of an English vocabulary free from the "birdsong" or "tweet-tweet" of connotation.

It is unlikely that the dream will come true in the near future. The most familiar phrases from Gertrude Stein—"A rose is a rose is a rose" and "Pigeons on the grass alas"—are rich in associations. Whatever Shakespeare may have said about a rose by any other name smelling as sweet, the very word gives off a special fragrance. And James Thurber has devoted an entire essay to pointing out that *alas* carries too many pathetic overtones for pigeons. Even the scientists' technical terms have unscientific overtones. E. B. White writes in *The Wild Flag:*

The latest element to turn up is called plutonium—which is Disney with a touch of mineral water. The word uranium had a mighty sound, a solemn sound, an awful sound. Plutonium is a belly laugh. Plutonium, incidentally, is not known in the stars; the stars are too high-minded. Plutonium is just a mouthwash used by Mandrake. Plutonium is just something belonging to the comical race of people who started their first atomic fire under a football stadium.

This discussion brings us back to the point that all words have connotation as well as denotation. But a writer can still make a useful, if arbitrary, distinction between words that are *charged* with some degree of bias or emotion—and words that are relatively *neutral*. These differences should be obvious:

Charged	Neutral
economic royalist	wealthy man
bourgeois	middle class
red-baiting	opposition to communism
alien isms	foreign ideologies
propaganda	doctrine
bureaucrat	government official
drunkard	alcoholic
pedagogue	teacher
pig-headed	obstinate
cravat	necktie
Quoth the raven, "Nevermore!"	"Never again," said the blackbird

Since it cannot go far with connotation, a dictionary definition is often of little help to a writer making these distinctions. The definition of *propaganda* in WNC contains no hint of the odious connotations engendered in the word by a perverted master of the art such as Goebbels; and the definition of *bureaucrat*— "an official of a bureau, esp. one pursuing a narrow and arbitrary routine"—offers only a slight trace of the common caricature of an economic parasite living off the government. A writer must keep his ears and eyes open to the associations that such words acquire from their context. In a special context a harmless neutral expression like *that man* can be loaded with love or hatred ("I can't help loving *that man*" vs. *"That man* in the White House!").

Perfect neutrality is as unattainable in language as in diplomacy. One man's neutral expression is another man's euphemism: it can be argued that *public medicine* is biased as much on one side of the issue as *socialized medicine* on the other. But there are occasions when a responsible writer will carefully select neutral words. In technical exposition, where strict factual accuracy is all-important, emotional bias is out of place. A reputable newspaperman tries to make a careful distinction between objective reporting and editorializing, just as he distinguishes honestly between the legitimate slanting of a responsible columnist and the inflammatory diatribes of an irresponsible gossip-caster. Any writer trying to arrive calmly and objectively at the truth in a controversy will try to avoid overloaded words. They will lead him into the fallacy of begging the question—assuming in advance the truth of something that remains to be proved.

But in many kinds of writing neutrality is undesirable. The magic of words doesn't have to be the black magic of a propaganda minister. When a writer has no reason to steer a neutral course in the interest of accurate reporting or fair discussion, he may prejudice the reader in favor of beauty or wonder or terror or whatever emotion he is trying to convey. He may take every advantage of the connotative value of charged words.

Read these two passages carefully:

A very trivial circumstance will serve to exemplify this. Suppose you go into a fruiterer's shop, wanting an apple,—you take up one, and, on biting it, you find it is sour; you look at it, and see that it is hard and green. You take up another one, and that too is hard, green, and sour. The shopman offers you a third; but, before biting it, you examine it, and find that it is hard and green, and you immediately say that you will not have it, as it must be sour, like those that you have already tried.

Nothing can be more simple than that, you think; but if you will take the trouble to analyse and trace out into its logical elements what has been done by the mind, you will be greatly surprised. In the first place, you have performed the operation of induction. You found that, in two experiences, hardness and greenness in apples went together with sourness. It was so in the first case, and it was confirmed by the second. True, it is a very small basis, but still it is enough to make an induction from; you generalize the facts, and you expect to find sourness in apples where you get hardness and greenness. You found upon that a general law, that all hard and green apples are sour; and that, so far as it goes, is a perfect induction. —Thomas Henry Huxley, *Darwiniana*.

So I wandered through the labyrinth of sunlight and shadow in the bazaar, watching, smelling, hearing, touching. I saw the long serpentine threads of sunlight sifting through the shade and fingering the booths of the jewel merchants; earrings, anklets, bracelets, neckbands, headbands, amulets, talismans; tooled leather from the southern ports, varnished metals from Indo-China, glittering worthless stones from Ceylon, vermilion and magenta silks from Tashkent, blue velvets from Bokhara, green rugs from Syria, great rippling shawls from Kashmir—

no longer fresh, any of them, all of them spotted and stained by the wet seasons or the touch of hands. And beyond these the sweetmeats, clotted syrups soft in the sun's rays, raw spices, dark granular honey, dried citron and figs and dates buzzing with a thousand little golden flies; caskets and bowls and ewers and medicine-bottles twisted out of blue glass; strangely shaped receptacles of iron and bronze and copper; salves and perfumes sickening the nostrils. Something false and pathetic about it all, as pathetic as the faces that hovered over them like moths.
—Frederic Prokosch, *The Asiatics.*

The point is not, of course, that the first passage is bad writing because it is colorless and unexciting and the second good writing because it is colorful and exciting. Nor is the first passage good merely because it is plain talk for the man in the street and the second bad because it is fancy language for the poet in the attic. They are both good writing, but of two entirely different kinds. Huxley, a scientist and teacher, is defining the abstract process of induction with the help of a homely concrete illustration. He uses neutral words—*shop, apple, hard, green, sour*—because he wants nothing to distract the reader from the bare statement of a simple scientific fact. Prokosch, a poet and novelist, uses exotic language redolent with associations—*labyrinth, bazaar, serpentine, amulets, talismans, vermilion, magenta*—to awaken all the reader's senses to the atmosphere of Asia. One passage is first-rate exposition; the other is admirable description. Taken together, they are evidence that the choice between charged and neutral words depends entirely on the writer's purpose.

In most informal prose there is a happy medium between the unemotional neutrality of the passage from Huxley and the richly spiced poetic prose of Prokosch. A student with an ingrained prejudice against literature, especially poetry, will too often swing consciously or unconsciously to a prosaic extreme. Picturing himself, perhaps with some pride, as a straightforward, sensible, tough-minded, "practical" writer interested only in the hard, cold facts of a problem, he will squeeze all the warmth and color out of language leaving it as cold and pale as the directions on a box of baking powder. Another student—either sincerely in love with beautiful words or under the illusion that overloaded writing is expected in an English course—will flavor the most prosaic subject with inappropriate emotions and uncalled-for emphasis. Of the two extremes, the second writer is doing more damage to the language. The undergraduate who pours strong emotions into trivial contexts is like the effervescent school-girl to whom anything good is *divine,* anything bad *frightful;* or the journalist to whom every sugar shortage is a *famine,* every political defeat a *landslide,* every diplomatic note an *ultimatum;* or the advertisers who have long since reached the dead end where even *super-deluxe* is a synonym for *commonplace.*

THE SOUND OF WORDS

"The mind's eye" is a familiar expression. We could as logically speak of "the mind's ear," for it is possible to imagine sounds as well as sights. Because the ear of a trained reader is never completely at rest, word sounds are important, even in writing not intended for oral delivery. The relation between sound and sense is extremely subtle. No word chemist, not even a poet, can separate the pure essence of audial beauty or ugliness from the other elements of connotation. Is *gush* as beautiful a word as *hush* or *ripe* as ugly as *gripe?* Is *lullaby* beautiful for its own sake or because it suggests madonnas and sleeping babies and Brahms? What's wrong with *cellar door,* Dorothy Parker's nomination for the most beautiful expression in the language, or *cuspidor,* Hendrik Willem Van Loon's? But every writer, even if he has neither the talent nor the ambition to write poetry, should be alert to unintentional violations of euphony and aware of the common sound effects in language.

The commonest violation of euphony in prose is the careless repetition of similar sounds. It may be unintentional true rhyme (*ice, nice*), identical rhyme (*vice, device*), or assonance (*vice, fine*). It shouldn't take a poet to catch the following discords:

I am not the *type* to *gripe,* but *I* don't see *why I* can't get a *high* grade in English.

My *reaction* to this *faction* is that they should keep their *dis-satisfaction* to themselves. (The writer of this sentence denied that he was playing with words.)

The introduc*tion* of the idea of muta*tion* marks nothing less than a revolu*tion* in our entire scheme of interpreta*tion*. What also is the no*tion* of emergent evolu*tion* save recogni*tion* of the novel, unexpected, unpredictable?

Marjorie Gregg, who cited the last example in a letter in the *Saturday Review of Literature,* aptly calls such bumping along from abstrac*tion* to abstrac*tion* *cobblestone rhetoric*. Special offenders are words ending in *-ation*. Tone-deaf experts in several fields are especially fond of cacophonous jargon like "the evaluation of the examination with relation to integration in education." The only way for many writers to avoid such doggerel is to read the first draft over out loud, listening carefully.

Except in experimental or facetious writing, intentional rhyme is seldom used in prose. Intentional assonance is a delicate device which even experienced writers must handle with care. Two other figures of speech are more common, *alliteration* and *onomatopoeia*.

Alliteration is the practice of beginning two or more words of a passage with the same letter. Except during the last two decades of the sixteenth century, it has never been as common in prose as in poetry. Today it is still widely used in advertising (Avoid Athletic Aroma; Better Buy Birds Eye; A Panoplied Pageant of Ponderous Pachyderms) and in flashy slick-magazine writing (An article calls soap operas "daily dilemma-dramas which ease drudgery at the drainboard"). Like parallelism and repetition, it can be effective in speechmaking. Only yesterday, when calculated rhetorical effects were still fashionable in serious writing, a passage like this was not rare:

The *i*ntense *i*nterest of the moment is that the Man of Science, the hero of the modern world and the latest of the great servants of humanity, has suddenly and dramatically refused to have anything to do with this dreary business of *n*ibbling *n*egation, and blind *s*cratching and *s*craping away of the very foundations of the *m*astery of *m*an. For the work of the sceptic for the past hundred years has indeed been very like the *f*ruitless *f*ury of some primeval monster; eyeless, mindless, merely *d*estructive and *d*evouring; a giant *w*orm *w*asting away a *w*orld that he could not even see; a *b*enighted and *b*estial life, unconscious of its own *c*ause and of its own *c*onsequences. But Man has taken to himself again his own *w*eapons—*w*ill and *w*orship, and reason, and the vision of the plan in things; and we are once *m*ore in the *m*orning of the world. —G. K. Chesterton, "The Return to Religion," *The Well and the Shallows.*

It is possible that the eloquence of such writing will keep the average uncritical reader from being distracted by the author's incessant alphabet game. But the tendency in prose today is not to take the risk of sacrificing matter to manner. Most serious modern prose writers consider alliteration a synthetic device that calls too much attention to itself.

Onomatopoeia—the use of imitative words and phrases—is a sound effect which beginners are less likely to overwork. It is a familiar device in storytelling and description, where the writer is inevitably confronted with capturing sounds on paper. The English language has a generous supply of onomatopoetic words, whatever their etymology: *crack, growl, hiss, murmur, mutter, roar, snarl, rumble, thunder, tintinnabulation, whistle*— to name a random handful. The writer's problem often consists of selecting audible words (The ice *cracked* open as the boulders *crashed* down from above) instead of leaving the sound to the reader's imagination (The ice opened up as the boulders fell on it). But if no appropriate word exists in the dictionary, this is one realm in which he may occasionally coin his own:

Analyzed, it is simply the old piano blues style (a sort of *oink*-ily, *oink*-ily, *oink*-ily effect). —Otis Ferguson, "Piano in the Band," *New Republic.*
The pounding of the cylinders increased: ta-pocketa-pocketa-pocketa-*pocketa-pocketa.* —James Thurber, "The Secret Life of Walter Mitty," *My World and Welcome to It.*
Tires *booped* and *whooshed,* the fenders *queeled* and *graked,* the steering wheel rose up like a spectre and disappeared in the direction of Franklin Avenue with a melancholy *whistling* sound, bolts and gadgets flew like sparks from a Catherine wheel. —James Thurber, "The Car We Had to Push," *My Life and Hard Times.*

SIMILE AND METAPHOR

Most high school graduates know that a *simile* is a direct comparison, usually with *like* or *as,* a *metaphor* an implied comparison without *like* or *as.* The definitions are accurate enough. But the common mistake is to assume that these two figures of speech are the monopoly of poets. This is far more misleading than to have the same illusion about alliteration and onomatopoeia. For simile and metaphor are not incidental ornaments (metaphor) to be laid on like the decorations on a birthday cake (simile). They are the lifeblood of language (metaphor). A dictionary is a cemetery of dead metaphors (metaphor); the word *metaphor* itself has a metaphorical origin (the Greek means *carry-over*). We could not *eliminate* them (a dead metaphor meaning *put them out over the threshold*) if we tried.

Here is a passage of informal prose:

The way our sophisticated modern critic will read complex innuendoes into what is elemental is enough to wear one's patience to the bone. Must poor old Homer father a lot of esoteric things? Is the *Iliad* to have four or five layers of meaning, one below the other, like a pile of sandwiches? This digging up of unsuspected meanings goes too far. It spoils a poem to be all the time spading it or boring through its imagery with a steam drill. These critics spend too much of their time underground, and they look pale and unwholesome when they come up. And it often happens that what they bring up is something they have dropped themselves. There are commentators who have been digging all their lives and come up with their own pocket handkerchief. They expect you to be glad about it. They think a poet, like a dog, no sooner happens on a good thing than he wants to bury it. —Frank Moore Colby, "Literary Burrowing," *Imaginary Obligations.*

Of the ten sentences in that paragraph only one is strictly literal, without a living simile or metaphor: *They expect you to be glad about it.* The key metaphor of burrowing is carried further than is common in modern prose; a humorist may take more liberties with figurative language than a more serious prose writer. But notice that in themselves the figures are all easy, natural, homely, essentially "unpoetic." And notice also that by using similes and metaphors, the writer is treating the highly abstract subject of literary criticism in the most concrete terms. This does not mean that he has consciously said to himself: "I shall sprinkle the page full of similes and metaphors to make my meaning clear." These figures are the natural result of an effort to make the abstract concrete. Similar figures inevitably come to any observant writer who is trying hard to express himself clearly and concretely.

Aristotle asserted wisely that a mastery of metaphor, based on "the intuitive perception of the similarity in dissimilars," cannot be learned from others. A beginning writer is in for trouble if he consciously sets out to write more metaphorically. But he can learn a few tests for measuring the effectiveness of the similes and metaphors that do occur to him. Most ineffective figures of speech are either (1) trite, (2) inappropriate, or (3) mixed.

1. TRITENESS: Trite similes and metaphors have already been considered in the discussion of clichés (see page 249). Such inevitable comparisons as *brown as a berry* and *brave as a lion* are similes; and many of the canned adjective-noun com-binations—*acid test, budding genius, clinging vine*—are metaphors, though custom has staled their metaphorical flavor. George Orwell's rule for avoiding such metaphorical clichés is strict but sensible: "Never use a metaphor, simile or other figure of speech which you are used to seeing in print." Their consistent use betrays a writer who is too lazy to create his own figures through the natural process of looking intently at his subject. They are annoying to a mature reader not only because he is tired of seeing them but because they have lost their power to evoke a clear-cut picture. And that is the only justification for the existence of a simile or metaphor.

The difference between trite and fresh figures should be obvious at a glance:

Trite	*Fresh*
He was as bald as a billiard ball.	The whites of his eyes were discoloured, like ancient billiard balls. —Aldous Huxley, *Young Archimedes.*

A man who is filled with the spirit of adventure will hitch his wagon to a star.

For an adventure differs from a mere feat in that it is tied to the eternally unattainable. Only one end of the rope is in the hand, the other is not visible, and neither prayers, nor daring, nor reason can shake it free. —William Bolitho, *Twelve Against the Gods.*

He is a complete bonehead.

Intellectually he is a nothingness, like interstellar space—a vast vacuum occasionally crossed by homeless, wandering clichés. —John Gunther, *Inside U.S.A.*

There is a grind in the class who is always shooting his mouth off.

The well-crammed youngster is like a siphon bottle. Press the handle and he fizzes in a welcome relief from pressure. —Henry Seidel Canby, *Alma Mater.*

2. INAPPROPRIATENESS: The test of appropriateness applies as surely to a figure of speech as to a single word. A simile or metaphor may be inappropriate because it is too grand for the context or too vulgar, too serious or too comical—because, in short, the picture it conjures up is hanging in the wrong gallery. Even without a broader view of their context, the following student figures are questionable:

The night was as dark as ink and the heavens were *perspiring a cold sweat* that blanketed everything.

He was in full evening attire except that his white tie had vanished and all that remained was a grey collar bent *like a river as it winds its way among the mountains.*

Beautiful colored evening gowns filled with *little bunches of mirth and laughter* flitted around the floor attracting the attention of many a young gentleman.

The radio certainly was an inspiring discovery, and its place in the average home is *like that of the saddle on a horse.*

In the first example, *dark as ink* is trite and the picture of a cold sweat blanketing might be condemned as mixed. But the main question is whether it is appropriate for the *heavens* to *perspire* a *cold sweat.* Heavens is poetic; *perspire* is a genteel euphemism; *cold sweat* is an informal phrase commonly used to describe a physical symptom of fear. In the second sentence, the student has used a forced pseudo-poetic simile absurdly out of place in a prosaic context, if not inaccurate geologically. The questionable image of the *gowns flitting,* in the third sentence, might be explained away as whimsy or *synecdoche,* a figure of speech in which the part is used for the whole. But *bunches,* a word commonly associated with celery or grapes or flowers, is a singularly inappropriate metaphor for young women. In the fourth example, the only point of comparison between the radio and the saddle is their presumed indispensability. If the student had written, "The radio is as important in a house as a saddle is on a horse," the comparison might be unobjectionable, though hardly inspired. But by failing to specify the point of comparison, he leaves the reader to conjure up such irrelevant images as that of grandfather sitting astride the new RCA Victor on the rooftree.

3. MIXED METAPHORS: It would be more accurate to call a *mixed metaphor* "a mixture of metaphors," for it usually consists of more than one. There are three common kinds:

a. *A mixture of living metaphors*

If the victorious allies try to put a fence around Japan and let her stew in her own juice, they will create a festering sore.

He is convinced that the gravy of the capitalist is the sweated blood of the struggling wage-earner from whom the cream of life has been taken and whose milk has soured.

In the first example, the writer has asked the reader to transfer his attention in rapid succession from a corral to a kitchen to a clinic. Though the pictures are consecutive, they follow each other so quickly that the reader gets the effect of a double exposure. In the second sentence, the switch from dining room to sweatshop to dairy is also too rapid. It is impossible to draw a hard-and-fast line between a legitimate switch from metaphor to metaphor and one that is too sudden. Occasionally a writer will prepare the reader for the change ("to change the metaphor"), but this sort of apology can become tiresome. A general rule of thumb is this: *Once you have set sail in a metaphor, don't change horses in midstream until you have at least finished the sentence.*

b. *Two or more dead metaphors:* These come to life and fight when they are put side by side.

> At present the United States is using atomic power as an ace in the hole to hold over the heads of other world powers.
>
> Some of them move outside the universities as well, joining hands with this or that political splinter. —Russell B. Lynes, "Intellectuals vs. Philistines," New York *Times Book Review.*

By itself, *ace in the hole* would probably not come to life in this context as a picture from card playing; it is a familiar idiom to people who have never sat in on a game of stud poker. Used alone, *hold over the heads* is a commonplace idiom, familiar to many who have never heard of the sword of Damocles. But when the two are brought together, the reader may get a ludicrous picture of a poker player flourishing an ace in the hole over other players' heads. This is, of course, the last thing in the world he would do with it. In the second sentence, *joining hands* and *splinter* both come to life, and the reader conceives an image of a hand full of splinters.

c. *A careless mixture of the figurative and the literal*

> Hester Prynne wore a scarlet A, while the Reverend Dimmesdale put on a false front.
>
> My aunt was instrumental in my musical studies. Being a rather adept pianist, she entertained high hopes that I should follow in her footsteps.

For all its symbolic overtones in *The Scarlet Letter,* Hester's A for adultery is actually sewed on her dress. Placed beside it in the same sentence, Dimmesdale's false front looks like a literal addition to his wardrobe. The writer of the second passage doesn't want the reader to take *instrumental* literally, but in a musical context, it evokes a picture of trumpets and trombones. Worse still, the dead metaphor in the second sentence—*follow in her footsteps*—is reincarnated in this context and presents a vision of the aunt tramping up and down the keyboard with both feet.

SUMMARY

The discussion of this chapter cannot be reduced to a simple formula. But these generalities are safe guides for a beginning writer if they are not taken too literally:

1. Use fresh words, not tired words, but beware of neologisms or straining to avoid clichés.

2. Prefer short words to long words if they will convey your meaning with equal accuracy.

3. Wherever possible, express yourself in concrete words, not in abstractions.

4. Try to use neutral words in objective reporting and honest argument: in other contexts use charged words freely without slipping into overemphatic, overloaded writing.

5. Beware of violating euphony or overworking sound effects that call too much attention to themselves.

6. Use similes and metaphors to make your writing more clear and concrete, not to decorate it.

7. The final test of any word or expression is this: Is it appropriate in its context?

The requirement of appropriateness transcends all others. William Hazlitt put the main lesson of this chapter briefly and simply more than a century ago: "The proper force of words lies not in the words themselves, but in their application. A word may be a fine-sounding word, of an unusual length, and very imposing from its learning and novelty, and yet in the connection in which it is introduced, may be quite pointless and irrelevant. It is not pomp or pretension, but the adaptation of the expression to the idea that clenches a writer's meaning. . . ."

EXERCISES

I. Correct the malapropisms in the following sentences by substituting, where possible, the word that the writer may have had in mind:

1. It will be some time before I convict myself that this was a fortunate event. *an event of a* *converse*

2. All the previous night the lightning of a fierce electrical storm had made darkened London light as day; those who remembered the blood-red sunset of August 3, 1914, said it was a potent.

3. Lincoln had proved to be one of the greatest, best-loved, most dependent presidents this great democracy ever had.

4. The suffrage in the United States is restricted to criminals, idiots, illiterates, and citizens under twenty-one.

5. The instance I heard the shot I ran into the woods to see if my brother had borrowed my rifle again.

6. One of the things I remember from my childhood is that my scraped knees were always painted with some red or brown mendicant against infection.

7. The reason he didn't win is that the students had become discouraged and indigent and set out with blood in their eyes after me, leaving the contest unfinished.

8. After a hard week's work, I needed a laxative evening of cards in order to ease the nervous tension.

9. Incoming officers should consult the bulletin board regularly because the notices below pertain valuable information for them.

10. As the movie pictured it, the wild, unsettled West, with its cowboys and ranches, reminded me of the days of futile knights and their ladies.

11. Since he had not had any eminent contact with women before this experience, Philip Carey remained very bashful.

12. It is difficult to estimate the debt which the world owes to the ingenuous inventions of Steinmetz and Edison.

13. When Philip noticed that Miss Price was no longer attending the art classes, his consciousness disturbed him.

14. After Prince Albert's immature death, Queen Victoria was despondent for years.

15. Florence Nightingale devoted years of untiring effort to increasing and maintaining mortality.

16. The work in the eighth grade was so difficult I could never phantom it.

17. A business firm should have all its bills paid in order to remain soluble.

18. In contrast to the major characters, the clowns are used mostly to create a little derivation for the spectators.

19. The Lady Macbeth who spurns her husband on to kill Duncan is a different character from the pathetic sleepwalker of the later scenes.

20. The line must be kept taunt so that you can tell when the crab starts pecking on the bait.

21. Adolf the calvary man and George Tesman the historian were well-educated men who were driven to distraction by their selfish wives.

22. Strindberg's Laura is a wife that one can feel no affection for, but of course, that is to be expected in a misogyny.

23. As any student of the American form of government knows, the final result of a presidental election depends on the electrical vote.

24. When two strong men meet face to face, no matter what their color may be, they are equally respective of each other.

25. Hamlet was finally killed in a duel with Laertes, the brother of his diseased girl friend.

II. The following sentences contain questionable expressions that are discussed in the GLOSSARY. Identify them and suggest substitutes that are more accurate or more generally acceptable in writing. Distinguish where necessary between levels of usage.

1. The professor was aggravated by the students' trite alibis for not reading the assignment.

2. Lake Hopatcong is all the farther I get away from New York in the summer, and I have never been anywheres west of the Mississippi.

3. After the dam had busted, the residents of the town had less than a half hour in which to flee from their homes.

4. The critics all enthused over the childish simplicity of the lyrics in his first book, and I agreed with them.

5. The handsome, dark-complected champion is the son of emigrants, who entered the country in 1920.

6. Irregardless of how incredulous it may seem, the story is too well authenticated for anybody who knows the facts to suspicion it.

7. In his first year as coach he fielded an elegant team with a quarterback who was right clever in deceiving the opposition.

8. He had a swell time at Ennui-by-the-Sea, swimming, fishing, sailing, golfing, and etc.

9. This is not as unique a specie as the one which inhabits the upper reaches of the river.

10. His feelings in regards to the governor's speech were that it was inexcusably lousy.

III. Discuss in detail the choice of words in the following passage:

Gentlemen, this is only the commencement. In these hallowed halls you have spent the four happiest years of your lives. But that is only a fraction of the three score years and ten which the finger of Fate deals us in this vale of tears. In the outside world you will find that there are two kinds of people playing the game of life: those who put their shoulders to the wheel and those who merely stand on the side lines. I don't mean to infer that you should be as busy as a bee twenty-four hours a day, for all work and no play makes Jack a dull boy. I mean that when you play, you should play hard, and that when you work, you should keep your nose to the grindstone. As the great poet Rudyard Kipling has well said, and I quote, you should fill the unforgetful minute with sixty seconds worth of distance run. Your Alma Mater sends you forth in troublous times. Life is no bed of roses, gentlemen; it is a fierce struggle for existence in which the law of the survival of the fittest prevails until the bitter end. But even though the strife of life is as keen as a knife, it is not for filthy lucre only but for all the wonderful things that money can buy in this prosperous land of ours. Last but by no means least, it is a struggle for the finer things in life which the almighty dollar can never buy. Gentlemen, I am green with envy when I consider your golden opportunities. You youth of today will be the adults of tomorrow. It is a challenge that I hope you will meet like men before the Grim Reaper cuts the threads of your existence. As I look into the sea of faces before me and know that you are part of the wave of the future, I feel confident that this nation cannot fail.

IV. Draw up lists of ten clichés and ten euphemisms that you have found especially annoying.

V. Without omitting any essential details, rewrite the following passages, substituting concrete words for fuzzy abstractions:

1. A female relative of mine made it financially possible for me to pursue the study of a musical instrument, and she followed my attainments with great interest until further practice was interrupted by illness.

2. Whenever any of the participants encountered any difficulty on the field, the coach always rendered counsel and assistance which would make a recurrence unlikely.

3. The acquisition of higher education cannot be attained without considerable amounts of both persistence and financial competence.

4. My relations with the opposite sex have never been entirely satisfactory as regards mutual participation in social occasions.

5. Anyone with radical ideas about the system in which all patriotic Americans believe should be denied the privileges of freedom.

6. The theory that differences in pupil capacity and status can be eliminated by uniform instruction and evaluation does not receive my approbation.

7. No individual can be properly comprehended unless both the temporal and geographical factors of his environment are taken into account.

8. It is inadvisable to attempt an evaluation of prospects that are still in an embryonic stage of development.

9. The actions and attitudes directed by one member of a group activity toward another should be such as the former would desire the latter to direct toward him in retaliation.

10. The sociologist maintained that individuals habituated to similar behavior are characterized by a tendency toward societal organization among themselves.

VI. Write a five-hundred-word theme in which you define and illustrate your conception of one of the abstract terms listed on page 258.

VII. Rewrite the following passages, removing as much of the emotional bias as you can by substituting neutral words for charged words. Do not attempt to translate word for word.

1. What men, in their egoism, constantly mistake for a deficiency of intelligence in woman is merely an incapacity for mastering that mass of small intellectual tricks, that complex of petty knowledges, that collection of cerebral rubber-stamps, which constitutes the chief mental equipment of the average male. A man thinks that he is more intelligent than his wife because he can add up a column of figures more accurately, and because he understands the imbecile jargon of the stock market, and because he is able to distinguish between the ideas of rival politicians, and because he is privy to the minutiae of some sordid and degrading business or profession, say soap-selling or the law. But these empty talents, of course, are not really signs of a profound intelligence; they are, in fact, merely superficial accomplishments, and their acquirement puts little more strain on the mental powers than a chimpanzee

suffers in learning how to catch a penny or scratch a match. The whole bag of tricks of the average business man, or even of the average professional man, is inordinately childish. It takes no more actual sagacity to carry on the everyday hawking and haggling of the world, or to ladle out its normal doses of bad medicine and worse law, than it takes to operate a taxicab or fry a pan of fish. No observant person, indeed, can come into close contact with the general run of business and professional men—I confine myself to those who seem to get on in the world, and exclude the admitted failures—without marveling at their intellectual lethargy, their incurable ingenuousness, their appalling lack of ordinary sense. The late Charles Francis Adams, a grandson of one American President and a great-grandson of another, after a long lifetime in intimate association with some of the chief business "geniuses" of that paradise of traders and usurers, the United States, reported in his old age that he had never heard a single one of them say anything worth hearing. These were vigorous and masculine men, but intellectually they were all blank cartridges.   —H. L. Mencken, *In Defense of Women.*

2. The kick was high and long. Everyone on the Seconds bench stood up. The new Varsity quarterback waited coldly beneath the unfinished arch of fall. He seemed to have set aside just enough mind for the catch and to have sent the rest of awareness ahead of him, where the brass and red adzehead of interference was hardening as it formed. Behind protection he ran for ten yards, but after two blackshirts broke through and touched his cleats with their fingers as they fell he cut at right angles across the field, running fiercely for the sideline in front of the Seconds bench. He was a man running along a beach through ankle-high surf, trying always to have white water underfoot and obliged to yield a little shoreward as the waves ahead of him grew ready for breaking. There was no contortion in his face. Icily as a surgeon he scanned what was offered him. Just as the Seconds quarterback leaped to where he would have been he halted and spinning half around, shifted the ball to his other arm. Two blackshirts went by, slant torsos trying to stop themselves. He jigsawed irregularly away from the deserted corner of the field on the Varsity side. Farley almost caught him but was indianized by the Varsity captain against the red wheels of an equipment wagon. He was over the goal line before Babb plowed with chin, knee and toecap a brown wet scar in the green turf behind him.

—George Anthony Weller, *Not to Eat, Not for Love.*

3. The radio is mom's final tool, for it stamps everybody who

listens with the matriarchal brand—its superstitions, prejudices, devotional rules, taboos, musts, and all other qualifications needful to its maintenance. Just as Goebbels has revealed what can be done with such a mass-stamping of the public psyche in his nation, so our land is a living representation of the same fact worked out in matriarchal sentimentality, goo, slop, hidden cruelty, and the foreshadow of national death.

That alone is sinister enough, but the process is still more vicious, because it fills in every crack and cranny of mom's time and mind—and pop's also, since he has long ago yielded the dial-privilege to his female; so that a whole nation of people lives in eternal fugue and never has to deal for one second with itself or its own problems. Any interior sign of worry, wonder, speculation, anxiety, apprehension—or even a stirring of an enfeebled will to plan sanely—can be annihilated by an electrical click whereby the populace puts itself in the place, the untenable place —of somebody called Myrt, for Christ's sake—and never has even to try to *be* itself alone in the presence of this real world.

This is Nirvana at last. It is also entropy. For here the spirit of man, absorbed, disoriented, confused, identified with ten thousand spurious personalities and motives, has utterly lost itself. By this means is man altogether lost. The radio, in very truth, sells soap. We could confine it to music, intelligent discourse, and news—all other uses being dangerous—but mom will not let us. Rather than study herself and her environment with the necessary honesty, she will fight for this poisoned syrup to the last. Rather than take up her democratic responsibility in this mighty and tottering republic, she will bring it crashing down simply to maintain to the final rumble of ruin her personal feudalism. Once, sentimentalism was piecework, or cost the price of a movie or a book; now it is mass produced and not merely free, but almost compulsory. —Philip Wylie, *Generation of Vipers.*

VIII. Rewrite the following passages to make them more euphonious:

1. As soon as the speaker said something serious concerning Shelley, I knew that I had chanced into one of the advanced courses in the Romantic Poets.

2. I don't like people who are too punctilious about punctuality at social functions.

3. Although he had to admit that the play was a bit of a hit, **he** was too modest to predict a long run for it.

4. He was as intensely interested in Italy's international integrity as in its internal security.

5. His relation to the organization hardly justified the Senator's blanketing the nation with impatient lamentations.

IX. Analyze the figures of speech in the following passages, distinguishing the effective ones from those that are trite, inappropriate, or mixed:

1. The switch about in the stands of various countries provides another piece of evidence to the effect that while politics makes strange bed fellows, wars, which so often spawn from politics, do not play second fiddle in that respect. —Easton (Pennsylvania) *Express*.

2. We demand the right to self-government and will oppose by every means at our command attempts to sell us down the river by those who want to gobble us up to make a Roman holiday for themselves.

3. To burn always with this hard, gem-like flame, to maintain this ecstasy, is success in life. —Walter Pater, *Studies in the History of the Renaissance*.

4. In the twentieth century there is hardly a realm of activity left in which the hand of woman has never set foot.

5. To some extent he has even influenced the naturally democratic Irish population of his city in this regard, so that they have become known for graduating through Family stages from "Shanty" Irish to "Lace-curtain" Irish, and finally to "Venetian-blind" Irish, and to look rather askance at those a rung below them on the shamrock path. —Cleveland Amory, *The Proper Bostonians*.

6. Onto the floor we went, Alice and I, and to the sweet strains of Horace Heidt's music, we were soon swept along in the maelstrom of dancers, much like a cake of ice on a flooded river in early spring, with a sea of smiling faces around us.

7. A healthy university in a healthy democracy is a free society in miniature. The pesky nature of democratic life is that it has no comfortable rigidity; it always hangs by a thread, never quite submits to consolidation or solidification, is always being challenged, always being defended. The seeming insubstantiality of this thread is a matter of concern and worry to persons who naturally would prefer a more robust support for the beloved structure. The thread is particularly worrisome, we think, to men of tidy habits and large affairs, who are accustomed to reinforce themselves at every possible turn and who want to do as much for their alma mater. But they do not always perceive

that the elasticity of democracy is its strength—like the web of a spider, which bends but holds. The desire to give the whole thing greater rigidity and a more conventional set of fastenings is almost overwhelming in these times when the strain is great, and it makes professed lovers of liberty propose measures that show little real faith in liberty.

—"The Talk of the Town," *New Yorker.*

8. Using Cyrano as their vehicle, actors have climbed the ladder of fame and producers have become happily dough-heavy.

9. Rostand reached back into the files of seventeenth-century France and plucked Cyrano from the well-padded bosom of obscurity and placed him once again in the limelight.

10. Soft-spoken men with the gift of gab who oil up internal turmoil by sneakily covering it up are a detriment to society.

11. A sentence begins quite simply, then it undulates and expands, parentheses intervene like quick-set hedges, the flowers of comparison bloom, and three fields off, like a wounded partridge, crouches the principal verb, making one wonder as one picks it up, poor little thing, whether after all it was worth such a tramp, so many guns, and such expensive dogs, and what, after all, is its relation to the main subject, potted so gaily half a page back, and proving finally to have been in the accusative case. —E. M. Forster, "Proust," *Abinger Harvest.*

12. Perhaps I am placing too much responsibility upon the teacher, but I think it is her duty to help students to interpret poetry by cutting it down to their size.

13. Strachey starts his biography of Florence Nightingale by having her up on a pedestal. Public opinion had nearly made a saint of her, and Strachey did his best to chop her down to her real size. Throughout the essay he seemed to have a chip on his shoulder.

14. The moving belt of industry has been adopted by education. The result is the same in both instances. The nut will fit only one kind of bolt. It cannot be used for any other purpose than to fit that certain bolt. It is a purely industrial robot. Those who come through the "pre"-courses and vocational courses, the product of the educational moving belt, are often educational robots—fit for just one thing and a poor fit at that. —Quoted by Robert Maynard Hutchins, "Education for Freedom," *Harper's Magazine.*

15. From the moment you press the Stop-Start Switch, the power-packed motor purrs its way through every bit of stubble, every patch of wire, from sideburn to sideburn. —Advertisement in the *Saturday Evening Post.*

16. His work [Coleridge's] is abundant in high promise and since the day of his death posterity has been trying to cash his I.O.U.'s. —H. V. D. Dyson and John Butt, *Augustans and Romantics.*

17. The campaign is well past the half-way stage, but contributors will have to cough up more money from their pockets if we are to carry the ball across the finish line.

18. The speaker certainly said a mouthful when he said: "An honest political platform is not one on which all politicians can stand." My opponent should put that in his pipe and smoke it.

19. Like another editor we talked to the other day, we are crazy to be *for* something, instead of being obliged to use so much space throwing punches at the restrictions, gremlins, regulations, barriers and mere anarchy which so many leaders of the misled human race seem determined to toss in the machinery, thereby postponing a good part of the things we should certainly be plugging for if the track were clear. —Editorial in the *Saturday Evening Post.*

20. His face was clean-shaven, rosy, and of cherubic fulness; his eyes beamed owlishly through spectacles which nobody had ever seen him take off. But for those spectacles he might have passed for a well-groomed baby in a soap-advertisement. —Norman Douglas, *South Wind.*

CHAPTER TEN

Style and Tone

Effectiveness of assertion is the Alpha and Omega of style. He who has nothing to assert has no style and can have none; he who has something to assert will go as far in power of style as its momentousness and his conviction will carry him.
—George Bernard Shaw.

A man's style in any art should be like his dress—it should attract as little attention as possible.
—Samuel Butler.

Although the word has seldom appeared in the discussion so far, this whole book has been about style. The general topics of the first two chapters; the organization of paragraphs; grammar, especially because it involves a choice among levels of usage; sentence structure, especially the problems of length, economy, variety, and emphasis; punctuation, when it extends beyond slavish obedience to black-and-white rules; spelling, to a relatively slight extent; and, most important of all, the choice of words and figures of speech—all are matters of style. For an effective prose style is not a mechanical mannerism that can be turned on like a spigot or a collection of glittering ornaments to hang on the bare limbs of sentences. In its broadest sense the elusive term *style* embraces the whole problem of how writing is written. The quotations from Shaw and Butler are only two small nuggets from a vast mine of critical commentary on the subject. Obviously, then, a single chapter can do no more than touch a few aspects of style, with a generous array of samples to keep the discussion as concrete as possible. But such a discussion should be a useful review of some of the important principles of good writing.

THE PLAIN AND ORNATE STYLES

Read the following passages aloud:

1. I ate the ham and eggs and drank the beer. The ham and eggs were in a round dish—the ham underneath and the eggs on top. It was very hot and at the first mouthful I had to take a drink of beer to cool my mouth. I was hungry and I asked the waiter for another order. I drank several glasses of beer. I was not thinking at all but read the paper of the man opposite me. It was about the break through on the British front. When he realized I was reading the back of his paper he folded it over. I thought of asking the waiter for a paper, but I could not concentrate. It was hot in the café and the air was bad. Many of the people at the tables knew one another. There were several card games going on. The waiters were busy bringing drinks from the bar to the tables. Two men came in and could find no place to sit. They stood opposite the table where I was. I ordered another beer. I was not ready to leave yet. It was too soon to go back to the hospital. I tried not to think and to be perfectly calm. The men stood around but no one was leaving, so they went out. I drank another beer. There was quite a pile of saucers now on the table in front of me. The man opposite me had taken off his spectacles, put them away in a case, folded his paper and put it in his pocket and now sat holding his liqueur glass and looking out at the room. Suddenly I knew I had to get back. I called the waiter, paid the reckoning, got into my coat, put on my hat and started out the door. I walked through the rain up to the hospital. —Ernest Hemingway, *A Farewell to Arms.*

2. And for a moment all the silver space was printed with the thousand forms of himself and Ben. There, by the corner in from Academy Street, Eugene watched his own approach; there by the City Hall, he strode with lifted knees; there, by the curb upon the step, he stood, peopling the night with the great lost legion of himself—the thousand forms that came, that passed, that wove and shifted in unending change, and that remained unchanging Him.

And through the Square, unwoven from lost time, the fierce bright horde of Ben spun in and out its deathless loom. Ben, in a thousand moments, walked the square; Ben of the lost years, the forgotten days, the unremembered hours; prowled by the moonlit façades; vanished, returned, left and rejoined himself, was one and many—deathless Ben in search of the lost dead lusts, the finished enterprise, the unfound door

—unchanging Ben multiplying himself in form, by all the brick façades entering and coming out.

And as Eugene watched the army of himself and Ben, which were not ghosts and which were lost, he saw himself—his son, his boy, his lost and virgin flesh—come over past the fountain, leaning against the loaded canvas bag, and walking down with rapid crippled stride past Gant's toward Niggertown in young pre-natal dawn. And as he passed the porch where he sat watching, he saw the lost child-face below the lumpy ragged cap, drugged in the magic of unheard music, listening for the far-forested horn-note, the speechless almost captured pass-word. The fast boy-hands folded the fresh sheets, but the fabulous lost face went by, steeped in its incantations. —Thomas Wolfe, *Look Homeward, Angel.*

Each of these passages comes near the dramatic close of a celebrated American novel published in 1929. Each passage portrays a moment of intense emotion in the life of the hero. Frederic Henry in *A Farewell to Arms* is trying to eat a calm supper between visits to the nearby hospital, where Catherine Barkley, who has just borne his child, is on the threshold of death. Eugene Gant in *Look Homeward, Angel* wanders in a dream through the city square of his birthplace, haunted by the inescapable memories of his dead brother. But there the resemblance ends. The ear alone can catch much of the difference. In the Hemingway passage the sentences are short and jerky; they are free from the traditional devices of platform rhetoric; their rhythm is the staccato pace of rapid conversation. Wolfe's sentences are long and swinging. He freely uses calculated repetition ("There, by the corner . . . Eugene watched . . . there by the City Hall, he strode . . . there by the curb . . . he stood"; "Ben, in a thousand moments . . . Ben of the lost years, the forgotten days, the unremembered hours . . . . deathless Ben in search of the lost dead lusts . . . unchanging Ben multiplying himself in form"). Through his sentences sweeps the music of a meter that soars above the irregular rhythms of conversation—time-honored blank verse:

> And for a moment all the silver space . . . .
> there, by the curb upon the step, he stood . . .
> that wove and shifted in unending change . . . .

And through the Square, unwoven from lost time,
the fierce bright horde of Ben spun in and out
its deathless loom. Ben, in a thousand moments . . . ;
Ben of the lost years, the forgotten days . . . .
his son, his boy, his lost and virgin flesh . . .
leaning against the loaded canvas bag,
and walking down with rapid crippled stride . . .
toward Niggertown in young pre-natal dawn. . . .

A superficial glance at the diction reveals a similar contrast. The first passage contains only one phrase (*paid the reckoning*) that might not fit naturally into the relaxed pattern of everyday talk. In fact, there isn't a single living metaphor in the entire passage. The quotation from Wolfe is a rich tapestry of metaphor: "all the silver space was printed with the thousand forms of himself and Ben"; "peopling the night with the great lost legion of himself"; "the fierce bright horde of Ben spun in and out its deathless loom"; "in young, pre-natal dawn"—to mention a random handful. It is not hard to see why a good-sized anthology has been quarried from the "poetical passages" in Wolfe's novels and short stories.

But it would be misleading to characterize the Hemingway passage as prosaic. For it conveys an underlying emotion that is intensified by the contrast with the matter-of-factness on the surface. In this selection Hemingway derives much of his effect from what he leaves unsaid. He soft-pedals the feelings of his hero, whereas Wolfe pulls out most of the stops. Hemingway understates, or at most merely states; Wolfe consistently overstates. Hemingway relies for effect on the eloquence of stark simplicity, Wolfe on the rhetorical artifice of traditional poetry or "poetic prose." The passage from *A Farewell to Arms* is written in a *plain style,* the passage from *Look Homeward, Angel* in an *ornate style.*

Sooner or later most discussions of prose style arrive at some such arbitrary distinction. In the nineteenth century Matthew Arnold characterized the plain manner as "Attic prose," the ornate as "Asiatic." In our time Cyril Connolly distinguishes between the "vernacular" and the "Mandarin" styles. A student of English literature will find both tendencies amply represented: Roger Ascham and John Lyly in the sixteenth century; Izaak Walton and Sir Thomas Browne in the seventeenth; Goldsmith and Burke in the eighteenth; Huxley and Ruskin in the nineteenth—plain and ornate existing side by side through the centuries.

Of course, the style of any writer, regardless of his personal trademark, will vary in accordance with his subject and his purpose. When he aimed only to clarify a scientific principle, Huxley could write the plainest down-to-earth prose (see page 265); when he mounted a rostrum to spread the gospel of evolution, he sometimes soared away on the wings of rhetoric. The purple patches of Ruskin's ornate prose are far more frequent in his praise of Turner's paintings than in his lay sermons on economics. Here are two passages from a celebrated modern writer:

1. I have myself, full confidence that if all do their duty, if nothing is neglected, and if the best arrangements are made, as they are being made, we shall prove ourselves once again able to defend our Island home, to ride out the storm of war, and to outlive the menace of tyranny, if necessary for years, if necessary alone. At any rate, that is what we are going to try to do. That is the resolve of His Majesty's Government—every man of them. That is the will of Parliament and the nation. The British Empire and the French Republic, linked together in their cause and in their need, will defend to the death their native soil, aiding each other like good comrades to the utmost of their strength. Even though large tracts of Europe and many old and famous States have fallen or may fall into the grip of the Gestapo and all the odious apparatus of Nazi rule, we shall not flag or fail. We shall go on to the end, we shall fight in France, we shall fight on the seas and oceans, we shall fight with growing confidence and growing strength in the air, we shall defend our Island, whatever the cost may be, we shall fight on the beaches, we shall fight on the landing grounds, we shall fight in the fields and in the streets, we shall fight in the hills; we shall never surrender, and even if, which I do not for a moment believe, this Island or a large part of it were subjugated and starving, then our Empire beyond the seas, armed and guarded by the British Fleet, would carry on the struggle, until, in God's good time, the New World, with all its

power and might, steps forth to the rescue and the liberation of the old. —Winston Churchill, *Blood, Sweat, and Tears.*

2. I continued in this unpretentious situation for nearly a year. However, by being so long in the lowest form I gained an immense advantage over the cleverer boys. They all went on to learn Latin and Greek and splendid things like that. But I was taught English. We were considered such dunces that we could learn only English. Mr. Somervell—a most delightful man, to whom my debt is great—was charged with the duty of teaching the stupidest boys the most disregarded thing—namely, to write mere English. He knew how to do it. He taught it as no one else has ever taught it. Not only did we learn English parsing thoroughly, but we also practised continually English analysis. Mr. Somervell had a system of his own. He took a fairly long sentence and broke it up into its components by means of black, red, blue, and green inks. Subject, verb, object: Relative Clauses, Conditional Clauses, Conjunctive and Disjunctive Clauses! Each had its colour and its bracket. It was a kind of drill. We did it almost daily. As I remained in the Third Fourth . . . three times as long as anyone else, I had three times as much of it. I learned it thoroughly. Thus I got into my bones the essential structure of the ordinary British sentence—which is a noble thing. And when in after years my schoolfellows who had won prizes and distinction for writing such beautiful Latin poetry and pithy Greek epigrams had to come down again to common English, to earn their living or make their way, I did not feel myself at any disadvantage. Naturally I am biassed in favor of boys learning English. I would make them all learn English: and then I would let the clever ones learn Latin as an honour, and Greek as a treat. But the only thing I would whip them for is not knowing English. I would whip them hard for that. —Winston Churchill, *My Early Life, A Roving Commission.*

When Winston Churchill faced the House of Commons in a critical hour after the retreat from Dunkirk, he rose to the historic occasion. The carefully wrought balance and rhythm of the sentences; the richly charged words (*duty, resolve, His Majesty's Government, British Empire, native soil, struggle, New World, power, might, rescue, liberation*); the taut alliterative phrases (*do their duty, nothing is neglected, defend to the death, grip of the Gestapo, flag or fail, subjugated and starving*); above all, the lavish expenditure of repetition—these are marks of the oratorical grand manner. But in one of the more peaceful chapters of a book of reminiscences, where the thunder roll of the rostrum would be inappropriate, Churchill could write plain, relaxed prose with the flavor of genuine, if somewhat genteel, conversation.

Again the discussion comes back to *appropriateness*. This book has been slanted in favor of the plain style partly because the most characteristic American prose in the middle of the twentieth century is plain and unadorned, partly because the ornate style is inappropriate to the subjects on which the college undergraduate usually writes. A simple narrative, a simple piece of description, a simple explanation of an idea or a process—to deck these out in the grand manner, whether in an English course or a course in reinforced concrete, is like hiring a philharmonic orchestra to play a fugue or mounting a platform to harangue friends in your own living room.

FLAT WRITING AND FINE WRITING

It is important to remember that the plain style is seldom as simple as it appears. The trick is not to ignore art, but to conceal it: to create the illusion of artlessness. Hemingway's simplicity is misleading, as many of his imitators have learned to their sorrow. A careful examination of the second passage from Winston Churchill gives the game away. Listen again to these four sentences: "They all went on to learn Latin and Greek and splendid things like that. But I was taught English. We were considered such dunces that we could learn only English. Mr. Somervell—a most delightful man, to whom my debt is great—was charged with the duty of teaching the stupidest boys the most disregarded thing—namely, to write mere English." After the sentence about the splendors of Latin and Greek, the brief second sentence is a calculated anticlimax. The repetition of *English, only English,* and *mere English* is obviously no accident. Here is a schoolboy at England's fashionable Harrow in 1887 who is denied the traditional privilege of wrestling with the classics in company with his more scholarly classmates and is penalized with a triple exposure to—of all things—his native tongue, English. Imagine that! From his perspective of 1930 the author is enjoying the wonder of it, and he wants the reader to enjoy it too. Thus the drill with Mr. Somervell becomes, not a prosaic statement of fact, but a vari-colored miracle. In a series of blunt short sentences Churchill carefully emphasizes his teacher's thoroughness ("He knew how to do it. He taught it as no one else has ever taught it. . . . It was a kind of drill. We did it almost daily. . . . I learned it thor-oughly"). By the time he comes to the key sentence ("Thus I got into my bones the essential structure of the ordinary British sen-tence—which is a noble thing") the reader is prepared for the trenchant metaphor and the romantic adjective *noble*. But this is not all. The writer must clinch the paradox of a triumph born in defeat by contrasting the solid, practical value of "common English" (the phrase is obviously ironic by now) with the elegant veneer of "such beautiful Latin poetry and pithy Greek epigrams" (equally ironic). And in driving home the pedagogical point, again he resorts to repetition: "Naturally I am biassed in favor of boys learning English. I would make them all learn Eng-lish . . . . But the only thing I would whip them for is not know-ing English. I would whip them hard for that." In its way, this plain paragraph is more artfully contrived than the impassioned oration after Dunkirk.

Reduce this passage to a mere statement of essential facts and what do you get?

I was so stupid in school that while all the bright boys were learning Latin and Greek, I had to study English. My teacher, Mr. Somervell, was a good English teacher, and he taught me grammar very thoroughly. When I grew up, I found that I was just as well off as my schoolmates, who had to learn English after all to get ahead in life. Latin and Greek are all right in their place, but I think everyone should be made to learn English.

Simple, natural, clear, correct English—but completely without flavor. The plain style doesn't have to be a bald style. Good plain writing is not flat writing.

At the other extreme, the student who sincerely attempts an ornate prose style must beware of the false rhetoric of "fine writing." A book reviewer discerns this common fault in a pro-fessional novelist:

Mrs. Janeway's over-writing is so strident, so full of top-heavy imagery, that she actually seems reluctant to say a simple thing simply. A fountain pen doesn't merely leak; it "hemorrhages." The lights of a passing train aren't merely lights; they are "long, low, little fires like the ones that lick up through the pavements of hell." The bitterness between John and his wife is not just bitterness; it is "the terrible ulcerous bedsores of marriage." This is bad writing because it is lazy writing, which eventually arrives at nothing whatever except the irritation induced by a conversation carried on in shouts. —John K. Hutchens, New York *Herald Tribune*.

An intelligent college freshman, who eventually learned to write with admirable simplicity, launched his first theme with this fanfare:

At my arrival at college I gazed in open-mouthed naïveté after the manner of all freshmen, at the spectacular galaxy of character and personality, including the best and the worst, the most common and the most unique that paradoxical humanity has to offer its apprentices. It was not until several months after my violent introduction into this seething maelstrom in which learning battles ignorance that I got a finger-hold on the drifting straw of perception and was carried to an elusive conclusion on which to buoy my mental weight. I found that I had lost my inspiration where the road forks toward wisdom or knowledge. This change of attitude altered my conviction that knowledge is the doorway to accomplishment and showed me that knowledge is merely the key to the door of the palace of wisdom. This ideal thrusts me far back into the kindergarten of wisdom's school. I find that I am not well on the road to education, but merely on a footpath leading to the highway or wisdom. Truly, I cannot expect startling and spectacular revelations at every bend in the road, but the trek to wisdom is a gratifying journey.

That is bad writing because it is not natural writing. It is too self-consciously "literary." The student's genuine emotion is not strong enough to carry the heavy cargo of his metaphors.

The problem then is not for a writer to cultivate *a style* and cling to it stubbornly regardless of what he is writing or why. The problem is to find the right balance between the aim and the art, between the emotion and the language chosen to convey it.

Reduced to its lowest terms, a good style is an appropriate adjustment of the means to the end.

GOBBLEDYGOOK

Self-consciousness about style may result in unnatural writing. But complete indifference to style may leave the writer an easy prey to a disease that has become fashionable in recent years. In a famous lecture published in 1916, Sir Arthur Quiller-Couch called it *jargon*.[1] In a violent diatribe from Washington in 1944, Maury Maverick brought it out of the Freshman English laboratory and renamed it *gobbledygook*. Because it applies more accurately to the vocabulary of a special group, the word *jargon* is misleading as a synonym for gibberish-in-general. *Gobbledygook*, an onomatopoetic imitation of the gobbling of a Texas turkey, has apparently found a permanent place in the language.

When the symptoms of gobbledygook are isolated, they turn out to be time-honored failings of bad writing which English teachers have been fighting for decades. But they are especially prominent in the writing of experts, who have never learned or have forgotten the lessons of Freshman English. Since most college undergraduates will some day be experts in something, gobbledygook is analyzed here as a final review and a warning: (The reader of the "improved" versions must remember that genuine gobbledygook defies accurate translation.)

1. INVOLVED SENTENCE STRUCTURE

Gobbledygook	*Improved*
It is difficult to find a word which expresses the whole self which is involved here as clearly and intelligibly as *behavior* and *attitude* describe the parts of the self which are involved in the first two learning reactions I have illustrated.	It is hard to find a word expressing the whole self as accurately as *behavior* and *attitude* describe the parts of the self involved in the first two learning reactions illustrated.

---

[1] *On the Art of Writing*, New York, 1916, pp. 100–126.

This is a relatively inoffensive example, but the Chinese box construction (*which*-within-*which*-within-*which*) presents the reader with a puzzle, not a clear statement.

2. UNNECESSARY REPETITION

Gobbledygook

A contract shall be considered a single premium life insurance or endowment contract if substantially all the premiums on such contract are paid within a period of four years from the date on which the contract is purchased.

When the tax liability of an individual for 1942 is discharged and such tax liability is greater than the tax for 1943, the excess of 1942 over the 1943 tax liability is added to the 1943 tax liability.

Improved

A single premium life insurance or endowment contract is one on which most of the premiums are paid within four years of its purchase date.

If you have paid all your tax for 1942 and it exceeds your liability for 1943, add the difference between them to your 1943 liability.

3. CIRCUMLOCUTIONS

Gobbledygook

Wherever children are dealt with by schools or other agencies, there has been relatively little clarity in making the differentiation as to whether the problem is primarily a lack of intrinsic stuff or whether the primary problem is a disorder in capacity to form relationships.

In the case of the fourth child or student, however, a problem is presented which is insoluble.

Improved

Wherever schools or other agencies deal with a child, it is seldom clear whether his primary problem is a lack of intelligence or an inability to form relationships.

The fourth child, however, presents an insoluble problem.

Experts in gobbledygook display a special fondness for the passive voice ("It must be recognized that"; "It can be observed that"; "The taxpayer's home address must be supplied and a permanent business address may be added"). They also like circumlocutions pivoting on the word *case:* When the author of a tax form writes, "In the case of a husband and wife living together," he apparently means, "When a husband and wife live together"; when he writes, "Except in the case of amounts attributable to deductions," he means simply, "Except for amounts attributable to deductions." Other circumlocutions abound in the jungle of gobbledygook: *due to the fact that* means *because; to the extent that* sprawls in place of *if; for the purpose of determining* equals *to determine.* The taxpayer does not *pay;* he *makes payment of.* Property is not *bought;* it is *acquired by purchase.* The list is endless.

4. A GOBBLEDYGOOK VOCABULARY

When concrete nouns are replaced by abstractions, simple words by pseudo-technical jargon, the result is gobbledygook.

Gobbledygook	*Improved*
Two important factors constitute the grounds for the uniqueness of supervision as educational method: first, the content of social case work and its training goals for the worker; and second, the learning situation composed of two people, a supervisor and a student, instead of a class situation.	In two important ways supervision in social case work differs from other teaching: (1) the worker has different problems and training goals; and (2) the teacher has only one student instead of an entire class.

Dressed in sober gobbledygook, that relatively unobjectionable passage has an awesome academic air. Eliminate the pseudo-technical jargon (*factors,* a favorite in gobbledygook; *learning situation; class situation*) and the assertion becomes absurdly simple. The gobbledygook expert is especially fond of cobblestone rhetoric (see page 268). Deprive him of the abstract nouns in *-ion* and *-ation* and he is inarticulate:

Gobbledygook

During the days of the development of intensive psychiatric services, case work found in psychiatric and psychoanalytic knowledge the greatest contribution to its own equipment; today an equal absorption of economic information is essential for intelligent operation as a case worker in the field of relief administration.

In each semester in every higher institution, a relatively small proportion of students tends to consume a disproportionate amount of institutional effort, for a variety of reasons. These causes may have been nonexistent or impossible to discern and unpredictable as of the date of the student's admission. The consequences appear as unsatisfactory deviations from original reasonable expectations of the University and of the student and his parents. On the basis of the propositions that "A stitch in time saves nine" and "an ounce of prevention is worth a pound of cure," it is clearly desirable that such deviates be identified as early as possible as a first step in the direction of remedy of the unsatisfactory situation.

In view of the foregoing, your cooperation is hereby invoked as follows: If (and when) you observe in student performance indications which point your thought toward this request, pen-

Improved

During the early days of their development, the case worker leaned most heavily on psychiatry and psychoanalysis; today he cannot administer relief intelligently without knowing as much economics.

I would like you to help me find problem students so that I can help them before it is too late. If you know of any, will you please write me a note or phone 6–4831?

cil an informal memorandum including the student's name and an outline of your observation and send it to this office through campus mail. Or, if you prefer, telephone 6–4831.

There are many species of the genus gobbledygook. The dean's memorandum just quoted is a mixture of *Pedagese,* the jargon of educationists (*institutional effort, deviations from original expectations, remedy of the unsatisfactory situation*) and *Officialese,* the private language of bureaucrats big and little (*as of the date of, on the basis of the propositions, in view of the foregoing, is hereby invoked*). Pedagese is merely one branch of the tangled tree of academic jargon; psychologists, anthropologists, sociologists, and literary critics can write equally offensive prose. Officialese is related to *Commercialese,* the jargon of business, and both are close relatives of *Legalese. Journalese,* which usually reveals a snappier, more economical style than true gobbledygook, is a distant cousin of the rest.

Some of the commonest terms in these special vocabularies are discussed in the GLOSSARY. Obviously an expert should not be condemned for using technical terms intelligently, especially if he is writing for other experts. Genuine technical terms are more accurate, less ambiguous, than the lay synonyms. But an expert must not become so completely dependent on technical jargon that he is unable to make sense to anyone who has not been initiated in the cult. And he must not habitually use high-sounding pseudo-technical jargon when familiar language will accurately convey his meaning. The psychologist who indiscriminately calls every quirk a *complex,* every worry a *neurosis,* every dislike a *phobia* is as guilty of using counterwords as the undergraduate whose only adjectives are *swell* and *lousy.*

But the jargon of special groups does not become an alarming symptom of gobbledygook until it begins to permeate the general vocabulary. The lawyer may be unable to avoid occasional reference to *the aforesaid party of the first part;* the businessman may be unable to carry on without perpetually *contacting prospects* about a *deal;* the bureaucrat may be lost without *personnel,* the engineer without *factors,* the educationist without *integration.* But the layman can leave this jargon generously to the experts.

The relation of technical jargon to gobbledygook has been emphasized because many undergraduates assume that as soon as they survive the elementary English courses of the first two years and enter the ranks of the majors, they can stop writing English and begin writing Economics, or Psychology, or Sociology, or Law. An expert understanding of the jargon of a single field presumably gives them a special license to violate the law of saying simple things simply. Genuinely distinguished men are seldom victims of this illusion. Take this passage, for example:

Persecution for the expression of opinions seems to me perfectly logical. If you have no doubt of your premises or your power and want a certain result with all your heart, you naturally express your wishes in law and sweep away all opposition. To allow opposition by speech seems to indicate that you think the speech impotent, as when a man says that he has squared the circle, or that you do not care wholeheartedly for the result, or that you doubt either your power or your premises. But when men have realized that time has upset many fighting faiths, they may come to believe, even more than they believe the very foundations of their own conduct, that the ultimate good desired is better reached by free trade in ideas—that the best test of truth is the power of the thought to get itself accepted in the competition of the market, and that truth is the only ground upon which their wishes safely can be carried out. That, at any rate, is the theory of our Constitution. It is an experiment, as all life is an experiment. Every year, if not every day, we have to wager our salvation upon some prophecy based upon imperfect knowledge. While the experiment is part of our system, I think that we should be eternally vigilant against attempts to check the expression of opinions that we loathe and believe to be fraught with death, unless they so imminently threaten immediate interference with the lawful and pressing purposes of the law that an immediate check is required to save the country. —Justice Oliver Wendell Holmes, Dissenting opinion, *Abrams v. United States* (250 U.S. 616), 1919.

There is a paragraph by an expert. The most distinguished jurist of his time, he could easily have cluttered up the page with *whereas's* and *aforesaid's,* learned parenthetical allusions and high-sounding legal abstractions. Instead, he wrote simply, directly, concretely, without pomp or pretense, and gave posterity one of the clearest statements on one of the most important problems of civilized government. Nobody has to write gobbledygook, not even an expert.

TONE

Read these two passages carefully:

1. Meanwhile in his classes the student will have been required to purchase certain books for study, and the mastery of them will be demanded by his teachers; but, in addition to this, he will be sent to the college library to consult other books without any intimation from his instructors that he should purchase them. He is only to learn how to consult these books, how to bring the information that he will find there into relation with the subject as set forth in his text-book. He will then learn that no book can be adequately understood by itself alone, but will yield up its treasure only when its words are compared with those of other books, and its truths tested by the experience of other men. The student will find that some of the books to which his attention has been directed are to be quickly consulted and quickly laid aside, as containing but little—though that little may be of great importance—that is related to the subject which he is investigating. Others may well seem to him more important than his text-book, and he may indeed in certain cases come to realize that his text-book has been quarried out of some larger and grander treatise on the subject. Gradually he will come to understand the truth of Bacon's words, "Some books are to be tasted, others to be swallowed, and some few to be chewed and digested; that is some books are to be read only in parts; others to be read, but not curiously; and some few to be read wholly, and with diligence and attention." Such counsel as this of Bacon's implies the guidance of a teacher and the existence of a library to which the student may be sent. No teacher will be content if his instruction ends in his class-room, and a student will have begun the educational process only when he carries away the lessons which he has received in the class-room, not as a body of dogma, to be received as *de fide,* but as an organic and growing thing to be constantly nourished

by human intercourse and by private study. —Chauncey B. Tinker, "The Library," *On Going to College*.

2. Beyond all this a college library needs open shelves. A college dean once boasted in a newspaper interview that his instructors could always be found "surrounded by their books." Well, the students should be besieged in the same manner. They must live close to books: it is part of the definition of the word "student." They must find, on the shelves, books that they were not looking for and that they did not know existed. They must be able to go from shelf to shelf, tracking down an idea, a name, or a picture. And all this freely, in a mood of peaceful *laissez faire*. It is absurd to have in a large library one room set apart as a Browsing Room. Reading and browsing are not separate functions of a double-action intellectual stomach.

Nor is a businesslike routine conducive to mental absorption. Going up to a Loan Desk with a slip which you have had to stop and write out, handing it to an attendant who stamps the date on it with a loud bang, shoves it down a pneumatic tube, and tells you to wait, makes the student life too much like the struggle for ration cards and three-cent stamps. Ordinarily, for "standard courses," college practice is to have a reserve of identical books which are doled out to the students, sometimes with a limit of two hours' reading time. What could be more discouragingly anti-cultural? A boy's will is the wind's will and even the second volume of *Tom Jones* could not, under those adverse conditions, anchor it. —Jacques Barzun, *Teacher in America*.

The difference between those passages is less a matter of style than of tone. The tone of the first passage is sober, earnest, dignified, impersonal, perhaps a trifle austere. Although it is not pontifical or condescending, it is essentially didactic. The somewhat ponderous sentences, involving careful balance and the continual repetition of the passive voice; the rather formal diction (*mastery, yield up its treasure, educational process, organic, human intercourse*); the prominent introduction of a lesson from the standard canon of English literature; the Latin phrase *de fide* for the more natural *on faith*—all contribute to give the passage an "academic" tone.

In the second passage the sentence structure is less involved, the diction less formal. The colloquial pause (*Well*), the familiar pronoun (*you*), and such direct monosyllables as *stop, stamp, loud, bang,* and *shoves* have a conversational flavor that makes *conducive to mental absorption* seem comic by contrast. The unobtrusive literary allusions (*A boy's will is the wind's will, Tom Jones*) are balanced by allusions from the market place (*double-action intellectual stomach, struggle for ration cards and three-cent stamps*). The contrast between the ideal of a free student surrounded by books and peace and the actuality of a slave harried by a noisy mechanical routine is coated with irony: the ironic quotes around *standard courses,* the carefully chosen verb *doled,* the exasperated rhetorical question (*What could be more discouragingly anti-cultural?*)—all conspire to evoke a tone of light ridicule.

Style and tone are closely related, but they are not the same. The style of a piece of writing includes both the choice of ingredients and the method of mixing them; the tone is the flavor or seasoning. A piece of plain prose may have a gay or somber tone, a literal or an ironic tone, a sentimental or a cynical tone. There is no textbook formula for distilling these elusive essences, but a few general hints may help:

1. *Adopt a tone appropriate to the subject:* This is really a matter of good taste. A tone of flippant banter is hardly fitting in a funeral oration or a sober air of pedantry appropriate in a discussion of the operation of a pinball machine.

2. *Beware of sudden shifts of tone in the middle of a paper:* Consistency of tone is as important as consistency in levels of usage. Do not burst out in a guffaw in the midst of a serious discussion or suddenly lapse into irony after a strictly literal introduction. The reader has a right to know when the tongue is in the cheek.

3. *Be personal but not familiar:* One trouble with Officialese is that it is so utterly impersonal. It is a machine grinding out directives for personnel, not a human voice talking to human beings. A distinctive prose style always has an authentic personal note. That is the implication of Buffon's time-worn epigram: "The style is the man." In most undergraduate papers it is natural for a student to write frankly in the first person about his

own prejudices, opinions, and experiences, whether or not the assignment is labeled "a personal essay." Only occasionally, as in a research paper or a technical report, is a personal tone likely to be out of place. This does not mean, however, that a student should slip into the common undergraduate habit of treating the reader habitually as one of the boys or making every theme a chatty, friendly letter to the teacher.

4. *Beware of both dogmatism and false modesty:* A college undergraduate is hardly expected to write on any subject with the tone of a pundit who knows all the answers. He should be wary of pontifical pronouncements and glib, unsupported generalities. But he is not required to wear his ignorance and immaturity on his sleeve, hedging every assertion with a humble apology ("It seems to me"; "Of course, this is only my personal opinion based on very little experience").

5. *Beware of exaggeration (hyperbole):* Exaggeration is presumably one of the traits that distinguish the ebullient American from the more phlegmatic Englishman. It permeates American advertising ("the longest and tastiest hot dogs east of the Rockies"); it flavors political oratory ("the most dastardly act of treason ever perpetrated against the American people since the Founding Fathers wrote the Constitution"); it is the lifeblood of sports reporting (Twenty-two college boys playing a game on Saturday afternoon become "gallant warriors locked in a titanic struggle for supremacy in the gridiron world"); it has been both the blessing and the bane of American humor ("Bless your heart, Cooper hasn't any more invention than a horse; and I don't mean a high-class horse either; I mean a clothes-horse."—Mark Twain). But it is a dangerous weapon in the hands of a novice. By exaggerating his feeling about his fraternity brothers, his alma mater, or his favorite cocker spaniel, a student can easily pervert genuine emotion into sentimentality. By overdramatizing a story, he can bludgeon the reader into boredom so that the big moment reads like just another incident. By overloading his argument with superlatives, he can leave himself wide open to the counterpunches of a more cautious opponent. Exaggerated irony

—the "oh yeah" tone that creeps into many student editorials—degenerates into sneering sarcasm. Exaggerated humor becomes tiresome farce.

Generally speaking, the intelligent modern reader does not like to be written *at*. If he feels that a writer is struggling too hard to open his tear ducts or tickle his ribs, he will automatically set up a resistance to tears or laughter. The subtle seasoning of tone should be blended with other ingredients, not laid on in a thick, soupy sauce. A general rule follows from this: *Let the emotion arise naturally from an honest presentation; infuse it into the material but don't superimpose it.*

6. *Handle humor with special restraint:* Undergraduate writing contains a great deal of genuine humor. But the weekly theme pile sometimes turns up a student with a bad case of chronic wisecracking. He can't begin his autobiographical first theme without straining for something funny in the simple fact that he was born ("In the beginning, of course, I was born"; "I was born in a little log cabin, which I did not help my father to build"). He cannot make a serious critical comment without killing it with an adolescent quip ("If I were asked to recite a few lines from any of Shakespeare's plays, I couldn't do it, because my teachers have never succeeded in getting me interested in Willy's weary works." "What political orator of today can compare with Antony in *Julius Caesar* as he sways his audience with a speech that would bring credit to Dale Carnegie?"). He cannot refer to a member of the faculty or student body without a pseudo-Dickensian tag-name (Professor Fossilpuss, Joe Bigshot, Bessie Birdbrain). Humor to him is a series of forced gags strung together with all the irrelevance of a radio comic's repertoire.

The student who wants to write humorously can learn a lot from his professional masters. Take, for example, this paragraph:

I passed all the other courses that I took at my University, but I could never pass botany. This was because all botany students had to spend several hours a week in a laboratory looking through a microscope at plant cells, and I could never see through a microscope. I never once saw a cell through a microscope. This used to enrage my

instructor. He would wander around the laboratory pleased with the progress all the students were making in drawing the involved and, so I am told, interesting structure of flower cells, until he came to me. I would just be standing there. "I can't see anything," I would say. He would begin patiently enough, explaining how anybody can see through a microscope, but he would always end up in a fury, claiming that I could *too* see through a microscope but just pretended that I couldn't. "It takes away from the beauty of flowers anyway," I used to tell him. "We are not concerned with beauty in this course," he would say. "We are concerned solely with what I may call the *mechanics* of flars." "Well," I'd say, "I can't see anything." "Try it just once again," he'd say, and I would put my eye to the microscope and see nothing at all, except now and again, a nebulous milky substance—a phenomenon of maladjustment. You were supposed to see a vivid, restless clockwork of sharply defined plant cells. "I see what looks like a lot of milk," I would tell him. This, he claimed, was the result of my not having adjusted the microscope properly; so he would readjust it for me, or rather, for himself. And I would look again and see milk.
—James Thurber, "University Days," *My Life and Hard Times.*

There may be a trace of exaggeration in this well-known passage: possibly the author did see a cell through a microscope. But this tendency to overstatement is neatly balanced by simple statement verging on understatement ("I would just be standing there." "And I would look again and see milk.") The author has not souped up his material with a will to move the reader to hysterics at any price. In the whole paragraph there is not a wisecrack, not a cute or clever comment, not a single smart aside. The effect is produced almost entirely by straight reporting. Whether this particular incident ever happened at Ohio State University is beside the point. It is the kind of incident that has happened in every college laboratory in the country. Thurber has let the humor rise from his material. The passage is appealing not because it is so clever but because it is so genuine.

THE LIGHT TONE

Frederick Lewis Allen once made a useful distinction between the *goon* and the *jigger*. "A goon is a person with a heavy touch as distinguished from a jigger, who has a light touch.

While jiggers look on life with a genial eye, goons take a more stolid and literal view."[2] The goon may have a standardized sense of humor: he can laugh long and loud at a joke—if it is properly labeled. But he is baffled by people who can see anything funny in situations or magazine cartoons that are obviously not jokes. When he writes, the goon writes in a goonish style. "It is thick and heavy. It suggests the sort of oatmeal served at lunch counters, lumpy, and made with insufficient salt." In short, it is strangely like gobbledygook.

To the goon, serious writing is sober writing, and humorous writing is funny writing, and never the twain shall meet. It doesn't strike him as somewhat absurd that many a college campus has a literary magazine that must not be humorous and a humor magazine that must never be either serious or literary. On the other hand, the playful mind of the jigger enables him to see that a light surface tone may add life to a piece of writing that is fundamentally serious. He knows that a writer can be serious without being solemn. Take this passage, for example:

Clearly, Thursday shouldn't throw me into a dither, but I think I know why it does. Every waking hour of every day affects me more or less the same way. I am constantly reminded of how little I know about the world I live in. Putting paper into a typewriter simply emphasizes the predicament. What ought to be a statement of truth turns into verbal manipulation of ignorance. Not that I'm against verbal manipulation. I love puns, limericks, double-crostics. Life would be poor without word games. But the trouble is that we are living in a world of word games, most of them so seriously contrived that we don't take them for games at all. We can't tell a White paper from a charade. We read something about India or Russia without realizing that the man who wrote it didn't know what he was talking about. He was just a monkey with the typewriter keys falling his way. He keeps up with the fashions in words, inexorable as fashions in lipsticks—the central fact, the foreseeable future.   —Thomas Hornsby Ferril, *I Hate Thursday.*

Obviously that has a light surface tone. The tone is conveyed by the colloquial contractions, the natural use of the first

[2] "The Goon and His Style," *Harper's Magazine,* December, 1921, 144: 121.

person pronoun, the informal use of prepositions at the end of two sentences, the incomplete sixth sentence, the frank affection for puns and limericks, the candid snapshots of the writer in an undignified dither and the monkey at the typewriter. Yet the whole point is extremely important in an age of semantic confusion and naïveté, and the writer is evidently serious about it. To be sure, the tone would be too light for some contexts. But it would be old-fashioned to restrict such writing to a quaint bailiwick called the *informal* (*personal* or *familiar*) *essay*. The light tone has long since escaped from those confines. As Rudolf Flesch has said, "Casualness, the light touch, is what makes modern English sound modern."

EXERCISES

I. Answer these questions about the style of each of the following passages, supporting your conclusions with specific examples: (1) Is it plain or ornate writing? (2) If plain, is it effective or merely flat? (3) If ornate, is it genuinely eloquent or "fine writing"?

1. At sunrise a Negro on his way to the big house to feed the mules had taken the word to Colonel Henry Maxwell, and Colonel Henry phoned the sheriff. The sheriff had hustled Jim into town and locked him up in the jail, and then he went home and ate breakfast.

Jim walked around the empty cellroom while he was buttoning his shirt, and after that he sat down on the bunk and tied his shoelaces. Everything that morning had taken place so quickly that he had not even had time to get a drink of water. He got up and went to the water bucket near the door, but the sheriff had forgotten to put water in it.

By that time there were several men standing in the jailyard. Jim went to the window and looked out when he heard them talking. Just then another automobile drove up, and six or seven men got out. Other men were coming towards the jail from both directions of the street.

"What was the trouble out at your place this morning, Jim?" somebody said.

Jim stuck his chin between the bars and looked at the faces in the crowd. He knew everyone there.

While he was trying to figure out how everybody in town had heard about his being there, somebody else spoke to him.

"It must have been an accident, wasn't it, Jim?"

A colored boy hauling a load of cotton to the gin drove up the street. When the wagon got in front of the jail, the boy whipped up the mules with the ends of the reins and made them trot. —Erskine Caldwell, "Daughter," *Jackpot*.

2. Early in September the stock market broke. It quickly recovered, however; indeed, on September 19th the averages as compiled by the *New York Times* reached an even higher level than that of September 3rd. Once more it slipped, farther and faster, until by October 4th the prices of a good many stocks had coasted to what seemed first-class bargain levels. Steel, for example, after having touched 261¾ a few weeks earlier, had dropped as low as 204; American Can, at the closing on October 4th, was nearly twenty points below its high for the year; General Electric was over fifty points below its high; Radio has gone down from 114¾ to 82½.

A bad break, to be sure, but there had been other bad breaks, and the speculators who escaped unscathed proceeded to take advantage of the lesson they had learned in June and December of 1928 and March and May of 1929: when there was a break it was a good time to buy. In the face of all this tremendous liquidation, brokers' loans as compiled by the Federal Reserve Bank of New York amounted to a new high record on October 2nd, reaching $6,804,000,000—a sure sign that margin buyers were not deserting the market but coming into it in numbers at least undiminished. (Part of the increase in the loan figure was probably due to the piling up of unsold securities in dealers' hands, as the spawning of investment trusts and the issue of new common stock by every manner of business concern continued unabated.) History, it seemed, was about to repeat itself, and those who picked up Anaconda at 109¾ or American Telephone at 281 would count themselves wise investors. And sure enough, prices once more began to climb. They had already turned upward before that Sunday in early October when Ramsay MacDonald sat on a log with Herbert Hoover at the Rapidan camp and talked over the prospects for naval limitation and peace. —Frederick Lewis Allen, *Only Yesterday*.

3. It ran in his knowledge before he ever saw it. It looked and towered in his dreams before he even saw the unaxed woods where it left its crooked print, shaggy, huge, red-eyed, not malevolent but just big—too big for the dogs which tried to bay it, for the horses which tried to ride it down, for the men and the bullets they fired into it, too big for the very country which was its constricting scope. He seemed to

see it entire with a child's complete divination before he ever laid eyes on either—the doomed wilderness whose edges were being constantly and punily gnawed at by men with axes and plows who feared it because it was wilderness, men myriad and nameless even to one another in the land where the old bear had earned a name, through which ran not even a mortal animal but an anachronism, indomitable and invincible, out of an old dead time, a phantom, epitome and apotheosis of the old wild life at which the puny humans swarmed and hacked in a fury of abhorrence and fear, like pygmies about the ankles of a drowsing elephant: the old bear solitary, indomitable and alone, widowered, childless, and absolved of mortality—old Priam reft of his old wife and having outlived all his sons. —William Faulkner, "The Bear," *Saturday Evening Post.*

4. It is with the highest appreciation I venture to convey the admiration for your excellent editorial, "August's Deepening Colors." The rich flow of expression, as well as the marked significance of August's manifestations in the revealing of her natural pigments, brings the reader nearer, and at home, with the hidden gems, of nature's distant unfoldments.

There is no doubt that he who has been unacquainted with the many expressions of the season's splendor is brought face to face with the living disclosures of her wonders in this presentation. Could anything be more sublime? The richness of letters are to be found in the distinct and prolific rendition of all compositions. Truth needs no embellishment for the apprehension of its idea. Life needs only the cognizant to give utterance to her features.

Only he who is capable of understanding nature in her true light and giving expression thereunto can leave the lasting impressions of beauty in poetry and epistolography. It is to him alone man may pay homage for the spark of the imagination that he may behold in the abstract that which has been already visibly concrete. —Letter by George F. Burnett in the New York *Herald Tribune.*

5. It is this method, I gather from rumors which trickle from the educative fields, which is in vogue just now, and even then there were a few instructors who took the larger view. I had one or two of them; one particularly I remember. He was an odd, impassioned gentleman, and he used to act out the beauties of literature for us on occasion. One of the grimmest memories of my youth concerns an afternoon when we all came to his classroom and found the shades drawn, so that the room was an unhealthy, yellow murk—the shades were a rather tired

yellow. He was sitting at his desk, with his gray hair pulled down, and was staring in a rather awful way at a bottle of ink. We crept in, silenced and a little frightened, and nobody said anything for several minutes. We just sat there, troubled. Then, with no warning, the instructor let out a little shriek. We all jumped and wished we could get out. In another minute, I think, we would have gone out, but then the instructor spoke.

"Is this a dagger which I see before me?" he screamed, in tones of anguish. We all settled back then, of course, and quieted down, although he grew noisier and noisier. After a while it began to seem, in a rather unpleasant way, a little funny, and it still does. —Richard Lockridge, "The Grammarian," *New Yorker*.

6. It fell to Trelawny to accomplish the last rite. On the fourteenth of August Williams's body was consumed on the shore. The following day Mary was taken to see the three white wands that marked the spot under which Shelley lay buried, and then, when she had gone, the pyre was erected.

No grander scene could have been chosen for a poet's funeral. The waves in quiet sorrow moaned against a stretch of golden sand, luminous in the sunlight. Behind, a great line of pine trees lifted their branches, their trunks rearing back as with fear of the sea that had been known to rip off their living bark in anger. The mountains glistened in the sun, reflecting the light from their marble veinings. No human abode but the watchman's temporary hut near the graveyard disturbed the immense solitude.

When Byron and Hunt arrived, the body was exhumed, the remains laid in the iron furnace, and the pyre lighted. Byron, bitterly cynical the previous day at Williams's cremation, on mankind's pride and folly in cherishing what in the end is but a mass of decay, stood silent and thoughtful while the flames wrapped all that remained of one who had been as a torch in the world's darkness. Where was that bright spirit? Not here, where the consuming heat laid bare the heart of him before whose purity all other men were as beasts. Not in that seething brain, uncovered by the burst skull. Not anywhere in those white ashes over which, with shrill cries, a sea bird circled, undaunted by the heat that made the air a quivering veil. Byron could bear no more, and, plunging into the sea, swam off to the *Bolivar*. —Frances Winwar, *The Romantic Rebels*.

7. The springs of your body release. You hurtle into the blast. Your ears "pop" in the sudden pressure. Your body falls and starts to

turn. Then, with a sudden jerk, your body is stopped and yanked upright. Your helmet snaps down over your nose and bruises its bridge. The risers slap your shoulders and welt your neck. You recover quickly and push your helmet back out of your eyes. You pull a forward slip and check your canopy. Perfect! Everything's all right! You sag in the harness with a sigh of relief. You glance down at the fast approaching ground. You spot your landing point and slip towards it. You can relax for a few seconds and enjoy the view. A feeling of superiority sweeps over you as you float slowly and magnificently downward. You admire the sun shining through your canopy, dousing your body in splashes of green and brown reflections from your camouflaged 'chute. Then you realize that the landing is due. You glance around and see that the earth below is clear. You slip and turn until you are in a position to hit. You pull down on your risers. The ground comes nearer and nearer. Your knees are bent, your head up, your legs relaxed. You release your risers with a "pop," and your fall is momentarily checked. There is a slight pause. Wham! You hit and roll. It is all over. —Student theme.

8. Communication by the written word is a subtler (and more beautiful) thing than Dr. Flesch or General Motors imagines. They contend that the "average reader" is capable of reading only what tests Easy, and that the writer should write at or below this level. This is a presumptuous and degrading idea. There is no average reader, and to reach down toward this mythical character is to deny that each of us is on the way up, is ascending. ("Ascending," by the way, is a word Dr. Flesch advises writers to stay away from. Too unusual.)

It is our belief that no writer can improve his work until he discards the dulcet notion that the reader is feeble-minded, for writing is an act of faith, not a trick of grammar. Ascent is at the heart of the matter. A country whose writers are following a calculating machine downstairs is not ascending—if you will pardon the expression—and a writer who questions the capacity of the person at the other end of the line is not a writer at all, merely a schemer. The movies long ago decided that a wider communication could be achieved by a deliberate descent to a lower level, and they walked proudly down until they reached the cellar. Now they are groping for the light switch, hoping to find the way out. —"The Talk of the Town," *New Yorker.*

9. The gentle jog of John Brown's trot set ajar the brittle woods; sycamores released their spice-brown leaves in a rain of October: like veins dappled trails veered through storms of showering yellow; perched on dying towers of jack-in-the-pulpit cranberry beetles sang of their

approach, and tree-toads, no bigger than dewdrops, skipped and shrilled, relaying the news through the light that was dusk all day. They followed the remnants of a road down which once had spun the wheels of lacquered carriages carrying verbena-scented ladies who twittered like linnets in the shade of parasols, and leathery cotton-rich gentlemen gruffing at each other through a violet haze of Havana smoke, and their children, prim little girls with mint crushed in their handkerchiefs, and boys with mean blackberry eyes, little boys who sent their sisters screaming with tales of roaring tigers. Gusts of autumn, exhaling through the inheriting weeds, grieved for the cruel velvet children and their virile bearded fathers: Was, said the weeds, Gone, said the sky, Dead, said the woods, but the full laments of history were left to the Whippoorwill.   —Truman Capote, *Other Voices, Other Rooms.*

10. There are three reasons why I think college students should be deferred from the draft until they graduate. The first is that the country needs educated men as never before. A country can't get along in war or peace without them. Secondly, if a student's education is once interrupted, there is a good chance that he won't continue it after he has served his time in the Armed Forces. It would be better for him to finish it first and then go in. My final reason is that I think it is wasteful to take men who have the capacity to become leaders and just give them the regular training that anybody gets regardless of his intelligence or ambition. This may seem very democratic, and I think democracy is a fine thing. But in the long run a country has to be practical about these matters.   —Student theme.

II. Without essentially changing the meaning, rewrite the following passages in simpler, clearer English:

1. The salesmanlike abilities and the men of affairs that so are drawn into the academic personnel, are presumably, somewhat under grade in their kind; since the pecuniary inducement offered by the schools is rather low as compared with the remuneration for office work of a similar character in the common run of business occupations, and since businesslike employés of this kind may fairly be presumed to go unreservedly to the highest bidder. Yet these more unscholarly members of the staff will necessarily be assigned the more responsible and discretionary positions in the academic organization; since under such a scheme of standardization, accountancy and control, the school becomes primarily a bureaucratic organization, and the first and unremitting duties of the staff are those of official management and account-

ancy. The further qualifications requisite in the members of the academic staff will be such as make for vendibility,—volubility, tactful effrontery, conspicuous conformity to the popular taste in all matters of opinion, usage and conventions.

The need of such a businesslike organization asserts itself in somewhat the same degree in which the academic policy is guided by considerations of magnitude and statistical renown; and this in turn is somewhat closely correlated with the extent of discretionary power exercised by the captain of erudition placed in control. At the same time, by provocation of the facilities which it offers for making an impressive demonstration, such bureaucratic organization will lead the university management to bend its energies with somewhat more singleness to the parade of magnitude and statistical gains. It also, and in the same connection, provokes to a persistent and detailed surveillance and direction of the work and manner of life of the academic staff, and so it acts to shut off initiative of any kind in the work done. —Thorstein Veblen, *The Higher Learning in America.*

2. I cannot deny that we did include, in our perfunctory readings, all the poets of eminence from Wordsworth through Tennyson, Browning, and Longfellow, and when class recitations were ordered and again when examinations were held, I could without difficulty spew from memory famous quotations from their poetic achievements. That may be a useful method for exercising the memory segment of the mind, but the tool for that exercising does not necessarily have to be poetic sayings, regardless of their eminence. It would be perfectly satisfactory to read well-known poetry in conjunction with memory work under this stipulation: to extract the foremost thoughts and thoroughly understand, to the best of your ability, the significance and experience the poem has to offer. Do not embroil the contents in an unnecessary puzzle, as so often is the case, for in that event you are only intensifying the difficulty. The authors are human just as you and I, but their use of words is very often quite connotative; therefore our minds in order to digest and receive the correct message after a perusal of the material have to be trained in special reading techniques. This stipulation should be the prime factor involved in the process of learning poetry, and unless this approach is employed in the schools with perseverance, children of today will be denied a wonderful opportunity to develop a lasting sense of poetry equally as pleasurable as that derived from music appreciation. No one will question the esthetic values music holds in store for us; similarly poetry, if handled and conveyed to the

student properly, will give him the same cherished, intangible values. But only by better teaching and thorough revision of poetry presentation in the schools will this ever be achieved. —Student theme.

III. Write a five-hundred-word theme expressing your own reaction to one of the following discussions of style:

1. Canby, H. S., "From Stevenson to Pegler," *Saturday Review of Literature*, February 5, 1938, 17:3–4, 16–17

2. Connolly, Cyril, *Enemies of Promise,* rev. ed., New York, 1948, chaps. 2, 3, or 4

3. Dobrée, Bonamy, *Modern Prose Style,* Oxford, 1934, pp. 210–229

4. Flesch, Rudolf, "What the War Did to Prose," *Saturday Review of Literature,* August 13, 1949, 32:6–7, 36–37

5. Graves, Robert, and Alan Hodge, *The Reader over Your Shoulder,* New York, 1943, chap. 4 or 9

6. Jones, Merwyn, "The King's Gobbledygook," *New York Times Magazine,* July 11, 1948

7. Little, A. H., "The King's English," *Printer's Ink,* December 17, 1936, or *Reader's Digest,* March, 1937, 30:69–70

8. Maugham, W. S., *The Summing Up,* New York, 1938, chaps. 8–14, pp. 19–46

9. Maverick, Maury, "The Case against Gobbledygook," *New York Times Magazine,* May 21, 1944

10. Montague, C. E., "Three Ways of Saying Things," *Century Magazine,* April, 1929, 117:691–698

11. Orwell, George, "Politics and the English Language," *New Republic,* June 17, 24, 1946, 114:872–874, 903–904

12. Quiller-Couch, Sir Arthur, "Interlude: On Jargon," *On the Art of Writing,* New York, 1916, chap. 4, pp. 100–126

IV. Discuss the tone of each of the following passages, illustrating in detail how the author achieves it. Do you think he is successful?

1. Oft in the stilly night, ere slumber's chain has bound me, I find myself sweating over a problem both philological and psychological; to wit, why in hell have the used-car dealers of this great republic never devised a better term to designate their profession? What could be more soaring than their idealism—I always think of them, in fact, as one of the great glories of the Rotarian metaphysic—and yet what could be more prosaic and forbidding than the name by

which they call themselves? The realtors, if they were of like back-wardness, would still be *real-estate agents* and brothers to the ox, and the morticians would still be *undertakers* and brothers to the buzzard. Are the used-car boys, then, too dumb to invent a match for *realtor* and *mortician?* Hardly, for haven't they already got rid of the vulgar and sordid *second-hand* by substituting the tasty *used,* and do not some of them proceed from *used* to *nearly new* and *experienced?* No, it can't be that. They are smart enough to excogitate something as far beyond *realtor* and *mortician* as either is beyond *mixologist,* for bartender, or *commissionnaire,* for door opener. They have simply fumbled their chance and neglected their duty. They suffer from a form of aphasia, and every lover of beauteous words must hope that it will be as evanescent as it is deplorable.   —H. L. Mencken, "Scented Words," *New Yorker.*

2. I have a mackintosh that is the apple of my eye, two topcoats, and a smoked melton, yet when a plugger in a clothing store recently detained me with a quick-change skit in which he whipped off a raglan, turned it inside out, and whipped it on again, with a hanky-panky on its behalf as a garment suitable for wet days, I bought it. Why? Because I am unable to rescue myself from demonstrators. Once my attention has been speared by a pitchman paring a potato with a trick knife, I stand mesmerized by the lengthening peel, powerless to move on till the operation is over and I have plunked down my quarter. I have thought of hiring an analyst to clean my coils, but the matter isn't really complicated enough for that. I'll give a few more examples of my trouble and then say what I think is at the bottom of it.

Not long ago, I was sauntering up Seventh Avenue in the Forties when a rap on the window of a store I was passing brought my head around in a reflex. Behind the glass, a man in a barber's tunic buttered his palms with a pomade called Lustrine and ground it into the noodle of a Latin youth seated before him on a three-legged stool. The stooge had dark, liquid eyes, which sought mine with a look of mute patience, as though for me alone was he taking this drubbing. When it was over and his locks were being combed into glossy undulations, I stepped inside for my trial size.   —Peter De Vries, "Through a Glass Darkly," *New Yorker.*

3. His house rested on the adjoining hill. It was a small frame house, amply windowed, with a large, red-roofed porch to one side. The placement of the structure was such that the sloping ground to all sides gave it a certain eminence by exaggerating its not unusual height. The boy had a den beneath the porch which was referred to

principally as "the cave." It was a black hole—at least half carved from
the cold, musty earth itself. It had the smell of dampness and mold, and
to be there was like being buried alive. Its drafts covered you. Its raw-
ness ate beneath your skin. The boy loved it there, but often when he
entered, his flashlight caught the shoe string tails of rats scampering
nervously into the shadows. Often the gang—that was Jim and Chuck
and Dick—held meetings there, in which they burned candles and sat
shivering as the restless light did things to their faces. But the cave
was not important only for the atmosphere it evoked. It was also
unsurpassed as a hiding place for certain invaluables. The various
nooks and crannies concealed obscure literature which dealt intimately
with the great, the infinite, the mysterious. There was a book on black
magic which explained the complex symbolism of beech trees and disclosed the variety of effects arising from the intelligent employment of
two aspen limbs and a dead rat. The most valuable possession of all,
however, was a fifty-page picture playground in which the sun-bronzed
students of Charles Atlas paraded in spotted skins, cloths, and belts.
The mighty man himself was on one of the pages—his seventeen-inch
arm cocked like a steel spring. He could pull a freight car as most men
would pull a wagon. Tenpenny nails became like rubber under his
grip. His signature was as forceful as a slap in the face and it seemed
chiseled into the page. This was the greatest man in the world. A book
on crime detection was also of unusual interest. It told how criminals
are brought to justice by means of fingerprints. Crime does not pay, it
said. Toward the front cover was a picture of a woman gangster. She
had a rather sweet face, and Chuck said she looked like Mrs. Kuntz
(Mrs. Kuntz lived up by the hospital and was having trouble with
Mr. Kuntz at the time). Because of the atmosphere and the treasures
it held, the cave was a big part of the boy's life. It excited him like
Stevenson's picture. It was dark and changeful. It was the Soho Street
of Mr. Hyde. —Student theme.

4. By her side, on the little reading-desk, was a survival from the
ages of litter—one book. This was the Book of the Machine. In it
were instructions against every possible contingency. If she was hot or
cold or dyspeptic or at loss for a word, she went to the book, and it
told her which button to press. The Central Committee published it.
In accordance with a growing habit, it was richly bound.

Sitting up in the bed, she took it reverently in her hands. She
glanced round the glowing room as if some one might be watching her.
Then, half ashamed, half joyful, she murmured "O Machine! O
Machine!" and raised the volume to her lips. Thrice she kissed it, thrice

inclined her head, thrice she felt the delirium of acquiescence. Her ritual performed, she turned to page 1367, which gave the times of the departure of the air-ships from the island in the southern hemisphere, under whose soil she lived, to the island in the northern hemisphere, whereunder lived her son.

She thought, "I have not the time."

She made the room dark and slept; she awoke and made the room light; she ate and exchanged ideas with her friends, and listened to music and attended lectures; she made the room dark and slept. Above her, beneath her, and around her, the Machine hummed eternally; she did not notice the noise, for she had been born with it in her ears. The earth, carrying her, hummed as it sped through silence, turning her now to the invisible sun, now to the invisible stars. She awoke and made the room light. —E. M. Forster, "The Machine Stops," *The Eternal Moment*.

5. In an effort to supplement the family income and earn the dime the Saturday matinee at the Wilbur cost, my brother and I once organized a popcorn company. I say we organized it, but the organization took place only after my mother bought fourteen gross of the stuff and told us we were going to sell it.

I was to be district vice-president in charge of salesmen. Brother was to be president in charge of business in the home office. This meant I would have to peddle popcorn all over the Borough while he stayed home and counted the money I was earning. I felt that this was unfair. My mother's feelings concurred with my own, so a reorganization took place. We now had two district vice-presidents, each supplied with a basket of popcorn and some change, and a new president whose duties at home would keep her from taking unfair advantage of the other two members of the company. So one bright sunny morning I sallied forth into the business world with the enthusiasm of a man who has just eaten his first mashed potato sandwich.

You who have not sold popcorn at the tender age of nine and a half cannot imagine the heart-rending anxiety I felt as I approached the door of my first would-be customer. They say a dying man will have his life flash across his mind during his last moments. They say a condemned man will repent of his sins while he walks to the electric chair. I was firmly convinced that a fate as terrible as these lay behind the door in front of me. Summoning all the courage in my quivering little body, I reached for the bell. I rang the bell. I said a prayer. My prayer was answered. Nobody came to the door. I ran down the street.

—Student theme.

CHAPTER ELEVEN

Clear and Cloudy Thinking

> Bad writing is nothing more than the outward and visible
> sign of bad thinking.
>
> —Oscar James Campbell.

> The new tinge to modern minds is a vehement and passion-
> ate interest in the relation of general principles to irreducible
> and stubborn facts.
>
> —Alfred North Whitehead.

⇛⇛⇛⇛⇛⇛⇛⇛⇛⇛⇛⇛⇛⇛⇛⇛⇛⇛⇛⇛⇛⇛⇛⇛⇛⇛⇛⇛⇛

In refuting the familiar argument that the minimum voting age in the United States should be lowered to eighteen, a college freshman wrote this:

An important aid to political judgment is business experience. Any man of wide experience in business knows which candidate for public office will do him the most good. Since democracy is a form of government based on the will of the majority, the man who attains office by giving the majority what they want is the right man for the position. Most of our eighteen-year-olds have not had much business experience and would not, therefore, make responsible voters.

In a passage of only eighty words the student has made six general assertions, none of them supported by evidence elsewhere in the theme:

1. Business experience aids political judgment.
2. Any experienced businessman knows which candidate will do him the most good.
3. Democracy is based on the will of the majority.
4. The man who gives the majority what they want is the right man for the office.
5. Most eighteen-year-olds have not had much business experience.
6. They would not make responsible voters.

Without quibbling over the meaning of such broad phrases as "political judgment," "the most good," or "business experience," a highly sympathetic reader might concede numbers one, two, three, and five—after warning the student that his generalization count is dangerously high. But what rule of logic justifies the deceptive transition from two to four? While uttering a traditional definition of democracy, the writer performs the remarkable sleight-of-hand trick of equating the desires of any experienced businessman with those of the majority. Do not experienced businessmen belong to a minority? Is the reader to infer from assertion number four that "the majority" is always right or that the most astute politician in the country can consistently manage to give at least 51 per cent of the people what they want, even assuming that they always know what they want? And finally, what of the swift leap from number five to number six? If lack of "business experience" makes a voter irresponsible, perhaps the Constitution should be amended to disenfranchise thousands of loyal, intelligent American citizens. The student writer had a point lurking in the inner recesses of his brain, but he was looking at it with his mind's eye half shut. In putting his point on paper, he violated some of the fundamental principles of clear thinking.

As the first quotation at the beginning of the chapter implies, cloudy thinking may be reflected in faulty organization, incorrect grammar, loose sentence structure, or careless choice of words. But this chapter is primarily concerned with *errors in reasoning* that cannot be defined in terms of "correct English." Although these *fallacies,* as logicians call them, are rare in narrative and descriptive writing, they are by no means confined to the process of "taking sides" on a controversial question. If a man says, "All footballs are made of pigskin," he is committing, not a fallacy, but an error in fact. If he says, "All footballs are made of pigskin because many people call them *pigskins,*" he is guilty of an absurd, but alarmingly common fallacy. He may have no desire of "starting an argument," but he has set one forth. By merely pretending to give a reason for his assertion, he has entered the realm of *opinion,* a treacherous region beset by fallacies on every hand.

OPINION VS. PREJUDICE

When Ambrose Bierce defined *prejudice* as "a vagrant opinion without visible means of support," he treated it as an inferior species of opinion. But it is a useful aid to clear thinking to keep the two as distinct as possible.

A prejudice is a *pre*judgment, a conclusion reached *before* any genuine evidence is in. It has no basis in observable facts or sound reasoning. Born in ignorance, it lives in mortal fear of knowledge, for knowledge can quickly slay it. Its natural habitat is the brain of the bigot, from which it emerges skulking behind dogmatic generalities, charged words, epithets, and exaggeration. Although a prejudice may be cool or even cold, it commonly generates heat and often explodes in a blast of hot air, sealing the mind with debris.

An opinion is a judgment resulting from an honest attempt to examine the evidence and reason logically from it. It is based on knowledge, however inadequate, and though new knowledge may destroy it, it is not afraid to succumb to a better opinion. Most at home in the mind of the responsible citizen, it expresses itself openly in tangible examples, neutral, unambiguous words, calm, reasonable tones. However strong, it is always flexible, never petrifying into dogma. However warmly held, it always aims to supply not heat but light.

If the writer of a familiar essay expresses a frank prejudice against parsnips, it is foolish to condemn him for not listing logical reasons. Lovers of Charles Lamb willingly regard his myriad prejudices as charming eccentricities. But in any serious attempt to express a point of view on paper, prejudice hath no charms to soothe the educated reader. He wants evidence. To be sure, the evidence may be a strenuous effort to defend a preconception. When a writer begins organizing his thoughts on any serious subject, it is probable that, from reading and listening and random reflecting in the past, his mind has already taken a tentative stand. But if he frankly recognizes this preliminary bias and is careful not to confine himself only to the evidence supporting it—a mental process inappropriately called *rationalizing*—he can still express a logical opinion. Even if he has allowed his bias to harden into a prejudice, his case is not hopeless unless he stubbornly insists on pawning it off as a valid opinion. The most tightly closed mind can still be pried open. As Thoreau said, "It is never too late to give up our prejudices."

DEFINITION AGAIN

"If you wish to converse with me," said Voltaire, "define your terms." If the first step toward intelligent discussion is abolishing prejudice, the second is a clear understanding of what the discussion is all about. A writer must make an unambiguous statement of his point of view, for it is obviously futile to assert *why* he takes his stand until he shows clearly *where* he takes it. In some discussions this involves a careful definition of words. Not that every essay in opinion must begin with a dictionary definition (see page 28). Arguments centering in "what Webster says" are notoriously futile. But a writer should leave no doubt about what he himself means by the pivotal words of his argument.

The danger of loose, ambiguous terms and the problem of defining abstract words have been considered in detail elsewhere (see pages 255–261). It should be clear by now that the most eloquent mouthing of abstractions is not opinion, whether they are charged with noble sentiments (liberty, loyalty, Americanism, free enterprise) or with venom (tyranny, disloyalty, treason, fascism). Von Bülow's arrogant boast—"To the meaningless French idealisms, Liberty, Equality, and Fraternity, we oppose the German realities, Infantry, Cavalry, and Artillery"—contains a sobering lesson in semantics. Moreover, the student should not forget that it is often wise to evade the problems of definition entirely by simply limiting the scope of a discussion. For example, a writer is beaten at the start if he tries to argue for or against "Communism" or "Socialized Medicine" or "Progressive Education" in five hundred words without any attempt at definition. If he sets out to define them, fully aware of the complexity of the task, he can hardly avoid readjusting his lens to bring a formless blur into sharper focus. Thus a cloudy indictment of communism can become a clear argument against one aspect of the foreign policy of the Soviet Union; a fuzzy attack on "socialized medicine" can become a clean-cut objection to a single provision of one bill before Congress; a hopeless jumble of jottings about something called "progressive education" can be reduced to a convincing defense of the old-fashioned policy of teaching children the alphabet before puzzling them with reading and writing and spelling. The writer, to be sure, has fled from the disturbing dilemma of defining his terms. But he has succeeded in defining his subject: *limiting* it to a reasonable size, making it more *definite*. He has shifted the grounds of the argument from words to issues. It is more rewarding to discuss issues.

One of the virtues of definition is that it is a safeguard against the common error of letting a word slip from one meaning to another in the course of the same argument:

> I have no objection to the sincere humanitarian aims of the proponents of this measure; they are all idealists of the highest order. But this is a hard, cruel, practical world, a world in which our leaders should keep their feet firmly planted on the ground. It is an age for practical men who are familiar with the problems of meeting a payroll. It is not an age for fuzzy-minded idealists.

All words change color from context to context, but the word *idealists* behaves in that passage like a chameleon. When first used, it carries approximately the first meaning listed in the ACD: "one who cherishes or pursues ideals, as for attainment." Surely the writer could make no objection to such an idealist in any generation; the most practical of men is trained to hitch his wagon to a star. But three sentences later the same *idealists,* with no warning from the writer, have acquired the odious connotation of meaning number two: "a visionary or unpractical person," and the reader is left wondering whether the ambiguous author has any faith in ideals.

This fallacy—known to logicians as the fallacy of *equivocation*—may also crop up in arguments between two or more persons. Many a dormitory joust goes on most of the night before somebody asks, "What do you mean by so-and-so?" and the disputants, finding themselves using the same label for two or more markedly different meanings, become suddenly aware that they have been tilting for hours at verbal windmills. When they have clearly defined the equivocal terms and thus isolated the issues, the contestants often prove to have surprisingly similar views—a discovery they might have made in the beginning at a considerable saving of time and vocal energy.

FAULTY ASSUMPTIONS

Here is a passage from an editorial in which a student argues against converting his Alma Mater to coeducation:

It is obvious that women require a different kind of education from men. Thus, to establish coeducation would mean, not only the expense of building new dormitories, with a fat salary bill for house mothers and additional campus policemen, but also the cost of establishing new courses in such fields as Domestic Science and Child Psychology. The number of women attracted would not justify the added expense. If our aim is to attract more good students to the campus, it would be simpler and cheaper in the long run to put the college "on the map" with a winning football team.

Whenever a writer confidently begins an argument with such a phrase as "It is obvious that," "As everybody knows," or "All sound-thinking people agree," he is probably about to produce a dubious generalization. Generalizations are inevitable in argument, and the problem of supporting them with adequate evidence will be discussed in detail later. The warning here is against building an argument on a generalization supported by assumption only.

An adversary searching for a flaw in the editorial need look no further than the first premise. If it were obvious that women require a different kind of education from men, one of the hardiest perennials among educational squabbles could be permitted to die a peaceful death. Since the student has built his argument on a dubious premise, it is fundamentally unsound, and the most solid logic in the superstructure won't keep it from tumbling down when an opponent attacks it. Of course, the superstructure is not solid. The student's third sentence contains another assumption, and the final sentence—a sort of superfluous cupola on the main structure—contains no less than three: (1) that winning football games would be simpler than converting to coeducation; (2) that it would be cheaper; and (3) that it would attract more good students to the college. An unmerciful opponent might point out that the evidence of recent years makes all three assumptions highly questionable. The most unassuming argument often conceals a tangled network of the most dubious assumptions.

BEGGING THE QUESTION

The fallacy of assuming the truth of something that remains to be proved is known in logic as *begging the question.* A simple form of question-begging is *reasoning-in-a-circle:* "The Robinsons are an undesirable family because they moved into the Fifth Ward, where the homeowners don't want undesirable families like the Robinsons." In an article entitled "The Alleged Failure of Democracy," Ralph Barton Perry shows that question-beggars— as they have been called—are often more subtle:

> People do not as a rule beg a question explicitly: they do not say in so many words that democracy is a bad thing because democracy is a bad thing. But there are those who argue against democracy in theory from their dislike of it in practice. Since the practice is precisely what the theory means, these critics are really not arguing at all, but are only expressing a prejudice.

The commonest kind of question-begging is the use of charged words or phrases (see pages 262–267), especially the resort to *name-calling.* Thus Henry Morton Robinson, arguing against students' working their way through college, begins by slanting the title ("Working Your Way—or Your Professor?") and throughout the discussion brands his victims as "scholastic hitch-hikers," "academic parasites," "academic rabble," and "academic gate-crashers." And any newspaper is likely to reveal a columnist or a congressman who has discovered that it is easier to beg the question of a man's guilt by pinning a label on him than to argue the question with impartial evidence. Despite the old proverb, names can hurt worse than sticks and stones. The game of fair argument should not be played with loaded dice.

IGNORING THE QUESTION

Closely related to begging the question is the fallacy of *ignoring the question* or *evading the issue*. There are many kinds of red herring in the marketplace, and the accomplished demagogue or propagandist is an expert at dragging them all across the trail to distract attention from the real point under discussion. The "band wagon" device ("Everybody's voting for Wintergreen. Don't you be left out."); the "plain folks" appeal ("Our candidate is just a plain humble farmer whose heart is still in the soil"); the testimonial (" 'Peppermint is my candidate,' says Rita Sheridan, distinguished star of stage and screen"); the appeal to flattery ("the thoughtful voters of this great city of Wilkes-Barre"), or pity ("He left the sick bed of a dying mother to speak to you tonight"), or fear ("Do you want your life savings swept away by economic crackpots?")—these are only a few of the emotional gambits used to convert an audience from thinking to throbbing.

The conscientious citizen, with no desire to imitate the demagogue, will often drag a red herring across the trail without being in the least aware that there is anything fishy about his argument. A familiar kind of unconscious evasion (though it may be conscious too) is the *argumentum ad hominem*—or "argument against the man." A speaker in a debate suddenly shifts from attacking his opponent's arguments to ridiculing his manners or his morals; or a writer, pretending to discuss the shortcomings of a proposed law, concentrates his attack—with or without explicit name-calling—on the family background of the senator proposing it. There are, to be sure, occasions where the issue is the man—the wisdom of a presidential appointment, for example—and others where the man has made such an issue of his own personality that it is difficult for the fairest opponent to judge his achievement impersonally. But despite the time-honored proverb, it is still not a pertinent criticism of the accuracy of a stone-thrower to point out that he lives in a glass house. Personal ridicule—"stooping to personalities"—is a favorite pastime with politicians, but it is not fair argument.

A less obvious but extremely common kind of evasion is the

false dilemma. This is the popular device by which a speaker or writer reduces a many-faceted problem to a neat argument with only two sides: his own, which is presumably pure white, and a hypothetical opponent's, which is clearly jet black. The propounder of the false dilemma is fond of saying, "All who are not with me are against me." He commonly denies that there can be any compromise between two extremes, any conceivable M between his irreproachable A and his adversary's impossible Z. If he does concede the existence of more than one argument besides his own and his target's, he is likely to maintain that, since the opposition's proposals "differ only in degree," they are really the same—a technique as logical as protesting that gray cats of all shades are really black because they are not white. Thus the traditional debating society assumes that all controversial questions can be deftly divided by two, Affirmative and Negative, with never a fraction left over. The professional politician presents the voter with a simple choice between absolutes: between "free enterprise" and "government planning," between "freedom from entangling alliances" and "involvement in international war," between "our whole ticket and honest government" and "their whole ticket and corrupt bureaucracy." The packages are neatly wrapped in the oversimplification factory and plainly labeled *either this* and *or that* by experts in "potted thinking."

The thoughtful voter knows better. This doesn't mean that a writer limited by time and space can always examine "all sides of an issue" or that he should timidly avoid conclusions because "there is much to be said on both sides." It means that the dilemma with only two horns is a much rarer animal than proverbial wisdom implies and that the unicorn is still a myth. Even with a two-horned dilemma the horns have a disturbing way of branching out like a deer's antlers.

THE ARGUMENT FROM ANALOGY

Which of the following arguments is the more convincing:

1. But the tendency of the time is much better illustrated by a group of professors of education who have just recently proposed that

the list of "required reading" in schools should be based upon a study which they have just sponsored of the tastes of school children. . . . Would any pediatrician base the diet which he prescribed for the young submitted to his care simply on an effort to determine what eatables they remembered with greatest pleasure? If he knew that the vote would run heavily in favor of chocolate sodas, orange pop, hot dogs and bubble gum, would he conclude that these should obviously constitute the fundamental elements in a "modern" child's menu? —Joseph Wood Krutch, "Should We Bring Literature to Children, or Children to Literature," New York *Herald Tribune Book Review*.

2. For instance, the author may be arguing against social security or the theory that it is the Government's business to provide for its people individually as well as collectively. On the face of it, the author's contention seems inhuman. But the principle involved—the reason behind the reason—is that life is a struggle, only the fittest survive; that men become fitter only by struggling; and that the progress of civilization depends upon the survival of the fittest. Therefore, handouts undermine the will and the ability to stay fit. —Alvan E. Duerr, *Pledge Training*, National Interfraternity Conference, 1946.

Krutch compares the educator prescribing a diet for children's minds to the pediatrician prescribing for their stomachs. Duerr supports a hypothetical argument with an implied comparison between the "struggle for existence" of man in modern society and the evolutionary process by which *homo sapiens* has descended through untold ages from the primordial ooze. Both arguments employ the extremely common device of *analogy*.

This book contains other analogies: for example, Heggen's comparison of heroism with the knee jerk (page 55), Martin's use of the subway rider to exemplify the unconscious, and Huxley's customer in the grocery store unconsciously illustrating the process of induction. But in those specimens the writer is primarily bent on exposition, and the chief test of their effectiveness is whether they help to make the point clearer. Krutch and Duerr are using analogies to carry the burden of argument. The main question is: Do they logically support that argument?

From the strict standpoint of logic all analogical arguments are false. No matter how many points two things may have in common, the comparison always breaks down somewhere along the line. But a useful distinction can still be made between a *tight* analogy, which, though it may actually prove nothing, helps to support the argument, and a *loose* analogy, which leaves the writer wide open to attack from a skillful adversary.

Regardless of his convictions about education or politics, a trained reader could hardly fail to see this difference in the passages cited. Why, says Krutch, should an educator let a child draw up his own mental menu when no responsible pediatrician would dream of letting him prescribe his own physical menu? The question is hard to answer. It can be pointed out, of course, that pedagogues are not pediatricians and the mind is not the stomach. But are these differences significant in this context? Is there any reason why a child needs less guidance in feeding his mind than in feeding his body? On the contrary, whereas the stomach might teach him an immediate lesson, rebelling violently against a surfeit of chocolate sodas and orange pop, the brain could survive for years on a diet of comics and picture magazines before its owner became aware that chronic illiteracy had set in. Krutch has thrown an embarrassing spotlight on the professors' proposal; although his tight analogy is only a small part of the argument of a long article, it helps to support that argument.

By contrast, the analogy in the second passage conceals a fallacy that Huxley exposed more than fifty years ago:

> There is another fallacy which appears to me to pervade the so-called "ethics of evolution." It is the notion that because, on the whole, animals and plants have advanced in perfection of organization by means of the struggle for existence and the consequent "survival of the fittest"; therefore men in society, men as ethical beings, must look to the same process to help them towards perfection. I suspect that this fallacy has arisen out of the unfortunate ambiguity of the phrase "survival of the fittest." "Fittest" has a connotation of "best"; and about "best" there hangs a moral flavour. In cosmic nature, however, what is "fittest" depends upon the conditions. —Thomas Henry Huxley, "Evolution and Ethics," *Evolution and Ethics and Other Essays* (1893) .

In other words, the familiar analogy between the "fittest" man in the economic struggle of modern times and the animal or plant best adapted to survive the evolutionary process through the ages—a fallacy based on the careless use of loose terms—is too loose to clothe even the ghost of an ancient argument. It is easier to find biological evidence for the contrary conclusion that the price of distinction is extinction.

An analogy is merely an extended simile or metaphor (depending on whether the comparison is stated or implied) and can be put to the same tests of originality, appropriateness, and consistency already discussed in Chapter Nine. For example, the "survival of the fittest" analogy not only is inappropriate but had already crystallized by 1893 into a trite metaphor. Today it takes its place beside Carlyle's scornful comparison of Democracy to a ship in a storm being run by the entire crew instead of by the captain, and Lincoln's analogy between swapping presidents in 1864 and swapping horses in midstream. These corroded coins still have a rhetorical glitter, but it is not the pure gold of sound logic.

FACTS VS. FOLKLORE

The student who has conscientiously read this chapter so far may vow to avoid prejudice, loose terms, faulty assumptions, evasions, and loose analogies, and anchor his opinions firmly to "irreducible and stubborn facts." This commendable vow is not easy to keep. Like Dickens' Thomas Gradgrind ("In this life, we want nothing but Facts, sir; nothing but Facts!"), we pay lip service to the worship of fact while we calmly subscribe to the prejudices of popular superstition. Our hard, cold facts are often hard and cold only because enlightened minds have long since consigned them to the grave. The discoveries of modern science are a sobering reminder that some of our most cherished axioms no longer qualify as facts.

Is it a fact that parallel lines never meet, that a straight line is the shortest distance between two points, or that the sum of the angles of a triangle equals two right angles? These are not facts; they are merely the convenient assumptions of plane geometry. Is it a fact that blood is a transmitter of heredity? Studies in heredity present not the slightest evidence for it. Is it a fact that all peoples resort to war as a solution of their problems? Ruth Benedict, in *Patterns of Culture,* presents evidence that some "primitive" cultures cannot even conceive the possibility of a state of war. Is it a fact that you can't change human nature, that there are superior and inferior races, that every question has two sides? Barrows Dunham, in *Man against Myth,* maintains that not one of these is a fact. And any student who is convinced that superstition is dead should consult Bergen Evans' *Natural History of Nonsense* to see how folklore still masquerades as fact. As Evans says, "the civilized man has a moral obligation to be skeptical, to demand the credentials of all statements that claim to be facts."

FACTS VS. JUDGMENTS

Many "facts" are not disguised folklore but concealed judgments. A fact is a report based on accurate observation or a reliable record; it cannot reflect in the slightest degree the personal bias of the reporter. "The New York Yankees are a baseball team"; "oranges grow in California"; "stealing is a criminal offense in New York City"; "Shakespeare was born in 1564"— these are all facts that can be readily verified, the first three by firsthand observation, the last by reference to dependable documents. A judgment is a conclusion involving a personal evaluation of evidence. Even if the evidence overwhelmingly corroborates the conclusion, it can never be a fact. "The New York Yankees are the best baseball team in the world" is not a fact, even if they have just won the World Series for the third straight year. "Delicious oranges grow in California" may not be a fact to a fanatical citizen of Florida. "Crime doesn't pay" is the expression of an ethical judgment bolstered by the sturdiest evidence from criminology—but it remains a judgment. And even if every responsible critic in the world supported it, the statement that "Shakespeare is the greatest playwright in English literature" could never become a fact. A careful writer doesn't lead off with "It's a well-known fact that" and follow with a judgment.

UNRELIABLE AUTHORITIES

In his search for facts a writer can't always limit himself to firsthand evidence; sooner or later he must depend on the authority of others. Modern man likes to draw odious comparisons between his passion for reasoning *inductively* from his own observation and the medieval habit of arguing *deductively* from the dogmatic generalization of an authority whose word was law. But the medieval faith in Aristotle could hardly have been more submissive than our slavery to the power of print and the pronouncements of experts. Many people in this pundit-ridden age put implicit belief in what "it says here" without ever stopping to ask themselves who says it where. In a century when it has been pretty conclusively proved that millions will believe the most incredible lie if it is repeated often enough, this is a dangerous habit.

The problem of discriminating among sources is discussed in more detail in the next chapter. But the student should be reminded now that he should be wary of citing any source in support of an opinion when his knowledge is limited to the fact that the author's name is John Doe, that he has a Ph.D., and that his book has a blue cover. It is equally questionable to cite a distinguished expert in one field (the social life of fruit flies) as an authority on a problem that lies in another (Far Eastern diplomacy)—even though it is standard practice for advertisers to imply that a star second-baseman becomes automatically a connoisseur of cigarettes, whiskey, and shaving lotion. Finally, the most convincing evidence in an argument doesn't come from an authority biased by personal or party prejudice. A rabid Republican newspaper is not the best authority on the sins of the Democrats or a Democratic National Committeeman the most detached critic of the corruption of the Republicans. Obvious as this may appear, many students remain uninterested in whether an authority is disinterested.

MISREPRESENTING AUTHORITIES

A conscientious writer should take care not only to choose authorities carefully but to represent them accurately. An obvious kind of misrepresentation is inaccurate paraphrase or misquotation. A more subtle and therefore more insidious kind is ignoring the context of a quotation. This is a calculated trick of the experienced demagogue, who is a master of ripping a suspicious phrase from its setting and challenging his opponent to prove that he didn't utter it. It is a natural technique in movie promotion, where the critic's assertion that "Miss Sheridan's acting is a brilliant contrast to the listless performances of the rest of the cast" becomes in the advertisement "Sheridan's acting . . . brilliant"—with or without the triple period denoting an omission. A more innocent student will sometimes build an entire theme or examination answer on a single phrase quickly read without benefit of context. "Lincoln was a radical," writes Rollo Walter Brown, and one student, leaping at the offensive adjective like a bull at a red rag, comes angrily to the great emancipator's defense without carefully reading the essay in which the author systematically defines his use of the word. "Even A.B.'s Must Eat," asserts Ernest Earnest in a title, and another student automatically assumes that the author is maintaining the impracticality of liberal education, though a careful reading of the article would show that he is doing nothing of the kind.

In the broadest sense, the context of a quotation not only includes the sentences immediately surrounding it but extends beyond the source to involve all the circumstances of its composition. Who said or wrote it? What were the circumstances of time and place? What was his intention? Considering the author, the circumstances, and his intention, what can be inferred about the tone of the quotation? Are the words to be taken seriously or humorously, literally or ironically? All these questions are essential in honest criticism. Take, for example, the classic argument that America should isolate herself from the affairs of the world because our first president warned against "entangling alliances" in his Farewell Address. In the first place, it is pertinent to point out that the phrase is not Washington's but Jefferson's; Washington wrote (and incidentally both Madison and Hamilton contributed to the speech): "'Tis our true policy to steer clear of *permanent* alliances, with any portion of the foreign world." A glance at the immediate context of the phrase would reveal that, among other things, Washington condemned "infidelity to existing engagements" and specifically advocated "temporary alliances for extraordinary emergencies." Finally, the most superficial study of the larger context would raise the natural question of whether a policy, recommended in the days of sailing ships, warning an infant republic against involvement in European wars can have any logical application to the world's most powerful democracy in a time of long-range bombers carrying atomic doom.

MISINTERPRETING STATISTICS

In his search for irreducible facts modern man has developed the science of statistics to an astounding degree. Techniques of mass interviewing and rapid calculating have been perfected to a point where the poor citizen untutored in the mysteries of modes and medians and graphs and incidences and correlations often feels strangely illiterate. In some circles there is no deity but the digit and the pollster is his prophet. It is an established article of twentieth-century faith that "figures don't lie."

Unfortunately they often do. The lies of statistics range all the way from the little white lies that only slightly mislead to the most bare-faced falsifications. The responsible men who live with statistics are thoroughly aware of their limitations. For example, the celebrated "Kinsey Report" (*Sexual Behavior in the Human Male*), after devoting 118 pages to a discussion of the complicated problem of collecting and evaluating statistical data, sounds this warning:

Throughout the remainder of this volume, the raw data and the calculations based on the raw data are treated with a precision that must not be misunderstood by the statistically inexperienced reader. It has not been practical to carry this warning in every paragraph of every chapter. Neither has it been possible to qualify every individual statistic, as every statistic in any study of the human animal should be qualified. For the remainder of the volume it should, therefore, be recognized that the data are probably fair approximations, but only approximations of the fact.

"Only approximations of the fact." That is all a reader can demand of statistical evidence involving complex, fallible human beings. More dramatic warnings are contained in the notorious *Literary Digest* poll predicting Landon's election in 1936 and the numerous polls prophesying Truman's defeat in 1948. Yet careless speakers and writers still throw around "facts and figures" with the calm assurance that every figure is a fact.

The most elementary study of statistics is a whole course in the catalogue. There is room here only to remind the reader with a general rule of thumb: *Do not put your faith in what statistics say until you have carefully considered what they do not say.*

Take a simple example. A newspaper story reports that, according to a poll, "the average annual income of the members of the class of 1930 twenty years after their graduation from Lackawanna College is $6,234.27." (Figures calculated to the last red cent carry statistical illusions more confidently than "round numbers.") This is an interesting figure, but what does it mean? "Average annual income" for how many years? Twenty or only for the year 1949–1950? Was the question worded so that "income" clearly included such items as dividends on stock, or could it have implied salary alone? Does the arithmetic average give any evidence about the distribution of incomes? How many members of the class make over a hundred thousand dollars a year and how many are wrestling with the wolf in the vestibule? Is the phrase "members of the class" restricted to graduates or does it include those who fell by the wayside in their first freshman term? How many answered the poll, four fifths of the class or less than half? And if four fifths appear to be a representative sampling, isn't it likely that the answerers include most of the financially successful members and the silent group contains most of the failures? So much is omitted from the newspaper report that the presumably accurate figure is all but meaningless.

Examples could be multiplied indefinitely to support the

rule that in almost all statistical evidence something is left out. Thus figures that announce a distressingly higher rate of insanity in our age of anxiety than in 1900 omit a half century's progress in psychiatric diagnosis and institutional growth. Statistics indicating a much higher per capita "crime rate" in A town than in B berg may ignore the point that a crime in A town, which has an alert modern police force and an uncorrupted judiciary, is merely a harmless wild oat in B berg, where the sheriff is not only in the pay of John Q. Gambling but married to the judge's favorite sister. And a student who comes to the common conclusion that Y College, where the passing grade is 70, has higher standards than Z University, where it is 60, may overlook the evidence tending to show that a 90 at Y is easier to get than a 75 at Z.

Finally, one of the biggest troubles with "hard, cold figures" is that they are hard and cold. The statistics on the number of people killed by the first atomic bomb dropped on Japan—an item that one commentator summarized as "considerable personnel damage"—cannot speak as eloquently as the human argument in John Hersey's *Hiroshima*. For all its virtues, our modern tendency to worship statistics can be dangerously inhuman. Charles Dickens tried to teach this lesson in *Hard Times* when statistical method was still in its infancy. Sissy Jupe confesses to her friend Louisa Gradgrind how miserably she has failed in Mr. M'Choakumchild's school of hard facts:

"And he said, Now, this schoolroom is a nation. And in the nation there are fifty millions of money. Isn't this a prosperous nation? Girl number twenty, isn't this a prosperous nation, and a'n't you in a thriving state?"

"What did you say?" asked Louisa.

"Miss Louisa, I said I didn't know. I thought I couldn't know whether it was a prosperous nation or not, and whether I was in a thriving state or not, unless I knew who had got the money, and whether any of it was mine. But that had nothing to do with it. It was not in the figures at all," said Sissy, wiping her eyes.

Statistics are often indispensable in supporting opinions. But a writer must be forever aware of what is "not in the figures at all."

LEAPING AT CONCLUSIONS

Paul B. Sears, in his study of Charles Darwin, tells the story of two scientists at the University of Illinois in the 1920's who were investigating the sense of balance, which is so important in aviation. They found that white rats, after long internment in whirling horizontal cages, "naturally showed some motor disturbance, but usually recovered." However, when some of the offspring of these whirling vermin were born with a tendency to travel in circles, it looked as if the old moot problem of the inheritance of acquired characters had finally been solved. Cautious excitement prevailed until a skeptical fellow scientist at a convention raised a pertinent question: "Are you sure that those animals did not have a hidden strain of the 'waltzing' habit in their inheritance to start with?" Further investigation revealed that the waltzing offspring all had a disease of the inner ear having no apparent relation to inheritance.

The history of science is studded with such tales, and every one is a further warning to the scientist not to announce a conclusion until he has made the most exhaustive investigation of the evidence—and even then to regard that conclusion as no more than a credible hypothesis. Thus Whitehead cautiously defines induction, not as "the derivation of general law," but as "the divination of some characteristics of a particular future from the known characteristics of a particular past."

Unlike the scientist, the average writer can't seek sanctuary in the laboratory for years before he ventures humbly forth with a tentative inductive conclusion. But there is a happy medium between a Charles Darwin studying evolution for more than twenty years before he printed his tentative conclusions in *On the Origin of Species* and a William Jennings Bryan thundering from the lecture platform: "If man is descended from the monkeys, why cannot we go into Africa today and see monkeys turning into men?" No writer can wait until "all the evidence is in" before coming to a conclusion; sooner or later he must take the "inductive leap" from the specific instances to the general rule. A careful writer will look before he leaps.

The soundness of a generalization depends on whether the evidence presented is accurate, typical, relevant, and adequate. Obviously a conclusion cannot be valid if it is based on errors in fact or on a discriminating selection of exceptional instances, ignoring typical evidence. And only the flimsiest hasty generalization can be based on evidence having no discernible relation to the conclusion. For example, a luncheon speaker is reported in a newspaper to have said: "Members of service clubs become tolerant of each other's views and therefore are in a better position to fight the 'isms' which threaten our economic and political system." Even if the first of these two generalities is accepted as evidence, by what logic does the second follow? The assertion is an extreme example of a *non sequitur:* "it does not follow." Another kind of *non sequitur* is represented by the common assumption that because B follows A, it was necessarily caused by A: "As soon as Coach Smith took over, the team lost to State for the first time in twenty-three years. Obviously bad coaching is the answer." The rabid alumnus guilty of this typical leap from fact to fancy probably doesn't know that the Latin has a phrase for it: the fallacy of *post hoc ergo propter hoc*—"after this, therefore because of this."

The meaning of the arbitary term "adequate evidence" will vary with the length and nature of the argument. A short essay in opinion may convincingly present three examples to "prove" a point; a doctoral dissertation may display three hundred. But the student should be warned against leaping to a generalization from a single piece of evidence, however accurate, typical, and relevant. College undergraduates have no monopoly on this common human habit. Abbott Lawrence Lowell, late President of Harvard, once wrote in a discussion of college athletics: "Nor is there any evidence that athletic contests interfere seriously with scholarship; for good scholars on a team are not uncommon, and occasionally the very highest are found among the players." Here the conclusion comes first, the "proof" follows. Even if the dual assertion after the semicolon is accepted at its face value, it is inadequate support for the opening generalization.

Even when a generalization is supported by adequate evidence, it is wise to present it with caution. Words such as *all* and *every, never* and *always, best* and *worse, certainly* and *undoubtedly* may exude a dogmatic cocksureness unjustified by the evidence. A writer would do well to remember that, when Sir Joseph Porter, K.C.B., boasts that he is "never, never sick at sea," the skeptical chorus of the sisters and the cousins and the aunts makes him qualify it with "well, hardly ever." Notice the number of qualifying words and phrases in a passage of about five hundred words from a magazine report of a scientific survey of radio listening habits (Edwin Muller, "Radio vs. Reading," *New Republic*):

The writer says:	*He does not say:*
"The study *suggests* . . . ."	The study proves . . . .
"A *general* conclusion *appears to be* . . . ."	The obvious conclusion is . . . .
"Radio . . . *tends* to play safe . . . ."	Radio plays safe . . . .
"Radio, *generally speaking,* does not attack people or things . . . ."	Radio does not attack people or things . . . .
"If . . . radio is *probably* not displacing the printed word . . . ."	If . . . radio is not displacing the printed word . . . .
"The material of the survey *suggests* some interesting comparisons . . . ."	The material of the survey makes inevitable some interesting comparisons . . . .
"The most characteristic listener to serious broadcasts *tends to be* the educated small-town man . . . ."	The most characteristic listener . . . is the educated small-town man . . . .
"There *would seem to be* less and less likelihood . . . ."	There is less and less likelihood . . . .
"Radio *may well become* . . . ."	Radio will undoubtedly become . . . .

A writer who overdoes such qualifying, even in scholarly articles, may some day find himself permanently stuck on the fence. But it is better to do a little extra hedging than to let an opponent invade your generalizations and rip them full of holes.

EXERCISES

Analyze the reasoning reflected in the following passages, distinguishing any flaws which make them illogical or unconvincing:

1. In a democracy the office of president goes to the candidate receiving the largest popular vote. The election is over; the people have spoken. The winner has not yet made one official utterance or performed one official act. How then can my opponent argue that he is not popular?

2. The results of a poll published in *Fortune* in September, 1949 clearly support my argument against required courses in science in college. The editors asked this question: "In grade school almost all students are required to study subjects like arithmetic, spelling, and geography. Now in college, are there any subjects you think all boys (girls) should be required to study no matter what they are going to do afterwards?" In answering this question only seven per cent of the respondents named one of the natural sciences as a requirement for boys and only three per cent named science for girls. And nearly thirty per cent didn't name any subject at all! How can higher education, which pretends to serve the public, ignore this evidence by insisting on required science courses?

3. To argue that because once in a while we get a picture like *The Informer*, Hollywood is justified, is just about the same as to argue that you should be forgiven for theft because you have used some stolen money for the remission of punishment, due to sin, of souls in Purgatory. —James T. Farrell, *The League of Frightened Philistines.*

4. Another advantage of football is that it builds strong physical specimens. It is no game for weaklings. You have to have a real physique to play sixty minutes of rugged football—strong legs and good wind and lots of coordination. The reader can see from this that football's value in building physiques can't be surpassed by any other sport.

5. Since it is obvious that the ultimate aim of all writers is to sell their books, the only reasonable standard by which to judge a writer is his royalty statements. They are a measure of his popularity, and he writes to be read by as many people as possible. How can anyone argue, then, that T. S. Eliot is a more successful poet than Edgar A.

Guest? From the statistical evidence of their royalties, Guest is far more successful. The inevitable conclusion is that he is a better poet.

6. We cannot protect the planet Mars against our enemies from the Earth if we permit these Earthists to flourish in our midst. Glog believes in freedom of speech; so do the Earthists. He believes in the right of trial by jury; so do the Earthists. He hates war as the Earthists do. He subscribes to the well-known Earthist philosophy that sin is a bad thing. I accuse him of being an Earthist of the most dangerous kind.

7. In our country the common man cannot be overlooked. The common man governs our democracy. He decides who operates the government. Actually the government is nothing but the servant of the common man. Throughout the years he usually has chosen men of his caliber to the important offices. Seldom has a learned scholar with an I.Q. comparable to Einstein's been elected President of the United States. Because the common man prefers material progress to spiritual progress, he should be given the kind of education that will allow him to make a direct material gain from it.

8. The one important difference between men is the difference in what they hold valuable, and in the degree of passion and conviction with which they adhere to and pursue that. The rest is embroidery. To the man who has the religion of peace, the supreme value is love. To the man who has the religion of war, the supreme value is strife. There can be no reconciliation between these attitudes. Men have simply to discover which it is they stand for. And it is these ultimate antagonisms that constitute the tragedy of life. —G. Lowes Dickinson, *The Choice Before Us.*

9. In arguing against David Lilienthal's appointment to the Atomic Energy Commission, Senator Wherry reminded Congress of Lilienthal's record administering the Tennessee Valley Authority. The senator pointed out that in his five years on the Appropriations Committee they had appropriated $626,000,000 to the TVA, and it had paid back only $17,000,000. And this was the man defenders were praising for his business ability! As Senator Wherry said, "The measuring stick for financial ability and for business ability is dollars and cents."

10. Before that fatal day of July 4th I had not been swimming once all summer. That afternoon some friends and I went into the woods to the old swimming hole for a dip. The outlet had been clogged with leaves and branches, and the water was stagnant and uninviting. But boys will be boys—especially on a hot summer day. The very next morning I was seized with the mysterious aches that turned out later

to be the dreaded symptoms of polio. My system had obviously been invaded by some kind of bug in the polluted pool.

11. My worthy opponent calls himself a progressive because he advocates such "forward-looking" measures as higher salaries for teachers, fairer wages in industry, and a new town sewage system. Then he ridicules me for what he calls my "Victorian faith in the inevitability of progress." How can a man call himself a progressive when he doesn't even believe in progress?

12. In regard to the college magazine the administration can do one of two things. It can either abolish the office of the so-called "faculty adviser" and give the magazine back to the students, making them and them alone responsible for what appears in print, or it can give him unlimited power to crib, cabin, and confine creative writing at this college with the most odious form of censorship. One course is democracy; the other is—fascism. As for me, give me journalistic freedom or require me to withdraw from college.

13. This man's reputation as a reformer of public morality has been built up amid the glamor of the television screen. How well it is deserved can be seen from a look at his own personal morality. The record shows that he has been twice divorced and that his first wife was given custody of the children by that "marriage." And this is the man who dares to prescribe public morality! Practice what you so unctuously preach, Smathers!

14. Freedom anyhow? The land of the free! This is the land of the free! Why, if I say anything that displeases them, the free mob will lynch me, and that's my freedom. Free? Why I have never been in any country where the individual has such an abject fear of his fellow countrymen. Because, as I say, they are free to lynch him the moment he shows he is not one of them.

No, no, if you're so fond of the truth about Queen Victoria, try a little about yourself. —D. H. Lawrence writing about America in "The Spirit of Place," *Studies in Classic American Literature.*

15. A college is a business just like a copper mine or a cement mill or a paper cup factory. No business can exist without advertising. Then why shouldn't those who run the business of the college be allowed to spend a decent amount of money for a good football team to advertise their plant and their product?

16. These so-called liberals must be seen for what they really are. The dictionary defines *liberal* as "favorable to or in accord with the policy of leaving the individual as unrestricted as possible in the opportunities for self-expression or self-fulfillment." It is the self-styled

liberals who have voted for the laws that have crippled American industry in recent years. They are not worthy of the name. The real liberals are the conservatives.

17. When a government passes an unjust law, a citizen can either obey it without a murmur and be a slave or refuse to obey it and be a man. The law requiring employers to collect taxes from their employees on a pay-as-you-go basis is obviously unjust. By what authority can the Congress compel me to be a tax-collector without pay? I see no alternative but to refuse to conform to this tyrannical law.

18. To get a clear picture of Shakespeare's taste in play-writing, one has only to look at *Titus Andronicus*. In the first act the hero sacrifices one of the three sons of the captive Gothic Queen, Tamora, and slays one of his own. In the second act the remaining two sons of Tamora murder Bassianus, and, after ravishing his wife, Lavinia, tear out her tongue and cut off her hands so that she can't squeal or put the finger on them. In the third act Titus cuts off one of his own hands, and two of his sons are decapitated. In the fourth act, after Tamora gives birth to a "blackamoor," her villainous lover, Aaron, kills both the nurse and the midwife to insure secrecy. In the last act, Titus cuts the throats of Tamora's two remaining sons, and Lavinia, after catching their blood in a basin, serves them up in a pie. But why pile on more evidence? How can anyone seriously argue that the author of this bloody butchery is a better playwright than the author of *Death of a Salesman?*

19. All voting is a sort of gaming, like checkers or backgammon, with a slight moral tinge to it, a playing with right and wrong, with moral questions; and betting naturally accompanies it. The character of the voters is not staked. I cast my vote, perchance, as I think right; but I am not vitally concerned that the right should prevail. I am willing to leave it to the majority. Its obligation, therefore, never exceeds that of expediency. Even voting *for the right* is *doing* nothing for it. It is only expressing to men feebly your desire that it should prevail. A wise man will not leave the right to the mercy of chance, nor wish it to prevail through the power of the majority. There is but little virtue in the action of masses of men. When the majority shall at length vote for the abolition of slavery, it will be because they are indifferent to slavery, or because there is but little slavery left to be abolished by their vote. *They* will then be the only slaves. Only *his* vote can hasten the abolition of slavery who asserts his own freedom by his vote.

—Henry David Thoreau, "Civil Disobedience" (1849)

20. This policy is unsound because it is the work of crackpot col-

lege professors. How can anybody have faith in a plan drawn up by fuzzy-minded planners in mortar boards? If they had been kept in their ivory tower where they belong and never allowed to flock to Washington to run the government with their bureaucratic meddling, a plan as impractical as this would never have been born.

21. As an example of what I mean by saying that the romantic poets are poor guides for modern living, take Keats. At the end of his famous *Ode on a Grecian Urn,* he argues that "Beauty is truth, truth beauty." I don't deny that this may be true. But when he goes on to say:

that is all

Ye know on earth, and all ye need to know

I rebel. How can a man possibly get along in the modern world if all he knows on earth is that beauty is truth, truth beauty? This is poetic nonsense of the silliest kind.

22. Everybody knows that the Wagner Act was an evil piece of legislation. To quote Westbrook Pegler, "the Wagner Act was put over on the American people by a confused, unfaithful Congress at the order of a bad, reckless president whose wickedness in many other particulars is no longer disputed." Other leading authorities on labor problems have condemned it with equal force.

23. A student can memorize and cram for a test and ring up a ninety-five, while another student won't study at all but rely entirely on what he learned at a lecture and emerge with an eighty. But some time later, the latter has a better chance of retaining all he learned than the former. This proves that grades signify nothing as far as intelligence is concerned.

24. To say that college does something to the average student's religion is to state a truth which will be conceded by anyone who has given the matter a moment's thought. Nine young men and women out of every ten who will receive their degrees this June would probably admit, if they were called to testify, that education has acted as a poison to their faith. . . .

In these pages I propose to show how higher education reacts upon faith by describing my own religious crisis just as it occurred while I was in college. —Philip E. Wentworth, "What College Did to My Religion," *Atlantic Monthly.*

25. Let pedants quibble about the differences between communism, socialism, and fascism. As all sound-thinking people know, they are only different names for the same thing. If they differ at all, they differ only in degree. There is no room in this country for any ism except one hundred per cent Americanism.

CHAPTER TWELVE

The Library Research Paper

Research is but diligent search which enjoys the high flavor of primitive hunting.
—James Harvey Robinson.

Some articles are born documented, others achieve documentation, but a good many have footnotes thrust upon them.
—William Riley Parker.

⫸⫸⫸⫸⫸⫸⫸⫸⫸⫸⫸⫸⫸⫸⫸⫸⫸⫸⫸⫸⫸⫸⫸⫸⫸

WHAT RESEARCH IS

In the highest sense of the word, research is investigation resulting in an original contribution to knowledge. The scientist may discover a new alloy or drug in the laboratory; the historian, pursuing his quarry through faded newspapers and forgotten documents, may throw new light on the causes of a devastating war; the literary scholar may edit an unpublished manuscript or add an important piece to the puzzle of a great writer's life.

On rare occasions college undergraduates have made contributions of this sort. An undergraduate at Oberlin College was the first American to work out the method by which aluminum is produced. But when the teacher assigns a library research paper, he doesn't expect revolutionary discoveries. Much of the time the student will be laboring in a field that has been thoroughly combed and countercombed by scholars who have recorded their findings in books and articles readily available in any good library. He will be expected to track down these references, sift out the materials that best suit his purpose, and synthesize them in a well-planned, well-written essay, carefully acknowledging indebtedness in accordance with a standard technique. He may also be expected to go one step further and come to intelligent conclusions of his own on the basis of the evidence presented.

Library research is not restricted to scholars, feature writers,

344

and historical novelists. It is a task for thousands of unliterary citizens who are required to collect accurate information, not only for speeches and reports but in the routine pursuit of their daily jobs. The research paper is an assignment that the student will meet again and again in college. The experience of writing one paper cannot make him a trained research man; but it can introduce him to the library, teach him to organize materials more complex than the facts and fancies of his shorter themes, show him the proper technique of scholarly acknowledgment, and help him to develop the resourcefulness and independence without which genuine education is impossible.

WHAT A RESEARCH PAPER IS NOT

A research paper is not a series of quotations loosely stitched together with the tenuous threads of transition. (Zilch says this: Quote at length. Zupitz, on the other hand, maintains this: Quote at length.) This is not a research paper; it is an anthology. *a collection of choice passages*

A research paper is not a paraphrase of a single book or article, or even of two or three laid end to end. This is a précis, *a brief summary* synopsis, or digest.

A research paper is not a simple transfer without acknowledgment from the printed page to the typed manuscript, however skillfully disguised with occasional alterations. This is larceny.

CHOOSING AND LIMITING A SUBJECT

In writing a five-hundred-word theme, the problem of selecting a subject and "staking out a claim" (see pages 20–22) is relatively simple. The preliminary choice of a topic for research is often highly tentative; the precise subject may not come clearly into focus until the student has spent many hours in the library. During the hunt for material, a vast area (marine disasters) may be narrowed down to a workable claim (the sinking of the *Titanic*). The search for the answer to a presumably simple question (How did President Truman win the nomination for Vice-President in 1944?) may lead into an intricate maze (American political strategy). A student beginning with a subject as infinite as evolution may run across accounts of the Tennessee "Monkey Trial" of 1925, become interested in the spellbinding politician who led the prosecution, and end up by writing on William Jennings Bryan's "Cross of Gold" speech in 1896.

Of course if the teacher selects the topic he will not expect it to undergo a complete metamorphosis. But he will expect the final size and shape of the subject to be intelligently adjusted to the length of the paper and the amount of information available. A two-thousand-word paper entitled *The Uses of Atomic Energy, The Poetry of Lord Byron,* or *Labor Unions* can be nothing but the most superficial synopsis. *Radioactive Isotopes in Cancer Detection, History and Fiction in "The Prisoner of Chillon," The Labor Policies of David Dubinsky*—these titles reflect a better sense of proportion. Occasionally a student chooses a subject so limited that he quickly exhausts its possibilities. But it is far more common for an inexperienced investigator to bite off more than he can even begin to taste.

FINDING MATERIAL

The only way to learn to use the college library is to walk in and go to work. But the student who is familiar with some of the important sources common to all good-sized libraries can get off to a faster start than a classmate who wanders vaguely up to the delivery desk and asks the nearest assistant librarian where to look for a book on model airplanes. The following list may seem imposing, but it is only a limited selection of sources that may be consulted, especially during the earliest stages of the hunt. Those marked with an asterisk (*) should be familiar to every undergraduate. He should know where they are in the library, what they are for, and how to use them.

* THE CARD CATALOGUE

A complete card catalogue lists every book in the library on at least three separate cards: by author, title, and subject. See the accompanying representative author card from the series issued by the Library of Congress.

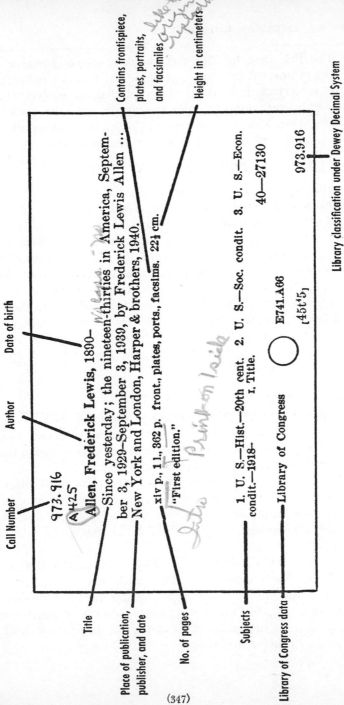

The title card for this same book is identical except that the title is inserted in black type above the author's name. Each of the subject cards is identical except that the subject (U.S.—Hist.—20th cent., for example) .appears in red type above the author's name. Most libraries would list this book under all three subjects indicated on the Library of Congress card.

PERIODICAL INDEXES

Although the card catalogue may list the titles of all the magazines and newspapers in the library, giving a complete record of volumes, numbers, and dates, it cannot possibly index all the articles in those periodicals. The student who reports that there is "nothing in the library" on *Color Television* because he has found no books listed under that subject in the card catalogue is ignoring the most obvious sources of information on such a recent development. Even if his subject is as old as *The Battle of Marathon,* his most valuable source may be an obscure article tucked away in one of the bound volumes of a magazine. A well-equipped reference room contains both general and specific periodical indexes.

GENERAL INDEXES

√* *Book Review Digest* (1905–). Contains excerpts from representative book reviews indexed by author, title, and subject. A quick way to find an exact reference to a review and get a bird's-eye view of a book's reception on publication.

√* *International Index to Periodicals* (1907–). Indexes by author, title, and subject the articles in many scholarly magazines not recorded in the *Reader's Guide* (see below), including those in foreign languages. "Devoted chiefly to the Humanities and Sciences."

√* *New York Times Index* (1913–). A monthly index to the New York *Times* since 1913. This guide not only directs the student to the files of a newspaper notable for its complete, objective reporting, but also helps him to date the events of recent history, and to determine dates when the same event will be reported in other newspapers.

* *Poole's Index to Periodical Literature* (1802–1906). A subject index to articles appearing in English and American periodicals for a century before the *Reader's Guide* (see below) was established.

* *Reader's Guide to Periodical Literature* (1900–). An indispensable reference that indexes articles in the best-known current magazines by author, title, and subject. It appears monthly, and the bound volumes cover periods of two or three years.

SPECIAL INDEXES

Agricultural Index (1916–)
Art Index (1929–)
Dramatic Index (1909–)
Education Index (1929–)
Engineering Index (1906–)
Index to Legal Periodicals (1926–)
Industrial Arts Index (1913–)
Public Affairs Information Service (1915–)
Quarterly Cumulative Index Medicus (1927–)

DICTIONARIES

The use of a standard desk dictionary is discussed in detail in Chapter Eight. The following are either more comprehensive or more specialized:

GENERAL UNABRIDGED DICTIONARIES

* *Dictionary of American English on Historical Principles,* 4 vols., Chicago, 1938–1944

* *Oxford English Dictionary,* 12 vols. and supplement, Oxford, 1933. Originally issued as the *New English Dictionary,* 10 volumes and supplement, 1888–1933. The OED or NED not only lists meanings in historical order but cites and dates passages in which those meanings appear. It gives the "complete history" of a word. Thus it is indispensable not only to students of language and literature but to all investigators who need an accurate understanding of any English word as a key to the past.

* *Webster's New International Dictionary,* 2d ed., Springfield, Mass., 1934

SPECIAL DICTIONARIES

Fowler, H. W., *A Dictionary of Modern English Usage*, Oxford, 1926

Horwill, H. W., *A Dictionary of Modern American Usage*, Oxford, 1935

Kenyon, J. S., and T. A. Knott, *A Pronouncing Dictionary of American English*, Springfield, Mass., 1944

Partridge, E., *A Dictionary of Slang and Unconventional English*, 2d ed., New York, 1938

Perrin, P. G., *An Index to English*, rev. ed., Chicago, 1950

Roget's Thesaurus of Words and Phrases, new ed., New York, 1947. (See page 240.)

Webster's Dictionary of Synonyms, Springfield, Mass., 1942. (See pages 240–241.)

BIOGRAPHICAL REFERENCES

Current Biography (1940–)

* *Dictionary of American Biography*, 20 vols., New York, 1928–1937, supplement, 1944. Contains brief lives of distinguished dead Americans.

* *Dictionary of National Biography*, 63 vols. and supplements, London, 1885–1937. Lives of distinguished dead of Great Britain.

International Who's Who, London, 1936–

Webster's Biographical Dictionary, Springfield, Mass., 1943

Who's Who, London, 1849–. An annual guide to living British subjects.

* *Who's Who in America*, Chicago, 1899–. A biennial guide to the lives of noteworthy living Americans.

ENCYCLOPEDIAS

GENERAL

Columbia Encyclopedia, 2d ed., New York, 1950

* *Encyclopedia Americana*, 30 vols., New York, 1948. The annual supplement is *The Americana Annual*.

* *Encyclopedia Britannica,* 14th ed., 24 vols., New York, 1929. The annual supplement is *The Britannica Book of the Year.*

New International Encyclopedia, 2d ed., 24 vols., New York, 1918

SPECIAL

Agriculture

Bailey, L. H., ed., *Cyclopedia of American Agriculture,* 4 vols., New York, 1907–1909

Art and Architecture

Bryan, M., *Bryan's Dictionary of Painters and Engravers,* rev. ed., 5 vols., London, 1903–1905

Harper's Encyclopedia of Art, 2 vols., New York, 1937

Fletcher, Sir B. F., *A History of Architecture,* 14th ed., New York, 1948

Business and Economics

Munn, G. G., *Encyclopedia of Banking and Finance,* 5th ed., New York, 1949

Education

Monroe, P., ed., *Cyclopedia of Education,* 5 vols., New York, 1911–1913

Monroe, W. S., ed., *Encyclopedia of Educational Research,* rev. ed., New York, 1950

Government

McLaughlin, A. C., and A. B. Hart, eds., *Cyclopedia of American Government,* 3 vols., New York, 1914

History

Adams, J. T., ed., *Dictionary of American History,* 5 vols., New York, 1940

Cambridge Ancient History, 17 vols., including plates, Cambridge, 1928–1939

Cambridge Medieval History, 16 vols., including maps and plates, Cambridge, 1911–1936

Cambridge Modern History, 2d ed., 13 vols. and atlas, Cambridge, 1926

Langer, W. L., ed., *An Encyclopedia of World History,* Boston, 1940

Literature and Quotations

* *Bartlett's Familiar Quotations,* 11th ed., by C. Morley and L. D. Everett, Boston, 1942

Bateson, F. W., ed., *Cambridge Bibliography of English Literature,* 4 vols., Cambridge, 1941

Cambridge History of American Literature, 4 vols., Cambridge, 1917–1921

Cambridge History of English Literature, 15 vols., Cambridge, 1907–1927

Hart, J. D., *Oxford Companion to American Literature,* 2d ed., New York, 1948

Harvey, Sir Paul, ed., *Oxford Companion to Classical Literature,* New York, 1937. *Oxford Companion to English Literature,* 3d ed., New York, 1946

Millett, F. B., *Contemporary American Authors,* New York, 1940

——, J. M. Manley, and E. Rickert, *Contemporary British Authors,* 3d ed., New York, 1935

Smith, H., ed., *Columbia Dictionary of Modern European Literature,* New York, 1947

Spiller, R. E., and others, *A Literary History of the United States,* 3 vols., New York, 1948

* Stevenson, B., *The Home Book of Quotations,* New York, 1934

Music

Grove's Dictionary of Music and Musicians, 3d ed., 5 vols. and supplements, London, 1935

Thompson, O., *International Cyclopedia of Music and Musicians,* 5th ed., New York, 1949

Philosophy and Psychology

Baldwin, J. M., ed., *Dictionary of Philosophy and Psychology,* new ed., 3 vols., New York, 1940

Warren, H. C., *Dictionary of Psychology,* Boston, 1934

Religion

Catholic Encyclopedia, rev. ed., 17 vols., New York, 1936–

Hastings, J., ed., *Encyclopedia of Religion and Ethics,* 13 vols., New York, 1911–1927. *Dictionary of the Bible,* 5 vols., New York, 1898–1902

Jackson, S. M., ed., *New Schaff-Herzog Encyclopedia of Religious Knowledge,* 12 vols., New York, 1908–1912

Jewish Encyclopedia, new ed., 12 vols., New York, 1925

Science

Tweney, C. F., and F. P. Shirshov, eds., *Hutchinson's Technical and Scientific Encyclopedia,* 4 vols., New York, 1935–1936

Van Nostrand's Scientific Encyclopedia, 2d ed., New York, 1947

Social Science

Seligman, E. R. A., and A. Johnson, *Encyclopedia of the Social Sciences,* 15 vols., New York, 1930–1935

YEARBOOKS

In addition to the annual supplements to the *Encyclopedia Americana* and *Encyclopedia Britannica,* the following yearbooks contain valuable factual information:

American Year Book (1910–)

New International Year Book (1907–)

Statesman's Year Book (1864–)

* *World Almanac and Book of Facts* (1868–)

THE PRELIMINARY BIBLIOGRAPHY

After a student has consulted the card catalogue and the pertinent books in the reference room, he should be able to make a preliminary list of sources he may use in preparing the paper. This bibliography will, of course, be highly tentative. A book or article with a promising title may be crossed off the list when a quick survey of its contents reveals that it doesn't cover the phase of the subject in which the student is primarily interested; another may turn out to be merely a rehash of a more thorough and reliable source. But it will save time and trouble in the long run if all the items in the preliminary list are carefully recorded as they would appear in the final bibliography. This can be conveniently done by entering each item on a separate 3 x 5 card and alphabetizing the cards—by author's last name or, if no author is given, by title. Bibliographical entries must contain a prescribed minimum of essential information. The following typical entries conform to one of several acceptable methods. A teacher may recommend another form, but whichever one the student adopts, he should be consistent down to the last mark of punctuation.

For a book:
1. Author's name, last name first, followed by first name or initials
2. Title underlined (italicized)
3. Place and date of publication

Turner, F. J., *The Frontier in American History*, New York, 1920

The name of the publisher is optional; it may be supplied between place and date: New York, Henry Holt, 1920.

For a magazine article:
1. Author's name, last name first, followed by first name or initials. If no author is given, list alphabetically by title
2. Title of article in quotes
3. Name of magazine underlined (italicized)
4. Date, volume, and page numbers

Sheean, Vincent, "My Last Visit with Shaw," *Atlantic Monthly*, January, 1951, 187:19–24

For a newspaper article:
Name of newspaper underlined (italicized) date, and page number

New York *Times*, July 13, 1951, p. 17

If the paper has two or more sections with separate paging, the section number should be supplied: sec. 4, p. 13.

In addition to this minimum of information, it is convenient to enter the library call number in the upper left-hand corner of each bibliography card.

DISCRIMINATING AMONG SOURCES

The writer's ability to judge his sources will depend to a great extent on his previous knowledge of the subject under investigation. But this doesn't mean that a student starting from scratch may indiscriminately accept as gospel anything he finds in print. Before relying on any source, the investigator might consider these points:

1. *Who is the author?* Is he a scholar pursuing the truth or a propagandist grinding an ax? Do other sources refer to him as a recognized authority? Is he merely a name or can you find reliable information about him in one or more standard reference works?

2. *How was the book received?* Technical books are often reviewed by experts in the field. A glance at the *Book Review Digest* or the book review section in a pertinent scholarly periodical may serve as a rough guide to a book's reliability.

3. *Where did the article appear?* An article in a reputable professional journal is likely to be more trustworthy than one in a popular magazine; a news story in the New York *Times* will probably be more reliable than one in the New York *Daily News*.

4. *How recent is the source?* The latest word may not be the most dependable, but in many fast-changing fields, timeliness is highly important. An article on atomic energy published in 1935 would probably be an untrustworthy guide in 1951. The date of a book is often sufficient evidence that the book is dated.

5. *How far is the author of the source removed from his material?* An undergraduate will usually be organizing second-hand material from the first-hand research of others. He will seldom use primary sources in the most limited sense of the term: unpublished diaries, memoirs, and other manuscripts. But he can learn to get as close to first-hand material as time and the resources of the library will let him. If he is writing on a literary subject, for example, he may safely assume that an author knows more about his own works than his critics do. If a point turns on

what happens in Act Four of *Hamlet,* he will read *Hamlet*—not confine himself to what Jones says about *Hamlet* or, worse still, to what Smith says Jones says.

6. *Does the source sound reliable?*   A good liar can create the illusion of truth; a quack can sometimes pass as a scholar. But often an unreliable book or article will be betrayed by its own inconsistencies, unsound generalities, or obvious sensationalism. An experienced reader can detect quackery in a field where he is a rank beginner.

NOTE-TAKING

A seasoned scholar may have developed his own personal method of taking notes on his reading. An inexperienced student would do well to follow a common procedure such as this:

1. Take notes on one side of 4 x 6 cards, limiting each card to a single source.

2. Identify each card at the top with a caption concerning the subject of the note and with the source of the material. If the source is already listed in your preliminary bibliography, you don't need to add place and date of publication.

3. In the left-hand margin write the number of the page from which each part of the material is taken, clearly indicating the exact point at which you go from one page to the next.

4. Distinguish carefully among (1) direct quotations—in quotation marks— (2) paraphrase, and (3) your own incidental comments [in square brackets]. When you quote directly, *quote exactly*—word for word, punctuation mark for punctuation mark. Check all quotations back against your source to make sure you have done this. If you omit part of a direct quotation, insert three periods, plus end punctuation if the omission comes at the end of the sentence. When you paraphrase or summarize a pas-sage, put it as nearly as possible into your own words. If your paraphrase retains a key phrase from the original, set it off in quotation marks. (See pages 359–361.)

5. If material from a single source covers more than one note card, number each card and identify it with caption and source.

Here is a sample note card:

[handwritten note at top:] Has to be one part of outline. Same as a paragraph—topic + subj.

[handwritten note card:]

① Public Reaction to Welles Broadcast
Cantril, The Invasion from Mars

58 28% of listeners thought it was news
bulletin. 70% of them "frightened or
disturbed."

60 Increase of 39% in phoning in metro-
politan No. Jersey during broadcast hours.
[which doesn't seem like much.]

67 Quotes Dorothy Thompson (N.Y. H-Trib.,
Nov. 2, 1938): "Nothing whatever about
the dramatization was in the least
credible, no matter at what point the
listener might have tuned in." Cantril
adds that first few minutes were
67/68 "almost credible to even relatively sophisticated and well informed listeners....
The sheer dramatic excellence of the
broadcast must not be overlooked."

[handwritten margin note:] 3-(3)

THE OUTLINE

A five-hundred-word theme may be neatly organized without
an outline, but the more complex problem of weaving together
the materials from a number of sources into a research paper
four or five times as long makes some sort of outline indispensable.
If the student is required to submit one with his paper, he should
observe these conventions:

1. *Use the standard system of subordination:*

I.
   A.
   B.
     1.
      a.

[handwritten in margin:] I. A. 1. 2. a. b. B. II.

2. *Make either* a topic outline (*words or phrases*) *or* a sentence outline (*complete sentences*). For the sake of parallelism,
avoid mixing the two.

Part of a topic outline:

I. Renaissance forerunners of modern thought

[handwritten in margin:] Use either one or the other

A. Copernicus
B. Machiavelli
C. Montaigne *Key nouns and modefiers*
    1. Comparison between man and animals
    2. Man's ignorance of nature
    3. The failure of man's senses

Part of a sentence outline:

I. Modern thought was influenced by three great renaissance minds.
  A. Copernicus upset the Ptolemaic concept of the universe.
  B. Machiavelli called man incapable of good action.
  C. Montaigne questioned man's traditional place in the "great chain of being."
    1. He found man only another animal.
    2. He stressed man's ignorance of nature.
    3. He maintained that man cannot even trust his senses.

3. *Avoid overlapping, illogical subordination, and single subdivision:*

Overlapping:

I. Kinds of fruit
  A. Oranges
  B. Apples
  C. Melons
  D. Canteloupes

Illogical subordination:

I. Kinds of fruit
  A. Oranges
  B. Apples
  C. Vegetables

Single subdivision:

I. Kinds of fruit
  A. Oranges
  B. Apples
    1. Crabapples
II. Kinds of vegetables

A complete topic outline for a research paper appears on page 367.

After finishing the outline, the student can go back through his notes, mark them with an appropriate symbol from the outline (I,A; I,B,1), and arrange them in the approximate order he will follow in the first draft.

WRITING THE PAPER

The actual work of writing presents two more problems that do not loom large on a five-hundred-word theme: (1) the use of quotation and paraphrase; and (2) the acknowledgment of indebtedness in footnotes.

QUOTATION AND PARAPHRASE

The amount of quoting will vary greatly with the nature of the research; the study of a poet's works is more likely to contain frequent direct quotations than does an analysis of economic theory. As a general rule, undergraduates quote too much. Although direct quotation is extremely common in dealing with primary sources, with secondary sources paraphrase will more often suffice. Generally speaking, quote directly:

1. When you are clinching an important point.

2. When the exact phrasing of the source is essential to clarify a controversial detail or illustrate a writer's style.

3. When the passage is so strikingly written that a paraphrase would squeeze out all the flavor.

4. When the phrasing of the original is so well known that paraphrase would sound like parody.

Never quote at length unless the passage is supremely important. Enclose all short direct quotations in quotation marks. Longer quotations (of about five lines or more) do not require quotes if they are indented and typed single-space. If you do not distort the essential meaning, you may omit words either in the middle or at the end of a quotation; when you do this, inform your reader by inserting three periods plus end punctuation (see page 184). If you interpolate a comment of your own in the middle of a quotation, set it off in square brackets [thus].

Much of the confusion and unintentional dishonesty in undergraduate research papers results from ignorance or carelessness about the difference between quotation and paraphrase. Study the following illustrations carefully:

1. DIRECT QUOTATION

Since this is a long quotation, it is indented single-space without quotation marks. Notice also the use of periods to indicate an omission, the careful reproduction of the author's italics (underlining), and the interpolation of the quoter in brackets.

In his candid analysis of the English character E. M. Forster carefully distils the essence of English hypocrisy:

> The Germans are called brutal, the Spanish cruel, the Americans superficial, and so on; but we are perfide Albion, the island of hypocrites, the people who have built up an Empire with a Bible in one hand, a pistol in the other, and financial concessions in both pockets. Is the charge true? I think it is; but while making it we must be quite clear as to what we mean by hypocrisy. Do we mean *conscious* deceit? Well, the English are comparatively guiltless of this . . . . Do we mean *unconscious* deceit? Muddle-headedness? Of this I believe them to be guilty. When an Englishman has been led into a course of wrong action, he has nearly always begun by muddling himself. A public-school education [Americans would say private school] does not make for mental clearness, and he possesses to a very high degree the power of confusing his own mind.

2. HALF-BAKED PARAPHRASE

The words of Forster and the student are indiscriminately confused. *Unacceptable.*

Forster says that, whereas Germans are called brutal, the Spanish cruel, the United States citizens superficial, the English are perfide Albion, the people who have built up an Empire with a Bible in one hand, a gun in the other, and pockets full of financial concessions. He goes on to say that, though this charge is true, English hypocrisy is not conscious deceit, but unconscious deceit. When an Englishman has been misled into a wrong action, he has nearly always begun by muddling himself. A public-school education, says Forster, does not make for mental clearness, and the Englishman possesses to a great degree the power of confusing his own mind.

3. PARTIAL PARAPHRASE

Brief quotations from Forster are properly identified. *Acceptable.*

In his analysis of the English character Forster carefully considers the indictment of England as "the island of hypocrites," a nation of Empire-builders "with a Bible in one hand, a pistol in the other, and financial concessions in both pockets." Although admitting the essential truth of this charge, he finds his countrymen guilty not of conscious hypocrisy but of *"unconscious deceit"* or "muddle-headedness"—a quality which the public schools have helped to develop.

4. COMPLETE PARAPHRASE

Forster's main point is put into the student's own words. *Acceptable.*

Although Forster admits that the English have built an Empire on hypocrisy, he concedes that their hypocrisy is usually the unconscious by-product of a mental confusion partly fostered by the public schools.

FOOTNOTES

In a short theme indebtedness to others may be acknowledged informally in the text in accordance with the general principles listed in Chapter One (page 6). In a research paper the writer cites sources specifically in footnotes. Use a footnote:

1. Whenever you quote another person's actual words.

2. Whenever you use another person's idea, opinion, or theory, even if it is completely paraphrased in your own words.

3. Whenever you borrow facts, statistics, or other illustrative material.

These principles must, of course, be applied with discretion or the text of the manuscript will be drowned by the rising tide of footnotes. As Frank Sullivan has said, if you give a footnote an inch, it will take a foot. A writer doesn't need to cite a reference for quotations that are familiar to any educated reader, ideas that are generally accepted, or facts that are well known and undisputed.

Footnotes may also be used—sparingly—not to acknowledge indebtedness but to record interesting sidelights and explanations that do not fit conveniently into the text of the paper.

A complete footnote contains the same information as a bibliographical entry except that there is no point in putting the last name of the author first, and the exact page number is regularly cited:

1. Author's name: First name or initials first.

2. Title: If a book, underline it; if a periodical article, put the title of the article in quotes and underline the name of the magazine.

3. Facts of publication: If a book, give place and date; the publisher's name may be supplied between them. If a periodical, give date and volume number. Separate these items by commas.

4. Page number(s): In a periodical reference the abbreviation for *page* (*p.*) may be omitted after the volume number.

Give a complete footnote the first time you refer to each source:

C. B. Tinker, *Young Boswell,* Boston, 1922, p. 49.

E. E. Leisy, "Folklore in American Prose," *Saturday Review of Literature,* July 21, 1951, 34:6.

Subsequent references to the same sources may be abbreviated:

Tinker, p. 49.
Leisy, p. 6.

The following Latin abbreviations may also be used for all footnote references after the first:

Ibid.   Refers to the same page of the same source to which you have just referred in the footnote immediately preceding.

Ibid., p. 324.   Refers to another page of the same source to which you have just referred in the footnote immediately preceding.

Tinker, *op. cit.*, p. 84. Refers to page 84 of the *work cited* several footnotes back.

Op. cit., p. 84. The author's name may be omitted if it is mentioned or clearly implied in the text.

Loc. cit. Means the "place cited" instead of the "work cited." This is commonly used in referring to magazine articles.

The student may also have occasion to use the following abbreviations in either footnotes or bibliography:

c. or ca.	Abbreviation for Latin *circa* (*about*), used with approximate dates (c. 1568)
cf.	Compare (cf. p. 83). Being rapidly replaced by *see*.
ch. or chap.	chapter
ed.	editor, edition (R. W. Chambers, ed., *Beowulf*, 2d ed., Cambridge, 1932.)
f.	and the following page (pp. 13 f.)
ff.	and the following pages (pp. 13 ff.)
l.	line
ll.	lines
n.	note
n.d.	no date (inserted in brackets when the date of publication is not given)
pp.	pages
sic	thus (inserted in a quotation in brackets to indicate that you are quoting exactly when an error or an obviously absurd or extreme statement is made [see page 192])
vol., vols.	volume, volumes (E. K. Chambers, *William Shakespeare*, 2 vols., Oxford, 1930.)

The most convenient place for footnotes is the foot of the page, but it is better for an inexperienced typist to list them neatly at the end of the paper than to crowd them helter-skelter into inadequate space. Use Arabic numerals for footnotes, either beginning each new page with number one or numbering con-

Revise footnote numbers (pencil annotation)

secutively throughout the paper. Avoid asterisks, daggers, and other cryptic symbols. *Don't use period after footnote number when in draft of footnote (pencil annotation)*

When drawing facts consistently from one source, a writer may occasionally avoid a profusion of unnecessary *Ibid.*'s with a general footnote of this sort:

> The facts in my account of Chaucer's life are taken from Marchette Chute, *Geoffrey Chaucer of England,* New York, 1946.

The sample research paper beginning on page 365 contains a variety of representative footnotes. Unless the teacher recommends a different form, follow these models carefully. *Do not manufacture your own systems.* Notice, for example, that the standard abbreviation for *page* is a small *p,* not a capital or a *pg.,* and that it is followed by a period. Notice that *Ibid.* begins with a capital, is underlined (because it is from the Latin), and is followed by a period (because it is an abbreviation). Notice that a comma separates the period after *Ibid.* from the page number. Remember that the titles of magazine articles are in quotation marks and the titles of books are underlined. Trivial as these matters seem, they are important simply because if every individualist had his way, the international language of scholarship would quickly degenerate into a Babel.

THE FINAL BIBLIOGRAPHY

Do not confuse footnotes and bibliography. Footnotes give exact page references for specific borrowings and are commonly listed at the foot of the page. A bibliography is a general list of sources; it is usually placed at the end of the paper and commonly contains no page references to books and only general page references to periodical articles. In a short research article, where the writer has acknowledged indebtedness carefully in footnotes, a bibliography is hardly necessary. If the teacher requires one, the student must decide whether to present an extensive bibliography which gives a complete picture of available source material on the subject or a selected bibliography which simply lists the sources the writer found most useful. Since many long undergraduate bibliographies are copied uncritically from the card catalogue and *Reader's Guide,* most college teachers would rather see a bibliography limited to ten or a dozen sources actually used.

In listing sources in the final bibliography, use the same form prescribed for the preliminary bibliography. Alphabetize sources by author's last name, either in a single list or in separate lists according to classification; it is common in a bibliography of some length to list books and magazine articles separately, but this is unnecessary in a short bibliography. When no author exists, alphabetize an entry by the first important word in the title. A sample bibliography appears on page 380.

A SPECIMEN RESEARCH PAPER

The following research paper should be studied as a review of the principles and details stressed in this chapter:

Watch spicery

MARTIANS AND MASS HYSTERIA *What Happened At the Battle of Lake Erie*

all large caps.

by
Woodruff Howe

Lafayette College   May 12, 1951

Kent State University

-1-

OUTLINE

I. The Impact of the Orson Welles broadcast

   A. The initial panic

   B. Later public reaction

II. Reasons for panic

   A. The jittery America of October, 1938

   B. Faith in radio news reporting

   C. Effective acting

   D. Good theater in the script

      1. The warnings against credulity

      2. Alternation of calm and crisis

III. Incredible aspects of the script

   A. The defiance of time and distance

   B. The unbelievable Professor Pierson

   C. Familiar literary devices

      1. Martians in science fiction

      2. "On-the-spot" reporting in other literature

      3. "The thing"

IV. The neglect of other evidence

   A. Failure to check on the story

   B. Rationalizing the evidence from inadequate checks

V. The lesson: a challenge to education

Don't use it on last page of text.

MARTIANS AND MASS HYSTERIA

When it swings nearest to the earth, the planet Mars is still thirty-four million miles away.[1] Despite the marvels of science fiction, the most reputable astronomers are highly dubious that living beings could even exist on Mars, let alone travel earthward and arrive hale and hearty.[2] Yet on Halloween in 1938 a fictitious Martian invasion of the Earth broadcast over the Columbia network by Orson Welles and the Mercury Theater of the Air frightened a million American radio listeners.[3]

The fear was nation-wide. In Newark, one of the primary objectives of the invaders, more than twenty families in a single block rushed from their houses, their faces covered with wet handkerchiefs and towels as protection against a gas attack. In the same city, physicians and nurses called police headquarters to volunteer their services in the emergency, while city officials phoned City Hall to make arrangements for evacuating the population. In one New York theater the audience was thrown into confusion when the hysterical wives of two playgoers insisted that their husbands be paged. A woman in Pittsburgh was found in a bathroom with a bottle of poison in her hand screaming: "I'd rather die this way than like that." In "a small southwestern college," sorority girls "huddled around their radios trembling and weeping in each other's arms."[4]

---

1 H. J. Bernhard, D. A. Bennett, and H. S. Rice, New Handbook of the Heavens, rev. ed., New York, 1948, p. 68.
2 See, for example, Sir James Jeans, "Is There Life on Other Worlds?" in H. Shapley, ed., A Treasury of Science, enlarged ed., New York, 1946, pp. 83-88.
3 Hadley Cantril, The Invasion from Mars, Princeton, 1940, p. 58. Unless otherwise noted, all details concerning the invasion are from the New York Times, October 31, 1938, pp. 1 and 4.
4 Cantril, op. cit., p. 53.

The Invasion of Mars, p. 53. (since he has 2 books use title)

2 collected essays from other people

Detail

H.

w Jersey and Indianapolis,
han three thousand miles away
fainted from fear when the
the broadcast.[5] Police depart-
ations, and newspaper offices
calls. The mass hysteria rose so
re they actually _saw_ the invasion.
g System had repeatedly reminded its
only a Halloween adaption of H. G.
. The War of the Worlds, did the
embling to their beds.
had passed, the general public
nation, admiration, and amusement.[6]
newspapers and magazines advocating
e Columbia Broadcasting System and
rship. Others railed against the
ic and the stupidity of the American
nothing but praise for the dramatic
Still others exploded in laughter. To
of "little people scurrying in all direc-
" offered "a spectacle fit for laughter of
inceton undergraduates promptly formed a
"League for Interplanetary Defense," with a platform advocating an
embargo on all Martial - with a capital _M_ - music. Four days after
the broadcast, Brooks Atkinson signed off a favorable notice of
Welles' new Broadway stage venture with the following guarantee:
"Ladies and gentlemen, you have just been reading a review of a

5 F. L. Allen, Since Yesterday, New York, 1940, p. 329.
6 See, for example, the letters in the New York Times, November
2, 1938, p. 22 and in Time, November 21, 1938, 32:4.
7 New Republic, November 9, 1938, 97:1.

-4-

performance of 'Danton's Death' at the Mercury Theatre last evening. It is a play of imagination based on history. There is no cause for alarm."[8]

Undoubtedly the radio public had been conditioned for disaster by the recurrent shocks of recent history. Frederick Lewis Allen neatly portrays the atmosphere of doom that hung over the Depression Decade:[9]

A feeling of insecurity and apprehension, a feeling that the world was going to pieces, that supposedly solid principles, whether of economics or of politics or of international ethics, were giving way under foot, had never quite left thoughtful Americans since the collapse of Coolidge-Hoover prosperity in 1929 and 1930. It had been intense during the worst of the Depression, had been alleviated somewhat as business conditions improved, and had become more acute again as the international aggressors went on the rampage (and as, simultaneously, the United States slid into the Recession).

In September, 1938, Hitler, already master of Austria, had put the finishing touches on the coup that brought Czechoslovakia into the Nazi fold. On September 30, after frantic days of dread, Chamberlain returned to Munich from London to tell cheering crowds that a pact with Hitler had brought "peace for our time." And day and night through it all, the precise, jerky voice of H. V. Kaltenborn had carried the crisis into every living room with a radio, making the American people suddenly aware of the alarums and excursions of European diplomacy and the dark threat of Nazi domination. It was the eerie twilight before the darkness of total war, and Americans, for all their traditional isolationism, were acutely jumpy. "I doubt if anything of the sort would have happened four or five months ago," wrote Heywood Broun after the Welles broadcast. "The course of world history has affected national psychology. Jitters have come to roost."[10]

---

8 New York Times, November 3, 1938, p. 26.
9 Op. cit., p. 327.
10 Quoted by Cantril, op. cit., p. 202, from the New York World-Telegram, November 2, 1938

-5-

II.

B. During the weeks before the Martian invasion, the radio had done more than give America a bad case of jitters. It had given the nation a brave new faith in radio news reporting. Many listeners, especially those with little education, had succumbed to the easy habit of listening to the news rather than reading it. In answer to the question, "Which of the two - radio or newspaper - gives you news freer from prejudice?" 17 per cent of those questioned in a contemporary *Fortune* poll had voted for newspapers, while 50 per cent had put their faith in radio.[11] The thousands of listeners who had been kept in a state of nervous excitement by the radio flashes on the Munich crisis, and who believed implicitly that radio news was always news, were likely to be ready dupes of a Martian melodrama masquerading as a sensational scoop - even without the customary voice of H. V. Kaltenborn.[12]

But neither the jitters of the age nor its childlike faith in Marconi's miracle is enough to account for all the hysteria of the invasion Halloween. What of the broadcast itself?

To anyone who has recently seen Orson Welles mugging his way through the movies of *The Third Man* and *Macbeth*, it is difficult to consider him as a credible Professor of Astronomy from Princeton (for that was his role), or even the disembodied voice of one. Nor is it easy to understand why so many listeners were taken in by the steady voice of "The Secretary of the Interior" urging the people to be calm in the face of Martian invasion when one is aware that the speech was delivered by Kenneth Delmar - alias Senator Claghorn, the stereotyped

---

11 Cited by Cantril, *op. cit.*, p. 69, from *Fortune*, August, 1939, 20:65.
12 In his radio version of the Mercury *Julius Caesar*, Welles had already helped to obscure the difference between radio news and radio drama by having Kaltenborn read a running commentary out of Plutarch's *Lives*.

-6-

Dixie demagogue of Fred Allen's more recent program.[13] But some aspects of the performance must have been unusually effective. The key role during the early part of the broadcast was that of Carl Phillips, the radio announcer. It demands a credible transition from the matter-of-factness of the reporter interviewing Professor Pierson about the strange new "meteorite" that has landed near Princeton to the horror of the stunned earthling watching his first Martian monsters wriggling through its topside exit:[14]

Just a minute! Something's happening! Ladies and gentlemen, this is terrific! This end of the thing is beginning to flake off! The top is beginning to rotate like a screw! The thing must be hollow! ... Good heavens, something's wriggling out of the shadow like a grey snake. Now it's another one, and another. They look like tentacles to me. There, I can see the thing's body. It's large as a bear and it glistens like wet leather. But that face. It...it's indescribable.

Ripped from its context, this pulp-fiction excitement is hardly believable. But Frank Readick, the actor who played the part, had an inspiration. He obtained the recording of the Hindenburg disaster – the famous report in which Herbert Morrison, covering a routine landing, is suddenly aware that the giant zeppelin has burst into flames in mid-air – and he played it over and over until he captured the authentic note of horror in his own voice.[15] The effect must have been convincing.

Apart from the authenticity of the acting, the script itself is effective theater. The martian invaders were not permitted to spring fully armed upon the listener the moment the program was introduced. The script writer, Howard Koch, prepared for their entrance with the care of a master playwright paving the way for the first appearance

---

13 John Houseman, "The Men from Mars," Harper's, December, 1948, 197:51.
14 Cantril, op. cit., pp. 15-16. Cantril reprints the entire script.
15 Houseman, loc. cit., p. 79.

-7-

of his leading lady. He conditioned the audience to accept the
fantastic climax, not only by the dry factual tone of the first
reports of "gas explosions" on Mars, but by insisting, through his
"scientific experts," that the listener attach no undue importance
to these phenomena. The first direct word from Professor (Orson
Welles) Pierson is a calculated anticlimax - "Nothing unusual at the
moment" - followed by the incidental information that the chances
are a thousand to one against "living intelligence as we know it"
existing on Mars.[16] Mars, he reminds us, is approximately forty
million miles from the earth. "Well," answers Carl Phillips, making
the obvious banal comment of the lay interviewer, "that seems a safe
enough distance." Later, when word comes of the shock near Princeton,
the Professor calmly denies that it can have any connection with the
disturbances on the planet: "This is probably a meteorite of unusual
size and its arrival at this particular time is merely a coincidence."[17]
Even after the "meteorite" has turned into a Trojan horse and the
first leathery monsters have emerged, a news bulletin cautions the
listener against credulity: "Professor Indelkoffer, speaking at a
dinner of the California Astronomical Society, expressed the opinion
that the explosions on Mars are undoubtedly nothing more than
volcanic disturbances on the surface of the planet."[18]

The script writer not only prepared the audience psychologically
for the climax, but made full use of the playwright's device of
alternating calm and crisis. The first intimations of trouble on
Mars are carefully interspersed with selections from "the music of
Ramon Raquello and his orchestra" playing in "the Meridian Room in

---

16 Cantril, op. cit., p. 8.
17 Ibid., p. 10.
18 Ibid., p. 18.

-8-

the Hotel Park Plaza in downtown New York."[19] The maestro's program
includes "the ever-popular Star Dust." When the landing of the "huge,
flaming object" at Grovers Mill, New Jersey, is reported and the
broadcasting system's "special mobile unit" is hurrying to the scene,
the listener's excitement is suspended in midair while he hears
twenty seconds of dance music by "Bobby Milette and his orchestra"
from the "Hotel Martinet" in Brooklyn.[20] When the monsters are
wriggling toward Phillips and he retreats desperately to a new position, the interlude is filled with the music of a lone piano. A
moment later when the broadcast from Grovers Mill is cut off amid
"screams and unearthly shrieks," the noise of a crashing microphone
is followed by dead silence; then comes the reassuring bulletin from
California, then the piano again, playing "Clair de Lune,"[21] then a
flash bringing the startling bulletin that at least forty people,
including six State Troopers, lie dead in a field east of the village,
"their bodies burned and distorted beyond all possible recognition."[22]

Poring smugly over the script a dozen years after the original
broadcast, it is easy to smile at such obvious contrivances and to
wonder how any acute listener could have missed the cosmic variation
on the old gag about the Californians and their weather or the
obvious double entendre in the song titles. But it is hard to deny
that on Halloween in 1938 the production was convincing enough to
induce, even in a sophisticated listener, "that willing suspension of
disbelief for the moment which constitutes poetic faith." Still it
is one thing to surrender one's skepticism temporarily to the wiles
of the playwright and another to give way to genuine panic. Even an

19 Ibid., pp. 5-7.
20 Ibid., p. 11.
21 Houseman, loc. cit., p. 79.
22 Cantril, op. cit., pp. 18-19.

-9-

inexperienced theatergoer can be thoroughly convinced of the reality
of Othello's jealousy without rushing onto the stage in Act Five to
save the life of hapless Desdemona. Neither the anxiety of the times
nor the effectiveness of the presentation could adequately explain the
fears of a million radio listeners - if those listeners had reacted
like intelligent adults. "Nothing whatever about the dramatization was
in the least credible," wrote Dorothy Thompson after the invasion.[23]
This may be an exaggeration, but it is closer to the truth than the
praise of other writers who freely bandied about the much-abused word
realistic. For the script of the broadcast bristles with incredibility
on every page.

In an age of scientific marvels, a listener might be forgiven
for his failure to consider the improbability of invasion from another
planet. But the immutable laws of time and space and common sense,
though they might not apply to Martian monsters, would hardly be suspended in New Jersey for the special benefit of the Columbia Broadcasting System - even on Halloween in an eerie decade. As Orson
Welles was quick to point out in his own anguished defense, the tale
is actually not told in the present at all: "The broadcast was performed as if occurring in the future and as if it were then related by
a survivor of a past occurence."[24] The total destruction was carried
out in less than twelve minutes; the entire broadcast from the first
faint Martian rumors to the fall of Manhattan took less than forty;

23 Quoted by Cantril, op. cit., p. 67, from the New York
    Herald Tribune, November 2, 1938.
24 New York Times, November 1, 1938, p. 26. The New Yorker,
    however, blamed the confused time picture for all the
    trouble: "People anchored to the present listening to a
    future event described by an invisible man to whom it
    happened in the past are in a bad way to start off with,
    and are going to be uneasy no matter what is said."
    (November 12, 1938, 14:15).

-10-

yet in that time "men traveled long distances, large bodies of troops
were mobilized, cabinet meetings were held, savage battles were fought
on land and in the air, and millions of people accepted it emotionally
if not logically."[25] A patently incredible detail, for example, is
the trip of Pierson and Phillips from Princeton to Grovers Mill to
investigate the "meteorite." Eleven miles in ten minutes we are told -
phenomenal time at night on country roads jammed with the traffic of
the curious; but the actual radio time interval is occupied by one
announcement of less than two hundred words followed by twenty seconds
of the inevitable swing band - about a minute in all. Martians may
travel on land at eleven miles a minute, but not Princeton professors.

Other improbabilities should have struck home even to listeners
with no time sense. Confronted with the problem of supplying on-the-
spot accurate information about the "meteorite" to the radio audience,
Professor Pierson throws scientific caution to the winds:[26]

Phillips: Can you tell us the meaning of that scraping noise inside
           the thing?
Pierson: Possibly the unequal cooling of its surface.
Phillips: Do you still think it's a meteor, Professor?
Pierson: (who has been standing at a safe distance) I don't know what
           to think. The metal casing is definitely extra-terrestrial...
           not found on this earth.

Obviously this is no time for careful laboratory experiments. But, of
course, Pierson has an extra-terrestrial quality himself; he leads a
charmed life. The last gasp of the ill-fated Phillips describes the
Professor fearlessly reconnoitering around the mysterious object while
three of Grovers Mill's finest advance toward the emerging Martians
hopefully flaunting a white handkerchief tied to a pole. Phillips has
retreated to a distant point; but after the invaders launch their first
attack with their deadly weapon, the announcer's charred body is found

---

25 Houseman, loc. cit., p. 80.
26 Cantril, op. cit., p. 15.

-11-

in the wreckage, while the Professor, now safely ensconced in a farm-
house, ventures a "conjectural explanation" of the death-dealing heat
ray.[27] He lives on in accordance with the inexorable law that a lone
survivor can and must survive anything – especially if he is played by
Orson Welles.

Without either scientific knowledge, time sense, or common sense,
any listener with the thinnest veneer of literary sophistication
should have been insulated against belief in the broadcast. By 1938,
more than half a century of farfetched science fiction, from Jules
Verne and H. G. Wells to Buck Rogers and Flash Gordon, had reduced the
man from Mars to a cliché no more horrendous than a Halloween goblin.[28]
As one unfooled listener remarked, "just the word Martian was enough
even without that fantastic and incredible description....I knew it had
to be a play."[29] The technique of radio news broadcasting may have
been new, but the technique of disguising a fantastic fiction as sober
fact, painstakingly documented with credible details of real time and
place, is as old as literature itself. What reader of Defoe's Robinson
Crusoe or his deadpan fabrications about the Plague Year could have
believed in Welles' Martians merely because the invasion itinerary
could be followed on a real map of New Jersey? Finally, the very
language of the script, once it moves into high gear, has telltale
traces of the jargon of amazing stories. Take, for example, the
repeated references to the "meteorite" as "the thing;" by 1950 "the
thing" had become such a commonplace epithet for an anonymous horror
that it was entombed in a tiresome popular song. The more one contem-
plates the script of the invasion, the less he wonders that the author
himself considered abandoning it in embryo as too fantastic even for

27 Ibid., p. 20.
28 See Life, November 14, 1938, 5:25.
29 Cantril, op. cit., p. 91.

-12-

radio. "Under no circumstances," Koch had feared, "could it be made interesting or in any way credible to modern American ears."[30]

It can be argued, of course, in defense of the duped that many of them switched from Charlie McCarthy only after the Martians were devastating New Jersey and that they didn't stay with the program long enough to hear any of the three subsequent announcements clearly identifying it as a dramatization. But the disturbing fact remains that thousands of these listeners believed the evidence of their ears implicitly without making any intelligent effort to check on it. If a spin of the dial had taken them from Charlie McCarthy to Martian monsters, another spin would have taken them back again to a station that was carrying on its routine broadcast calmly while Manhattan fell to the invaders. Many of those who did check made the mistake of rationalizing the new evidence as consistent with their worst fears. Thus one person spun the dial, heard church music, and, without remembering that this was not unusual on a Sunday night, immediately leaped to the conclusion that the congregation was pleading with God for intercession against the monsters.[31] One scared listener would run to the window, and, seeing no cars in the street, conclude that they had all been obliterated by the Martians; another would see the street teeming with traffic and assume that everyone was fleeing for his life.[32] All this in a nation that prides itself on its mastery of the careful techniques of scientific investigation.

The lesson is clear. Orson Welles may have sworn never again to play hobgoblin on Halloween, but the difference between a Martian heat ray and the devastating flash of an atomic bomb is of little importance

30 Houseman, loc. cit., p. 76.
31 Cantril, op. cit. p. 94.
32 Hadley Cantril, The Psychology of Social Movements, New York, 1941, p. 71.

-13-

to the victims. Whether confronted by an actual invasion or by the
scares and rumors of an enemy skilled in propaganda, the nation can
ill afford to behave like the frightened million of October, 1938.
The cure is not to train every citizen in the facts of science or the
intricacies of propaganda analysis. The cure is to develop in as
many citizens as possible the sound judgment and healthy skepticism
which distinguish the educated adult from the easy victim of the
propagandist, the rumormonger, and the demagogue. Cantril's researches
indicate a clear relationship between the radio listener's lack of
education and his gullibility.[33] The story of the radio invasion from
Mars is a challenge to American education.

---

[33] Cantril, _Invasion from Mars_, pp. 112-13, 157.

-14-

SELECTED BIBLIOGRAPHY

Allen, F. L., _Since Yesterday_, New York; 1940

Bernhard, H. J., D. A. Bennett, and H. S. Rice, _New Handbook of the Heavens_, rev. ed., New York, 1948

Cantril, Hadley, _The Invasion from Mars_, Princeton, 1940

The Psychology of Social Movements, New York, 1941

Gurko, Leo, _The Angry Decade_, New York, 1947

Houseman, John, "The Men from Mars," _Harper's_, December, 1948, 197:74-82

Jeans, Sir James, "Is There Life on Other Worlds?" in H. Shapley, ed., _A Treasury of Science_, enlarged ed., New York, 1946, pp. 83-88

Life, November 14, 1938, 5:2-5

Nation, November 12, 1938, 147:498

New Republic, November 9, 1938, 97:1

New York Times, October 31, 1938, pp. 1,4; November 1, pp. 1, 22, 26; November 2, p. 22; November 3, p. 26

New Yorker, November 12, 1938, 14:15

Time, November 21, 1938, 32:4

Glossary of Usage

>>>->>>

To make the most intelligent use of this glossary, the student should first read (or reread) the following pages:

Chapter One, pages 9 through 18: "Correctness," "Appropriateness," "Levels of Usage"

Chapter Eight, pages 231 through 239: "Definitions"

Chapter Ten, pages 294 through 300: "Gobbledygook"

The following abbreviations are used:

ACD   *The American College Dictionary* (text edition, New York, Harper, 1948)

WNC   *Webster's New Collegiate Dictionary* (Springfield, Mass., Merriam, 1949)

a, an. *A* is commonly used before all consonant sounds (*a* hotel, *a* union, *a* one dollar bill). *An* is used before all vowel sounds (*an* opening, *an* hour). Some reputable writers still use *an* where *h* is pronounced in an unaccented syllable. (Select any burning issue of the day, and see how quickly it becomes both *an* historical and a philosophical problem.—H. M. Jones, "The Place of the Humanities in American Education"). But this practice seems to be disappearing.

above. The use of *above* as an adjective, adverb, or noun, referring to a point previously made, is not grammatically incorrect (the *above* point, the point made *above*, the *above*). But this use is commonly classified as Commercialese or Legalese, along with *above-mentioned, aforementioned, before-mentioned, aforesaid,* and *said. Above* is not as awkward, however, as *foregoing,* which is often recommended in its place. The main trouble with all these expressions (*above-mentioned* in the *foregoing* sentences) is that they call too much attention to the writer's blueprint. Usually *the point I have just made* or merely *this point* is an accurate and natural substitute. See page 298.

above-mentioned. See *Above.*

accept, except. *Accept* is a verb meaning *receive. Except* is a preposition meaning *excluding* or *but,* or a formal verb meaning *exclude, omit.* (The fraternity *accepted* everyone *except* George. It was easy to see why they *excepted* him.)

ad. Colloquial shortening of *advertisement.* Acceptable in informal writing.

adviser, advisor. *Adviser* is more common but either is acceptable.

affect, effect. *Affect* is a verb meaning *influence* or *pretend.* (Her attitude *affected* me deeply, but I *affected* indifference.) *Effect* is a verb meaning *bring about* or a noun meaning *result.* (The weather *effected* a change in his disposition; the total *effect* was disastrous.) Remember that, except as a technical term in psychology, *affect* is never a noun.

aforementioned, aforesaid. See *Above.*

aggravate. In formal English *aggravate* means *increase an evil* or *make worse.* (Exposure to the sun *aggravated* the wound.) As a loose synonym for *annoy, disgust, displease, irritate, madden, offend,* or *provoke,* it is a common colloquialism.

agree to, agree with. One agrees *to* a plan and *with* a person. (The only members of the faculty who *agreed to* the president's proposal were those who always *agreed with* him.)

ain't. There is no need for *ain't* as a contraction of *is not, are not, has not,* or *have not.* All these expressions have their own logical, legitimate contractions. By the same token, *I'm not* makes *I ain't* hard to justify. But there is no satisfactory contraction for the first person singular in asking a question, and the language needs a substitute for the awkward *am I not.* Some speakers use *ant I* with the *a*-sound about halfway between *a* in *art* and in *man,* but this has no standing in written English. *Aren't I,* common in England, is apparently gaining in America despite the absurdity of *are I not. Amn't I* is too hard to pronounce. In view of this dilemma some hardy authorities now accept *ain't I* as a legitimate colloquialism. But since *ain't* is still widely condemned as a mark of illiteracy, however used, educated people avoid it in serious speech and writing.

airplane, aeroplane. The spelling *aeroplane,* still common in England, is now almost extinct in the United States, where *airplane* has been officially adopted by the Army, Navy, and Bureau of Standards.

alibi. Formal English still sticks to the strict legal use of *alibi:* the defense of an accused person that he was elsewhere when the crime was committed. In colloquial English, as in Ring Lardner's famous *Alibi Ike* stories, the word means *any kind of excuse.* Now, in the heyday of detective fiction, it even turns up as a verb meaning *lie one's way out of a tight spot.*

all. The traditional rule that *all* should not be followed by *of* before a noun has been disregarded too often to be taken seriously. *All the people* may be slightly more formal and slightly less redundant than *all of the people,* but a writer would do better to consider the rhythm of the passage than be enslaved by a dying rule.

all-around, all-round. See *Around.*

all the farther. This expression and others like it (*all the faster, all the higher, all the quicker*) are colloquial at best when used in place of *as . . . as.* (Colloquial: This is *all the farther* the trolley goes. Formal: This is *as far as* the trolley goes.) Another common use of the same phrases is acceptable in informal writing: When the woman came out with the broom, the cat climbed *all the higher.*

allude, elude. *Allude* means *refer to,* usually indirectly. *Elude* means *escape.* (The speaker *alluded* to the time when Robin Hood *eluded* the sheriff.)

allusion, illusion, delusion. An *allusion* is a passing reference, usually indirect. (See pages 250–251.) An *illusion* is a misconception which may be either pleasant or harmful. The word *delusion* may refer to anything from a strong *illusion* to a fixed *misconception* requiring drastic psychiatric treatment. (The *allusion* in my speech was to the common *illusion* that every patient who suffers from *delusions* thinks he is Napoleon.)

almost. See *Most.*

aloud. See *Out loud.*

already, all ready. The single word *already* is an adverb meaning *previously*. *All ready* is a phrase meaning *completely ready* or signifying that every member of a group is ready. (He had *already* had his swim before we were *all ready* to set out for the lake.)

alright. Since the English language distinguishes between *all together* and *altogether* and between *all ready* and *already*, there is no *logical* reason why it should not accept a similar distinction between *all right* (Six students had the problems *all right*) and *alright* (He felt *alright* after the doctor came). But here again usage disregards logic. Regardless of meaning, the spelling *alright* is largely restricted to experimental writing and advertising. The ACD notes that it is "not generally regarded as good usage," and WNC says it is "not recognized by the authorities as proper."

alternative. Strict formal usage limits a choice of alternatives to two. But except in the most formal writing, *alternative* is commonly used for one of several choices.

although, though. As conjunctions these words are practically interchangeable. *Though* is more common. *Although* appears more often when the subordinate clause precedes the main clause; *though* occurs more often when it follows. But a writer is safe in using whichever sounds better in the passage. As a synonym for *however* in the middle or at the end of a sentence, *though* is a colloquial adverb. (I did not think, *though*, that he would come. He did, *though*.) Neither should be used in place of *however* at the beginning of a sentence. See pages 127–128.

altogether, all together. The single word *altogether* is an adverb meaning *entirely*. *All together* is an adjective phrase meaning *united*. (He was *altogether* wrong when he implied that the politicians were *all together* in their belief in the candidate.)

alumnus, alumna. An *alumnus* is a male graduate; an *alumna* is a female graduate. In strict accordance with the Latin plurals, male graduates are *alumni* (rhyming with *rum nigh*), females are *alumnae* (rhyming with *bum knee*). But *alumni* is now widely used for both sexes. Although the word *gradu-ates* is becoming more common, *alumni* has the advantage of including those who leave college without diplomas.

America, American. *The United States* is a more formal and accurate designation for the country than *America*. Despite efforts to confine the meaning of *American* to *inhabitant of the Western Hemisphere,* the word is acceptable on all levels as an adjective meaning *pertaining to the United States* or a noun meaning *an inhabitant of the United States. Americanism* and *un-American* are being reduced to meaninglessness by demagogues and gossips.

among. See *Between.*

amount, number. *Amount* refers to things considered in bulk or in the aggregate; *number* refers to things which can be counted separately. (Correct: a large *amount* of ink, a *number* of bottles of ink. Incorrect: a large *amount* of bottles.)

and etc. See *Etc.*

angle. As a synonym for *approach, aspect, phase, point of view, angle* has become a counterword. It is weary from working overtime in business, journalism, and detective fiction.

any place. *Any place* (sometimes spelled *anyplace*), *every place, no place,* and *some place* are colloquial when used in place of the adverbs *anywhere, everywhere, nowhere,* and *somewhere.* (Colloquial: He was going *no place* fast. Formal: He was going *nowhere* fast.)

anybody's else. However logical grammatically, this and similar clumsy phrases are no longer in general use. *Anybody* (*anyone*) *else's, everybody else's, nobody else's,* and *somebody else's* are now acceptable on all levels.

anyone. This indefinite pronoun is sometimes spelled as two words regardless of use, but it is logical to discriminate between *anyone* meaning *anybody* and *any one* person singled out of a group. The same logic applies to *everyone* and *someone.* (*Everyone* is going with *someone; every one* of the boys plans to go with *some one* of the girls.) *No one* is either two words or hyphenated. For number, see pages 108–109.

anyways. When it means *in any way, anywise,* WNC accepts it without restriction, the ACD calls it colloquial. (His behavior was not *anyways* offensive.) In the sense of *in any case*, it is listed in WNC as dialectal. (*Anyways* the rumor was brought into the open.)

anywheres, everywheres, nowheres, somewheres. Vulgate for *anywhere, everywhere, nowhere, somewhere.*

apt, liable, likely. These three words have distinct meanings in formal English. *Apt* means *quick to learn* or *inclined to.* (An *apt* student of languages, he is *apt* to do better in French than in mathematics.) *Liable* implies exposure to danger, risk, or punishment (*liable* to fall downstairs, *liable* to fine or imprisonment). *Likely* merely suggests probability. (It is *likely* to rain before tomorrow.) In informal English *apt* is often used as a synonym for *likely.*

around, round. The following uses of *around* are acceptable in formal English: As an adverb meaning *in a circle* or *here and there* (He walked *around* and *around*. He drove *around* in his car); as a preposition meaning *encircling, on all sides* (*Around* her neck she wore a yellow ribbon. They gathered *around* the campfire). The following uses are still considered colloquial: As an adverb meaning *in the general vicinity* (I'll be still *around* when you get back); as a preposition meaning *here and there in* or *near in time, amount, or number* (He went *around* the country. *Around* six o'clock he made *around* five dollars). In American English, except perhaps on the formal level, *around* and *round* are often interchangeable. Thus a versatile athlete can be either *all-around* or *all-round.*

as. Colloquial as a substitute for *who, that,* or *whether* (ACD). (Anyone *as* wants to can learn to speak English, but some students don't know *as* they should bother.) A common connective as a substitute for *because, for, while,* or *since,* but these conjunctions are more accurate, especially in writing. (Weak: *As* I was looking out of the window, I noticed that, *as* it was snowing, my neighbor was putting on his chains. Better: *While* I was looking out of the window, I noticed that, *because* it was snowing, my neighbor was putting on his chains.) The old rule that *so* should be used after a negative instead of *as* is now observed only by the most formal writers. (I am *as* old as John but not *so* old as Mary.) *Not . . . as* has achieved wide respectability. (His fate, however, was not *as* terrible as that of another adventurer who became involved in a remarkable which-mire.—James Thurber, *Ladies' and Gentlemen's Guide to Modern English Usage.*) See *Like.*

as per. See *Per.*

as regards. See *Regard.*

as to. Acceptable in the sense of *in regard to, about, of.* (*As to* his qualifications, I cannot speak with authority.) Redundant before *whether.* (I do not know [*as to*] whether he was coming.)

asset. As a general synonym for any useful thing or quality, this word is overworked and has a commercial flavor.

at. *At* adds emphasis in speech when used as an extra adverb with *where.* (He didn't know where he was *at.*) But it is redundant in writing.

at about. This colloquialism is redundant and ambiguous. In writing, it is more logical to make a choice between *He went at midnight* and *He went about midnight,* depending on which is closer to the truth.

athletics. When the word refers to specific sports, it is usually plural; when it refers to sports in general, it is usually singular. (Our only important *athletics are* football and baseball, though we preach the doctrine that *athletics is* beneficial to all.) This hairline distinction is not as important as learning to pronounce and spell the word with only three syllables. Contrast the spelling with that of *mathematics.*

author. The use of *author* as a verb (He has *authored* fourteen books) appears to be spreading in the magazines and newspapers, but it is still unlisted in WNC and the ACD.

auto. Now that this abbreviation for *automobile* has finally arrived on the informal level, it has become almost extinct, largely replaced on all levels by *car.*

awhile, a while. The single word *awhile* is an adverb meaning *for a short time.* When the noun *while* occurs in a prepositional phrase, it should stand alone. (He stood *awhile* in thought but only for *a while*.)

back of, in back of. The ACD classifies both *back of* and *in back of* as U.S. colloquial. (Colloquial: He stood [*in*] *back of* me. Formal: He stood *behind* me.)

balance. This word is properly used as a noun in a commercial context. (His *balance* at the bank was $1.99.) Because of its commercial ancestry and flavor, many object to its use as a general synonym for *rest* or *remainder*. (He stayed for the *balance* of the week.) WNC classifies this use as colloquial; the ACD labels it *U.S.*

bank on. Colloquial for *count on, depend on*.

because. See *Reason is because*.

being as, being that, it being. *Being as* and *being that* are vulgate for *because, since*. (*Being that* she was sick, he couldn't get away.) Though probably more common among educated people than the other two, *it being* is both awkward and ungrammatical. (*It being my* birthday, I felt like celebrating. Better: Since it was my birthday, I felt like celebrating.)

beside. *Beside* is nearly always used as a preposition meaning *at the side of*. *Besides,* meaning *in addition to,* is most common as an adverb, but it can also be a preposition. Despite widespread interchange between the two words, a careful writer will distinguish between *"Beside* the three girls there were three boys" and *"Besides* the three girls there were three boys."

between, among. According to a time-honored rule, *between* is used with only two objects, *among* with more than two (*between* you and me, *among* the trees in the forest). But this rule has never been faithfully followed, and now *between* is commonly used with more than two objects, especially when each is individually related to the others. (In a memorandum made by the Prince, about this time, of an interview *between* himself, the queen, and the Prime Minister, we catch a curious glimpse of the state of mind of those three high personages.—Lytton Strachey, *Queen Victoria.* Suppose that you in the audience are witnessing a scene *between* four of the characters, and that . . . this scene must be followed by one *between* two of the characters only.— A. A. Milne, *By Way of Introduction*.) Like all prepositions, *between* governs the objective case. See page 92.

blame on. WNC classifies this expression as colloquial. (Don't *blame* it *on* me.) Formal writing and most informal writing would use the following more logical expressions: Don't blame me; don't blame me for it; don't put the blame on me.

blond, blonde, brunet, brunette. In strict accordance with their French origins, formal usage decrees that *blond* and *brunet,* whether used as nouns or adjectives, are masculine, *blonde* and *brunette* feminine. But on the informal level the distinction is not so carefully kept as that between *fiancé* and *fiancée.*

born, borne. *Born* is used for *given birth to* except after *have* or before *by.* (Lincoln was *born* in a log cabin. Nancy Hanks had *borne* a great man. Edward VII was *borne* by Queen Victoria.) For other meanings of the verb *bear, borne* is the past participle. (He was *borne* aloft by his excited teammates. I had *borne* his insolence too long.)

boughten. A localism unacceptable in writing. Once widely used before the noun to distinguish store goods from homemade (*boughten* bread), it is probably disappearing in the age of the chain store. The past participle of *buy* is *bought.*

broke. Archaic or poetic as the past participle of *break. Broken* is the standard form. Used to mean *out of funds, broke* is slang.

bunch. When applied to a group of people, this word is colloquial. (A *bunch* of the boys were whooping it up.) *Group* would be more acceptable in a formal context.

burst, bust. The principal parts of the verb *burst* are *burst, burst, burst. Bursted* is no longer acceptable for the past tense or past participle. *Bust* is one of the most useful verbs in the language. (The balloon *busted.* He was flat *busted.* He *busted* out of college. He *busted* his roommate on the nose.) But all these uses are still generally classified as slang, colloquial, "ineloquent," or humorous. WNC classifies the noun *bust* as slang when applied to a drinking bout or a failure. In formal writing *bust* is permissible in such combinations as *trust-busting, bronco-busting,* and *boom and bust.*

bust. See *Burst.*

but that, but what. In such expressions as "I have no doubt *but that* (*but what*) he is right," *but that* is sometimes considered more proper than the colloquial *but what.* Formal English would use *that* alone.

calculate. A localism when used to mean *plan, intend, expect, think.* (I don't *calculate* to lose the nomination this year.)

can, may. The traditional distinction between *can* (*be able to*) and *may* (referring to probability, possibility, or permission) is apparently on its way out. But the difference is still observed in formal writing. Without it, such a sentence as "You *may* if you *can*" is impossible.

cannot, can not. Although *cannot* is more common, *can not* is equally acceptable and puts more emphasis on the *not.*

cannot help but. See Double negative.

can't hardly, scarcely. See Double negative.

can't seem. See *Seem.*

censor, censure. *Censor* is a noun standing for an official who examines books, plays, and so forth in order to suppress objectionable matter; or a verb denoting the act of censorship. *Censure* is a noun meaning *an expression of disapproval,* or a verb meaning *disapprove* or *condemn.* (The city *censor censored* the movie by cutting out half the plot This action was met with *censure* by the producers, who *censured* him for his ignorance of art.)

center around. A common colloquialism. (The industry was *centered around* Pittsburgh.) Formal usage decrees *center in, center on,* or *center upon.*

childish, childlike. Two words with the same denotation and vastly different connotations. *Childish* refers to the unpleasant or immature characteristics of children or, more commonly, to the infantile activities of adults. *Childlike* summons up the pleasant qualities. (The Dean looked at George with an air of *childlike* innocence and said: "This college is no place for *childish* freshmen.")

claim. In American English acceptable use of the verb *claim* is no longer confined to the meaning *demand as a right.* (The exiled prince *claimed* his father's throne.) WNC and the ACD place no restrictions on its use as a synonym for *assert* or *maintain.* (I *claim* that the Notre Dame team is better than Army.)

combine. When it means *an alliance for political or commercial purposes, combine* is colloquial. *Combination* is preferable in formal writing.

common. See *Mutual.*

company. *Company,* meaning *guests* or *visitors,* is classed as colloquial in WNC but is unrestricted in the ACD.

compare. The verb can mean either *liken* (The relatives all *compared* the baby to her father) or *set together to reveal both likenesses and differences* (The students were asked to *compare* Dante with Milton). In the first sense, *compare to* is slightly more common; in the second sense, *compare to* and *compare with* are used with equal frequency. *Contrast with* is preferred to *contrast to.*

complected. Such expressions as *dark-complected* and *light-complected* are colloquial or dialectal. The verb *complect* means *interweave. Dark-complexioned* is acceptable but rather clumsy. It is simpler to say: "He had a dark complexion."

consensus of opinion. Since *consensus* usually implies *agreement in matters of opinion,* some argue that only the one word is necessary. But usage has made the phrase generally acceptable.

considerable. An adjective meaning *important* or *rather large in extent or amount.* (He was a *considerable* financier who had lost a *considerable* amount in the market crash.) Used as a noun (He lost *considerable*), it is colloquial. As an adverb (He worked *considerable* harder than before), it is used in careless speech but has no standing in writing. The correct adverb is *considerably.*

contact. The use of *contact* as a verb meaning *communicate with* is classified as colloquial by both WNC and the ACD. WNC adds: "a use avoided by careful writers and speakers." Actually the verb is widely used by careful writers and speakers in the business world, especially when the user can't or doesn't want to cite a specific means of communication (*write, phone, wire, make a personal call*). The objection to its general use is not that *contact* is properly a noun, for nouns have been used as verbs in English for centuries. The objection is that it has become Commercialese.

continual, continuous. "*Continual* implies that successive recurrences are very close together, with only small breaks between them, or none at all: *continual misunderstanding between nations. . . . Continuous* emphasizes the idea that the succession is unbroken: *the continuous life of the universe.*" (ACD)

could of. Misspelling of *could have.*

couple. The noun is generally acceptable when meaning *two things or persons combined* (a married *couple*, a *couple* on the dance floor). The colloquial meaning of *approximately two* is common in informal writing. *Of* is sometimes omitted in speech but seldom in writing.

credible, creditable, credulous. *Credible* means *worthy of belief.* (His tale was too *credible* to be doubted.) *Creditable* means *worthy of praise.* (His performance was *creditable.*) *Credulous* means *quick to believe, gullible.* (*Credulous* children believe in Santa Claus.)

criticism, criticize. The meaning of these words is often confined to faultfinding. (Perhaps it would be wise not to carp or *criticize.*) But in a literary context, *criticism* often implies *judgment* or *evaluation,* whether the final verdict is favorable or unfavorable. Thus *censure* and *condemn* are more accurate synonyms for *find fault.*

cunning. Colloquial in the sense of *appealing.* (Isn't Junior a *cunning* little fellow!) The formal meaning is *skillful* or *sly.* (He was both a *cunning* artist and a *cunning* politician.)

curious. In the sense of *odd, eccentric,* the word is still classified as colloquial, but it is common in informal writing. (The explorer discovered a *curious* tribe of pinheaded pygmies.) See pages 226–227.

cute. When used to mean *clever* or *shrewd,* this shortened form of *acute* is now archaic or dialectal (ACD). In the sense of *attractive, appealing* (What a *cute* baby!), it is a badly overworked colloquialism, especially in feminine vocabularies.

data. In origin *data* is plural, but the singular *datum* is now seldom found. *Data* as a singular noun (This *data* proves it conclusively) is now common, even in scientific writing. *These data* is more formal.

date. Colloquial as a noun meaning *appointment* (My *date* with Destiny) or a verb meaning *make an appointment with* (He *dated* her all summer). Slang when applied to the person with whom an appointment is made. (His *date* couldn't come.)

deal. The noun is acceptable when meaning an *amount* (a great *deal*), or when used literally or metaphorically in regard to card playing (a new *deal*, the New *Deal* party). As a general synonym for *business transaction* (a big *deal* in stocks), it is colloquial and commercial. When it means an *arrangement for mutual advantage* (a political *deal* in a smoke-filled room), WNC calls it colloquial, but the ACD does not restrict it.

delusion. See *Allusion.*

different from, than. *Different from* is more formal (His house is *different from* mine), but *different than* is common in reputable writing. (Dewey, if he got the nomination after refusing to compromise . . . would be quite a *different* President *than* a Dewey who got a synthetic nomination. . . .— Walter Lippmann in the New York *Herald Tribune.* Such instruction in English composition as is consistent with sound pedagogic procedure . . . demands entirely *different* methods *than* those employed in Freshman English.—O. J. Campbell in the *English Journal.*) When a clause follows the expression, *different than* is more economical. (This was *different than*

I had anticipated vs. *from what* I had anticipated). In spite of such evidence, some people still consider *different than* incorrect.

disinterested, uninterested. *Disinterested* means *impartial, neutral, unbiased. Uninterested* means *lacking in interest.* (A baseball umpire should be *disinterested* if he wants to be fair, but he cannot afford to be *uninterested* if he wants to see what's going on.) Originally *disinterested* meant *uninterested,* but WNC classifies this use as rare and the ACD calls it colloquial.

dived, dove. Either is acceptable as the past tense of *dive.*

double negative. From Old English times down into the nineteenth century the double negative was commonly used to intensify negative statements. But in more recent times fashion has consigned the expression to the vulgate level, where it flourishes profusely. ("We are *not* gonna fight *no* Lesneviches, we are *not* gonna fight *no* Maxims at the present time."—Jake Mintz, manager of Ezzard Charles, quoted by Red Smith in the New York *Herald Tribune.*) With adverbs which are negative by implication (*can't hardly, can't scarcely*), the same rule applies: Formal and informal usage now insist on *I can hardly do it. Can't help but* is more controversial. Although it is common in educated speech and appears in some writing (I *can't help but* do it), most authorities still require the gerund in informal writing (I *can't help doing it*). I *can but do it* is the approved formal idiom. Chaucer, who piled up double and triple negatives with vigorous abandon, would surely laugh at our attempts to justify these vagaries of usage by solemnly parroting the rule from formal logic that two negatives make an affirmative.

doubt if, that, whether. Despite some expert opinion to the contrary, *if* and *that* are both acceptable in writing after the verb *doubt.* (I *doubt if* George will come; I *doubt that* Mary will care.) *Doubt whether* is the most formal of the three. After negatives the standard idiom is *doubt that.* (I don't *doubt that* he will run again.) See *But that, but what.*

due to. Some people still argue that this expression is improper unless the adjective *due* has a noun to modify. They assert, in other words, that it is correct to write, "His pneumonia was *due to* exposure" (where *due* modifies *pneumonia*) and incorrect to write, "*Due to* pneumonia, he died." For the presumably improper use of the phrase, they suggest the substitution of *because of, on account of,* or *owing to.* Others point out that *due to* has been used as a preposition by respectable writers ever since the seventeenth century. (*Due to* Mr. Redgrave and Mr. Houghton, it has its good scenes and its many exciting moments.—John Mason Brown in the *Saturday Review of Literature*.) They remind us that *owing to* was originally adjectival. In view of the evidence there is no reason why a student should worry about the prepositional use of *due to* unless he is writing with the most punctilious formality.

due to the fact that. Like other expressions including *the fact that,* this phrase is often wordy. The simple word *because* is often an adequate subsitute. (Wordy: In high school, life became more interesting *due to the fact that* there were more extracurricular activities. Economical: In high school life became more interesting *because* there were more extracurricular activities.) See *Due to* and page 149.

dumb. In the sense of *dull* or *stupid* (He was just plain *dumb*) , this overworked word is still classified as colloquial.

effect. See *Affect.*

either, neither. Strictly speaking these words should refer to *one of two.* (He did not like the play of *either* team.) But their use with more than two appears to be increasing in reputable writing. For number see page 107.

elegant. This word means *characterized by taste, refinement, luxury.* In the general sense of *excellent* (an *elegant* football team) it is an overworked colloquialism.

else. See *Anybody's else.*

elude. See *Allude.*

emigrate, immigrate. *Emigrate* means to *migrate out* of a country, *immigrate* to *migrate in.* (The Pilgrims *emigrated* from Europe and *immigrated* to America.)

enthuse. The English language needs a single word in place of such circumlocutions as *make enthusiastic, become enthusiastic,* and *wax enthusiastic. Enthuse* is a "back formation" (like *donate* from *donation*) widely used for that purpose. But for some reason the word has never risen above the colloquial level, where it is frowned on by many educated people.

entitle, title. Either verb is correct. (The book was *entitled* or *titled The Disenchanted*) . *Entitle* is more formal.

etc. Although this common abbreviation is occasionally handy to indicate that a series could go on indefinitely, it is more often used as an easy way out of the problem of selecting details in a series. Literally it means *and other things,* but in many sentences there is no indication of what the other things can possibly be. Moreover, since the ending is the strongest position in the sentence, it is hardly the place for a vague abbreviation. At its worst *etc.* is meaningless; at best it is anticlimactic. Except in technical writing, where abbreviations are more at home, it should be avoided entirely; if a substitute is needed, *and so forth, and so on,* or *and the like* may be appropriate. *Such as . . . etc.* is redundant, for the *such as* indicates that the writer is making a selection. *And etc.* (literally *and and other things*) is bad Latin. *Ect.* is a common misspelling.

every place. See *Any place.*

everybody's else. See *Anybody's else.*

everyone. See *Anyone.*

everywheres. See *Anywheres.*

exam. A colloquial shortening of *examination.* It would not be out of place in informal writing with a campus context.

except. See *Accept.*

expect. Colloquial in the sense of *suppose.* (I *expect* he will come before morning.) Used more formally, it means *look forward to.* (I *expect* his arrival at any *minute.*)

extra. Used as an adverb in such expressions as *extra good, extra fine,* this word has a commercial flavor. *Unusually* is preferable in most contexts.

factor. As a synonym for *aspect, cause, circumstance, element,* or *phase,* this word is a favorite with lovers of gobbledygook (see page 296). Its use should be limited as much as possible to such contexts as biology or mathematics, where it has a genuine technical meaning.

falls, woods. Formal English keeps the distinction between the plural (The *falls* are as high as Niagara) and the rarer singular (A small *fall* comes over the cliff). Colloquially both *falls* and *woods* are used with singular verbs.

famed, famous, noted, notorious. Both *famed* and *noted* are Journalese for *famous. Notorious* means *widely known but not in good repute.* (John Wilkes, a *notorious* assassin, killed Lincoln, a *famous* president.)

farther, further. According to the traditional distinction, *farther* refers to physical distance, *further* to degree or quantity. (The man *farther* down the road went *further* in his attack on the mayor.) But this hairline distinction is now seldom kept, even by careful writers. As an adjective meaning *more* or *additional, further* is preferred. (*Further* reports place the battle lines south of Seoul.)

faze. Colloquial verb meaning *worry, disconcert, disturb.* Distinguish carefully from the noun *phase,* meaning an *aspect* or *stage.*

feature. As a verb meaning *emphasize, exhibit prominently, give special attention to,* this word is too common in business to be entirely appropriate in other contexts. (Commercialese: *The Lady in Ermine features* the new starlet, Wanda Beverly, who wears the new furs *featured* this year by I. J. Fox.) As a verb meaning *imagine,* it is slang. (*Feature* a winning football team without athletic scholarships!)

fellow. Formal when it means *the holder of a fellowship, a member of a society, an associate, a mate.* (He was a Guggenheim *fellow,* and his cousin was a *fellow* of the Royal Society. He was admired by his *fellows.* He threw the shoe after its *fellow.*) Colloquial when it means *boy friend* (She was out with her latest *fellow*) or merely *male person* (George is a decent *fellow*). But American English needs such a neutral word. *Male* is too biological, *chap* too British, *guy* and *gent* are too colloquial, *man* and *boy* are too chronological.

fewer, less. *Fewer* refers to number, *less* to amount, degree, quantity, or value. (*Fewer* knives and forks, *less* silverware; *fewer* difficulties, *less* trouble; *fewer* cars, *less* traffic.) Although *less* occurs occasionally with a plural noun in educated writing, this use is generally frowned upon.

fiancé, fiancée. *Fiancé* is masculine, *fiancée* feminine. They are pronounced alike: *fee-on-say,* with the accent on either the the third or second syllable. The French accent mark is often dropped in informal writing.

field. When applied to a study or occupation, *field is* overworked and frequently useless. (Wordy: I studied in the *field* of psychology; I am now in the teaching *field.* Economical: I studied psychology; I am now in teaching. See *Line.*

fine. Colloquial as a substitute for *well.* (The tomatoes are coming up *fine* this year.) See pages 247–248.

first-rate. WNC places no restriction on its use as an adjective meaning *excellent.* (Her term paper was *first-rate.*) It is colloquial as an adverb meaning *excellently.* (She performed *first-rate.*) It is often spelled without the hyphen and occasionally as one word.

fix. The ACD lists twenty-four meanings for the verb alone, eloquent testimony that this word is badly overworked. In the sense of *arrange, prepare, repair,* the verb is acceptable in informal writing. (She *fixed* the food while we *fixed* the flat tire.) More strictly confined to colloquial use are these meanings: *to arrange dishonestly* (The race was *fixed*); a *dishonest arrangement* (The gambler was involved in a basketball *fix*); *to get revenge* (The Lone Ranger *fixed* the cattle rustlers); and a *predicament* (He was in a pretty *fix*).

folks. Acceptable in informal writing to designate *people in general* or *people in a group.* (*Folks* are funny. Poor *folks* have a hard time these days.) But the word carries a rustic, homey, "folksy" connotation. Colloquial for *relatives.* (My *folks* are coming for the week end.)

foot, feet. When used after a number before a noun, *foot* is the proper collective plural in both written and spoken English. (A four-*foot* fence, a six-*foot* man.) Before an adjective or adverb it is colloquial at best. (Five *foot* away, six *foot* two inches tall.)

foregoing. See *Above.*

former, latter. The *former* is the *first of a pair,* the *latter* the *second.* It is improper to use them with more than two or to use one in the absence of the other. (Wrong: Of her three sons, Tom, Dick, and Harry, the *latter* is the handsomest. I don't like people who are always talking about themselves. The *latter* bore me.) Even if used properly, these words are likely to be awkward because they often send the reader back to check on their antecedents. This can usually be avoided by using a pronoun with an unmistakable antecedent or by innocent repetition. *Former* may, of course, mean *previous, past,* or *ancient.* (The *former* heavyweight champion. Memories of *former* days.) *Latter* may mean *later* or *toward the end.* (In the *latter* years of his life he wrote his autobiography.)

formulas, formulae. Either plural is acceptable, but the English (*formulas*) has apparently passed the Latin in popularity.

freshman, freshmen. The adjective is *freshman.* (He was a member of the *freshman* class.) *Freshmen* is the plural of the noun. (He was one of three hundred *freshmen.*) They are usually not capitalized.

funny. WNC and the ACD do not restrict the word when it means *laughable* but label it colloquial when it means *queer* or *odd.* Since many things are laughable because they are queer or odd, the distinction is rather farfetched. Probably the best objection to using the word in informal writing is that it is inaccurate and overworked. Even in speech there is a question of whether the user means *funny* funny or *queer* funny.

further. See *Farther.*

gentleman, lady. *Man* and *woman* are more natural unless the writer wishes to put special emphasis on a person's refinement or breeding. (He saw two *men* and two *women* in the restaurant. Her manners are vulgar, but her mother was a real *lady* and her father a *gentleman*.) The word *gentleman* has lost caste since the days of Victoria, and *lady* has been misapplied so often that it sometimes has a vulgar connotation. Its widespread use in business (*saleslady, ladies'* garments, tables for *ladies*) and in general demands (Step to the back of the bus, *lady*) has hastened this degeneration. Both are still proper in special contexts (*Ladies and gentlemen* in introducing a speech; *Gentlemen:* in a business letter). *Gent* is vulgar or presumably humorous.

get, got, gotten. Of eighteen meanings of the verb, not including numerous idiomatic phrases, the ACD restricts the following: Colloquial: *to be obliged to* (I have *got* to do it); *to kill* (They just *got* Lefty); *to puzzle* (That *gets* me); and *to understand* (Do you *get* me?). Slang: *to hit* (The ball *got* him in the eye). *Have got* in the sense of *possess* (I *have got* five dollars) is colloquial and redundant. *Got* in "I *got* to do it" is vulgate. Many verb phrases (*get across, get along, get even with*) are acceptable idioms in informal writing. In the United States both *got* and *gotten* are correct as the past participle. (He had *got* or *gotten* a new car.)

good, well. In formal and informal English, *well* is either an adverb (He played *well*) or an adjective (He was *well*). *Good* is an adjective only. (His playing was *good;* he felt *good*.) As an adverb, *good* is usually classed as vulgate (He did *good*), though its wide use has led some authorities to consider it colloquial. The difference between *feeling well* and *feeling good* is one of meaning, not grammar: *well* suggests only that a person does not feel ill; *good* carries a more positive connotation of health or happiness.

got, gotten. See *Get*.

guess. Neither WNC nor the ACD places any restrictions on *guess* in the sense of *believe, suppose, think*. But some handbooks still classify it as colloquial, or, like *calculate* and *reckon,* local. At best the verb is badly overworked and should probably be limited in writing to the more specific meanings, *judge at random* and *conjecture.*

gym. Like *exam,* this colloquial shortening of *gymnasium* would be out of place in formal writing but not in informal writing with a campus context.

had better, best. Both *had better* and *had best* are acceptable idioms in writing. (You *had better* do it.) Without the verb the expressions are colloquial. (You *better* do it.)

had have, had of. It is illiterate to say, "If I *had have* (or *had of*) known." Correct: "If I *had* known."

had ought, hadn't ought. These common expressions (You *had ought* to go) may result from an attempt to supply the missing past tense of *ought.* They are colloquial at best. In writing, use *ought* or *should,* supplying *have* with the infinitive if the sense requires the past. (You *ought* to do it. He *should* do it. They *oughtn't* to have done it before.)

hang, hanged, hung. In formal English, following traditional legal usage, *hanged* is still used for capital punishment or suicide. (He was *hanged* for murder. She *hanged* herself.) For all other uses the principal parts are *hang, hung, hung.*

hardly. See Double negative.

hardly ever. See *Rarely ever.*

have got. See *Get.*

healthful, healthy. According to WNC and the ACD, the traditional handbook distinction between *healthful* (*giving* health) and *healthy* (*having* health) is not justified by educated usage. *Healthy* is now commonly used for both. (The *healthy* climate made him *healthy.*)

heighth. A misspelling of *height* apparently by analogy with *length, width, depth.*

herself. See *Self.*

highbrow, lowbrow. Still generally classified as slang but surely acceptable in informal writing. WNC still hyphenates both words. *Middlebrow* appears to be taking its logical place between them. See page 236.

himself, hisself. See *Self.*

hoi polloi. Since *hoi polloi* means *the masses, the hoi polloi* is as redundant as *and etc.*

home, homely, homey. Formal: Madame is *at home.* Informal: She is *home.* Vulgate: She is *to home.* Except in advertising English, a *home* is usually a house that has been lived in. In the United States *homely* is usually applied to people and means *very plain.* (She had a *homely* face.) In formal contexts it occasionally means *simple, unpretentious, homelike.* (He dined on *homely* fare.) The common American adjective for *homelike* is the folksy colloquialism *homey.*

honorable, reverend. Strict formal usage of these titles requires that they be preceded by *the,* capitalized, and followed by either initials, first name, *Mr.,* or *Dr.* (The *Honorable* R. A. Taft; the *Honorable* Robert A. Taft; the *Honorable* Mr. Taft; the *Reverend* H. E. Fosdick; the *Reverend* Harry Emerson Fosdick; the *Reverend* Dr. Fosdick.) In less formal usage *the* is sometimes omitted and abbreviations *(Hon.* and *Rev.)* are sometimes used. Neither expression should be used alone or with the last name only (the *Reverend;* the *Reverend* Fosdick). Because of the flattery oiling the wheels of politics, there is no foolproof formula telling a writer when to use *Honorable.*

however. An old rule that *however* should not begin a sentence is seldom followed today. It is entirely proper to write, *"However,* I do not agree with him" or *"However* right he may be, I do not agree with him." It is common, *however,* to insert the word between commas in a less obtrusive part of the sentence or to begin the sentence with *but.* The important point for beginners is to distinguish between the *however* that begins a new sentence and the *however* that is merely an interrupter in the middle of a sentence. See page 174.

human, humane. Authorities still differ on the use of *human* as a noun. (After all, we are *humans,* not apes.) WNC places no restrictions on it; the ACD calls it colloquial or humorous. Because of the humorous connotation, it is safer to use *human beings* in a serious, formal context. As an adjective, *human* may refer to any aspect of human nature (*human* kindness, *human* wickedness). The older form *humane* is now restricted to the credit side of the ledger. (Lincoln was a *humane* president. The SPCA is *humane* to dogs. The humanities are sometimes called *humane* learning.)

hung. See *Hang.*

if. See *Doubt if.*

ill, sick. *Ill* is a fashionable and formal word for *unwell.* In England *sick* usually implies nausea or vomiting, but in America it is entirely acceptable for any *illness* (or *sickness*). It is commonly used instead of *ill* before a noun (a *sick* child), as a collective noun (good care for the *sick*), and in numerous pat phrases (*sick* at heart, *sick* for home). The absurd taboo on the thoroughly respectable word *sick* leads some people to the ridiculous euphemism *violently ill* for *vomiting.*

illusion. See *Allusion.*

immigrate. See *Emigrate.*

imply, infer. The traditional distinction between these two words is clear: One person *implies* something in his speech, writing, or manner; another *infers* something from it. (Although he meant to *imply* that I was right, I *inferred* from his remarks that I was wrong.) *Infer* is often used by reputable writers where others would insist on *imply.* (But we do speak of a civilized state . . . and thereby *infer* something about the institutions and law courts of that state. . . .—George Catlin, "T. S. Eliot and the Moral Issue," *Saturday Review of Literature.*) Thus the ACD lists *imply* without restriction as one of the meanings of *infer,* whereas WNC labels this use as "erroneous." The distinction between the two words is worth keeping.

in, into. *In* refers either to a *state of rest* or to *motion within; into* indicates *motion toward* or *direction.* (They were either standing or swimming *in* the ocean when he dove *into* the water.) Colloquially *in* is often used where careful writers would use *into*.

in back of. See *Back of.*

in regard(s) to. See *Regard.*

incredible, incredulous. See *Credible.*

individual, party, person. *Individual* is widely used as a synonym for *person,* but more careful writers use it either to distinguish a person from a group or to stress a person's special qualities, his individuality. (Democracy emphasizes the rights of the *individual.* America is full of funny men, but Danny Kaye stands out as an *individual.*) Fowler exaggerates in calling the loose use of *individual* "one of the modern editor's shibboleths for detecting the unfit"; but its indiscriminate use is draining it of individuality. *Person* is the neutral everyday word for human being. *Party* is Legalese (*party* of the first part), Commercialese (Did I connect you with your *party,* sir?), or colloquial (Who was that *party* I saw you with last night?).

infer. See *Imply.*

ingenious, ingenuous. *Ingenious* means *clever, resourceful, full of ingenuity. Ingenuous* means *frank, candid, naïve.* (Although he was the *ingenious* inventor of the phonograph, Edison had a strangely *ingenuous* attitude toward grand opera.)

inside. As a noun, *inside* is properly followed by *of* (the *inside of* the house). When *inside* is used as a preposition, the *of* is often superfluous (a room *inside* the house). *Inside of* in reference to time (I'll return *inside of* two minutes) is often called colloquial, but the ACD does not restrict it. "I'll return *in* two minutes" and "I'll return *within* two minutes" are more generally acceptable in writing.

instance, instant. An *instance* is an *example;* an *instant* is a *moment in time.* (Here is an *instance* of how he tends to make up his mind in an *instant.*)

intermural, intramural. *Intermural* is a common undergraduate misspelling. The word is *intramural* meaning *within the* *walls* (*intramural* athletics). *Intermural* would mean *between the walls* as *intercollegiate* means *between colleges.*

invite. The noun, with the accent on the first syllable (He sent her an *ínvite* to the party), is slang for *invitation.*

irregardless. A double negative for *regardless,* sometimes dignified as colloquial but more often classed as vulgate. It is as logical as saying *unhopeless.*

is when, is where. These expressions are often inaccurately used in definitions involving neither time nor place. Inaccurate: Chauvinism *is when* patriotism is carried too far. Onomatopoeia *is where* the sound of words suggests the sense. Accurate: Chauvinism is patriotism carried too far. Onomatopoeia is the use of words whose sound suggests the sense. On the other hand, there is no legitimate grammatical objection to introducing a noun clause with *when* or *where* after the verb *to be.*

it being. See *Being as.*

job. When it means a *position* or *situation, job* is still classed as colloquial by WNC; but the ACD merely labels it *U.S.* The distinction between a job and a position is as much a question of salary as of language. *Situation* is even more formal than *position.* Both have tended to become euphemisms for *job,* like *perspiration* for *sweat.*

just. Colloquial when used as an intensive meaning *very, truly, simply* (*just* wonderful, *just* fine, *just* grand). Unrestricted uses of *just* as an adverb are *precisely* (He is *just* six weeks old); *barely* (She *just* missed making Phi Beta Kappa); *only* (A professor is *just* a human being); and *only a moment ago* (He was *just* here).

kid. The verb meaning *tease* is slang. The noun meaning *youngster* is either slang (ACD) or colloquial (WNC).

kind of, sort of. Widely used in speech as adverbs where written English would normally use *rather* or *somewhat.* (Colloquial: They were *kind of* annoyed. He looked at me *sort of* queerly.) When these phrases are followed by a noun (a *kind of* cheese, a *sort of* intellectual) , they are acceptable in formal writing if the *of* is not followed by an indefinite article (*kind of a* cheese, *sort of an* intellectual).

know-how. A counterword much overworked recently in describing the technical competence of American industry.

lady. See *Gentleman.*

later, latter. *Later* is the comparative of *late. Latter* is a separate adjective that is usually coupled with *former.* Used by itself, it may mean *later* or *toward the end.* It is correct to say either "the *later* years" or "the *latter* years of Shakespeare's life." See *Former.*

lead, led. When *lead* is pronounced to rhyme with *bread,* it is a noun meaning *a heavy metal.* It should not be confused in spelling with *led,* the past tense or past participle of the verb *to lead.* (Correct: He *led* the *lead* soldiers as they had never been *led* before.)

learn. Vulgate when used in place of *teach.* Vulgate: I guess that'll *learn* you a lesson. Informal and Formal: I guess that'll *teach* you a lesson if you are willing to *learn* it.)

leave, let. Generally speaking, *leave* means *depart, desert, abandon; let* means *allow, permit.* (Don't go away and *leave* me; *let* me go with you.) The distinction between "*let* me alone" (don't bother me) and "*leave* me alone" (depart hence) is close but kept by most careful speakers and writers. The difference between "*let* me out" (allow me to get out) and "*leave* me out" (don't count me in) is clear-cut. The most important rule is that only *let* should be followed by an infinitive. (*Let* George *do* it.) "*Leave* George *do* it" is vulgate.

led. See *Lead.*

lend. See *Loan.*

less. See *Fewer.*

let. See *Leave.*

liable. See *Apt.*

lighted, lit. Either of these forms may be used for the past tense or past participle of *light.*

like, as. In formal writing and in most informal writing, the traditional distinction is still kept between *like,* a preposition, and *as,* a conjunction. (He walks *like* me, but he doesn't run *as* I run.) But *like* is common as a conjunction in colloquial English and is often found in reputable informal writing. (I wander around the world of advertising pretty much *like* Alice wanders around Wonderland.—John Crosby, New York *Herald Tribune.* On the news map the most you could hope for was breaking out of the open arena of the researcher, where men engage facts *like* toreadors do bulls. . . .—Norman Cousins, *Saturday Review of Literature.*)

likely. See *Apt.*

line. A *line* of talk is slang. (Falstaff gave Prince Hal an amazing *line.*) Applied to an occupation (He was in the old-clothes *line*) or goods (a *line* of new sport jackets), the word is Commercialese. Like *case* and *field, line* is also common in circumlocutions. (Redundant: He did work along the *line* of chemistry. Better: He did work in chemistry.)

lit. See *Lighted.*

loan. Acceptable as a verb meaning *lend,* though its use is largely restricted to the United States. (I *loaned* him money, patched up a quarrel between himself and his wife.—Stuart Chase, "The Luxury of Integrity.")

locate. As an intransitive verb meaning *settle* (She *located* in Pocatello), *locate* is usually classified as colloquial. Its transitive uses are acceptable in both formal and informal writing.

loose, lose. *Loose* can be both an adjective meaning *free from restraint, unfastened* and a verb meaning *set free, unfasten.* (The ropes were *loose* because somebody had *loosed* them.) *Lose* is a verb meaning *suffer loss.* (Heads I win, tails you *lose.*) A convenient mnemonic device for poor spellers is that *lose* loses and *o.*

lose out, win out. Still often classed as colloquial, these idioms are more emphatic than the unsupported verbs and are hardly objectionable in informal writing.

lot, lots. Common colloquialisms for *much, a great deal, a large amount.* They sometimes appear in reputable informal writing. (*Lots* of people seem to think that fashionable words like *Blitzkrieg* or things like college slang or jive talk are the important feature of current English.—Rudolf Flesch, *The Art of Plain Talk.*) *A lot* should not be run together as one word.

lousy. A slang word so widely used to express all degrees of disapproval that it has become completely deloused. This leaves us with the absurd word *pediculous* or the redundant *really lousy* to mean *infested with lice*.

lovely. Still listed in the dictionaries to apply to delicate, exquisite beauty (a *lovely* orchid) or spiritual beauty (a *lovely soul*). But it has been spoiled by colloquial use as a counterword to express any degree of approval (a *lovely* ashtray, baby, campus, dog, or zebra). See pages 247–248.

luxuriant, luxurious. *Luxuriant* means *abundant, exuberant* (the *luxuriant* growth of the tropics). *Luxurious* refers to man-made luxury (the *luxurious* homes of the movie stars).

mad. In the sense of *angry, enraged,* this word is usually classed as colloquial. But WNC places no restrictions on this use, which appears often in informal writing. Its use in the literal sense of *insane*—traditionally the proper meaning—is now comparatively rare. It often means *insane* with an ironic or facetious overtone. (His *mad* antics at parties made his wife *mad* as a hatter.)

majority, plurality. In counting votes, a *majority* means *more than half the total cast;* a *plurality* means *more than the next highest candidate. The majority* may also be *the group or party with the most members or votes,* as opposed to one or more minorities. Used colloquially as a synonym for *most* (a *majority* of the guests, the *majority* of the students), the expression is heavy.

mathematics. Singular when used as the name of a science. (*Mathematics* is an important subject for engineers.) Usually plural in other contexts. (It is impossible to solve the problem if your *mathematics* are incorrect.)

may. See *Can.*

may of. Misspelling of *may have.*

mean. Colloquial and overworked in the sense of *ashamed, peevish, selfish, unkind.*

medium. In general uses, the plural is usually *mediums.* Spiritualists are *mediums.* In scientific contexts, *media* is still common.

might of. Misspelling of *might have.*

mighty. Colloquial for *very.* (That's *mighty* nice of you.)

moral, morale. The noun meaning *attitude, spirit, mental outlook* is *morale.* (Fifth columnists are dangerous to military *morale.* The *moral* is that they should be exposed.)

most. In formal writing *most* may be used as an adverb meaning *to the greatest extent.* (I am *most* happy; he is *most* cordial.) Its use as a substitute for *almost* or *nearly* is colloquial. (He came *most* every day to see me.)

must of. Misspelling of *must have.*

mutual, common. Strictly speaking, *mutual* indicates an *exchange or interchange between two or more persons or things,* not merely something shared in common. (They had a *mutual* affection for each other because they shared *common* interests.) The exceptions (our *mutual* friend) are usually ascribed to the unfortunate ambiguity of the word *common.*

myself. See *Self.*

neither. See *Either.*

no one. See *Anyone.*

no place. See *Any place.*

nobody's else. See *Anybody's else.*

not as. See *As.*

noted, notorious. See *Famed.*

nowhere near. A common colloquial substitute for *not nearly.*

nowheres. See *Anywheres.*

number. See *Amount.*

O, oh. Both are interjections to express pain, surprise, or grief. *O* is more common before a name in direct address, as in a poetic invocation. (*O* wild West Wind, thou breath of

Autumn's being.) *Oh* is directly followed either by a comma or an exclamation mark, depending on the writer's emphasis, and it may be uncapitalized in the middle of a sentence. *O* is not directly followed by any punctuation and is always capitalized.

of. Beware of the substitution of *of* for *have* in *could have, might have, should have,* and so forth.

off of. The *of* is often redundant. (He jumped *off* the train, not *off of* the train.)

oh. See *O*.

O.K., OK, okay. An overworked colloquialism especially common in business. Despite long-standing arguments, its origin is still in doubt.

oral, verbal. According to their Latin origins, *oral* (*os, oris, mouth*) means *spoken,* and *verbal* (*verbum, word*) means *in words.* All writing is *verbal,* but it is *oral* only if it is delivered by a speaker. But this distinction has not been carefully kept. A *verbal* order in the Army means a *spoken* order; a *verbal* contract in the law is unwritten; a recommendation form from Columbia University lists: "Power of expression: 1. Verbal. 2. Written." Both WNC and the ACD list *oral* without restriction as one of the meanings of *verbal.*

ought. See *Had ought*.

out. See *Lose out*.

out loud. Often classed as colloquial, this common expression is certainly acceptable in informal writing. The difference between snoring *out loud* and snoring *aloud* (the more formal usage) can be measured in imaginary decibels.

outside of. Colloquial in the sense of *besides* or *except*. (No one was invited *outside of* him.) Acceptable in formal English when it means beyond (His house was *outside of* the city limits), though the *of* is superfluous.

over with. Colloquial and redundant in the sense of *ended, finished.* More formal and economical: The concert is *over.*

overly. Usually classified as colloquial when used as a synonym for *excessively*. (He was *overly* cautious.) *Over* in a compound word serves the same purpose more neatly. (He was *overcautious*.)

pair. The formal plural is *pairs,* but pair is acceptable after a number in informal writing. It is especially common in business usage (four *pair* of gloves).

party. See *Individual.*

peeve. Colloquial as a verb. WNC doesn't recognize the noun, but the ACD lists it without restriction as a back formation from *peevish.*

per. The traditional objection to *per* before English words is a pedantic distinction belied by usage. Expressions such as *per foot* and *per yard* are as common as *per annum* and *per diem.* But the preposition has a commercial flavor. Except in one or two very common expressions (*per capita, per cent*), *a* is usually preferable (twenty cents *a* pound). *As per* is pure Commercialese.

per cent, percent, percentage. *Per cent* may be either two words or one and does not have to be followed by a period. Most writers prefer *percentage* when a number is not mentioned (fifty *per cent,* a large *percentage*). But "a large *per cent*" is not incorrect. The symbol % should not be used except in business and technical reports.

persecute, prosecute. These two words are commonly confused. *Persecute* means *oppress, annoy, treat cruelly. Prosecute* means *to institute or carry on a legal proceeding.* (For *persecuting* the Jews, the Nazi leaders were *prosecuted* at the Nuremberg trials.)

person. See *Individual.*

personnel. This is a convenient counterword in Officialese and Commercialese, but it should not be used indiscriminately to mean *people in general.* As the London *Times* says, people to whom it is applied "do not go, they proceed. They do not have, they are (or, more often are not) in possession of. They do not ask, they make application for. . . . They cannot eat, they only consume; they perform ablutions; instead of homes they have places of residence in which, instead of living, they are domiciled. They are not cattle, they are not ciphers, they certainly are not human beings: they are personnel." If you must use it, spell it right.

phenomenon. In its philosophic use ("any object known through the senses") and its scientific use ("any observable fact or event") this word normally has a plural *phenomena*. When it means "an exceptional or abnormal person or thing," the common plural, according to WNC, is *phenomenons*. (The class was full of *phenomenons* who were brilliant at identifying *phenomena* viewed through a microscope.) Unlike *data, phenomena* has not crossed the line as a singular noun.

phone. This colloquial shortening of *telephone* is acceptable in informal writing either as a noun or a verb.

photo. Usually classed as a colloquialism, though WNC lists it as both a noun and a verb without restriction. Like *auto,* the word is rapidly becoming extinct. Except in compounds, it is now commonly replaced by *picture* or *snapshot*.

place. See *Any place.*

plan on, plan to. Either is an acceptable idiom. (I *plan on* reading the book; I *plan to* read it.)

playwrite. A logical misspelling of *playwright,* the second syllable of which means *workman,* as in *millwright, wheelwright.*

plenty. Colloquial when used adverbially. (My father was *plenty* mad.) It may be used in informal writing as a predicate adjective where formal English would use *plentiful*. (The harvest was *plenty*.) Its other use as an adjective is colloquial. (There were *plenty* apples.) When it is used as a noun, its number varies logically with the context. (Although there *are* plenty of windows, there *is* not plenty of light.)

plurality. See *Majority.*

politics. May be either singular or plural regardless of its meaning. (His politics *are* Republican, or His politics *is* Republican.)

practicable, practical. *Practicable* applies to a plan that has not been put in practice but appears feasible. *Practical* can be applied either to persons (*sensible, businesslike, aware of the realities of life*) or to things (*workable, useful, the opposite* *of theoretical*). The word *practical* has been so overworked and is so relative that a writer using it should first ask himself: *"Practical* in terms of what?" The answer will probably lead to a more accurate word.

preposition at the end of a sentence. When Winston Churchill was rebuked for ending a sentence with a preposition, he is supposed to have answered: "I agree. It is a practice up with which I cannot put." The old rule ("A preposition is a bad word to end a sentence with") has been ignored or violated for centuries. Reputable modern writers pay no attention to it. (The faculty of hearing is ours that we may find in its exercise that delight which arises from the unimpeded activity in the groove nature meant it to run *in.*—A. E. Housman, "Introductory Lecture." Writing for Adams was therefore a makeshift, and yet the thing he was born *for.*—Van Wyck Brooks, *New England, Indian Summer.* I am quite sure that the character I'm least likely to forget is a boy I grew up with and nowadays see little *of.*—E. B. White, "A Boy I Knew.") Even Emily Post ends an advertisement with a preposition. (Beneath its myriad rules the fundamental purpose of etiquette is to make the world a more pleasant place to live in, and ourselves more pleasant to live *with!*) There is some logic in the argument that an unimportant word should not come in the important final position in a sentence. But a gain in emphasis should not be made at the expense of natural word order. Moreover, students haunted by the ghostly rule often make the mistake of putting in two prepositions for good measure. (In 1920 Congress enacted an amendment giving the right to vote to all people, no matter *of* what sex they are *of.*)

pretty. Acceptable in informal writing as an adverb meaning *considerably, moderately, rather.* (It is *pretty* dark in here.)

principal, principle. As an adjective, *principal* means *chief* (the *principal* point involved); as a noun it means either *chief* (the *principal* of the school) or a sum of money (interest on a *principal* of ten thousand dollars). *Principle* is always a noun meaning a *ru(le), law,* or *fundamental truth.* (Appropriateness is an important *principle* of composition.)

proposition. Commercialese for *offer, proposal, scheme, under-taking.* (What's your *proposition,* J. B.?) Slang for a *person* or *problem.* (Both Coach Anthrax and the T formation present a tough *proposition* for Saturday's game.) Slang as a verb meaning *make a proposal or offer.* (He *propositioned* me about buying a new car.)

prosecute. See *Persecute.*

proved, proven. As the past participle of *prove,* either is accept-able in American English, though *proved* is the more com-mon.

provided, providing. Either is acceptable in writing, but the ACD makes a hairline distinction between them: "*Provided* always indicates some stipulation: . . . *provided* he goes, we can go along. *Providing* means 'just in case some certain thing should happen': *providing* he should come, we must have extra sup-plies ready."

put. Of the many idiomatic phrases with *put, put in,* in the sense of *spend,* is usually classed as colloquial. (He *put in* an eight-hour day.) *Put across* and *put over* are classed in WNC as slang.

quite. In formal English *quite* means *completely* (*quite* the op-posite) or *really* (*quite* an experience). In informal writing it often has its colloquial sense of *rather, somewhat,* or *to a considerable extent.* (Her face was *quite* attractive.) It should not, of course, be confused with the two-syllable word *quiet,* meaning *silent.*

raise, rise. *Raise* (*raised, raised*) is a transitive verb. (He *raised* the window.) *Rise* (*rose, risen*) is an intransitive verb. (He *rose* from his seat.) It is entirely proper to write in American English of *raising* a family. *Rear* is less common and more formal.

real. As an adverb for *very* or *really, real* is a common American colloquialism that sometimes appears in informal writing. (The odd thing about paranoia is, you take a good look at the patient and you can hardly tell it from a *real* bad case of nationalism.—E. B. White, *The Wild Flag*). But neither WNC nor the ACD lists *real* as an adverb.

rear. See *Raise.*

reason is because. A common argument against this construction is that, since *because* means *for the reason that,* the expression is redundant. But it is common in educated speech and often occurs in reputable writing. (The *reason* so much junk is produced on a mass scale *is because* this is so profitable.— J. T. Farrell, *The League of Frightened Philistines.*) More widely acceptable expressions would be: The *reason is that* it is so profitable, or The *reason is* the profit in it.

reckon. Dialectal (mostly southern) in the sense of *think* or *suppose.* (I *reckon* it will rain before morning.) In formal and informal writing the verb usually means *estimate* or *esteem.* (He *reckoned* that there were forty-eight miles to go; he was *reckoned* an excellent navigator.) Even these uses carry a strong colloquial flavor.

regard, regards. *As regards, in regard to, with regard to,* and *regarding* are equally acceptable in writing. *In regards to* and *with regards to* are vulgate. See *Irregardless.*

reminisce. This back formation from *reminiscence* was once classed as colloquial, but the best modern dictionaries place no restrictions on its use.

repeat again. The adverb is superfluous if the meaning is *say once again.* But it is logical to make a distinction between repeating once and repeating again.

reverend. See *Honorable.*

right. Common colloquialisms are: *right along (continuously); right away, right off (immediately).* In the southern dialect the word is a common colloquial substitute for *very (right* good, *right* smart, *right* soon) .

rise. See *Raise.*

round. See *Around.*

run. The use of *run* in the sense of *conduct* or *manage* (He *runs* the Stork Club) is classed as colloquial in WNC, but the ACD lists it without restriction. It is certainly acceptable in informal writing. See page 232.

said. See *Above.*

same. *Same* is common in conversation as a pronoun. (Make mine the *same.*) In writing it usually has a legal or commercial flavor. (He sent a package and she received the *same.*) It has been abandoned in the best business writing and should be replaced by a more natural pronoun in any general context. (He sent a package and she received *it.*) *Same* may be used without qualms as an adjective. (He returned the *same* day.)

scarcely. See Double negative.

seem. The use of *seem* after *can't* (I can't *seem* to do it) is sometimes classed as colloquial, but WNC accepts it without restriction. It is no more illogical than many other idioms. "I *seem* unable to do it" is more acceptable in formal writing, but it is wooden. The word *seem* is often overworked by students who use it as a cloak for their own uncertainty. A sentence such as "It *seems* that war is a great evil" can be cut down to "War is a great evil." The reader feels like saying with Hamlet, "Seems. . . . Nay, it is."

seldom ever. As in *rarely ever,* the *ever* is superfluous if the writer means merely *seldom.* If he means *hardly ever* or *seldom if ever,* he should say that. *Seldom ever* is colloquial at best.

self. In formal English, *himself, myself* and so forth are either reflexive pronouns (He hurt *himself*) or intensive pronouns (I'll marry her *myself*). Of their many colloquial uses in place of personal pronouns, two have been classified as acceptable in informal writing: after *than* in comparisons (Others with more vision or courage than *myself.* . . .—E. M. Forster, "I Believe"); and as the object of a verb or preposition (They gave George and *myself* a prize; he gave his to *myself*). *Hisself* and *theirselves* are vulgate. Compounds with *self* (*self-love, self-knowledge, self-control*) are regularly hyphenated.

set. See *Sit.*

shall, will. The traditional rules for *shall* and *will* are simple enough on paper: To express simple future, use *shall* in the first person, *will* in the second and third. (I *shall* go, but he *will* probably stay home.) To express determination or a command, reverse the process. (I *will* not go, and you *shall* not make me!) In asking a question, use the same word you expect in the answer. (*Shall* you go with me? Answer: I *shall. Will* he go with me? Answer: He *will.*) The only trouble with this doctrine is that it doesn't conform to usage. The tendency among reputable writers is for all forms to level to *will* for simple future. (I *will* go, but he *will* probably stay home.) *Shall* is now common in the first person to express determination. (We *shall* not flag or fail.— Winston Churchill.) *Will* is the natural form for the second person in asking a question. (*Will* you go with me?)

shape. When used in the sense of *condition* or *manner* (The team is in good *shape* for the game), it is classed as colloquial by WNC but not restricted in the ACD.

should, would

Use *should* in all persons:
1. To express obligation (You *should* study harder).
2. To express probability (They *should* be here by noon).
3. In conditional or hypothetical *if* clauses (If I s*hould* die, think only this of me).

Use *would* in all persons:
1. To express customary past action (He *would* sit there every day).
2. To express conditional willingness (I *would* if I could).
3. In place of *will* to make a statement more polite (*Would* you mind not blowing smoke in my face?).

Otherwise, the traditional formal rules for *should* and *would* follow those for the simple future use of *shall* and *will*. (I *should* like to go, you *would* like to go, and so forth). There is a marked tendency for *would* (like *will*) to take over for all persons.

should of. Misspelling of *should have.*

show, show up. As a noun standing for a *spectacle* (the greatest *show* on earth), it is acceptable on all levels. As a noun meaning *chance* (They don't have a *show* against Yale) or referring to any theatrical performance from burlesque to Ibsen (*Hamlet* is a good *show*), it is an overworked colloquialism.

Show up, meaning *expose, stand out,* or *appear* (sometimes without the *up*) is also colloquial.

sick. See *Ill.*

sit, set. *Sit (sat, sat)* is normally an intransitive verb meaning *to be seated* (He *sat* on the floor); *set (set, set)* is normally a transitive verb meaning *to cause to sit* (He *set* the table on the floor). *Setting hen* and *setting sun* are acceptable intransitive uses of *set.*

size, size up. Expression such as *a large size coat* (or *large-size*) are acceptable in informal writing where formal writing would probably have *large sized* (or *large-sized*). *Size up,* meaning evaluate, is often classed as colloquial, but the ACD puts no restrictions on it.

smart. *Sharp, severe, brisk, quick, clever, shrewd, neat, fashionable*—the fact that *smart* can double for any of these adjectives is ample evidence of why it has degenerated into a counterword of approval (see pages 247–248). The clothing industry is busy giving it the *coup de grâce.*

so, so that. There is nothing incorrect about using *so* as a conjunction; it is done by the most reputable writers. (Virtually everything he saw and heard was being seen and heard by him for the first time, *so* he gave it his whole attention.— E. B. White, "A Boy I Knew.") But inexperienced writers often overwork it. The trouble with the "so-habit" is not only the monotony of repeating one sentence pattern too often but the resulting neglect of the more emphatic periodic sentence with the main clause last. Compare "I didn't like it, so I went home" with "Because I didn't like it, I went home." As an intensive (*so* round, *so* firm, *so* fully packed), *so* is weak from overwork. The omission of *that* in *so that* is a colloquial shortcut. (More formal: I came early *so that* I could see you.)

some. Colloquial as an adverb meaning *considerable.* (That's going *some!*) Slang as an adverb meaning *somewhat* (He is *some* improved) or an adjective meaning *of considerable account or consequence.* (That was *some* storm!) — ACD.

some place. See *Any place.*

somebody's else. See *Anybody's else.*

someone. See *Anyone.*

somewheres. See *Anywheres.*

sort of. See *Kind of.*

specie, species. *Specie* means *coined money. Species,* meaning *kind* or *class,* has the same form in both singular and plural. (A piggy bank is a *species* of animal that eats *specie;* there are other *species* of pigs.)

split infinitive. George Bernard Shaw once wrote to the London *Times:* "There is a busy body on your staff who devotes a lot of his time to chasing split infinitives. Every good literary craftsman splits his infinitives when the sense demands it. I call for the immediate dismissal of this pedant. It is of no consequence whether he decides to go quickly or to quickly go. The important thing is that he should go at once." This neatly summarizes the enlightened modern view about the absurdity of covering split infinitives with a blanket ruling. The researches of Professor Curme reveal that reputable writers have been splitting infinitives since the fourteenth century and never with such abandon as during the past fifty years. But the little schoolmarmish ghost that throws up its hands in horror whenever an infinitive is split still haunts our national conscience. The question of whether to split or not to split depends, of course, on considerations of smoothness, rhythm, emphasis, and meaning. As Professor Curme points out, "He failed entirely *to comprehend* it" is ambiguous; the adverb is a squinting modifier. "He failed *to entirely* comprehend it" is both natural and clear. Some split infinitives can't be unsplit without rewriting the whole sentence: for example, "There should be enough evidence in five centuries *to about convince* the unregenerate." There is no place in that sentence where *about* can be put without reducing it to nonsense. Obviously, if a split infinitive is awkward, a sentence should be recast. This is especially true when the wedge consists of more than one word: "We do want *to,* *at this time, thank* those who supported us in our recent campaign for re-election." This would be a smoother sentence with *at this time* at the beginning. But any general condemnation of the split infinitive results either from ignorance or a stubborn refusal to face the facts of usage. (See page 139.)

stratum. The Latin distinction between the singular *stratum* and the plural *strata* is still kept. There is no tendency, as with the more popular word *data,* to use the plural form for both numbers.

such, such as. As an intensive followed only by a noun (I never saw *such* a day), *such* is informal at best. Do not follow *such as* with *etc.* See *Etc.*

sure. *Sure* is an adjective; its use as an adverb is still regarded as colloquial. (Formal and informal: He never bet except on a *sure* thing. Colloquial: But he *sure* bet a lot of money on them.)

suspicion. The accepted verb is *suspect.* It is colloquial or dialectal to *suspicion* anything.

swell. As a noun (He was a *swell* with that suit on), the word is slightly archaic. As an adjective meaning *elegant* (It was a *swell* layout) or *first-rate* (It was a *swell* dance), the word is badly overworked. All three meanings are colloquial, if not slang.

take. Of the many uses of this ubiquitous verb, the following are restricted: Colloquial: *take in* (He *took in* a show); *take off* (*to burlesque*); *take on* (He *took on* like a madman); and *take up with* (*associate with*) . *Take and* (He *took and* threw it across the river) and *take sick* are dialectal.

than. *Than* is usually a conjunction. (He is taller *than* I—*am* understood.) In formal writing it may be a preposition followed by a direct object in such a sentence as: Walt Whitman was a poet, *than* whom no one was a more loyal friend of democracy. In colloquial speech and in some informal writing, *than* is followed by an objective pronoun in less stilted expressions: He is taller *than* me, her, and so forth. It should not be confused with *then,* which means *at that time.* See *Different from, than.*

that there. *That there, this here,* and similar expressions are vulgate. (Vulgate: I'll take *that there* piece. Acceptable: I'll take *that* piece *there.*)

theater, theatre. *Theater* is the more common spelling in the United States, but either is correct.

theirselves, themselves. See *Self.*

this here. See *That there.*

though. See *Although.* The variant spellings *tho* and *tho'* are both recorded in the ACD, but they are not widely used. See page 207.

thro, thro', through, thru. WNC lists *thro'* and *thru* as variant spellings of *through.* The ACD also lists *thro. Through* is still the commonest spelling, the most acceptable in formal writing. Whichever a student uses, he should be consistent (see page 207). In the sense of *finished, through* is sometimes classed as colloquial.

till, 'til, until. A writer may take his choice between *till* and *until* depending on the rhythm. *'Til* has a quaint poetic flavor like *o'* in *bit o' sunshine.*

title. See *Entitle.*

today, tomorrow. These words are seldom hyphenated in America today and may never be tomorrow.

toward, towards. *Toward* is more common in the United States, *towards* in Britain. A writer may take his choice.

transpire. This word means *exhale, give off,* or *come to light.* As a synonym for *happen* (Much has *transpired* since Friday), it is condemned by some authorities, but both the ACD and WNC list it without restrictive labels.

try and. In formal writing, *try to* is more acceptable (I shall *try to* come); but *try and* is acceptable in informal writing (*Try and* stop me).

type. Since *type* is a noun, not an adjective, it should be followed by *of* in such expressions as *a different type of person.* But its use in hyphenated compounds is common in advertising (*Scotch-type* liquor) and appears to be filtering into informal writing of other kinds. (In order to save civilization, he said, we will have to go underground with it, out of reach of the *new-type* bomb.—E. B. White, *The Wild Flag*.)

typical. This overworked adjective often stands for a writer's failure to analyze the individuality of his subject. What is a *typical* lawyer, a *typical* American, a *typical* college professor?

ugly. WNC restricts *ugly* in the sense of *unpleasant* or *ill-tempered* to colloquial use. The ACD does not. Both note that the meaning *ill-tempered* is an Americanism.

uninterested. See *Disinterested*.

unique. In its strict literal sense, *unique* means *unequalled*, the only *one* (*unus*) of its kind. In formal writing there is no such thing as *more unique, less unique, most unique,* or *very unique*. But it is widely used as a counterword meaning *rare*, *unusual*, and the ACD recognizes its meaning without reservations. The main objection to this use in informal writing is that the word is overworked. The extent to which *unique* has lost its absolute quality is illustrated in a comment by Dr. Morris Fishbein on a news story about a ten-year-old mother. He called it *"unique*, but not extraordinary." See page 105.

United States. The official name of the country includes the definite article. (United States Steel is one of the largest industries in *the* United States.) Do not abbreviate to *the U.S.* See *America*.

until. See *Till*.

up. *Up* is so widely used as an adverb (close *up*, finish *up*, hurry *up*) that it is impossible to devise a formula to determine which expressions are redundant. The word usually adds emphasis: *beat him up* is more emphatic than *beat him*. Occasionally it makes an appreciable difference in meaning: to say that a man is *broken up* is not the same as to say that he is *broken*. Often it is superfluous: *closing up* a store is hardly more emphatic than *closing* it. Since these combinations are widely regarded as colloquial, they are usually avoided in formal writing. In informal writing, the writer must treat each case separately.

used. Beware of omitting the *d* from the past participle. (Wrong: He was *use* to it.)

verbal. See *Oral.*

very. According to a strict and subtle formal rule, *very* should not be used alone with a past participle unless the participle is common as an adjective before a noun. Thus "He was *very* disturbed" should be changed to "He was *much* or *very much* disturbed"; "He was *very* tired" is acceptable. But this questionable distinction is not carefully observed. (He was *very* embarrassed, having brought out this thing he had lived by. . . .—Ernest Hemingway, "The Short Happy Life of Francis Macomber.") A writer should beware of overworking *very* in an attempt at emphasis. See page 247.

viewpoint. Some authorities still insist on *point of view.* It would be as logical to insist on *point of standing* instead of *standpoint. Viewpoint* is widely used in reputable writing.

wait on. In the sense of *wait for* (Don't *wait on* me; I won't be back in time), this expression is dialectal.

want. The standard idiom after *want* is the infinitive. (I *want* you *to do* it. I *want to come* in.) The following expressions are dialectal: I *want* that you should do it; I *want* for you to do it; I *want* in; I *want* out. In the sense of *ought, want* is colloquial. (You *want* to do it before morning.)

way, ways. When it means *away* or *condition, way* is colloquial. (*Way* over in Japan he was in a bad *way.*) *Ways* is colloquial for *way.* (He went a long *ways* in his old car.)

well. See *Good.*

when. See *Is when.*

where. See *At, Is where. Where* is colloquial as a substitute for *that.* (I see *where* the President came out in favor of peace.)

whether. See *Doubt if.*

which. Common in informal writing as a substitute for *this* at or near the beginning of a sentence. (All of *which* does not make for a national school of music or any sort of art.—

Deems Taylor, *Of Men and Music.*) In a more formal context this example would be regarded as an illegitimate sentence fragment. See pages 127–129.

while. Overworked colloquially as a substitute for *and, but, though,* and *whereas.* It is used more accurately in expressions of time. (Colloquial: He is going to Yale, *while* she is going to Vassar. *While* I don't object strenuously, I hope she changes her mind. More accurate: He is going to Yale, *and* she is going to Vassar. *Though* I don't object strenuously, I hope she changes her mind. *While* I wait here, you talk to her.) See *Awhile.*

will. See *Shall.*

win out. See *Lose out.*

with regard(s) to. See *Regard.*

woods. See *Falls.*

would. See *Should.*

would have (of). Dialectal: If I *would have* known that, I never would have come. Correct: If I *had known* that, I never would have come. *Would of* is a misspelling of *would have.*

yourself. See *Self.*

Index

T

Taking notes, 24–25, 356–357
"Talk of the Town, The," *New Yorker,* quoted, 12, 156, 236, 282–283, 311
Taylor, Deems, quoted, 56
Tenses, 98–100
Term paper (*see* Library research paper)
Terms, grammatical, 81, 115–116
That and *which,* 90
There is, was, are, were, 110–111
Therefore, punctuation with, 173
These kind, those kind, 111
Thinking (*see* Clear and cloudy thinking)
Tho, 207, 421
Thoreau, Henry David, quoted, 321, 342
Thru, 207, 421
Thurber, James, quoted, 28, 155, 186, 269, 304–305, 387
Tight, tightly, 104
Time, quoted, 238
Tinker, Chauncey B., quoted, 300–301
Titles: capitalization of, 211; choosing, 34–35; position in the theme, 33; punctuation of, 186–187, 192
Titles and degrees, 180, 210
Together with, number with, 108
Tone, 300–307, 314–317; exercises, 314–317
Topic outline, 357–358
Topic sentence, 42–47
Toynbee, Arnold J., quoted, 70–71
Transitions: incomplete sentences for, 129; within the paragraph, 42, 47–49; between paragraphs, 40–41, 69; punctuation of, 178
Transitive verb, 96
Triteness, 4–5; *see also* Clichés
Twain, Mark, quoted, 247, 303
Typing, 32–33
Typographical errors, 10

U

Underlining, 192–193
Understatement, 305
Unemployed words, 149
Unfinished sentence, punctuation of, 189
Unity: in the paragraph, 42–47; in the theme as a whole, 68–69
Unreliable authorities, 331
Upside-down subordination, 134
Usage, glossary of, 381–424
Usage, levels of, 16–18, 234–239

V

Vagueness, 8–9
Variety in sentence structure, 151–152
Veblen, Thorstein, quoted, 312–313
Verbals, 100–102, 127–128
Verbs: agreement, 107–112; defined, 83–84; finite, 100, 127–128; kinds, 96; mood, 97; phrases, 113; principal parts, 102–103; tense, 98–100, voice, 97–98, 150, 295–296
Victoria, Queen, quoted, 193
Vocabulary building, 222–224
Voice, 97–98, 150, 295–296
Voltaire, quoted, 321
Vulgate, 16–17, 234

SYMBOLS FO[

▶ WITH PAGE REFERENCES TO THE BOOK

SYMBOL	MEANING	PAGE
Ab	Improper ABBREVIATION or number. Spell out	33–34
Ad	ADJECTIVE or ADVERB misused	103–106
Agr	Error in AGREEMENT { of pronoun and antecedent or of subject and verb	107–113
Ap	Omission or misuse of APOSTROPHE	212–213
Ca	Error in CASE of pronoun	89–94
Cap	Use CAPITAL letter(s)	210–212
Cl	Lack of CLARITY	7–9
CF	COMMA FAULT	173–175
Coh	Lack of COHERENCE	47–49, 69
Cst	Error in sentence CONSTRUCTION	126–157
Dng	DANGLING MODIFIER	136–138
D	Faulty DICTION	222 ff.
Div	Improper DIVISION of word into syllables	213
Emp	Lack of EMPHASIS in the sentence	152–157
Fig	Faulty FIGURE of speech	267–275
Frag	Sentence FRAGMENT (period fault)	127–130
Glos	Consult the GLOSSARY of usage	381–424
Gr	Error in GRAMMAR	79–115
Hy	Insert HYPHEN	213–214
Id	Faulty IDIOM	230
Ital	ITALICIZE (Underline)	192–193
K	AWKWARD expression	12
Log	Faulty LOGIC	318–338
lc	Change to LOWER CASE (small letter)	210–212
MM	MISPLACED MODIFIER	138–139
MS	Improper MANUSCRIPT form	32–34
No ¶	NO PARAGRAPH indention	36–42
¶	Begin new PARAGRAPH	36–42
¶U	Lack of PARAGRAPH UNITY	42–47
¶Coh	Lack of PARAGRAPH COHERENCE	47–49
¶Dev	Inadequate PARAGRAPH DEVELOPMENT	49–51